THE ROYAL PREROGATIVE AND THE LEARNING OF THE INNS OF COURT

MARGARET McGLYNN

CAMBRIDGE
UNIVERSITY PRESS

CAMBRIDGE UNIVERSITY PRESS
Cambridge, New York, Melbourne, Madrid, Cape Town, Singapore,
São Paulo, Delhi, Dubai, Tokyo, Mexico City

Cambridge University Press
The Edinburgh Building, Cambridge CB2 8RU, UK

Published in the United States of America by Cambridge University Press, New York

www.cambridge.org
Information on this title: www.cambridge.org/9780521187695

First published 2003
First paperback edition 2010

A catalogue record for this publication is available from the British Library

ISBN 978-0-521-80429-5 Hardback
ISBN 978-0-521-18769-5 Paperback

THE ROYAL PREROGATIVE AND THE LEARNING OF THE INNS OF COURT

Between the mid-fifteenth and mid-sixteenth century *Prerogativa Regis*, a central text of fiscal feudalism, was introduced into the curriculum of the Inns of Court, developed, and then abandoned. This book argues that while lawyers often turned their attention to the text when political and financial issues brought it to the fore, they sought to maintain an intellectual consistency and coherence in the law. Discussions of both substance and procedure demonstrate how readers reflected the concerns of their time in the topics they chose to consider and how they drew on the learning of both their predecessors and their peers at the Inns. The first study based primarily on readings, this book throws new light on legal education, early Tudor financial and administrative procedure, and the relationship between the ways that law was made, taught, and used.

MARGARET MCGLYNN is Assistant Professor of History at Wellesley College.

CAMBRIDGE STUDIES
IN ENGLISH LEGAL HISTORY

Edited by
J. H. BAKER
Fellow of St Catharine's College, Cambridge

Recent series titles include

The Private Trustee in Victorian England
CHANTAL STEBBINGS

The Fee Tail and the Common Recovery in Medieval England 1176–1502
JOSEPH BIANCALANA

Aliens in Medieval Law
KEECHANG KIM

A History of the Country Court, 1846–1971
PATRICK POLDEN

Literary Copyright Reform in Early Victorian England: The Framing of the 1842 Copyright Act
CATHERINE SEVILLE

CONTENTS

PREFACE

Maitland's famous comment in his equally famous Rede lecture that "law schools make tough law" has been often quoted, but little has been done to prove or disprove it for the period he discussed. The history, structure, and culture of the Inns of Court have been well studied, but little work has been done on the content of their teaching. Admittedly, the materials are unprepossessing, but they are voluminous, and they exert their own odd fascination, for they offer us the opportunity to understand how common lawyers were trained to think. Given the numerous roles that men trained at the Inns of Court played in sixteenth-century England, any insight into their understanding of the law, their role, and their society would seem to be of value. At the conclusion of this project I am not sure how much insight I have achieved into the lawyers, but I have come to truly appreciate Maitland's comment, and the depth and breadth of knowledge of the men who taught at the Inns of Court.

This was in many ways an unexpected project for me, and many people made it possible. My deepest thanks go to Ken Bartlett, who was an unending source of intellectual, moral, and practical support, and who gave freely of that most precious of all commodities, his time. I am also deeply grateful to John Baker for giving me the benefit of his vast knowledge of the manuscript readings on which this study is based at an early stage, and for keeping any misgivings he may have felt to himself. His work on the readings and on the Tudor reports made this project possible, and his support, encouragement, and advice have been invaluable. Richard Schneider argued over virtually every page with me, and constantly pushed me to think more deeply about the sources. I am also grateful for the insights of William C. Jordan, Thomas Mayer, and John Guy, as well as the readers from the Press. Others gave me help, advice, and criticism along the way. Brian Merrilees helped me wrestle with

Law French, Dr. Amanda Bevan of the Public Record Office very kindly provided me with a copy of sections of her unpublished PhD dissertation on the Tudor judiciary, and Dr. Lisa Ford both gave me a copy of her dissertation on Henry VII's Council Learned, and discussed Henry's aims with me at length. The members of the reading group at the Centre for Reformation and Renaissance Studies at the University of Toronto gave both support and stern criticism, both of which were greatly appreciated.

My research was supported by the University of Toronto, York University, and Wellesley College, and I am grateful for their help. I have also benefited greatly from the advice and support of my colleagues in the history departments of York University and Wellesley College. This work relies on manuscript materials held in the British Library, the Public Record Office, Cambridge University Library, the Harvard Law School library, and the library of Gray's Inn. I would like to thank the staff at those institutions for allowing me access to their collections and for their expertise and their helpfulness.

This book is dedicated to Richard, who has listened to me talk about the prerogative for many years, with every appearance of attention, and with real and constant encouragement. For this, and for everything else, thank you.

FIGURES

ABBREVIATIONS

Caryll's Reports	John Caryll. *Reports of Cases by John Caryll.* Edited by J. H. Baker. 2 vols. Selden Society vols. 115 and 116. London: Selden Society, 1998 and 1999
Constable	Robert Constable. *Prerogativa Regis: Tertia Lectura Roberti Constable de Lincolnis Inne Anno 11 H.* 7. Edited by S. E. Thorne. New Haven: Yale University Press, 1949
CUL	Cambridge University Library
Frowyk	CUL MS Hh.2.1, ff.1–26
Hall	Edward Hall. *Hall's Chronicle.* Edited by Henry Ellis. London, 1809
HLS	Harvard Law School
Port	BL MS Hargrave 87, ff.142–76
Port's Notebook	Sir John Port, *The Notebook of Sir John Port.* Edited by J. H. Baker. Selden Society vol. 102. London: Selden Society, 1986
Spelman	Gray's Inn MS 25, ff.302–18v. (Chaloner MS)
Spelman's Reports	Sir John Spelman, *The Reports of Sir John Spelman.* Edited by J. H. Baker. Selden Society vols. 93 and 94. London: Selden Society, 1976 and 1977
Staunford	Sir William Staunford. *An Exposicion of the Kings Prerogatiue, collected out of the great Abridgement of Iustice Fitzherbert, and other olde Writers of the Lawes of Englande, by the right Worshipfull Sir William Staunford Knight, lately one of the Iustices of the Queenes Maiesties Court of Comon Pleas.* London, 1567

YB	Year Books. *Les Reports des Cases en les Ans des Roys Edward V. Richard III. Henrie VII. & Henrie VIII. Touts qui par cy devant ont este Publies*. London, 1679
Yorke	BL MS Hargrave 253, f.77v
Yorke's Casebook	BL MS Hargrave 388, ff.211–72
Willoughby	BL MS Harley 1691, ff.197–201

INTRODUCTION

Throughout the Middle Ages, land was the central source of power in England. It was the basis for wealth, for authority, for jurisdiction, and for military strength. Despite ongoing arguments between historians about our construction of feudalism – the validity of the term, the breadth of its application, and the level of systematization it implies – the distribution and organization of land in England through the Middle Ages was in some way feudal. There is no doubt that what it meant to be feudal changed over the course of the Middle Ages, but to reduce the idea to its most basic level, land was held by tenants from lords and tenants returned service to their lords for that land. Lords retained certain rights over their tenants and their land, the most important of which applied at the death of their tenant, such as escheat for failure of heirs, and, for tenants who held in knight service, the wardship and marriage of minor heirs. The relationship between lord and tenant changed between the eleventh and fifteenth centuries, as did the kinds of service rendered, the kinds of jurisdiction exercised, and the ways in which military strength was exercised. However, the basic language of lordship and service remained intact.

Throughout this period, the king also remained the chief feudal lord of the kingdom. His power came both from his status as king and from his position as the most substantial landlord in the kingdom. He was the lord of the greatest lords, and also of the most lords. Besides the inherent power that kingship gave him, he also had the revenues of land that his lordship gave him, and the benefits of prerogative lordship that came from the combination of the two. Thus his rights to escheat and wardship were greater than those of any other lord, primer seisin was his alone, and he had procedural prerogatives in court which allowed him to further safeguard his rights. The origins and development of many of these rights are unclear, but in the reign of Edward I or Edward II they were encapsulated in the text *Prerogativa Regis*. From this point on, the king's rights were integrated into the common law, part of the common knowledge of the legal profession, and subject to the same kinds of development and interpretation as the rest of the common law.

The first place we look for interpretation is the courtroom, and the year books are legal historians' most common route to the legal mind of the Middle Ages. However, the discussion in year book cases generally focuses on the needs of the case at hand, more or less, and is usually not concerned with explaining the broader background to the dispute, or with placing it in the context of the common law as a whole. The participants spoke ad hoc, and, as a result, the legal profession recognized that year book cases could be wrong; they were examples of argument, but not necessarily guides to practice. However, from the early fourteenth century, a system was developing in the Inns of Court which did allow lawyers to consider the law in a more focused and coherent way, as part of the structure of legal education. Within this structure, prominent lawyers gave lectures on statutes, known as "readings," twice a year, during which the common knowledge on a text could be rehearsed, examined, and argued.[1]

The earliest known reading on *Prerogativa Regis* comes from the 1440s or 1450s, before Henry VI's ejection from France. The rest of the readings fall between the 1470s and the 1550s, with most of them in the reigns of Henry VII and Henry VIII. This can hardly be accidental. Although historians argue about "the New Monarchy" and whether it is Yorkist, Lancastrian, or Tudor, there can be no doubt that English kingship underwent startling changes between the second reign of Edward IV and the death of Henry VIII. While ideas of kingship, the methods and efficiency of royal administration, and the structure of the royal court all changed dramatically, the king remained, in theory and in fact, the chief lord of England. Land continued to be the basis of wealth, authority, and military power, if no longer always of jurisdiction. The lords of the land, and their tenants, continued to hold in feudal tenure, owing service for land, and the king continued to claim escheats, wardships, and primer seisin on his lands, together with other rights of lordship. While the late-fifteenth and early sixteenth-century monarchs

[1] A description of the educational system follows, below.

sought new expressions of authority, they did not neglect the elaboration of their traditional rights, and the counterpoint between the two reflects the process of transition apparent in this period.[2] Feudal forms continued well into the early modern period, and they operated, not in hidden and archaic corners, but in the most essential base of sixteenth-century life: land. This book will consider, from one particular point of view, how this worked and, a little more generally, what it meant.

The point of view is that of the legal profession. The common lawyers were charged with operating this system and operating it in a way that would make sense in contemporary society. What that meant changed over time, and the readings make it clear that the logic of the prerogative in the early fifteenth century was no longer the logic of the prerogative in the mid-sixteenth century. The function of the lawyers was to respond to changes in law and society, while maintaining the coherence of the principles within the law. However, they could not do this job in isolation, but had to respond to changing statutory law, changing administrative practices, and political pressure. The story of *Prerogativa Regis* in the early Tudor period, then, shows contemporaries, professional lawyers, grappling with the development of feudalism in a period that historians no longer see as feudal, and is a reminder that the ideas and structures of medieval society underpinned Tudor England long after the realities of that society had changed.

An examination of our base text, *Prerogativa Regis*, seems in order before we proceed any further.[3] The first three chapters of the text deal with the custody of the land and heir of the king's tenants-in-chief. Chapter one of *Prerogativa Regis* gives the king custody of all the lands of which those who held of him in chief in knight service were seised on the day they died, with the right to hold such lands until the heir is of full age. The fees of the archbishop of Canterbury, the bishop of Durham between Tyne and Tees, and the counts and barons of the March are excepted from the operation

[2] It is not unusual to find historians arguing that feudalism was irrelevant by the sixteenth century. See, for example S. E. Thorne, ed., *Prerogativa Regis: Tertia Lectura Roberti Constable de Lyncolnis Inne Anno 11 H. 7* (New Haven: Yale University Press, 1949), ix; and A. R. Buck, "The Politics of Land Law in Tudor England 1529–40," *Journal of Legal History* 11 (1990): 200–17. There are some exceptions to this, for example, Steven G. Ellis, *Tudor Frontiers and Noble Power: The Making of the British State* (Oxford: Clarendon Press, 1995).

[3] *Statutes of the Realm*, 11 vols. (London, 1810–22), vol. 1, 226.

of the statute.[4] Chapter two allows the king the marriage of any heirs in his custody, for whatever reason. Chapter three gives him primer seisin of all land held by his tenant on the day of his death, and the profits of all that land until an inquisition is held and the heir sues livery, at his majority. Though there is much of interest in the readers' discussions of the later chapters, I have restricted this study to the first three chapters of the text, partly for reasons of space, but primarily because they comprise the foundation of the statute.[5]

Though dating from the late thirteenth or early fourteenth centuries, *Prerogativa Regis* was not one of the classic statutes, and in fact its status is something of a mystery. It is presented as a list of the king's rights, for there are no words of promulgation in it, ordaining or commanding that these rules be kept. This, together with its somewhat anecdotal later sections,[6] led Maitland to conclude that it is not in fact a statute, but a treatise written by a member of the legal profession.[7] However, the definition of statutes in the thirteenth and fourteenth centuries was far from sophisticated. In this period, statutes were a relatively novel means of achieving legal change. Plucknett, for example, has looked at the nature of legislation in the first half of the fourteenth century by focusing

[4] The statute gives no reason for the exclusion of the archbishop of Canterbury. The earls and barons of the March are excepted because the king's writ does not run in the Marches, thus it is effectively an independent jurisdiction. Durham is, of course, a palatine jurisdiction, and Constable concludes that the bishop was excepted from the royal prerogative by the normal course of the law, even without the statute. This being the case, he argues that the law also excepts the other counties palatine, Lancaster and Chester, even though they are not mentioned in the statute. Robert Constable, *Prerogativa Regis: Tertia Lectura Roberti Constable de Lyncolnis Inne Anno 11 H. 7*, ed. S. E. Thorne (New Haven: Yale University Press, 1949), 26–27.

[5] The statute goes on to deal with widows and heiresses, alienation of lands, churches to which the king has right of presentation, custody of the lands of idiots and lunatics, the right to wreck, whales and sturgeon, the escheats of lands of Normans and other foreigners, and the king's right to the chattels of felons and fugitives.

[6] The chapter on the escheat of the lands of Normans gives the example of the barony of Monmouth, while another chapter relates the experiences of Matilda, daughter of the duke of Hereford.

[7] F. W. Maitland, "The *Praerogativa Regis*," in *Collected Papers* (Cambridge: Cambridge University Press, 1911), vol. 2, 183–89. Plucknett suggests that it could be a memorandum of prerogatives followed in the chancery sent by Edward II to Chief Justice Brabazon in 1314 after the judge had admitted his ignorance on the topic. T. F. T. Plucknett, *A Concise History of the Common Law* (5th edn, Boston: Little, Brown & Co., 1956), 542, n.2.

on the process of creating a statute and incorporating it in the common law. He argues that, in the early years of the common law, legislation was hardly a distinct function of king or parliament, but simply one way, and often an easy and informal way, of changing the common law.[8] Thus in the reign of Edward I and for some time thereafter, statutes did not differ in their nature from other forms of legal instruction, such as the king's instructions to judges on eyre, and might simply be the king's expression of his role as lawmaker.

This raises the question of how some texts came to be accepted as statutes, while others were not. The most important enactments, such as Westminster I, are clearly statutes, but the status of many other texts produced by the legal profession of the first three Edwards is more questionable. Plucknett concludes that the only reasonable way to deal with the problem is to accept the description of contemporaries, especially lawyers and judges, since they were the most qualified to calibrate the value and validity of any particular text. He also argues that this evaluation would take place fairly quickly after the production of the text, since most statutes are framed to deal with issues of current concern, and thus are likely to be tested fairly quickly.[9]

Richardson and Sayles also examined the early statutes, but rather than evaluating their status through the operation of the legal system, they looked at the physical recording and transmission of the early statutes and particularly the statute roll. They conclude that the statute roll is not complete, and was never intended to be either complete or authoritative.[10] The impression of uncertainty is supported by Plucknett's assertion that "reference by the court to an official copy of a statute was decidedly unusual and . . . the court did not possess a copy of its own for ready reference."[11] On the other hand, the statutes did circulate in private collections compiled for the use of lawyers. The collections were the result of private enterprise and were in no way standardized. They might include a variety

[8] T. F. T. Plucknett, *Legislation of Edward I* (Oxford: Clarendon Press, 1949), 13–15.

[9] *Ibid.*, 11.

[10] H. G. Richardson and G. O. Sayles, "The Early Statutes," *Law Quarterly Review* 50 (1934): 215. They point out that there continued to be omissions on the statute roll until the end of the reign of Edward III and beyond, but argue that the statute roll gradually acquired a peculiar authority.

[11] T. F. T. Plucknett, *Statutes and their Interpretation in the First Half of the Fourteenth Century* (Cambridge: Cambridge University Press, 1922), 104.

of statutory texts, and *Prerogativa Regis*, for example, is found in only about 25 percent of the surviving manuscript statute books.[12] Besides statutes, these books also contain collections of writs and other legal texts. Richardson and Sayles point out that "at any time in the thirteenth century, all the works of reference the practical lawyer needed could be contained in one moderate-sized volume; and the state of the texts is explained if we recognize such a collection for what it is, . . . a *vade mecum* aiming at being inclusive, but with no high standard of accuracy and certainly making no contemporary claim to authority."[13]

Thus the early statutes were recorded either on an incomplete and semi-official statute roll or in the catch-all unofficial collections of working lawyers. The situation was hardly conducive to the formulation of a definitive collection of authoritative texts or indeed an authoritative version of any one text. However, despite the confusion of the sources, Richardson and Sayles make at least a tentative attempt to define a statute. They conclude that there are three tests for a statute: whether the legislation arises from a petition of the *commune*; whether it will apply generally; and whether it is intended to be permanent. If the text misses any of these points, they conclude, it should not, strictly speaking, be considered a statute.[14] Though these criteria are simple, coherent, and practical, the authors go on to warn that they have been deduced from the texts and were not necessarily recognized, or accepted, by contemporary draftsmen.[15]

It seems, then, that modern scholars have found various methods of testing a text to determine whether or not it is a statute, but they warn that in the end none of these tests is beyond doubt. The safest method is simply to accept the word of contemporaries, for the practical needs of the court will determine whether a text has statutory force. A problem arises when we try to apply this criterion to *Prerogativa Regis*, for contemporaries were uncertain as to whether it was a statute or not, and modern scholars have remained equally unsure. The text is included in the *Statutes of the Realm*, but

[12] J. S. Arkenberg, "Statute Books and Medieval Legal Education" (paper presented at "Learning the Law," Thirteenth British Legal History Conference, Trinity Hall, Cambridge, 3 July 1997).

[13] Richardson and Sayles, "The Early Statutes," 544.

[14] *Ibid.*, 559. [15] *Ibid.*, 559–60.

there it is included with the statutes of uncertain date.[16] It is also in the early printed editions of the statutes, where it was assigned by tradition to 17 Edw. II.[17] It seems clear that it belongs to the reign of either Edward I or Edward II, for the text refers to "King Henry, father of King Edward." Maitland suggests that it belongs to the early years of Edward I,[18] but a year book case from the reign of Edward III refers to it as being made in the time of King Edward, the father of the present king,[19] while Staunford, in the mid-sixteenth century, argued that it must date from the reign of Edward II, since otherwise the text would have referred to King Henry our father, rather than King Henry father of King Edward.[20] Serjeant Kebell recognized that the date of the statute was "doubteous" in 1497, and his verdict still holds.[21] *Prerogativa Regis* is usually called a statute, but, in the period from which it dates, the two most common tests of authenticity for a statute were that it should be dated and sealed. *Prerogativa Regis* meets neither of these criteria.

This led to some discussion concerning its status among contemporary lawyers, and posed a problem for later readers, since it was generally accepted that readings must be based on statutes. Two year book cases raised this question. The first dates from about 1370 and hinges on the question of whether, when the king gives the gift of a manor with an advowson attached, the advowson automatically goes with the gift, or whether this must be expressly stated. Serjeant Cavendish argues that in the reign of Henry III the king was treated just like anyone else under the law, and that this changed with the statute *Prerogativa Regis*, made in the time of Edward II.[22] Kirton responds that *Prerogativa Regis* is not a statute, but a rehearsal of the king's prerogatives, since it is clear that the king had this prerogative before the time of the statute.[23] Fencotes

16 *Stat. Realm*, vol. 1, 226.

17 See, for example, *Magna Carta in F. wherunto is added more statutes than euer was imprynted in any one boke before this tyme* . . . (London, 1529), f.98. It was assigned this position because the miscellaneous undated statutes were gathered together on the statute roll at the end of the reign of Edward II.

18 Maitland, "*Praerogativa Regis*," 188.

19 YB Mich. 43 Edw. III, f.22, pl.12.

20 William Staunford, *An Exposicion of the Kinges Prerogatiue collected out of the great Abridgement of Iustice Fitzherbert, and other old Writers of the Lawes of Englande* (London, 1567), f.6–6v.

21 YB Trin. 12 Hen. VII, f.20, pl.1.

22 YB Mich. 43 Edw. III, f.22, pl.12.

23 *Ibid.*

is in agreement with Cavendish, that the words of the text clearly indicate that something new is being reserved to the king with this document, and therefore it is a statute.[24] The main criterion here for a statute seems to be that it changes the common law in some manner, though in this case the lawyers disagree on what has been changed and to what extent.

The second year book case dates from 1475 and it deals with the question of whether, if the king has the wardship of an heir of one of his tenants-in-chief, and the child inherits land held in socage, the king should have the wardship of this land also.[25] In this case, Serjeant Bryan characterizes *Prerogativa Regis* as an affirmation of the common law.[26] Pigot argues, based on the previous case from 1370, that it is not an affirmation of the common law, but a statute.[27] Littleton, however, chimes in on Bryan's side, arguing that *Prerogativa Regis* cannot be a statute, for it has no certain date and it is not obeyed in every point. He considers that it is just like the treatises *Dies Communes in Banco*, *Dies Communes in Dote* and *Expositiones Vocabulorum*, which were "written in our books and yet are not statutes, but were made for this purpose, that that which was in doubt in the common law should be made certain."[28] The earliest readings do not add much of use: the first reading agrees that the text is a statute, though it does not explain why, and adds that it was made "solement pur lauantage et profite de Roy."[29] The next reading argues that part of the statute is an affirmation of the common law and part is not.[30] A contemporary commonplace book rounds out the spectrum of opinion, arguing that "*Prerogativa Regis* is not a statute, because it does not specify the year it was made or the place," and quoting the exchequer chamber for its authority.[31] It seems, therefore, that the course of almost two hundred years of practical application had not settled the status of *Prerogativa Regis*. The text was used and applied because its provisions were a reasonable statement of the king's financial rights over his tenants-in-chief

[24] *Ibid.*

[25] YB Mich. 15 Edw. IV, f.12, pl.17. This is *Skrene's Case*, and we will return to a fuller discussion of its significance at pp. 43–45 below.

[26] *Ibid.* [27] *Ibid.*

[28] *Ibid.*, ff.12–13. It is worth noting that just a few years earlier Serjeant Pigot had denied that *Dies Communes in Banco* was a statute, but an affirmation of the common law, though the court had termed it a statute. YB Pas. 8 Edw. IV, f.4, pl.9.

[29] CUL MS Ee.5.22, f.338. [30] CUL MS Hh.3.6, f.55v.

[31] BL MS Harley 2051, f.40.

and reason was the central criterion by which any text of the common law was judged. Any attempt to apply the text to a situation not explicitly contained therein, however, led to discussion and debate about the nature and the applicability of *Prerogativa Regis*.

Discussion and debate were, however, an integral part of the educational programme of the Inns of Court. The Inns were both educational and social institutions, and as such they came to have a central role in the way the lawyers developed both their skills and their corporate identity. Both were necessary, for the lawyers played a crucial and complex role in the interpretation and maintenance of the common law. The structure of English law meant that the preservation and construction of law were inextricably connected. The administration of justice was based on the common law of the realm and statutory law. Statutory law could introduce new law or it could declare the common law more clearly, but in either case it had to be interpreted in light of the existing common law. This meant that in theory the entire body of existing law should be kept in mind when any new statute was being made. Though the king was at the head of the legal system, it was unrealistic to expect him to have this kind of knowledge of the law, as Sir John Fortescue's *De Laudibus Legum Anglie* makes clear. When Fortescue's chancellor urges the young prince to learn the laws of the land he will one day rule, the prince objects, on the ground that such knowledge takes many years to acquire. The chancellor responds that the prince need only know "the principles and causes of the law as far as the elements."[32] It was for others to know the details. This was an old issue, and one not confined to English law. Roman law placed a similar expectation on the king, requiring him to keep all the laws in the shrine of his breast.[33] In the English context, this could become more complex, for the royal advisors in the making of the law were not necessarily the same men as those who interpreted the law; *Bracton*, for example, says that the prince was counselled by the magnates of the realm, not doctors of law, and the prince was the voice of the law, for

[32] Sir John Fortescue, *De Laudibus Legum Anglie*, ed. S. B. Chrimes (Cambridge: Cambridge University Press, 1942), 23.

[33] This maxim was later also adopted by the canon law. The jurist Cynus of Pistoia (1270–1336) warned against a literal interpretation of the idea, arguing that it was to be understood in the sense of "his court which should abound of excellent Doctors of Law through whose mouths the most law-abiding prince himself speaks." E. H. Kantorowicz, *The King's Two Bodies: A Study in Mediæval Political Theology* (Princeton: Princeton University Press, 1957), 154.

the promulgation of law was by his *auctoritas*.[34] If the relationship between the king, the magnates, and the lawyers were not complex enough, by the fifteenth century this theory had further to consider the role of parliament.

In his classic fifteenth-century exposition of English government, Fortescue presents kingship as *dominium politicum et regale*, where the king is limited, though not controlled, by parliament. There was no doubt that the king had the power to declare law, but it was equally clear that he could do this only in conjunction with parliament. The exact role that parliament played is not explicitly stated by Fortescue. Bishop Russell, in the draft of the sermon he planned for the parliament of Edward V, compared parliament to Moses and Aaron "whych escend vnto the mownt where the lawe ys geven. The peuple must stond a forr, and not passe the lymittes; ye speke with the prince, whyche is *quasi deus noster in terris*."[35] Parliament thus appears as a mediator between the king and the people, intended to moderate the force of the king's presence. Bishop Russell pursues this idea further, pointing out that:

> when so euer the kynge in hys person, for the multitude of mysdoers, takythe vpon hym to visite hys Reame . . . the ministracion of justice is wont to be so terrible and precise in processe that alle the pertees and persones adioignaunt quake and tremble for fere . . . Wherefor it ys not to doulte but that the rule and governaile of the Reame appereth then in most temperaunce and moderacion when the kynges juges and commisses be obeyd at large in every parte of the londe.[36]

The king's personal administration of law was probably associated with extreme circumstances and harsh application because his judicial tours usually followed outbreaks of political violence. Under normal circumstances, according to Russell, while parliament represented the king's wishes to the people, it was left to the judges and commissioners to put them into practice throughout the land.

Bishop Russell's parliament is a rather passive body, and he has little to say about its role as counsellor or advisor in the law-making

[34] *Ibid.*, 154–55; Bracton, *On the Laws and Customs of England*, trans. S. E. Thorne (Cambridge, MA: Belknap Press of Harvard University Press, 1968), vol. 2, 305.

[35] Sermon printed in S. B. Chrimes, *English Constitutional Ideas in the Fifteenth Century* (New York: American Scholar Publications, 1966), 173.

[36] *Ibid.*

process. Nevertheless, this idea of parliament as a repository of legal knowledge, as well as a creator of law, was still important at the time he was drafting his sermon. Thus in the act recognizing Richard III's right to the throne, it is stated that, though his claim is lawful,

> the most parte of the people of this Lande is not suffisantly lerned in the abovesaid Lawes and Custumes, wherby the trueth and right in this behalf of liklyhode may be hyd, and nat clerely knowen to all the people, and thereupon put in doubt and question. And over this, howe that the Courte of Parliament is of suche auctorite, and the people of this Lande of such nature and disposicion, as experience teacheth, that manifestacion and declaration of any trueth or right, made by the Thre Estates of this Reame assembled in Parliament, and by auctorite of the same, maketh, before all other thyngs, moost feith and certaynte.[37]

Here parliament is presented as the guardian of the law, on behalf of the people. The act does not make or change any law, it simply states that according to the law of the land Richard III's claim is good and it is expected that such a declaration by parliament will satisfy the people.

This situation, though instructive, was unusual. Parliament's role as guardian of the law was generally much less dramatic. The king was still seen as the central figure in both creating and preserving the law. In his coronation oath, Henry VII made the traditional promises to "keepe to the people of Englande the Lawes and customes to them as olde rightfull and devoute kinges graunted, and the same ratifie, and confirme," to "make to be done after ... [his] strenght and power rightfull Justice in all ... [his] domes and iudgementes and discrecion with mercie and trowthe," and to "graunte the rightfull Lawes and customes to be holden and ... after ... [his] strenght and power such lawes as to the worship of god shalbe chosen by ... [his] people ... to be strenghthenid and defended."[38]

Such a promise remained important, for it was still believed that the well-being and prosperity of the land depended on the king's willingness both to protect the law and to listen to the advice of parliaments. This is clearly displayed in the act settling the crown on Richard III, which compares the ideal past when "this Lande many

37 *Rotuli Parliamentorum: ut et petitiones, et placita in parliamento*, 6 vols. (London, 1832), vol. 6, 241.

38 "Little Device" in *English Coronation Records*, ed. Leopold G. W. Legg (Westminster: A. Constable, 1901), 230.

years stode in great prosperite, honoure and tranquillite; which was caused, forsomoch as the Kings than reignyng, used and followed the advice and counsaill of certaine Lords Spirituelx and Temporelx, and othre personnes of approved sadnesse, prudence, policie and experience, dreding God, and havyng tendre zele and affection to indifferent ministration of Justice, and to the common and politique wele of the Land,"[39] with the more recent past.

In all this rhetoric, and in the sermons before parliament of the late fifteenth century which deal with the question of law, it is notable that the protection of the law is seen to be of equal importance for the maintenance of the country as the declaration of new law. Archbishop Warham touched on the crux of the issue in his sermon before parliament in 1503 when he quoted Ecclesiasticus, "Rule is transferred from peoples to peoples because of injustice,"[40] and went on to argue that "Justice is the best founder of laws and the best conservator of these foundations; since otherwise laws are either founded unjustly, in which case their authors are cursed... or well-founded laws are perverted."[41] The circumstances of the late fifteenth century made this a powerful argument for the proper administration of justice. It is also worth noting that Warham was directing his sermon on the love of justice to the parliament at large, but especially to those "who undertake the care of administering the Republic."[42] These ideas also circulated in the Inns; in the opening of his reading on *Quo Warranto* in 1519, John Spelman pointed to the Romans as an example of an empire that had fallen because justice was not well administered.[43]

If we can thus assume that king and parliament together were seen to create well-founded laws, how was it possible to prevent those laws from being perverted? Spelman's answer was through "the due administration of the laws and customs," which, "if administered well and righteously, according to the purpose for which they were ordained... furnish comfort to just men."[44] This statement would have occasioned no controversy, but establishing the due administration of the law and customs was a challenging process. The structure of the law presented a problem by itself, for it

[39] *Rot. Parl.*, vol. 6, 240. [40] Ecclesiasticus 10:8.
[41] *Rot. Parl.*, vol. 6, 520. [42] *Ibid.*
[43] John Spelman, *John Spelman's Reading on Quo Warranto*, ed. J. H. Baker, Selden Society vol. 113. (London: Selden Society, 1997), 76.
[44] *Ibid.*

was assumed that the common law and statute law together made up a complete and coherent body of law. As Kern argues, once the state had begun to create and codify law,

> it had set forth on the path which ended in the fiction that the written law is comprehensive, and the positive law a complete system. For the authority of legal scholarship or of the statute books, which is considered infallible, gives an answer even where it is silent. For this reason, the State, from the very first moment when it took upon itself to promulgate law, was compelled, in theory, to promulgate a complete law.[45]

English law was far from being complete or systematic. Yet there were practitioners of law whose function it was to expound and apply the law in a systematic way. Fortescue could tell the prince that he need only learn the principles of the law because it was not expedient for him "to investigate precise points of the law by the exertion of . . . [his] own reason, but these should be left to . . . [his] judges and advocates who in the kingdom of England are called serjeants-at-law, and also to others skilled in the law who are commonly called apprentices."[46] It was up to these practitioners to determine whether any alleged custom was part of the common law,[47] and it was up to them to interpret statutory law in light of that law. They can be seen, in Barton's words, as "repositories of the communal sense of right, with implied authority to consent to new customs on behalf of their fellow-countrymen."[48]

The legal profession occupied an ambiguous position in the system of governance. Fortescue presents the judges largely as an academic group. He describes a somewhat idyllic life in which, after they have spent the morning in court and meeting with counsel, they "pass the whole of the rest of the day in studying the laws, reading Holy Scripture and otherwise in contemplation at their pleasure, so that their life seems more contemplative than active."[49] Dudley's *Tree of Commonwealth* echoes Fortescue's sentiment when discussing the localities, for it argues that the chancellor should appoint "good men and suche as will deale indefferently bytwene the

[45] Fritz Kern, *Kingship and Law in the Middle Ages*, trans. S. B. Chrimes (New York: Blackwell, 1956), 178.

[46] Fortescue, *De Laudibus*, 23.

[47] Christopher St. German, *Doctor and Student*, ed. T. F. T. Plucknett and J. L. Barton, Selden Society vol. 91 (London: Selden Society, 1974), 47.

[48] St. German, *Doctor and Student*, li–lii.

[49] Fortescue, *De Laudibus*, 129.

subiectes, and in no wise to put in auctoritie those which are greate bearers of matters"[50] to administer justice in the shires. This idealistic picture does not ring true, and indeed both Fortescue's and Dudley's lives give the lie to any argument that the justices were free from politics.

The *Tree of Commonwealth*, however, goes on to deal with both the appearance and reality of judicial office in more detail. Dudley argues that justice must be one of the roots of the tree of commonwealth, and

> must nedes come of our souereigne lord hym self, for the whole auctorite therof is gyven to hym by god, to mynister by hym self or by his deputies to his subiectes. And though it be suffrid or permytted y^t^ a prince make or ordeyne his deputies in euery parte of this realme to mynister iustice, as his Chauncellor, his iustices of both benches, and other generall and speciall comyssioners in euery [countie] and Shere, yet the cheif charge is his owne. Wherfore, for the honor of god, lett it be forsene y^t^ his grace may make his Iustices of them y^t^ be well lernyd men and specially of good consciens.[51]

Dudley is concerned that the king should appoint men of good conscience, for he recognizes the pressures to which the judges were subject. He exhorts the king to urge the judges to the true administration of justice, and argues that "by hym they must be enformid and put in corage so to do, and y^t^ thei lett [not] for fere or displeasure of any of his one seruantes or counsellours to do trew iustice nor for fere of any great persons in his realme, for y^t^ that thei do is done by his auctorite, and not by ther owne."[52] Here Dudley points out that the judges are often under pressure from great lords to bend the administration of justice in their interests and he returns to the fact that the judges act on behalf of the king. In this he agrees with Fortescue, who told the prince that "none of the kings of England is seen to give judgment by his own lips, yet all the judgments of the realm are his, though given through others."[53]

[50] Edmund Dudley, *The Tree of Commonwealth*, ed. D. M. Brodie (Cambridge: Cambridge University Press, 1948), 34.
[51] *Ibid.* [52] *Ibid.*, 35.
[53] Fortescue, *De Laudibus*, 23. This also echoes Cynus of Pistoia's interpretation, p. 9 above. Spelman echoes both Fortescue and Dudley on the need for both learned and honest lawyers, and recognizes more bluntly than either that "these persons and their officials sometimes misuse their authority, and sometimes exceed it" (Spelman, *Reading on Quo Warranto*, 76.)

This raised a further problem for the judges, for the great lords were not the only ones who might seek to exert pressure on them to bend the law. What would happen if the king were to do the same? They acted by the king's authority and their judgments were in effect the king's judgments; did that mean that the king could require them to return the opinions he wanted? Dudley replies in the negative, arguing that "though the cawse toche hym self, yet he must put them in comfort not to spare to mynister iustice withowt fere: And this to do he shalhave greate meede, for without doubt fere is a great impedyment of iustice emongist the iudges and commyssyoners."[54] Dudley accepts that the king can interfere with the course of justice, but he cautions that he should not misuse his influence over the justices.[55] Of course, there was no guarantee that the king would choose to behave appropriately.

Thus the justices were in a difficult position. The law they administered was made by the authority of the king, but it could not be made or changed by his will alone without the consent of parliament. Their judgments were on behalf of and by the authority of the king, but they were expected to render judgment against the king when the law demanded it. They were guardians and interpreters of both common and statutory law and they were to protect the law against king, lords, and commons. A task of this complexity could not simply be carried out as part of the day-to-day work of the courts, for individual judgments were subject to inconsistency and debate. The lawyers needed an opportunity to examine the law they practised as a logical and coherent whole, and they could do this within the context of legal education.

By the Tudor period, the major institutions of legal education were the four Inns of Court: Lincoln's Inn, Gray's Inn, and the Middle and Inner Temple. The origins of these institutions are obscure. They were not incorporated, and so there are no charters giving their dates of foundation. Their own records begin at different times; the Black Books of Lincoln's Inn are the earliest, beginning in 1422, the records of the Middle Temple begin in 1501 and those of the Inner Temple in 1505, while Gray's Inn has no records until 1569. There is no relation between the dates of the records and the actual origin of the Inns, for a call of serjeants in 1388 demonstrates that the Middle and Inner Temple and Gray's

[54] Dudley, *Tree of Commonwealth*, 35. [55] *Ibid.*, 36–37.

Inn were established by that time.[56] It is notable that Lincoln's Inn is not represented in this call, and this, together with the lack of other contemporary evidence for its existence and the small number of students recorded when its Black Books open in 1422, suggests that it had in fact only come into existence shortly before that date.[57]

There is evidence that some form of learning exercises and even rudimentary lectures on the statutes were taking place in the Inns of Court in the first half of the fourteenth century.[58] If the learning exercises did in fact begin in the early fourteenth century, this provides a possible explanation for the dominance of the major statutes of the thirteenth century in the curriculum of the Inns. There can be no doubt of the importance of these statutes, but it is possible that, if the learning exercises had begun at a later period, the inclusion of contemporary statutes would have prevented their monopoly. The canon of statutes appropriate for readings may, however, have been fixed by the early fourteenth century, and the paucity of major new statutes in the following centuries would mean that this diet of statutes would continue to form the staple of legal education until the early sixteenth century.[59]

While legal education was probably part of the Inns from their inception, no record of it survives from within the Inns before the fifteenth century. In 1428, Lincoln's Inn ordained that members from London and Middlesex should pay commons for the two

[56] J. H. Baker, "The Inns of Court in 1388," in *The Legal Profession and the Common Law* (London: Hambledon, 1986), 4.

[57] The distinction between the Inns of Court and Chancery also seems to be clear by this date: all the serjeants called in 1388 came from what became known as Inns of Court, and, while a serjeant was called from Clifford's Inn in 1396, this was unusual enough to merit a commemorative inscription in the hall window. Baker, "The Inns of Court in 1388," 4.

[58] Paul Brand, "Courtroom and Schoolroom: The Education of Lawyers in England Prior to 1400," *Historical Research* 60 (1987): 162–63; J. H. Baker, "Learning Exercises in the Medieval Inns of Court and Chancery," in *The Legal Profession and the Common Law* (London: Hambledon, 1986), 14.

[59] Later statutes do appear in the readings, but they generally appear as modifications of the major statutes of the thirteenth century rather than as subjects of readings in their own right. Cf. G. R. Elton's argument about the basic requirements for reform and his contention that they only existed in the period of Cromwell's ascendancy, in G. R. Elton, *English Law in the Sixteenth Century: Reform in an Age of Change* (London: Selden Society, 1979), 7–11. He goes on to argue that the Cromwellian reform in law was equivalent to that of Edward I, since "by the middle of Elizabeth's reign it was these Acts of Henry VIII's reign that formed the substance of teaching at the Inns, whereas the Edwardian Acts, hitherto the main pabulum of the young student, lay forgotten and mouldering" (*ibid.*, 16).

weeks before the opening of the Hilary and Easter terms and the three weeks before the Michaelmas term.[60] This seems to have been aimed at ensuring that those who had to pay would in fact be in attendance at the Inn during those weeks and thus available to take part in the learning exercises to be held at that time. This was extended in 1442 by another ordinance of the Inn requiring that every member, after having graduated from the status of student to fellow, should remain at the Inn for the three learning vacations for three years after his admission.[61]

Thus by the mid-fifteenth century the Inns had an established educational system, together with an educational hierarchy. There were three basic ranks within the Inns, though there was some variation from Inn to Inn. These were: inner barristers, who sat within the bar at moots; utter barristers, who sat outside the bar at moots; and benchers, who made up the governing body of the Inn.[62] Progress within the Inn was closely related to its educational function. The inner barristers were the entering students, and they usually held this status for about three years. The utter barristers were those obliged to attend a specified number of learning vacations after their admission as fellows of the Inn, though they retained this status unless and until they became readers.[63] The readers were senior utter barristers who became benchers on the completion of their first reading, and usually completed a second or even a third reading before becoming serjeants, at which time they left the Inn.

Students became utter barristers when they had reached the appropriate standing within the Inn, as utter barristers became readers when they had reached the appropriate level of learning. The

[60] S. E. Thorne, "The Early History of the Inns of Court with Special Reference to Gray's Inn," in *Essays in English Legal History* (London: Hambledon, 1985), 145.

[61] *Ibid.*, 147.

[62] Gray's Inn differed from the others in this, as its governing body was made up of readers rather than benchers. See A. W. B. Simpson, "The Early Constitution of the Inns of Court," *Cambridge Law Journal* 28 (1970): 245–49; and A. W. B. Simpson, "The Early Constitution of Gray's Inn," *Cambridge Law Journal* 34 (1975): 139–41.

[63] The number of learning vacations required varied from Inn to Inn. In Gray's Inn, there was an intermediate class between the utter barristers and readers, called the ancients. Members became ancients through a formal call or election, and the readers at that Inn were drawn exclusively from the ancients. Simpson, "Early Constitution of Gray's Inn," 143–44.

promotions were probably regulated by customs within the Inns, but calls to the bar and bench were not recorded until the sixteenth century.[64] Lincoln's Inn first recorded its calls to the bar in 1518 and Simpson suggests that Gray's Inn began its records in 1523, though the other Inns did not do so until the reign of Elizabeth.[65] This indicates that progression through the Inns was a purely internal matter until at least the 1520s, when the call to the bar began to be seen as a basic prerequisite for practice in the central courts. The status of utter barrister, however, was only the beginning of a legal career for a man who wished to rise in the profession. It was possible to become an utter barrister after two or three years at an Inn, but Simpson argues that it could take anywhere from fifteen to over twenty years to become a reader and up to thirty to become a serjeant.[66] Clearly only a very small number of the men admitted to the Inns reached this exalted status, and most probably did not intend to do so.

Thus the audience at the readings covered the full range of knowledge. The readers were talking to advanced and able students of the law as well as respected practitioners, who might be expected to argue with their interpretations and help refine their understanding of the king's prerogative. However, to consider them simply as a group of serjeants-in-training is to misunderstand the nature of the Inns. Many of the students at the Inns had no intention of following a legal career. Young men of good family often attended an Inn for a couple of years to gain a grounding in the law, to enjoy the rich cultural and social life for which the Inns were famous, and to make useful connections for the future. Thus the readers might also be talking to young men who held or who expected to inherit land which might be held of the king, men who would have a particular interest in understanding the current state of the law and the new claims the king was making. Other students intended to make the law their career, but did not have the ability, the money, or the connections to follow the full course of study and enter the rarefied atmosphere of the Westminster courts. These men often returned to a legal practice in their own community but retained a link to Westminster and their friends and associates at the Inns.

64 Baker, "Learning Exercises," 10.

65 Simpson, "The Early Constitution of Gray's Inn," 140; Simpson, "Early Constitution of the Inns," 250.

66 Simpson, "The Early Constitution of Gray's Inn," 145–46.

These were the men who would be expected to advise their clients on the direction of legal change and the best way to avoid the long arm of the king.[67]

This multi-dimensional nature of the Inns of Court is often overlooked, leading to a somewhat artificial distinction between lawyers and laymen. Carpenter, for example, believes that the use made of law by landowners can tell us a great deal about their ideas of governance, and recognizes that many landowners had "at least a smattering of the law," but she warns that we should remember "that it is the consumers of the law, not the lawyers, that we want to learn about."[68] It is important to guard against this reaction, for the lawyers, besides being significant consumers of the law, regulated and determined the way in which the law was used, and were often the source for the landowners' law, both in terms of practical knowledge and in terms of legal ideas.

Lawyers were trained in two main learning exercises in the Inns: moots and readings. Moots were part of the basic educational structure for the inner and junior utter barristers, while readings on statutes were more advanced and formal exercises.[69] Simple readings were being given in the early fourteenth century,[70] and by the mid-fifteenth century they were quite elaborate.[71] Baker argues that the readings played a significant role in "the arrangement, consolidation and explanation of unwritten principles which are often glimpsed only fleetingly in the year books."[72] Each reader built upon the arguments of his predecessor, endorsing what had been accepted as "good" law, raising new questions which had emerged in

[67] E. W. Ives, *The Common Lawyers of Pre-Reformation England* (Cambridge: Cambridge University Press, 1983), 146.

[68] Christine Carpenter, "Political and Constitutional History: Before and After McFarlane," in *The McFarlane Legacy: Studies in Late Medieval Politics and Society,* ed. R. H. Britnell and A. J. Pollard, The Fifteenth Century Series No. 1 (Stroud: Alan Sutton, 1995), 197.

[69] Moots were pleading exercises held in the halls of the Inns. Some manuscripts of moots and moot cases have survived, though not in the same quantity as manuscript readings. The only moots in print are those in J. H. Baker, ed., *Readings and Moots at the Inns of Court in the Fifteenth Century*, Selden Society vol. 105 (London: Selden Society, 1989), vol. 2, and those included in Robert Keilway, *Relationes quorundam Casuum selectorum ex Libris Roberti Keilway Armiger* (London: 1602).

[70] Brand, "Courtroom and Schoolroom," 160–62.

[71] Thorne, "Early History of the Inns of Court," 149.

[72] J. H. Baker, "The Inns of Court and Legal Doctrine," in *Lawyers and Laymen*, ed. T. M. Charles-Edwards *et al.* (Cardiff: University of Wales Press, 1986), 278.

the courts since the last reading on the statute, and discussing hypothetical questions. The reader was not imposing his view of the law on his audience, however, for his auditors were expected to make it clear when they disagreed with his interpretation, so that discussion could ensue. The readers in the early Tudor period did not rely on a discussion of case law, whether recent or ancient. There are few year book references in the surviving lecture notes, and those few are often later additions. The readers instead seem intent on presenting the law as a clear and coherent structure which can be both explained and understood simply by the application of reason.[73] As Ives comments, legal education in the late fifteenth century "was less a cramming course in ancient precedent than an endeavor to develop forensic agility."[74] The year books provided useful illustrations of the law at work, but the readings were intended to explain why the law worked in that way.

The readings took place in the Autumn and Lent vacations, with the Autumn session usually being taken by a new reader, and the Lent vacation given to the more senior double reader. A report on the Inns of Court from 1540 states that the reader will choose to "reade some one such Act, or Statute as shall please him to ground his whole reading on."[75] Though this was probably true by 1540, it is less clear how texts were chosen in the fifteenth century. Thorne argues that readers had little say in their choice of text, but lectured on the statutes, following their predecessor in rotation through the major statutes from Magna Carta to the end of the reign of Edward II.[76] It seems, however, that Thorne's scheme is too tidy;

[73] See J. H. Baker, "English Law and the Renaissance," *Cambridge Law Journal* 44 (1985): 52–53; Baker, "The Inns of Court and Legal Doctrine," 276; Eric Ives, "A Lawyer's Library in 1500," *Law Quarterly Review* 85 (1969): 108.

[74] Ives, "Lawyer's Library," 108.

[75] Report of Thomas Denton, Nicholas Bacon, and Robert Cary, reprinted by D. S. Bland, "Henry VIII's Royal Commission on the Inns of Court," *Journal of the Society of Public Teachers of Law* 10 (1969): 186.

[76] S. E. Thorne, ed., *Readings and Moots at the Inns of Court in the Fifteenth Century*, Selden Society vol. 71 (London: Selden Society, 1954), vol. 1, xvi. Thorne, "Early History of the Inns of Court," 148–49. The surviving records of the Inns note when readers were appointed and when they read, but they do not mention the texts covered. J. H. Baker, *Readers and Readings in the Inns of Court and Chancery*, Selden Society Supplementary Series vol. 13 (London: Selden Society, 2001), details all the known manuscript readings, with their topics, their dates and their readers, as far as he could establish them. This remarkable volume has given us the clearest outline thus far of the readers in the Inns of Court and Chancery, but there are still some gaps in our knowledge.

though there were periods when a sequence of readers would follow texts in chronological order, there is no evidence that this was the norm, although there does seem to have been a practical desire to cover most of the major statutes on a fairly regular basis.[77]

The expectation that readings would be based, not only on a statute, but on an old statute, also meant that the readers often had to strain their text artificially in order to cover the topic they wished to discuss. For example, in 1503, Thomas Marow lectured on justices of the peace, but, instead of reading on a later act which dealt with them, Marow chose the opening chapter of Westminster I, which pre-dated the development of the office.[78] It was not impossible to read on a more recent statute; Marow's colleague at the Inner Temple, Gregory Adgore, lectured on a statute of 1484 in his first reading, given in 1489 or 1490.[79] The classic statutes remained the staple of the readings into the early sixteenth century, though they had increasingly to share the stage with newer material.

In the normal course of events, each reader was appointed a year before his reading in order to give him time to prepare. This routine was sometimes upset by death or illness, and in these circumstances a bencher might step in to fill the vacant place and deliver a third or even a fourth reading. Similarly, when a new group of serjeants was called, the serjeants-elect were expected to deliver the next reading at their Inn, or, if two were called from the same Inn, the junior man lectured. In either of these cases, the reader seems to have been allowed to expound any "old" statute that interested him.

Since readings on statutes are a largely neglected source, it is worth spending a little time on the manuscripts themselves, and the problems and possibilities inherent in their use. The first and most obvious limitation is the fact that the readings generally exist only in the notes taken by auditors. Though it is difficult to avoid presenting the texts as the words of the readers, we must always keep in mind that they are actually a record of the elements of the reading which were of most interest to the note-taker. This means that we have to be particularly careful in arguing from silence, for

77 Baker, *Readers and Readings*, 3.

78 Bertha Putnam, *Early Treatises on the Practice of the Justices of the Peace in the Fifteenth and Sixteenth Centuries*, Oxford Studies in Social and Legal History, ed. Sir Paul Vinogradoff (Oxford: Clarendon Press, 1924; reprint New York: Octagon, 1974), vol. 7, 167.

79 Baker, *Readers and Readings*, 69.

we have no guarantee that the notes do not simply omit a section of the lecture. This can cause problems of varying degrees. On the more basic topics of the prerogative, for example forms of tenure, this is generally not problematic, since, while the readers do not always cover the same points, they show no signs of disagreement. This is one of the more basic elements of the lecture, material with which the listeners were more likely to be familiar, and thus it is often recorded more sketchily. Where the material is more complex or more original, it is rather more difficult to handle. This is particularly true because there is generally no standard template for the lecture, and, while some readers lean on their predecessor's work, they do not follow it exactly in either content or structure.

While the readings present certain problems of interpretation, they are also replete with possibilities. The readings were first and foremost learning exercises. They were presentations of the law as it was understood by senior members of the profession, intended to instruct students on the issues they would face in court. This makes them a peculiarly direct route to the law of the day, comparable to the year books for immediacy, but more detailed and comprehensive. Although, as we will see, the readings were not free of bias, they were not in their nature polemical statements. Individual readers might have different interpretations of what the law was, and thus provide insight into both the law and politics of the issue under discussion, but the readers could not create a political case without a very strong basis in law, if they expected it to be accepted by their audience. The readings could not afford to be arguments as to how the law should be, or how it used to be, because that would not serve the needs of their audience. Those looking for an over-arching theoretical background for the readings will be disappointed, for they were simply expositions of the law as it stood, with little consideration of why it was that way, or whether it should be changed. The readers might, on occasion, express disapproval of a particular practice as being contrary to the law, but their reasons have to be inferred from the broader structure of their reading.

The readings are also invaluable because they allow us to see the law develop over time. Not only can we see the progression of ideas, we can also see the ways in which particular topics moved in and out of the readers' spotlight, and thus get a glimpse of changes of emphasis as well as doctrine. However, the nature of the texts can sometimes make this difficult, and the readings on *Prerogativa*

Regis are a good example of both the benefits and pitfalls of this exercise. The readings given by Thomas Frowyk and Robert Constable in 1495 are the first lectures to survive on the topic with known readers and clearly attributed texts. We are also sure of the content of John Spelman's lecture in 1521 and George Willoughby's in 1549. However, we have references to readings on *Prerogativa Regis* for which texts do not seem to survive, while there are numerous other manuscript readings on *Prerogativa Regis* which do not match the surviving texts of Frowyk's, Constable's, Spelman's, or Willoughby's lectures. However, identifying anonymous readings is more complicated than simply connecting texts to named readers, since readers quite commonly used the work of their predecessors, without indicating what they were doing. This practice, combined with the fact that the recorders could easily omit sections of the lectures, makes it difficult to tell if an anonymous manuscript is a different version of a known text, or a different reading. Since the readers were not particularly concerned with citing precedents, it is also difficult to date the texts from internal references. A consideration of the manuscripts will help to lay out the pattern of the readings on *Prerogativa Regis* and some of the problems with the readers and their texts.

There are three manuscript readings which appear to pre-date 1495. The first is in Bodleian MS Rawlinson C. 294. This is a brief text, only about two and a half pages, and there is nothing in it to allow any kind of definite dating. The second early reading is in CUL MS Ee.5.22. There are only a few internal pointers to the dating of this text. It makes no mention of *Skrene's Case*, which puts it before 1475, but it does refer to Henry VI's statute on farmers, which places it after 1430.[80] These are the only definitive parameters within the text though there is one other point which suggests that it belongs in the earlier part of this period: the mention of "opinio laikon," presumably William Laken, who became a serjeant in 1453.[81] Since Laken's opinion would have been of greater value when he had some

[80] For *Skrene's Case*, see below, passim. 8 Hen. VI, c.16, *Stat. Realm*, vol. 2, 252. This identification is not secure, since the reading actually refers to "vn estatut fait en temps del Roy H le iiij^{te}" (CUL MS Ee.5.22, f.343). There is no statute of Henry IV which fits the description, but the reference could also be to 18 Hen. VI, c.6, *Stat. Realm*, vol. 2, 306–07, which rehearses the earlier statute and refines it.

[81] CUL MS Ee.5.22, f.341; Baker, *Readers and Readings*, 21.

seniority, it seems likely that this reading belongs to the 1440s or 1450s. This would also fit with the parlous state of royal finances at the time: the 1440s were a desperate decade, and the looming collapse of the French lands made Henry VI's government consider some new, and occasionally unusual, financial expedients, some of which were based on the royal prerogative.[82]

The third early reading, in CUL MS Hh.3.6, can be dated more precisely. It discusses *Skrene's Case*, but it makes no mention of the statute of 4 Hen. VII, c.17 which changed the law on uses. This limits it to the period 1476–1489. It has more case, statute, and general references than the earlier text, but they do not help to date it any more precisely than this. Although we cannot establish it beyond a doubt, it seems likely that this is the reading of Edward Grantham of the Inner Temple, who seems to have given a reading on *Prerogativa Regis* at about this time.[83] Thorne argues that this was Brown's reading, but there is no evidence that Brown read on *Prerogativa Regis*.[84] His name appears in the text, but he seems to be attending the reader and raising questions for discussion rather than lecturing himself. Thorne also conjectures, based on a corruption in the text (which seems to refer to Richard IV), that the reading post-dates the reign of Edward IV, and suggests that it belongs to early Henry VII. However, there is an argument that the reading probably preceded Buckingham's revolt in October 1483.[85] If both conjectures were true, the reading could be dated quite precisely to the autumn of 1483, but this would probably be straining the evidence.

Following these early texts, we have the two 1495 readers, Thomas Frowyk of the Inner Temple, and Robert Constable of Lincoln's Inn.[86] They were probably followed in 1507 by John Port. This identification is not secure, but it seems likely. Internal evidence dates the reading in BL MS Hargrave 87 to between July 1507 and 1513, in the Inner Temple. Since all the readings from 1508 to 1512 are known, a process of elimination places it in the Autumn of 1507, when Port read.[87] The most troubling point about this

[82] R. A. Griffiths, *The Reign of King Henry VI* (Stroud: Sutton, 1998), 380–82 and 384–87.

[83] E.g. BL MS Harl. 2051, f.39v refers to "Grantham lector" and the context suggests a reading on the prerogative. Baker, *Readers and Readings*, 285 and 420.

[84] Thorne, *Prerogativa Regis*, xlix.

[85] See pp. 51–52 below.

[86] See Baker, *Readers and Readings*, lii.

[87] *Ibid.*, 324.

identification is that it would have been Port's first reading, following on the treatment of the topic by two serjeants-elect. If it is Port's reading, he took care to base it closely on Frowyk's text, and to refer continuously to Frowyk through the text.[88]

The next reader was also a serjeant-elect, John Spelman of Gray's Inn, who read during Lent 1521. His reading is preserved in the Chaloner manuscript, Gray's Inn MS 25. He was followed in 1531 by another Gray's Inn reader, Roger Yorke, whose text does not survive, though there are brief excerpts from it in BL MS Hargrave 253 and BL MS Add. 38133. Material on the prerogative in Yorke's notebook (BL MS Hargrave 388) also gives us some sense of his knowledge, but this is all fragmentary.

Following Yorke, there are two possible readings on the prerogative: Edward Mountague of the Middle Temple in the Autumn of 1531 and John Fitzjames, also of the Middle Temple, during Lent 1537. No text survives for either reading: Mountague's lecture is suggested in Pollard's reports, while Fitzjames' is suggested by Brooke's *Abridgement*.[89] These attributions are problematic; Baker bases his tentative identification of Mountague on the assumption that lectures on *Prerogativa Regis* were usually given by serjeants-elect, but, if the identification of Port in 1507 is correct, it would have been his first lecture, and Fitzjames' conjectural reading would have been his second. It is possible that by the 1530s *Prerogativa Regis* was no longer a challenging text for a reader to choose, and thus it might have been appropriate for a junior reader. The later readings on *Prerogativa Regis* were not given by serjeants-elect; the next known reading was by George Willoughby of the Inner Temple, during Lent 1549, and the last was probably given by William Staunford of Gray's Inn, during Lent 1551. The first three lectures of Willoughby's reading survive in BL MS Harley 1691, while Staunford's reading is mentioned in BL MS Harley 785. Staunford also wrote a treatise on the king's prerogative in 1549, which may be related to his text.

Thus the readings on *Prerogativa Regis* emerged in the mid-fifteenth century, were developed by the foremost lawyers of the day in the later fifteenth and early sixteenth century, and faded into obscurity in the reign of Edward VI. This book will examine how this happened, the actual development of the law from reader to reader,

[88] *Ibid.*, 74 and 324. [89] *Ibid.*, 154 and 341, and 156.

but it will also consider why it happened. Why did this problematic text arouse interest through this period, and why did the interest then fade? Significant attention was given to *Prerogativa Regis* in 1495 because Henry VII's political and financial policies exploited the king's fiscal prerogatives in an aggressive and imaginative way. The king could set these policies in motion, but the lawyers' role was to examine the details of their implementation, and determine whether his servants were operating within the bounds of the law. While Henry VIII's aims differed substantially from his father's, he too exploited his prerogative for financial and political reasons. However, the readers in the late fifteenth and early sixteenth century had demonstrated that there were limits to how *Prerogativa Regis* could be interpreted, and, as the pace of change quickened in the 1530s and 1540s, new legislation re-wrote the king's relationship with his tenants. *Prerogativa Regis* remained an important base text of the fiscal prerogative, and the treatments of Willoughby and Staunford show that a familiarity with its provisions remained necessary, but, following the Statutes of Uses and Wills, it was no longer a focus of debate and controversy.

Not only had new legislation changed the administration of the king's financial prerogatives, the conception of the prerogative itself was changing in the later sixteenth century. Though this development is outside our purview, readings like James Morice's on Westminster I, c.50 in 1578 demonstrate that not only had *Prerogativa Regis* been superseded as the focus of the prerogative, but the financial prerogatives were being diminished, dismissed as only some of the royal rights, and "those not the chiefest."[90] Between 1495 and 1578, both the law based on *Prerogativa Regis*, and the conception of king's prerogative, underwent substantial changes. In order to understand the extent of this change, we need to begin with the history of the royal lands and the king's exploitation of his feudal prerogative.

[90] BL MS Egerton 3376, f.7.

1

THE EARLY READINGS

The military importance of feudal tenures became subsidiary to their financial importance little more than a century after the Conquest. Richardson and Sayles argue that, by the time of Glanvill, "those who render and those who accept homage have no thought of arms, of service in the field: they think of reliefs, marriage and wardship, the profits, not the remotely ancient obligations, of military tenure."[1] Developments through the thirteenth century continued this trend. A royal ordinance of 1256 attempted to protect the incidents of feudal tenure by restricting the right of tenants-in-chief of the king to alienate lands held of him. Alienation at will meant that the king's control over his lands was weakened by subinfeudation, as the feudal ladder was stretched. Moreover, his dues were often reduced by the division of land into parcels too small to return the appropriate services. After 1256, alienation was only permitted by licence of the king. There is little evidence of the effect of this change under Henry III, but the records from the late thirteenth century suggest that licences were not easily available until the mid-1290s.[2] At this point, Edward I reversed his previous policy of opposing alienation of lands held in chief. Instead, he granted licences to alienate, under which the alienee would hold the land in chief of the king and for which a fine was paid. Thus the king's financial incidents were safeguarded and he made money from the licence. Bean sees this as part of the growing consciousness of the

[1] H. G. Richardson and G. O. Sayles, *The Governance of Medieval England from the Conquest to Magna Carta* (Edinburgh: Edinburgh University Press, 1963), 111. Susan Reynolds' discussion of the confusion between some military and socage tenures suggests that the distinction was no longer considered crucial to the safety of the realm. Susan Reynolds, *Fiefs and Vassals* (Oxford: Oxford University Press, 1994), 355.

[2] J. M. W. Bean, *The Decline of English Feudalism 1215–1540* (New York: Manchester University Press, 1968), 71–73.

royal prerogative in this period and the increased interest in defining the king's rights.[3] The statute of *Quia Emptores* of 1290 played a part in this process by conferring freedom to alienate on all men, but abolishing the process of sub-infeudation.[4] Throughout this period of change, there is no mention of any military drawbacks to alienation or sub-infeudation.[5] Both the king and the mesne lords are concerned with protecting the financial value of the wardships, reliefs, and escheats due from their tenants. Richardson and Sayles argue that, by this time, "the state is independent of feudalism, and if, perforce, its organization must at some points be accommodated to certain feudal ideas and forms, it cannot at any period be justly termed a feudal state."[6]

Thus it can be argued that, from the reign of Edward I and before, England was not a feudal state, but that her kings used the feudal forms as a source of income. The importance of the income garnered from the king's tenants-in-chief varied over the centuries. Wolffe argues that the royal estate was of little economic importance to the Angevin kings, whose "political power as kings was so great that, by comparison, their financial resources as landlords were insignificant."[7] He believes that English kings from the Conquest onwards relied mainly on taxation to finance their government and that contemporaries expected nothing else. In the thirteenth and fourteenth centuries, it was understood that the king would use the income from his own estates primarily to support his family, secondly to provide patronage, and finally, and only intermittently, to contribute to the expenses of government.[8] Wolffe points out that the idea that the king should live of his own is relatively late and that the phrase occurs for the first time in 1311. At that time,

3 *Ibid.*, 70.

4 Bean concludes that *Quia Emptores* did not apply to tenants-in-chief. He argues that the ordinance of 1256 had settled the question of their ability to alienate and the fact that they continued to need licences to alienate demonstrates that the new statute did not affect their position. *Ibid.*, 81–83.

5 Richardson and Sayles, *Governance of Medieval England*, 112.

6 *Ibid.*, 40. Pocock makes a similar point when approaching the issue from the vantage point of the seventeenth century. He comments that Coke "knew all there was to know about feudal law in England, except the single fact that it was feudal." J. G. A. Pocock, *The Ancient Constitution and the Feudal Law: A Study of English Historical Thought in the Seventeenth Century* (New York: W. W. Norton, 1967), 66.

7 B. P. Wolffe, *The Royal Demesne in English History: The Crown Estates in the Governance of the Realm from the Conquest to 1509* (London: George Allen & Unwin, 1971), 22.

8 *Ibid.*, 65.

contemporaries were arguing that the king should live on his rightful income and avoid the evil of purveyance, which was impoverishing the countryside. When they argued that the king should live of his own, they considered "his own" to include all the royal income, including direct and indirect taxation, not just the income of the royal estates.[9]

It was only with the accession of Henry IV and the addition of the Lancastrian family lands to the royal income that the importance of the revenue of the crown lands increased substantially. The overseas preoccupations of Henry V and the weakness of Henry VI meant that these resources were not exploited to their full extent, and the crown continued to rely heavily on parliamentary taxation to fund government. Wolffe maintains that, when Edward IV became king, he began a concerted effort to administer the crown lands effectively. He applied the principles of private estate management to the crown lands and resumed many of the estates granted away by his predecessors. Wolffe suggests that Edward IV was the first king to believe that the king should "live of his own" in the later sense of the phrase, rather than relying on taxation, and that he proposed to do so by the effective development of the crown's landed base.[10] Edward succeeded in making the royal estates profitable, but it was left to Henry VII to take the next logical step. Edward exploited the lands in his grasp effectively, but he made little progress in seeking out tenants-in-chief of the crown who had managed to slip through the feudal net in the chaos of the fifteenth century or in extending the services due to the king.[11]

Edward also made little progress in dealing with the problem of uses, which meant that the crown was consistently being deprived of income from the lands of its tenants-in-chief. In its simplest form, a use was where a tenant enfeoffed another with his land,

[9] *Ibid.*, 40–51.

[10] In his review of Wolffe's *The Crown Lands 1461 to 1536: An Aspect of Yorkist and Early Tudor Government* (New York: Barnes & Noble, 1970), G. L. Harriss argues that Edward's promise to live of his own was part of an attempt to soften up parliament in preparation for a request for taxation. *English Historical Review* 88 (1973): 172.

[11] Lander notes that, under Edward IV, exchequer officials made extensive searches for information. He points out that in 3 Edw. IV, the clerks of the Treasurer's Remembrancer were paid £20 for special work in compiling rolls of farms, wards, and marriages at the king's disposal, and the clerks of the Great Roll were also paid £20 for searching the rolls and books of the exchequer from Edward III to Henry VI. J. R. Lander, *The Limitations of English Monarchy in the Later Middle Ages* (Toronto: University of Toronto Press, 1989), 67–68, n.12.

thus transferring seisin, but kept the profits of the land for his own use, or for the use of a third party, known as the *cestui que use*. Since the king's prerogatives were due only on land held of him which passed by descent from a tenant-in-chief to his heir, if the tenant-in-chief enfeoffed another of his land, keeping the use of it for himself or for another, and then died, the king could not claim his feudal incidents, for neither the feoffor nor the *cestui que use* held the land at the time of the feoffor's death. The *cestui que use* would have the use of the land but, since the land itself had not passed by descent, the king lost his prerogative rights in it.[12] Not only did this practice rob the king of profit in the short term, the complex conveyancing which accompanied it also quickly obscured titles to land.

The responsibility for keeping track of the king's rights and his lands fell on the escheator. Each county had an escheator responsible for safeguarding the feudal incidents due to the king from his tenants-in-chief in that county, and it was this official's job to hold inquisitions.[13] The inquisition was the first step in claiming the king's feudal dues by establishing who his tenants were, when exactly they died, what they held, of whom and how it was held, what it was worth, who the heir was, and how old he was. This provided the necessary information to establish the king's rights over the land in question. The escheator was then responsible for seeing that these rights were protected. All of the surviving readings deal with the inquisition writs and, while important to an understanding of the process, they are generally not complicated. For these reasons, we can consider them here, before moving on to the more complex elements of both law and procedure.[14]

The escheator could carry out an inquisition either *virtute officii*, by virtue of his office, or *virtute brevis*, by virtue of a writ issued from chancery. An inquisition held *virtute officii* was returned by the

[12] The owner would usually convey the land to a group of co-feoffees, thus ensuring that the land would not fall to the king through the death of the feoffee. The feoffees in turn would pass the land on to others before the last one of them died and so it would continuously change hands through conveyance without ever passing by descent. Simpson notes that eminent lawyers were often used as feoffees to secure the conveyance and reduce the likelihood of fraud on the part of the feoffees. A. W. B. Simpson, *A History of the Land Law* (Oxford: Clarendon Press, 1986), 182–83.

[13] Bean, *The Decline of English Feudalism*, 19.

[14] We will return to the methods for dealing with problematic inquisitions at pp. 128–40 below.

escheator to the chancery or the exchequer. Having been returned, this writ meant that the lands in question were in the hands of the king as a matter of record. This was important, for in order for an aggrieved tenant to challenge the king's right to any seized land, he had to be able to object to information on record. An inquisition *virtute brevis* could be called by one of four writs. The most common was the *diem clausit extremum*, which had to be issued from the chancery within a year of the death of the tenant-in-chief. As with the inquisition *virtute officii*, when it was returned to chancery it became a matter of record and the land was properly in the hands of the king.[15] The second writ used to call an inquisition was *mandamus*. This was much the same as the *diem clausit extremum*, but it was issued after a year if there had been no *diem clausit extremum*, or if the first writ had not been returned to chancery. The third writ was used if the king had an heir in ward and the heir died. This writ of *devenerunt* ordered the escheator to enquire what lands were in the king's hands because of his wardship, and it was effectively a new enquiry into the reasons why the king had the ward in the first place. It also sought the heir of the ward and the heir's age. The fourth writ was *amotus*. This was sent out when the first writ issued had not been returned. *Amotus* rehearsed the first writ and required that it be returned. Beyond these four writs, there were two others, but these could not be issued unless one of the four had first been issued and returned. *Que plura* was applicable where, after the first writ was returned, the king was informed that his tenant held more lands than were named in the return. *Melius inquirendum* was used when the first writ had been returned with some necessary information missing, as for example when the inquisition jury did not know of whom the land was held, or how, and it ordered a second inquisition to discover the missing information.[16]

15 The writ of *diem clausit extremum* could only be sued once. In a case of 2 Hen. VII before the justices in the exchequer chamber, a plaintiff sought a commission to enquire concerning his title to land in tail of which his brother had died seised, and the justices concluded that such a commission was in effect nothing but a *diem clausit extremum*, and so his request was denied. M. Hemmant, ed., *Select Cases in the Exchequer Chamber before All the Justices of England*, vol. 2: 1461–1509, Selden Society vol. 64 (London: Bernard Quaritch, 1948), 128.

16 All of the readers cover this material: e.g. Bodleian MS Rawlinson C. 294, ff.205v–06v (this text does not discuss the writ *amotus*); CUL Ee.5.22, ff.342v–43; CUL Hh.3.6, ff.55v–56; Robert Constable, *Prerogativa Regis: Tertia Lectura Roberti Constable de Lincolnis Inne Anno 11 H. 7*, ed. S. E. Thorne (New Haven: Yale University Press, 1949, 42–45.

An inquisition held *virtute officii* gave the king title, but it did not give the heir title and the heir had to go through the process of an inquisition sued on a chancery writ. If the heir to the land was found to be a minor, he would become a ward of the king until he reached his majority, according to the age in the inquisition. He would then prove his age and retrieve his lands from the king. An heir found of full age in the inquisition avoided wardship, but the king still seized his lands and he had to pay relief before following the same process as a minor heir in swearing homage and getting livery of his lands.[17]

Although this process sounds fairly straightforward, by the late fifteenth century there were a number of problems with it. One was that inquisition juries were not always knowledgeable enough about the land under consideration, largely because of the growing complexity of land transfers. Worse still, they were not always impartial. They could be intimidated by the heirs of the deceased, or by the sheriff of the county, or they could be biased towards the heirs. In any of these cases, an injustice could result.[18] Thus, by the end of the fifteenth century, both the ongoing practice of enfeoffment to use and the turmoil of the civil wars, meant that the king had very little idea of who his tenants-in-chief actually were. The last feudal aid collected by a king was in 1428, when the commons made a grant of tonnage, poundage, a tax on parishes and towns, and a levy on knight's fees.[19] The next attempt to collect a feudal aid would be in 1504. Over the seventy-six years between them, much changed, both in the tenurial map of England, and in its politics. This was also the period in which readings on *Prerogativa Regis* began.

The first of the two anonymous fifteenth-century readings on *Prerogativa Regis* is CUL Ee.5.22, which probably dates from the

[17] The details of this process are covered in chapter 3, pp. 142–49, below.

[18] See D. A. Luckett, "Henry VII and the South-Western Escheators," in *The Reign of Henry VII: Proceedings of the 1993 Harlaxton Symposium*, ed. Benjamin Thompson, Harlaxton Medieval Studies V (Stamford: Paul Watkins, 1995), 54–64, for a consideration of the problems associated with inquisitions and some of the ways in which the administration dealt with them.

[19] H. C. Maxwell-Lyte, ed., *Calendar of Feudal Aids 1284–1431*, vol. 1 (London: HMSO, 1899), xxvii. Another similar aid was voted in 1431, but parliament petitioned for a remission, arguing that it was too complicated for assessment. *Ibid.*, xxviii–xxix.

1440s or 1450s.[20] As with every other reading on *Prerogativa Regis*, it opens with the question of whether the text is a statute, and answers with the assertion that it is, and is "made solely for the advantage and profit of the king."[21] From this assertion it moves on to consider what lands are held of the crown, for only lands held of the crown bring the full weight of the prerogative. The reader begins by arguing that, if an earldom or barony held of the crown escheats to the king, any tenant who holds of the barony will owe only the same service that he would owe his lord, so the king will not have his prerogative in these lands. The discussion which follows is rather confusing, but the reader seems to be arguing that, if the king grants escheated lands out again, they will once more carry the full weight of the prerogative for their new holder; thus, he argues that a modern grant of crown lands carries the same burden as an ancient grant.[22]

This issue will come up again in later readings, but this early reading does not linger over the problem, but moves on to the next element of the statute, the need for the king's tenant to die seised in his demesne as of fee. The reader points out that the words of the statute are not always taken literally, and his discussion of this point turns into an examination of the difference between reversion and remainder.[23] He argues that, if the king's tenant has leased the lands he holds of the king to another for term of the other's life, with the king's licence, and then dies with his heir under age, the king will still seize the wardship of the infant, and the wardship of any lands his tenant held of other lords, and will have any rent reserved on the

[20] The third anonymous fifteenth-century manuscript, Bodleian MS Rawlinson C. 294, is too short for effective dating, and its brief discussion adds little to our knowledge of the topic in any case. See pp. 23–25 above for the dating of these texts.

[21] CUL MS Ee.5.22, f.338. It cites 43 Edw. III in support of this point.

[22] *Ibid.*, f.338v.

[23] Land leased or alienated in fee tail often carried the condition that, if the donee died without issue, it should revert to the donor or his right heirs, an estate known as a reversion. Although the reversioner might not actually hold the land, a reversion was not considered to be a future estate in law, for the reversioner or his ancestor had held the land and maintained a continuous interest in it, though he was neither lord nor tenant. A remainder is created when land is alienated to someone for a stated term, and at the end of the term is to pass to a third individual. The recipient, the remainderman, had no previous connection with the land, and so a remainder, unlike a reversion, is a future estate.

leased land.[24] The reader does not give his reasons immediately, but when he returns to the point he says that some argue that, when the king's tenant leases his land in this way,[25] the king has the choice of taking the lessee, i.e. the tenant in possession, or the lessor, i.e. the tenant in law, as his tenant.[26] However, the reader disagrees with this and argues that the relationship between the king and the lessor remains the same, and so the lessor must remain the king's tenant. His reasoning is that the fee simple remains in the lessor, and so, if the lessee were to become the king's tenant, the holder of the fee simple would not hold of anyone, which would be unreasonable.[27] However, if the king's tenant leased the lands with the remainder over in fee, the tenancy did change, because the fee simple left the lessor, and the tenant in possession became the king's new tenant until the remainder was determined.[28] Therefore, if the potential remainderman died leaving an heir under age before the lessee died, the king would not have the infant in ward, since he already had a tenant, and the remainder was not determined.[29]

In the case above, the reversioner did not die seised, but his heir was still in ward. In the next case, the tenant's not dying seised changes the wardship. If the tenant is disseised, and the disseisor dies with an heir under age, and is found to be the tenant, the king will have his heir in ward. The right heir cannot enter on his lands during the wardship, because he cannot disturb the king's possession, but he can enter after the disseisor's heir sues livery. The reader's main concern is to maintain that "this descent does not defeat the entry, since he could not enter and thus no default or laxity may be adjudged in him [the heir of the diseissee]."[30]

In the third example, the king loses wardship of lands when the ancestor does not die seised. Thus, if the king has the wardship of an infant and afterwards other lands, not held of the king, descend to the infant from another ancestor, the king will not have the lands, because the tenant did not die seised. Instead, the lord of the lands will have them.[31] The reader goes on to point out that this is not

[24] CUL MS Ee.5.22, f.338v.

[25] He also uses the example of land given in tail, but I have stayed with the lease for clarity of exposition.

[26] CUL MS Ee.5.22, f.338v. [27] *Ibid.* [28] *Ibid.* [29] *Ibid.*, ff.338v–39.

[30] *Ibid.*, f.339. The same applies if a husband and wife are disseised during coverture or if the disseisee is under age at the time of death of the disseisor.

[31] CUL MS Ee.5.22, f.339v.

peculiar to the king, but works in the same way for any lord. Conversely, if a lord has the wardship of his tenant's heir and then land held of the king descends to the same infant, the king will have the wardship of the land, but he will not be able to claim the infant, since the body had legally vested in the first lord, and as a chattel it cannot be divested.[32]

The reader also points out that, although the statute says that the king will have all the lands of which his tenant dies seised, that does not always work. This is because the prerogative applied to land which passed by descent, but only when land passed by direct descent from the tenant-in-chief to his heir, whether an heir to land held in fee tail or fee simple. Land held in fee simple passed from the tenant to his heir without restriction. Land in fee tail passed from the tenant to the heirs of his body, but it could not go to a brother or cousin. This restriction was known as a fee tail general, but it could be further refined to a fee tail special, in which land would pass only to the heirs male of the tenant's body, or to the heirs of the tenant begotten on the body of a particular woman.[33] Thus, if a man held land in tail to the heirs of his body begotten on his first wife, any children born of his second wife would have no claim to it. It was fairly common for the heir general and the heir in tail to be the same person. For example, when a tenant-in-chief held land in fee simple and land in tail to the heirs of his body begotten on the body of his first wife, and the couple had a son, this son would be heir general of the land in fee simple and heir tail of the land in fee tail. In this case, the king would have his prerogative in all the land held. However, if the king's tenant was given lands in tail female, and he died leaving an heir male and female, the king would have the wardship of the heir male and the lands held of him, but the donor would have the wardship of the heir female and the lands held of him.[34] If the tenant died with no heir female, the lands would simply revert to the donor, and the king would still not have them,

[32] *Ibid.*

[33] Littleton states that "if a man give lands or tenements to another, to have and to hold to him and his heirs males, or to his heirs females, he, to whom such a gift is made, hath a fee simple, because it is not limited by the gift, of what body the issue male or female shall be." Thus the fee tail had to state that the heirs be begotten on the body of the tenant, but it could then go on to limit the inheritance to heirs male or female. Sir Thomas Littleton, *Littleton's Tenures in English*, ed. Eugene Wambaugh (Washington: John Byrne, 1903), § 31.

[34] CUL MS Ee.5.22, f.339.

even though his tenant was seised in his demesne as of fee on the day he died.[35]

However, if the tenant had married twice, and with each marriage he had received land in tail female, and he died leaving a daughter from each marriage, the king would have the wardship of both daughters, since both were co-heirs for the tenant's land held of the king. If one of them was of full age at the time of the tenant's death, the king would not have her in ward, but he would still seize all of the land of which the tenant died seised, since the king cannot be a joint tenant with anyone.[36] However, the elder daughter could sue by petition for her part, and the king would give her her lands.[37]

The reader completes his interpretation of chapter one with a note on the final branch, which deals with lands held of the archbishop of Canterbury, the bishop of Durham, and the lords of the March. He argues that their exception from the statute refers only to lands which have been held from time immemorial, and does not refer to any recently granted lordships.[38] This is in clear contrast with the extension of the royal prerogative to recent grants.

The second chapter deals with the king's rights to the marriage of his tenant's heir, and this prerogative is broader, for the king has it whether the tenant held of the crown, as of an escheat, or whether he is a ward by reason of wardship, and whether the king's tenant held of him by priority or posteriority.[39] The reader notes that this is simply an affirmation of the common law, for at the common law the king will get priority in those things which cannot be divided, like the body of an heir, or his marriage, thus reinforcing the point that the king cannot be a joint tenant made in the previous chapter.[40] For his illustration of this point, he returns to the example he had used above, and argues that, if land is divided between the king and

[35] *Ibid.*

[36] The reader has already made this point above, in an apparent non sequitur: he gives the example of the division of lands between Henry V and Anne Stafford.

[37] CUL MS Ee.5.22, ff.339–39v. [38] *Ibid.*, ff.339v–40.

[39] As it became more common for tenants to hold land of many lords, the question of wardship was aggravated. It was easy enough to settle the wardship of the land by agreeing that each lord should have the wardship of the land held of him. The body of the heir was not divisible, however, and a rule had to be established to determine where the body of the heir would go. The obvious choices were the lord of whom the deceased tenant held the most land or the lord by whom he was first enfeoffed. The latter was known as the lord by priority, in contrast to the lord by posteriority.

[40] CUL MS Ee.5.22, f.340v.

his aunt, and a man who holds of a manor divided in this way dies with his issue under age, the king will have the body of the ward because of his prerogative, even if he came to the land through the younger sister.[41]

The reader goes on to reiterate this point, arguing that, if someone gives the king the lordship of his tenant by knight service, who also holds of another lord by knight service, the king will again have the wardship of the body by his prerogative, even though he is the lord by posteriority.[42] This takes him into another detour, and from here he discusses the transfer of land to and from the king, arguing that the king can only receive and grant land by matter of record, "because otherwise the king may seize the lands of each man when it pleases him and the party would have no remedy except to sue to the king by petition, which would be a great mischief."[43] The only exception he allows is when lands descend to the king by inheritance, in which case he can proceed as a common person would.[44] The reader had earlier mentioned limits to the king's ability to grant, arguing that the king can only grant out things that he has in possession, and not things that he has in right; thus he cannot grant to his tenant that his heir will never be in ward, but when he has the possession of a wardship he can grant it out from heir to heir during his nonage; i.e. if the heir dies before he reaches his full age, the grantee will automatically get the wardship of the next heir, if he is under age.[45]

After this detour, the reader returns to wardship, opening with the general point that no lord will have the wardship of an infant except where the infant's ancestor died in the lord's homage, and died seised in fact or in right.[46] This latter point is important, because he argues that, if the tenant is disseised, the lord can seize the wardship of the body of the heir and enter on the disseisor.[47]

41 *Ibid.* 42 *Ibid.*

43 *Ibid.* This issue arises several times in the year books. See YB Mich. 37 Hen. VI, ff.9–11, pl.20; and Mich. 7 Edw. IV, ff.16v–18, pl.11. It was also discussed in an Inner Temple moot in the late fifteenth century, when Brudenell said that the king could have all chattels and everything which came to the king by his lordship, such as escheats and wardships, without an inquisition, but not other prerogatives, such as year, day, and waste. Sir John Port, *The Notebook of Sir John Port*, ed. J. H. Baker, Selden Society vol. 102 (London: Selden Society, 1986), 153.

44 CUL MS Ee.5.22, f.340v. 45 *Ibid.*, f.339.

46 *Ibid.*, f.340v. 47 *Ibid.*

He goes on to argue that, if the king has the wardship of an infant who does not sue livery of his lands when he comes to full age, and then a wardship by reason of wardship falls in to the king, even if the first heir sues livery immediately he will not have the second ward from the king, because the wardship is a chattel, or a profit which accrued to the king while he had possession of the lands.[48] The law is the same if someone leases a manor which has *villeins regardant* and during the term of the lease one of the villeins purchases lands; the lessee could seize the villein's lands and hold them in the same way as the villein would, for "during my term I shall do to him and with him in chastising, imprisoning or in taking his goods and all other points which the lord may do to him as well as the lord himself."[49] Furthermore, when the lease ends, the lessor will not retrieve from the lessee the profits which fell to him during his term.[50] If the king's ward does not sue livery of his lands out of the king's hands when he reaches his full age, the king will continue to take the profits from the land until he does, even if it takes him twenty years, "because the king's possession was lawful and it will be because of the heir's laxity that he did not sue livery before."[51] If some of the lands in the king's hands are held of other lords, they will suffer if the infant does not sue livery, since they will continue to lose their rents and other services, which will go to the king instead. The reader says that their only remedy is by petition to the king.[52]

In the next section, the reader examines the difference between the king's grant of a wardship, and the king's grant of land on which a wardship falls in. He argues that, in the first case, i.e. where the king grants a wardship but retains the lordship of the ward's land, the king's committee will have the same rights in the ward as the king would have, because he is the king's bailiff. Thus he will have the land until the ward sues livery from the king and if he is impleaded for the ward he can pray aid of the king. The law is the same for the committee of the committee. However, the committee also has his own rights in the wardship, for he can sue a writ of ravishment of ward or ejectment of ward against one who seizes the ward from him or ejects him.[53] However, when the king grants lordship of the

[48] *Ibid.*, ff.340v–41. [49] *Ibid.*, f.341. [50] *Ibid.* [51] *Ibid.*, f.338v.

[52] *Ibid.* If a ward by reason of ward is in the king's hands, on the other hand, he can sue livery of his lands so as not to be prejudiced by the first ward's negligence.

[53] CUL MS Ee.5.22, f.341. These points are argued in YB Hil. 12 Hen. IV, ff.18–19, pl.20; and Trin. 12 Hen. IV, f.25, pl.12, in the earl of Arundel's case.

land to a man in fee and then a wardship falls in on the land, the lord will have only the same rights as any other lord.[54]

From here, the reader moves on to an apparent diversion which results in one of his few points relevant to the avoidance of wardship. He argues that, if an infant purchases lands in knight service he will not be in ward for them, nor will the lands be in ward, unless he is already the king's ward and he purchased the lands without licence, in which case the king will seize them for the contempt and retain them until he sues livery of them.[55] From here, he moves on to a complex set of examples in which purchase also allows the heir to avoid wardship. He begins with the case where a tenant leases land held of a lord to another for term of life, with the remainder to a tenant of the king and his heirs in fee. In this case, the lessee becomes the lord's tenant. However, he argues that, if the king's tenant dies with his issue under age and the lessee then dies, the king will seize the lands held of the lord, "because these lands descended to the infant on account of the dying seised in fee of his father."[56] Thus, when the remainderman is the king's tenant, the remainder to the father and his heir is enough to bring the king's wardship, though in the discussion of chapter one, when the king's tenant leases land, the remainderman is not subject to the prerogative, since the fee simple has not yet passed to him.[57] The reader goes on to argue that, in the same case, if the remainderman held nothing of the king or any other lord in knight service, then the lord would have his heir in ward.[58] However, if the lease was for term of life, with the remainder to the heirs of X in fee, and then X died with his heir under age and then the lessee died, the infant would not be in ward, because the land did not descend to him through his ancestor, but instead "he came to them as a purchaser."[59] The reader is here making a distinction between conveying the remainder "to X and his heirs" and "to the heirs of X"; the former brings wardship, while the latter does not. This is, however, a cumbersome way to avoid wardship, with a clear practical problem: if the lessee died before X, the right heir would not be determined and the conveyance could fail. The reader's attention to this problem suggests that he is working in a period before uses had become the standard way of dealing with

[54] CUL MS Ee.5.22, f.341. BL MS Harl. 2051, f.39v makes the point that this also applies to the committee's rights to the heir of land held of the king by posteriority.
[55] CUL MS Ee.5.22, f.341. [56] *Ibid.*, f.341v. [57] See pp. 33–34 above.
[58] CUL MS Ee.5.22, f.341v. [59] *Ibid.*

this issue. The whole discussion also suggests that the principles behind the king's right to the wardship of remaindermen was not at all clear.

From here, the reader moves back to some standard issues. He points out that sometimes the king will not have the wardship of the body of his tenant's heir, even though the tenant died seised in his homage. For example, if there is a grandfather, mother, and son and the mother dies first, when the grandfather dies the king will have the wardship of the land, but the father retains the custody of his heir, and his marriage "because the law always understands that the father wishes to provide and is more profitable for his son than any other will be, and therefore the father shall always have the wardship of his son or daughter."[60] The reader notes that "the mother shall never have the wardship of her issue, except for nurture and this is where the lands are held in socage &c. because the law understands that a woman cannot provide as well for an infant as a wise man."[61]

The reader goes on to note that priority or posteriority cannot be changed by the lord, for even if the lord aliens his lordship and takes it back again, this does not change the relationship between the tenant and the lord. However, he argues that the tenant can change the relationship, for if he makes a feoffment of all of his lands in fee and takes them back in fee all at once, there will be no priority or posteriority. This will not affect the wardship of the lands, but the wardship of the body becomes problematic; the reader argues that it will go to "the first to grab."[62] This is effectively a minor tangent, since it is not a problem for the king, who always has the right to the body. This is fairly typical though, for although the reading is focusing on the royal prerogative, the reader is aware that many of the issues that affect the king also affect lesser lords.

From the right to wardship and marriage, the reader moves on to the process of marriage. He argues that, although Magna Carta says that the heir should be married without disparagement, if the king marries a ward badly the heir has no remedy except by petition under the statute of Merton.[63] The reader also argues that, if the king does not tender the ward a marriage, he will still have the value of the marriage from him before he can sue livery of his lands, since the king is not restricted by time. This is part of the prerogative,

[60] *Ibid.* [61] *Ibid.* [62] *Ibid.* [63] *Ibid.*

since normally the lord must tender a marriage during the nonage of a male heir, or under the age of sixteen for a female heir.[64] If the heir marries himself against the will of his lord, the lord will have double the value of the marriage, and this applies equally to the king and any other lord.[65]

Next, the reader rehearses the statute of Marlborough, which says that, if a tenant enfeoffs others by collusion with the intent of defrauding the lord of his wardship, the lord can seize the heir and bring a writ of right of ward against the feoffees. If collusion is found, the lord will recover the lands and the heir.[66] If the king is defrauded, the reader says that he can simply seize the wardship of the body and the lands without a writ of ward. However, it is not clear if this is because the enfeoffment is without licence, or simply a procedural prerogative.

From here, the reader moves on to the third chapter, which deals with primer seisin. According to *Prerogativa Regis*, the king is able to seize the lands and tenements of which his tenant died seised in his demesne as of fee, and to hold them, with their issues and profits, until the heir makes his homage and sues livery. The logic behind this is clear: the heir will be the king's tenant and thus he must receive his lands directly from the king and swear homage to him as his lord. However, the reader immediately argues that the statute will not be taken literally, for the king will only take the lands which are held of him, and not those held of other lords.[67] This is a substantial abridgment of the king's rights, and makes his right to primer seisin much narrower than his right to wardship. For those lands held of the king, the heir will only sue livery of those to which the king is entitled by a matter of record, such as a writ of *diem clausit extremum*.[68]

Having argued that the king will not have primer seisin of all the lands of which his tenant died seised, the reader goes on to argue that in some cases he will have primer seisin where the tenant did not die seised. Thus, if the king's tenant grants land in tail, and afterwards the tail is determined so that it reverts to the donor's heir, the king will have primer seisin, "because he will be judged in the demesne immediately after his ancestor by descent and if

[64] *Ibid.*, ff.341v–42. [65] *Ibid.*, f.342. [66] *Ibid.* [67] *Ibid.*, f.342v.

[68] *Ibid.* At this point, the reader enters into a discussion of the six inquisition writs and their uses, as well as the process for proving age.

he was under age he will be in ward."[69] Similarly, when a tenant by the curtesy dies, the king will have primer seisin, even though he was not seised in his demesne as of fee.[70] However, the reader clearly thinks that these are peculiarities of the law, and argues that in general dying seised is necessary. Thus, if the king's tenant is disseised and after his death his heir brings a writ of entry against the disseisor and enters, the king will not have primer seisin, because his tenant did not die seised, even though the heir holds the land by inheritance.[71]

After covering the basics of inquisitions and proving age, the reader moves on to discuss traversing the inquisition. He argues that no one who is next in blood to the tenant can traverse, but only a stranger. Thus, if the king's tenant is found to have died seised of an acre held of a stranger, when in fact the stranger held it, he can traverse the inquisition immediately, or whenever he wishes.[72] The reader notes that, by a statute of Henry IV, if the stranger brings the traverse within a month after the inquisition, he will have the land to farm.[73] He further argues that, if the king had committed these lands within the first month, the traverser could enter on the committee. However, as long as the traverse remains at issue, the heir will not have livery of the lands, since the farmer is responsible to the king for the farm. If the traverse is successful, the stranger will be restored to the lands with all of the accrued issues and profits.[74] There are some cases where the stranger cannot traverse, but will be put to his petition. For example, when the king's tenant is attainted and it is incorrectly found by a *diem clausit extremum* that he died seised of an acre held of a stranger, in this case the stranger must petition the king against the record of attainder.[75] The reader notes that the king's tenant's feoffees will have the same process as a stranger.

If the stranger traverses in the case above, but during the traverse someone brings an action on his title to the same land, the reader considers against whom the writ will be brought: the king, the heir or the stranger. He argues that it is brought against the stranger,

[69] CUL MS Ee.5.22, f.343v. [70] *Ibid.* [71] *Ibid.*, ff.343v–44. [72] *Ibid.*, f.343.

[73] *Ibid.* There is no statute of Henry IV which deals with this issue. The reader is probably referring to 8 Hen. VI, c.16, *Statutes of the Realm* 11 vols. (London, 1810–22), vol. 2, 252, though he may also be thinking of 18 Hen. VI, c.6, *Stat. Realm*, vol. 2, 306–07.

[74] CUL MS Ee.5.22, f.343v. [75] *Ibid.*

since the freehold remains in the stranger, as evidenced by the heir's inability to sue livery during the traverse, and the stranger's right to *ouster le main* if the traverse is successful.[76]

From here, the reader moves on to consider the difference between *ouster le main* and livery, arguing that livery affirms the king's possession, in which case the heir will not get the issues with the lands. Since *ouster le main* does not affirm the king's possession, the king will generally not have the issues, though there are exceptions. Thus, if the king seizes the land because of an alienation or an attainder, he will keep the issues.[77] This is the extent of the reader's discussion of livery, which obviously is not an area of great interest to him.

This earliest reading is generally fairly simple. It does not pursue the prerogative into great complexity, and it does not seek to explain all the elements of process involved in the administration of the prerogative. It makes no mention of many of the elements which will play a role in later lectures, most notably uses, and instead its most obvious concern is with the king's rights over reversions and remainders. This is a substantive issue of some complexity and interest; the passage of the fee simple is one of the most important elements of land transfer, and, when it is divided between the passage of the right and the possession, the implications for descent become quite complex. After adding the variable of the king's prerogative rights to wardship and primer seisin, it is not surprising that the reader has some difficulty in presenting a clear and coherent exposition. He was not alone in his confusion on this issue, and in fact *Skrene's Case* of 1475 raised many of the same issues.

A manor was given to William Skrene and Elizabeth, his wife, and to the heirs of the body of William, and for default of issue to the right heirs of William. William had issue, John Skrene, who was seised of a manor held of the king in chief as of his crown. William died, and Elizabeth held the land as survivor. John Skrene had a son, Sir John Skrene, and died seised, so the king seized the wardship of Sir John. Elizabeth then died, and a *diem clausit extremum* was issued, which found the gift of the manor, held of the bishop of Ely, and that Sir John, in the king's ward, was the heir. On the basis of this inquisition, the king seized the manor held of the bishop. Sir John then died without issue, and another *diem clausit extremum*

[76] *Ibid.*, f.344. [77] *Ibid.*

was issued, which found the manor held of the king, the manor held of the bishop, and that John died without an heir.[78] The case raised two major questions. The first was procedural, and centred around the writ used in the inquisition: was the second *diem clausit extremum* appropriate, or should it have been *devenerunt*?

The second question was substantive, and related to the issues raised by the first reader. Jenney, representing the bishop of Ely, argued that the king had no right to seize the manor, since "the manor of which Elizabeth died seised did not come to Sir J[ohn] Skrene through him by whose death he was in ward, but by the death of a stranger, for now he claims this manor as kinsman and heir of W[illiam] S[krene], son of J[ohn] S[krene], son of the aforesaid W[illiam] and not as heir of J[ohn] S[krene]."[79] Thus Jenney is arguing that Sir John received the land by remainder rather than reversion, since it came to him from his grandmother and not through his father. Danvers supports Jenney, making almost exactly the same argument as the reader, that "if my true tenant leased his land for term of life to a man, the remainder over in fee, now the remainderman does not hold of the lord, but the tenant for term of life, and if the remainderman dies with his heir under age, he will not be in ward, for his father did not hold of the lord, but it is otherwise if my true tenant leased his lands for term of life, saving the reversion to himself, now the lessor remains my tenant, and if he dies with his heir under age he will be in ward, for he held of the lord." He argues that, when William Skrene died, the fee simple descended to John, but Elizabeth held of the bishop, and "if there is no tenure then no-one can have the ward."[80]

Philpot quibbles, but Fincham agrees that "this is a maxim in our law, where the remainder is granted out and where the true tenant reserves a reversion in him, in the one case he holds of the lord, and in the other case not."[81] However, Brygges disagrees, arguing that the king will, on occasion, have the wardship of land where his tenant did not die seised, and he gives the same example as the reader: when one leases land for term of life, with the remainder over in fee to the king's tenant, and the king's tenant dies with his heir under age, the king seizes the wardship and then the tenant for term of life dies, in this case the king will have the manor, even

[78] YB Mich. 15 Edw. IV, ff.10–11, pl.16. [79] *Ibid.*, f.11.
[80] *Ibid.* [81] *Ibid.*, ff.11–12.

though his tenant did not die seised. Both Bryan and Littleton agree with this point.[82] This develops into a discussion on the nature of *Prerogativa Regis*, where the distinction between a statute and an affirmation of the common law is aired. Choke returns to the issue at hand, arguing that, even with the benefit of the prerogative, the king can only seize when his tenant has something "as possession in fact, or possession in law, but the king shall have nothing by the death of his tenant where there was nothing in him except only in right."[83] Bryan accepts part of Choke's point, but moderates it, arguing that the king will have the wardship when right and possession were joined, but, according to Bryan, if the heir recovered the land and entered, that was enough, for as long as "possession is joined to right, the king shall have the wardship."[84] In this view right and possession did not have to descend together: as long as they were joined at some point, the king would have his claim.

This raised a whole new set of problems. Allowing the king to have wardship wherever right and possession were joined would potentially extend his wardship over his disseised tenants. Digas recognizes this and challenges Littleton with a new case, where his tenant was disseised of lands he held of the king, and the disseisor died seised, and then his tenant died seised of an acre held of him, with his heir under age, and he seized the body and the land, and then the heir recovered the land held of the king by a writ of entry on disseisin. He accepts that the king would then have the wardship of the land held of him, but asks if he would also have the body of the heir and the other acre. Littleton answers that he would, "for by the recovery he is in the same condition as if the infant's ancestor had died seised of all." Digas responds that "this is a marvel, for I am seised and in possession of my ward."[85] Thus, by trying to draw out the implications of the king's rights to remaindermen, and more broadly to cases in which right and possession moved separately, Littleton ended up by challenging the lords' fundamental right to retain the body of an heir which had vested before the king's land descended.

This case clearly displays the complexity of the issues the readers were dealing with, and the difficulty of drawing out principles which would be consistent across a range of applications. As with most year book cases, there is no conclusion, and it is likely that

[82] *Ibid.*, f.12. [83] *Ibid.*, f.13. [84] *Ibid.*, f.14. [85] *Ibid.*

no agreement was reached. However, the discussion highlights the role of the readings in developing these points of principle, and the similarity of some of the arguments to the points of the reader is striking. The same issues returned in later readings and we will continue to see the interplay of reading and reported case as the law develops.

The next fifteenth-century reading, possibly by Edward Grantham, follows *Skrene's Case*, but it also deals with many of the same points as the earlier reading.[86] It opens with the question of whether the text is a statute or not, but it is much more ambiguous than the earlier reading, arguing that part of the statute is an affirmation of the common law, and part is not. Grantham goes on to say that the first article of the statute is clearly an affirmation of the common law, because the lands are in the lord's ward "for the defence of the realm, so that the power of the realm will not be enfeebled by the nonage of such an infant . . . Then if the lands shall be in ward for the defence of the realm and the king is the best protector and defender of the realm before any other, this was the cause and reason that the king shall have the lands held of him by knight service."[87] From here, he proceeds to a general consideration of the writs for inquisitions, and the use of commissions. Commissions could serve the same purpose as a *diem clausit extremum*, though they were usually used for broader inquiries into landholding.[88]

Next, Grantham follows his predecessor in considering the kinds of lordship that give the king prerogative wardship. Like the earlier reader, he seems to be arguing that the king would only have prerogative rights if the tenant's land is held of the crown. Thus, if there is a lord, mesne, and tenant, and the mesnalty escheats to the lord, who happens to be the king, the king will only have wardship of the lands that the tenant holds of him, and will have no rights in the lands he holds of other lords, since that tenant does not hold of him *ab antiquo ut de corona*.[89] He says that the law is the same for lands that the king has by reason of the duchy of Lancaster,

[86] The identity of the reader cannot be conclusively proved, but, since it seems likely, I will refer to this reader as Grantham.
[87] CUL MS Hh.3.6, f.55v.
[88] *Ibid.*, ff.56–56v. He uses *Skrene's Case* as an example of the complications attendant on the use of writs and the proper use of the *diem clausit extremum*.
[89] CUL MS Hh.3.6, f.56v.

and any other lands the king has inherited. However, if the king gives a lordship of the crown to another, and the lordship returns to the king by escheat, the king will have the wardship of all of the tenant's lands, both those held of him and those held of other lords.[90]

Similarly, if a tenant who holds of another lord is attainted of treason, the tenant's lands will escheat to the king. If a tenant who holds of that tenant then dies with an heir under age, the king will have the wardship of the land held of the attainted tenant, but not of the land held of any other lord. The reader says that the law is the same for attainder for felony, and for tenants in tail or for term of life: the king will have the lands for their lifetime and will have the wardships that fall due during that term, but only to the same extent as the original lord would have had. The reader explains that this is because "notwithstanding that he had all of the lordship by reason of his crown, still it is not part of his crown."[91] Thus this is a prerogative which is not based on the tenurial relationship. Grantham is not as concerned as the earlier reader to make the point that new grants of land carry the same prerogative as old ones, but he is clearer in his explanation of how the prerogative works, and in the limits on the king's rights.

The reader points out other places where the king will not have custody of lands not held of him. For example, if there is a grandfather, father, and son, and the father is the king's tenant and dies, the king will seize the wardship of the son and the lands held of him. When the grandfather dies and his lands descend to the son, the king will not have the wardship of them, unless they are held of him.[92] This is because the heir and his father's lands had vested in the king, and the lords of whom the grandfather's lands were held would get their wardship. When a female tenant of the king dies, leaving her heir and her husband, the king also loses his wardship, in this case of both the land and the heir, since the husband is now tenant by curtesy, and also guardian of his heir. If, however, the husband died first, and the wife married again, had another child and died, her second husband would be tenant by curtesy and guardian of the second child, but, if he surrendered his estate to the heir of the first husband, the king would have the wardship of both land and body.[93]

[90] *Ibid.* [91] *Ibid.*, f.57. [92] *Ibid.* [93] *Ibid.*

The king also loses his rights to land when his tenant does not die seised. Thus Grantham argues that, if his tenant is disseised of land held of other lords, and the disseisor's heir enters before the king's tenant dies, the king has no claim to that land. However, if the king's tenant's heir recovers the lost lands during his minority, the king will have them in wardship by his prerogative. The same principle applies if the king's tenant discontinues a tail and his heir recovers by formedon.[94] The reader does not explain why, but it seems that it is because both recoveries bring together right and possession in the way the judges discussed in *Skrene's Case*. In fact, the case is very similar to the one with which Digas challenged Littleton, with the difference that in this case the tenant was disseised of the land he held of the other lord, rather than the land he held of the king.[95]

The most common reason for the king's loss of wardships in the late fifteenth century was probably collusive enfeoffments or uses, but Grantham spends very little time on the former, and makes no mention of the latter; he simply says that, if the king's tenant makes a feoffment by collusion and dies, and this is found in the inquisition, the king will have the wardship of those lands, even though his tenant did not die seised.[96]

Although in all of these cases the king loses the wardship of some lands, there is one case in which his rights are extended: wardship by reason of wardship. Thus, if a wardship falls in to an heir in his custody, the king will have that wardship and retain it. The reader also implies that, if his tenant already held this wardship, it would pass to the king with the rest of his lands and his heir. However, there are some restrictions on the king even in this case: he will only have the lands that the second ward held of his tenant, and, if lands descend to the second ward while he is in the king's custody, the king will not have them unless they are held of him.[97]

Grantham disagrees with the earlier reader when it comes to the king's rights to wardship of a lessor; he argues that the king's wardship is delayed when his tenant makes a lease for term of life by licence, and the heir will not be in the king's wardship until the lessee dies.[98] Brown breaks into the reading to disagree, and accepts the earlier reader's point that the king would get the wardship of the

[94] *Ibid.*
[95] YB Mich. 15 Edw. IV, f.14, pl.17. See p. 45 above for the case.
[96] CUL MS Hh.3.6, f.57. [97] *Ibid.*, f.57v. [98] *Ibid.*

heir.[99] He also raises the question of what happened when the land was leased for term of years, as opposed to term of life. According to Baker, "the right of the [lessor's] lord to oust the termor during the wardship of the lessor's heir had been settled law – indeed 'common learning' – in the fifteenth century."[100] Brown does not disagree with this, but he states that the lessee would be allowed to finish his term after the heir retrieved his land from the king. This is a novel argument, for the term of years had a fixed beginning and end, and could not be broken up into segments, which seems to be what Brown is implying. However, it is clear that he was seeking to protect the rights of the lessee for term of years as well as the lessee for term of life. Brown's approach conflicted with the logic of the law, but this desire to protect the termor will appear again.

If the king's tenant makes a gift in tail, Grantham argues that the king will receive the rent for the land from the donee, "for the law presumes that the one who has the possession of the land should better pay the rent."[101] However, this does not mean that the donee is the king's tenant. The reader argues that, if the donee dies, the king will not have the wardship of his heir, because he was only the king's tenant in possession, and not in right.[102] This is the same debate that we have seen before; Grantham agrees that the king gets wardship when the right and possession are joined, but for him the corollary of that is that the king does not get wardship for possession without right, or right without possession.

Much of this discussion is drawn from *Skrene's Case*, and Grantham continues this thread in the next case, where he gives the example of a gift to a man with two sons. The land is given to the father for term of life with the remainder in tail to the elder, and, in default of issue, to the right heirs of the father. If the tenant in tail dies without issue, Grantham argues, the king will have the wardship of the heir, because he inherits the fee simple from the father.[103]

99 *Ibid.*, f.59.

100 John Spelman, *The Reports of Sir John Spelman*, ed. J. H. Baker, 2 vols, Selden Society vols. 93 and 94 (London: Selden Society, 1976 and 1977), vol. 2, 182.

101 CUL MS Hh.3.6, f.57v.

102 *Ibid.*

103 *Ibid.*, f.57v. The connection to *Skrene's Case* is made even clearer by the fact that Grantham picks up on Danvers' point about the application of this principle to half-brothers. He argues that the law will be the same if the sons had different mothers; the issue of half-blood does not matter here, since in either case the second son is the right heir of his father. YB Mich. 15 Edw. IV, f.11, pl.17.

As well as dealing with these substantive issues of interpretation, the reader also pauses to note some semantic points. He says that, although the statute says that the king will have the wardship of the lands held of other lords *per huiusmodi servicium*, and this implies knight service, in fact the king will also have socage lands in ward, as long as the tenant holds of him by knight service.[104] He also notes that full age is twenty-one for a male heir or a female heir, though sixteen was standard for an unmarried woman.[105] However, he goes on to argue that, if the heir does not sue livery out of the king's hands for fifty years, he will still be considered under age. Beyond this, if the king grants the wardship to another *quam diu infra minore etate extiterit*, then the committee will only have the wardship until the heir reaches twenty-one, but if the grant is *quam diu in manum nostrum extiterit*, then it will last until the heir sues livery.[106]

Having covered the semantic issues, Grantham turns to the substance of the king's right to the marriage of the heir. He agrees that this right is wider than the right to lands, since the king has the marriage of heirs in his wardship whether the lands are held of him by reason of his crown, escheat, wardship by reason of wardship, priority, or posteriority. Grantham heads off on a problematic tangent with this, for he argues that this is an affirmation of the common law, "for at the common law every common person shall have the advantage of his prerogative which was that he shall have advantage of the heir of his tenant if the land was held of him by priority. And also it is good reason that the king shall have advantage of his prerogative as a common person of his prerogative."[107] However, this does nothing to explain why the king has the marriage of heirs who hold of him by posteriority.

He gets even more confused as he continues, that "Henry IV had the first choice of lands which came to him by Lady Blanche, his mother, and yet she was the younger daughter and it was because of his prerogative that he shall be preferred before any common person, and the king chose the duchy of Lancaster. And then it was confirmed by parliament that this duchy followed the crown, viz. that whoever was king would always inherit it."[108] This entire passage seems to come from the earlier reading, which talked about

[104] CUL MS Hh.3.6, f.57. [105] *Ibid.*, f.57v. [106] *Ibid.*, ff.57v–58.
[107] *Ibid.*, f.58. [108] *Ibid.*

the division of lands between the king and his aunt in a number of places. However, the earlier reading never specified which king it was referring to. The most obvious royal inheritance in the period was the duchy of Lancaster, and it was also the one which had the most obvious implications for the prerogative and for administrative issues, since it was administered entirely separately from the royal lands. However, Grantham's description does not fit the inheritance of the duchy of Lancaster, since Blanche's sister died without heirs in 1362, leaving Blanche the sole heiress. The earlier reader was in fact referring to Henry V's division of the Bohun inheritance with his cousin Anne in 1421. The inheritance had previously been divided between Eleanor de Bohun and her younger sister Mary, wife of Henry IV, but Henry V was not satisfied with the division, and the death of the dowager duchess and the return of her lands to the inheritance provided an excuse for a re-consideration of the estate. In 1421, Anne, the daughter of Eleanor, re-divided the inheritance, and Henry V had first choice of the parcels. The parliament of that year recognized the division and annexed the Bohun lands to the duchy of Lancaster.[109]

Though this might seem to be of purely antiquarian interest, and a simple mistake for the reader to make, it does raise some questions about the timing of the reading and the environment of the reader. The division of the Bohun estates continued to have implications for English politics in the fifteenth century through Anne's heirs, the Stafford dukes of Buckingham. With the extinction of the Lancastrian line after the death of Henry VI and his son in 1471, the Staffords could argue that the other half of the Bohun inheritance should return to them, despite its annexation to the duchy of Lancaster, which had been annexed to the crown. Since the Staffords were already one of the wealthiest families in England, the addition of these lands to their holdings would be politically unwise, especially given Edward IV's circumstances in 1471, when they could pose a dynastic as well as a political threat. Buckingham continued to press Edward for restitution of the lands, however, and the rights that went with them, and his dissatisfaction may have played a role in his support of Richard III and his

[109] Carole Rawcliffe, *The Staffords, Earls of Stafford and Dukes of Buckingham 1394–1521* (Cambridge: Cambridge University Press, 1978), 12–15. *Rotuli Parliamentorum: ut et petitiones, et placita in parliamento* (London, 1832), vol. 4, 135–40. I would like to thank Anne Curry for her help with this point.

subsequent revolt.[110] It is hard to imagine that a reader after 1483 would have been completely unaware of this history, and the error suggests that the Stafford claims were not at the forefront of his mind, or his auditors', perhaps narrowing the date of this reading to between 1476 and 1483.

After this detour, Grantham moves to the question of granting wardships. While the earlier reader argued that the king could not give or receive anything without a matter of record, this reader argues that the king can seize a wardship without an inquisition, but he cannot give it away without one, "inasmuch as the king cannot give anything to someone else of which he does not know the value."[111] Thus he can give the wardship of an acre of land or a manor, because that is certain, but if something like a marriage is given and it is uncertain, the grant is void.[112]

He next goes on to deal with more complicated granting issues. He gives an example where the king's tenant died seised of two manors, but it is found in the inquisition that he had only one, and the king seizes the manor and the wardship and commits them to another. If the king then seizes the other manor as a result of another inquisition, the committee will not have the manor, "because the king did not have confirmation of this manor at the time of his grant."[113] If another wardship falls in by reason of wardship, the committee will have it, because it comes as part of the king's grant. However, if more lands come to the first ward through a different ancestor, the committee will not have them; instead they will go to the king, because the lands are not related to the lordship which was committed.[114]

Grantham then deals with cases where the king will have the wardship of the land, but not the body. The first and most basic one is where lands held of a lord descend first, and the wardship of the body is legally vested in the lord before lands held of the king descend to him.[115] However, Grantham argues that, if the heir was not yet married, the king will have the wardship of the marriage, without the body.[116] The earlier reader explained that, if the king

110 Rawcliffe, *The Staffords*, 30–32.

111 CUL MS Hh.3.6, f.58. However, if the king's tenant is disseised and dies leaving an heir under age, the king cannot seize the ward without an action or inquisition to that effect. *Ibid*. f.58v.

112 *Ibid*., f.58. 113 *Ibid*. 114 *Ibid*., ff.58–58v.

115 *Ibid*., f.58v. 116 *Ibid*.

tenders a marriage to the heir and the heir refuses, the king (or any lord) will have double the value of the marriage. Grantham does not explain this principle, but he argues that, if the king's tenant married his son under the age of four years and died, and the king seized the body of the infant and tendered him a marriage when he reached the age of fourteen, the boy could refuse it without penalty.[117] This is because the first marriage is good, but not binding; the child could refuse to consent to the marriage made under age when he reached the age of consent. However, if he accepted it, the king had no right to oppose him.[118]

The second case where the king will have wardship of lands without body is where the infant inherited lands held of the king from his mother; in this case, the king has the lands, but the father retains custody of his heir.[119] Grantham goes on to note that this only applies to a father, as he points out that there is a writ *de consanguineo et herede rapto*, but argues that "this is not law" since no one could have the value of the marriage of his cousin, but only of his son or daughter.[120] There is another limit to the king's rights: if the king's ward is fifteen or older, the king will not have his marriage, presumably since the child was over the age of consent. He agrees with the earlier reader that the king will have the value of the ward's marriage even if he does not offer him a marriage, unlike a common person who must offer a marriage and have the ward reject it to get the value of the marriage. However, apart from this point, he says that the rules about disparagement and forfeiture are the same for the king and a common person.

The next point may be an interjection in the reading by Brown, though it is not clearly indicated in the reading that this is the case. In structure it returns to the earlier topic of cases where the king will have the land without wardship, which suggests that it is an interjection, but the organization of the readings is not coherent enough to make this a compelling argument. Thus the reading argues that, when the heir is married in the life of his father, he will

117 *Ibid.*

118 Payling notes that the crown did not refuse to be bound by marriages contracted before the age of consent until the reign of Henry VII. Simon Payling, "The Politics of Family: Late Medieval Marriage Contracts," in *The McFarlane Legacy: Studies in Late Medieval Politics and Society*, ed. R. H. Britnell and A. J. Pollard, The Fifteenth Century Series No. 1 (Stroud: Alan Sutton, 1995), 24.

119 CUL MS Hh.3.6, f.58v. 120 *Ibid.*

not be in wardship, even if the spouse has since died. It also argues that, if the heir was legally vested in a lord who made waste and from whom the heir recovered his land, even if lands held of the king then descend to the ward, the king will have the lands but not the heir, though this point is marked with a query. Finally, it argues that, if the lord releases the heir's marriage to him, or takes homage from him, the law will work in the same way. In all of these cases, the heir was once in ward, but, having been officially released, he could not be taken into ward again.[121]

From here, the reader moves on to cases where the king will not have wardship of the lands or the body, suggesting that the tenant might be seeking to avoid wardship. Thus, he outlines a case where the king's tenant enfeoffs two men of his land for a year, with the king's licence, and holds of them and the heirs of one of them. The feoffee with the fee dies with his heir under age, but, Grantham argues, the king will not have the wardship of him, because the land would pass to the other feoffee as survivor, and from the survivor either to the heir of the other feoffee who would then be in ward, or to the heir of the feoffor, who would not.[122] He goes on to argue that, if the tenant enfeoffs certain people by collusion and the lord brings a writ of right of ward against them, and land held of the king descends while the writ was pending, the king will seize the wardship of the land and the heir. If the lord recovers against the feoffees, Grantham argues that he will recover the heir from the king, presumably because the infant should have vested with him before the descent of lands held of the king. However, the point is marked with a query in the text, and it seems likely that the audience could have objected either on the ground that the body has vested in the king, or on the ground of the prerogative.[123]

The reader opens his discussion of chapter three with a general statement of primer seisin, pointing out that it is an affirmation of the common law. He argues that those who hold by knight service cannot sue livery until they reach the age of twenty-one, and that the king will have the seisin of everything held of him in socage or otherwise, but that the heir can sue livery of the land held in socage whatever his age.[124]

There seems to be another interjection by Brown here, and the discussion of primer seisin opens with an explanation of the

[121] *Ibid.* [122] *Ibid.* [123] *Ibid.* [124] *Ibid.*, f.59v.

structure of the section: first, an examination of when the king will have primer seisin; then when he can seize without inquisition and when not; and, finally, when he cannot seize based on an inquisition without needing a *scire facias* or any other process. The reading seems to skip the simpler elements of this topic, however, for the first case discussed jumps into a fairly complicated point. The reader argues that, if land is given to the king's tenant in tail and he has issue, when the tenant dies the king will have primer seisin of everything. However, if the tenant dies without issue, the donor will enter and the king will not have primer seisin of the land in tail.[125] If the same gift was made with a remainder and the tenant died with issue, the king would also have the primer seisin, but, if there was no issue, the remainderman would enter and the king would again lose.[126] This differs from wardship: there, if the fee simple remains in the donor, the king does not get custody, but, if it passes to the remainderman, he does.

If the king's tenant dies disseised of lands held of other lords and this is found in the inquisition, the king can seize the lands in the hands of the disseisor.[127] However, if the heir of the disseisor is in by descent and this is found in the inquisition, the king will not have primer seisin. Equally, if the heir of the disseisee brings a writ of error or a writ of entry on disseisin, or formedon, the king will still not have primer seisin, since the heir will not have received the land by descent in those cases.[128]

The ways in which the king's tenant holds land can also affect the king's rights to primer seisin. Thus land held jointly is exempt, since it passes to the survivor.[129] However, the reader argues that the king will have primer seisin of land in borough English or gavelkind, though this is queried. The reader also notes that in all of these cases the king must have an inquisition before he can seize the lands.[130]

This provides the transition to the discussion of when the king needs an inquisition and when not. If the abbot of a royal foundation dies, the king can seize the abbey lands during the vacancy without

125 *Ibid.*

126 *Ibid.* He notes that the law is the same if the land was given in tail male and the donee had a daughter.

127 *Ibid.*, f.60. The reader also argues that the law is the same if the tenant makes a feoffment of lands held of another lord under age and it is found in the inquisition, though this point is queried.

128 *Ibid.* 129 *Ibid.* 130 *Ibid.*

inquisition; the law is the same for a bishop, but in this case the exchequer must then issue a writ to the escheator to seize the lands and enquire into the death.[131] The king can also enter without an inquisition in the following cases: when he has leased lands of his crown in tail and the donee dies without heirs, or for term of life and the tenant dies; when land is leased to a tenant for term of life with the remainder to the king in fee and the tenant dies; when land escheats to the king for a lordship in his hands; when his villein purchases lands; and when lands descend to him from any of his ancestors.[132] In all of these cases, either the transmission of the land is already a matter of record and so the tenant's rights are protected, or the land is not part of the crown, and is not subject to the prerogative, so the king has the same rights as any other lord would have.

Finally, the reader moves to the third point, arguing that in some cases the king could not seize lands in primer seisin based on the inquisition alone, but that he required further process such as a *scire facias* or an original writ. Thus, if the inquisition found that the king's tenant had committed waste, or the abbot of a royal foundation had aliened land given in free alms, the king could not seize the lands without further process.[133]

After this interjection, Grantham returns to a simpler exposition, pointing out that primer seisin applies to tenements and lands held in knight service or socage. He argues that this is based on common law, for two reasons:

> one is because the king shall have the knowledge of his land, for by the intention of the law the king has more land than any other man and for this reason the king shall have primer seisin with the intention that his tenant should sue livery out of his hand, by which suit the king shall have notice and knowledge of him. And also the second reason why the king shall have primer seisin of lands held of other lords is because by suing livery he shall have notice of the quantity of land which was held of him and thus for these reasons it was common reason that he should have the primer seisin of lands held of him and of others &c.[134]

Thus Grantham assumes that the king has the right to know the quantity and type of land his tenant holds of him, and to update this knowledge regularly. He makes the same point later in the reading, when he states explicitly that "in each case where the king's tenant

[131] *Ibid.* [132] *Ibid.* [133] *Ibid.*, ff.60–60v. [134] *Ibid.*, f.60v.

in right or the tenant in possession is changed, the king shall have a fine."[135] The earlier reader made the same point in a later section of his reading.[136]

From here, he moves on to the process involved in primer seisin and the suing of livery. Some of this material deals with the problems caused by mistaken inquisitions. Thus, he argues that, if two different heirs are found by two different inquisitions, the two must interplead in chancery, when the chancellor will send the issue into king's bench to be tried. When the issue is tried, the result will be returned to chancery, and the one for whom title is found will have livery there.[137] If, on the other hand, the inquisition finds the younger son to be the heir, the elder son has no remedy, for he has no inquisition giving him title, and he cannot have a petition of right if the inquisition does not give the king any right.[138] The reader points to Sir John Paston, who found himself in this situation, arguing that his only remedy was by an act of parliament.[139]

Much of his discussion, however, is focused on the king's rights to primer seisin in more complex situations. Thus he argues that, if there is a lord who is the king, a mesne, and a tenant, and the mesne becomes the tenant's wife, and then dies, the mesnalty, which was in suspense during the marriage, will revert to the heirs of the wife and the tenancy to the heirs of the husband (since in this case they had no issue). Even though the wife was not possessed of the mesnalty at the time of her death, she passed a fee on to her heirs, and so the king has the right to primer seisin.[140]

If the king's tenant makes a lease of lands for term of life, reserving a rent, and dies, Grantham argues that the king will have primer seisin of the rent, because the king's tenant died seised in fee of it, since it was annexed to the reversion of the land.[141] If, however, the rent was not connected to the fee, then it would simply be a chattel, and the king would have no rights to it, so the tenant's heir would sue livery of it.[142] When the tenant for term of life then died, the king would have primer seisin of the land, and the heir would have to sue livery again; Grantham argues that this is because "this tenancy was twice changed in his tenant."[143] Thus he is following

135 *Ibid.*, f.69v. 136 CUL MS Ee.5.22, ff.350v and 351.
137 CUL MS Hh.3.6, ff.60v–61.
138 Petitions of right are dealt with later. See pp. 130–35 below.
139 CUL MS Hh.3.6, f.61. 140 *Ibid.* 141 *Ibid.* 142 *Ibid.*
143 *Ibid.* The law is the same if the gift was in tail with a rent reserved.

through on his argument that the king has the right to examine land held of him every time it changes hands.

He next turns to the process for retrieving the lands from the king, noting that the king will have the profit of lands as long as they remain in his hands for primer seisin.[144] He notes that the tenant can have land out of the king's hand in four ways: by suing livery, by traversing an inquisition, by *monstrans de droit*, and by petition of right. All of these are based on the findings of the inquisition, which must have been held *virtute brevis*. The only exceptions to this are cases where the tenant's title is recorded as a matter of record elsewhere, such as where the king seizes land by reason of attainder for felony; after the year and day, the lord will have livery of the lands without an inquisition.[145]

An inquisition can serve as the basis for livery for more than one heir, such as an heir male and heir female of lands in tail. An heir cannot traverse any part of the inquisition on which he sues livery; thus if, for example, the inquisition was correct in everything but the heir's age, he has no remedy except a petition of right to the king.[146] Grantham also notes that livery must be sued on the entire estate at one time, or the king can re-seize everything, but if the heir has livery and then inherits more land from the same ancestor, for example by the descent of a remainder in tail or a reversion in curtesy or dower, then the king will not re-seize everything, as long as the heir has a separate inquisition for the new land.[147] The need to preserve the integrity of the inquisition is so strong that coparceners must also sue jointly; if one does not wish to sue the other is put to a petition of right.[148]

Grantham next considers the king's profits from his primer seisin. He argues that, if the king has a lordship by primer seisin and a wardship falls in before livery is sued, the king will retain the wardship after giving livery of the rest of the estate, since the wardship is a chattel.[149] The law will be the same if a villein of

[144] *Ibid.*, f.61v. [145] *Ibid.*

[146] *Ibid.*, ff.61v–62. The judges, meeting at Blackfriars in the first year of Henry VII's reign, discussed this very question. They agreed that there was no remedy for this situation at common law and it was suggested that a remedy could only be provided through parliament. YB Mich. 1 Hen. VII, f.3, pl.3. A traverse is also inappropriate if the inquisition found that the heir held two manors where he only held one, or if the elder son is found heir in one county and the younger in another.

[147] CUL MS Hh.3.6, f.62. [148] *Ibid.* [149] *Ibid.*

the lordship purchases lands. However, if a tenant who holds of the lordship dies without an heir, the king will have the escheated lands while he holds the primer seisin, but the heir will retrieve the tenancy when he sues livery, since otherwise "he will suffer a great mischief."[150] In the same way, if a tenant alienates land in mortmain, the king will hold it until livery is sued and then return it to the heir.[151] There appears to be an interjection in the reading here, as the text continues "it seems he has the land purchased by a villein &c."[152] This presumably represents discussion with the audience on the status of the villein's land and the heir's claim to it as a chattel or a fee.

The reader concludes with a brief description of the difference between suing livery and *ouster le main*: in the first case, the heir affirms the king's title and loses the profits, while in the latter case he denies the king's right to the lands and takes the profits which had accrued while the king held it.[153] Thus, if the king's tenant dies without issue, the next heir will sue livery and lose the profits, while, if the king's tenant held the land jointly with another, the joint tenant would sue *ouster le main* and recover the profits.

Neither of these readings suggests much urgency in the development of the prerogative. They both deal with fairly fundamental elements of both landholding and of the king's position as chief lord. The discussions in *Skrene's Case* represent the central controversial element of both readings: the explication of the transmission of the fee through gifts with reversions or remainders, and the implications of such gifts for the king's rights. On one level, it is striking that such a fundamental issue remained so controversial, and was clearly not settled in these discussions. On the other hand, the complexity of the arguments raised, and the need for the principle to be broadly applicable, display the importance of the process of argument visible in the readings and the year books, and the role of the readings in fostering those skills and contextualizing the arguments.

The lawyers' role was to become more important in the years following Grantham's reading, for the first Tudor king showed more interest in the potential of the royal prerogative than the Yorkists had done. These rights represented a valuable, if irregular, addition

150 *Ibid.* 151 *Ibid.*

152 *Ibid.* Cf. Christopher St. German, *Doctor and Student*, ed. T. F. T. Plucknett and J. L. Barton, Selden Society vol. 91 (London: Selden Society, 1974), 63.

153 CUL MS Hh.3.6, f.62v.

to the royal income, but, when Henry came to the throne in 1485, they had been allowed to lapse in many cases. Often the king no longer knew his tenants-in-chief, and many of them had succeeded in settling their lands in a way which placed them out of the king's reach. Henry VII set out to remedy this situation and regain the income to which he was entitled, and which he needed to establish himself securely on the throne. His resuscitation of *Prerogativa Regis* also had the benefit of allowing the king to assert his authority as feudal sovereign, a position which still held some meaning in fifteenth-century England. In order to carry out this plan, the king constructed a new network to identify tenants-in-chief, evaluate their debt to the crown, and collect and administer feudal payments as they fell due.

As we might expect, Henry VII's new policy was not greeted with great enthusiasm by his tenants, and many historians have joined contemporaries in criticizing "the revival of feudalism" under the early Tudors. Hurstfield, for example, argues that already by the middle of the thirteenth century feudal wardship had "lost its chief moral and political justification."[154] The structures of feudalism were thus retained for their fiscal value to king and lords, while they became increasingly unrelated to the realities of the developing economy and polity. Thorne believes that by the late fifteenth century it proved "impossible to justify or explain successfully all the aspects of an unpopular and paradoxical policy that set itself to meet the expanding financial requirements of a modern state by means of a set of rules framed for his tenants-in-chief by a feudal suzerain."[155] While the revival of *Prerogativa Regis* in the late fifteenth century was indeed unpopular, it was not as paradoxical as Thorne suggests. Henry VII was in many ways continuing and enlarging the practices of his predecessors, both immediate and more distant, in the same way that the readers in his reign would expand on the ideas of their predecessors. He was not trying to create, nor did he realize that England was becoming, "a modern state." In turning his attention to his feudal prerogatives, Henry was looking to a traditional source of income which had played an important, if varying, role in the finances of

[154] Joel Hurstfield, "The Revival of Feudalism in Early Tudor England," *History* 37 (1952): 133.

[155] S. E. Thorne, ed., *Prerogativa Regis: Tertia Lectura Roberti Constable de Lincolnis Inne Anno 11 H.* 7 (New Haven: Yale University Press, 1949), ix.

the monarch from the Conquest to his immediate predecessors. It seems somewhat harsh to castigate Henry VII for attempting to return to the exploitation of "feudal" revenues which had ceased to be feudal some time in the late twelfth or early thirteenth century and which had provided a base for relatively stable government under Edward IV.

Henry sought to build up the crown's landed base from the very beginning of his reign. The resumptions and confiscations he made in the parliament of 1486 more than doubled the value of the royal estates, and though that money was quickly devoted to other purposes, the attainders and resumptions of the next ten years further augmented royal holdings.[156] The mere fact of acquiring land was only the beginning, however. Henry's exploitation of his feudal dues is closely connected with his development of the chamber as the centre of his revenue system. The chamber was the king's personal financial office, and its informality provided him with a more flexible tool for revenue control than was available from the traditional methods of the exchequer.[157] Henry VII was not the only king to develop the chamber system, nor was he the first to do so. In fact, his immediate predecessor, Richard III, used the chamber in preference to the exchequer for the receipt of income from crown lands.[158] It seems, however, that in the early years of his reign Henry allowed the chamber machinery to decay. Wolffe argues that because of Henry's ignorance of estate management (the kingdom of England was, after all, the first land he had owned and administered) he did not at first recognize the value of the system, and the exchequer enjoyed a brief revival.[159] The exchequer procedure was too cumbersome to manage the scattered crown lands, however, and by the early 1490s Henry VII had begun to use his household in the same way as his predecessor. This machinery was governed simply by the king's authority, and the informality of its methods, as well as the unpopularity of the policy itself, led to a number of objections to the revived prerogative.

156 F. C. Dietz, *English Government Finance 1485–1558* (2nd edn, London: Frank Cass, 1964), 25–26.

157 See W. C. Richardson, *Tudor Chamber Administration 1485–1547* (Baton Rouge: Louisiana State University Press, 1952), and Dietz, *English Government Finance*, for detailed discussions of the chamber system.

158 Dietz, *English Government Finance*, 65–67.

159 B. P. Wolffe, "The Management of English Royal Estates under the Yorkist Kings," *English Historical Review* 71 (1956): 24–25.

Though it took the king some time to develop the structure he would use to organize the crown lands, he began investigating their current administration almost immediately. In 1486, Sir Reginald Bray, chancellor of the duchy of Lancaster, was ordered to carry out a review of officials in charge of royal lands, and the following year parliament annulled all grants of such offices, as well as all leases on the king's manors and lordships, in order to allow a complete overhaul of the system.[160] The income garnered from this revitalization of the system was to be paid into the chamber, which was far easier to access than the exchequer. These activities in the early years of Henry VII's reign established the core of his new system. Bray remained one of the king's chief financial advisors until his death, and he was always closely connected with the administration of the crown lands, while the chamber became one of the chief treasuries of the reign. The household system thus established by the king allowed him to control this administration personally.

This household system at the centre was linked with the localities through officers appointed by the king. By May 1488, a commission was appointed to nominate auditors and receivers, together with other accounting officers, to all crown lands, and to let the lands themselves to appropriate tenants.[161] Although no complete list of the appointees has survived, enough is known to make it clear that many of them had worked for the Yorkists, and were accustomed to working under the chamber system. While these officers managed the revenues of the known crown lands, the king used commissions to identify concealed lands and investigate his feudal rights. Such commissions could issue on the death of a tenant-in-chief and take the place of the escheator's inquisition, they could supplement a faulty inquisition, or they could have more general instructions to survey the area for evasions of the king's rights. Commissions to inquire of the lands of particular tenants-in-chief were quite common in the later years of Edward IV. These commissions were usually made up mainly of members of the local gentry, and they were sent out with specific instructions to enquire into the lands of a particular tenant after his death. Edward's commissions seem to have focused on prominent lords who could be expected to have extensive lands, or lords who had been attainted. Richard III continued this practice of sending out commissions, but he seems to

160 *Ibid.*, 26.
161 S. B. Chrimes, *Henry VII* (London: Eyre Methuen, 1972), 124.

have recognized that they could be used for wider purposes than simply examining the lands of particular tenants. Richard did not have time to develop the implications of the commissions, and it was left to Henry VII to bring them to their final pitch of development. Henry sent out commissions with a general brief to survey particular areas and to enquire into concealments of lands held of the crown, suppressions of wardship and other feudal dues. He also staffed the commissions with lawyers as well as local gentry, and, as his reign progressed, the lawyers came to outnumber the gentry. Henry's aim in the early years of the commissions seems to have been mainly to find out exactly what he should have, and in this he was quite determined.[162] The escheators were also part of the extended search for royal rights, as they were prompted by information from the centre to re-examine old cases in new inquisitions.[163] The success of these procedures in identifying and realizing the value of the king's feudal incidents is made apparent by the need for a further refinement of the chamber system in 1503, when a surveyor of the king's wards was appointed.[164]

The growing exploitation of crown finances in this period is further supported by the appearance, at about the same time, of the Council Learned in the Law. Somerville first identified the records he found among the duchy of Lancaster papers as relating to the Council Learned, a part of the king's council, which seems to have begun operating around 1500. The Council was largely concerned with government prosecutions, and evasions of feudal dues seems to have been a large part of its business. Its surviving records are meagre, but it seems clear that, as Henry used the chamber administration to bypass exchequer control over the gathering of his feudal dues, he used the Council Learned to bypass its role in examining his rights in many cases. Though Bayne, for example, obviously saw the Council Learned as somewhat sinister,[165] Elton felt that it was

[162] Henry's commissions were deeply resented by the population at large. In 1504, parliament refused to sanction the use of the commissions, and when Henry sought a feudal aid to marry his daughter and knight his son Arthur (then already dead) parliament voted instead to grant him a gift of £40,000. It was cheaper to give him the money than to be identified as a tenant-in-chief and made subject to the ongoing claims of the prerogative.

[163] D. A. Luckett, "Crown Patronage and Local Administration in Berkshire, Dorset, Hampshire, Oxfordshire, Somerset and Wiltshire, 1485–1509" (PhD diss., Oxford University, 1992), 302–08.

[164] Chrimes, *Henry VII*, 129.

[165] C. G. Bayne, ed., *Select Cases in the Council of Henry VII*, Selden Society vol. 75 (London: Bernard Quaritch, 1958), xxviii.

a typical early Tudor court, "a weapon of the king's policy rather than a means for settling the subject's disputes."[166] Ford takes the normalization of the Council Learned a step further, arguing that Henry was simply administering his kingdom as his personal estate, and that the Council "was a place for the king's essentially personal staff of lawyers and fiscal administrators . . . to sort and act upon complaints of the king against his subjects, or the tenants of crown lands to complain to the king as landlord."[167] Thus the chamber and the Council Learned were both part of Henry VII's personal financial machinery, and both had a role in the administration of the king's lands and his prerogative, as well as in other areas where the king's role as king, lord, and landlord intersected. Although historians have sought to disentangle different elements of their business, the records of Henry's legal and financial servants display the unity of approach which lay behind them.

Thus, for example, the chamber treasury was also responsible for obligations and recognizances due to the king. Obligations and recognizances were bonds which provided for the payment of a debt due to the king, or the forfeit of a certain sum of money, at some point in the future, contingent on a future event. John Heron, the treasurer of the chamber, and one of Henry's trusted servants, kept careful lists of the obligations and recognizances due to the king. They related to matters as varied as the hire of royal ships and the payment of customs duties, the restitution of bishops' temporalities, pardons for murder, rape, and felony, the sale of wardships, and the faithful performance of duties by the king's officers.[168] Thus they were generally either fees which were due to the king, or bonds for good behaviour. It has been argued that these bonds were used to keep the nobility in a state of submission to the king,[169] and that many of the pardons were for offences committed under outdated statutes, discovered by paid informers, and prosecuted by Dudley and Empson. It is true that Henry VII revived a number

[166] G. R. Elton, "Henry VII: Rapacity and Remorse," in *Studies in Tudor and Stuart Politics and Government, Papers and Reviews 1946–1972* (London: Cambridge University Press, 1974), vol. 1, 51.

[167] Lisa Ford, "Conciliar Politics and Administration in the Reign of Henry VII" (PhD diss., St. Andrews University, 2001), 143.

[168] Dietz, *English Government Finance*, 39.

[169] J. R. Lander, "Bonds, Coercion and Fear: Henry VII and the Peerage," in *Crown and Nobility 1450–1509*, ed. J. R. Lander (London: Edward Arnold, 1976), 293–300.

of statutes which had fallen into disuse during the period of civil war, but in doing so he was simply responding to a generally felt need. Furthermore, there was no doubt that the king had the right to resuscitate a law that had fallen into disuse. Fortescue tells us that:

> oftentimes the written law lies as it were dead under a covering of words, though not wholly lifeless, and then the Prince, by means of equity, rouses its vital spirit as if from sleep . . . so that then that saying of the Gospel may be used concerning two laws reposing under one covering – "There shall be two in one bed; one shall be taken and the other left." Often, also, the mind of the lawgiver did not perceive all that the words of the law embrace. Wherefore in such case the office of a good prince, who is called a living law, supplies the defect of the written law.[170]

There is no doubt that Henry set his lawyers, particularly Empson and Dudley, to find and supply the defects of the written law. It is also true that paid informers were used to root out offenders, and these informers, particularly the infamous Grimaldi, were subject to particular vituperation.[171] The system was not one calculated to make friends, and Empson and Dudley have borne the brunt of historical censure of this work. Much of their notoriety rests on the *Anglica Historia* of Polydore Vergil, which complains that "every day even laws which had been anciently revoked and invalidated they [Empson and Dudley] called into use again, brought into the light of day and at their discretion whom they would they judged to have offended against these old laws. And they proceeded against not the poor but the wealthy, churchmen, rich magnates, even the intimates of the king himself, and any and every individual of fortune – not only the living, but the dying, and those who were long since dead, if by chance they had left property."[172]

170 Sir John Fortescue, *De Natura Legis Naturae: The Works of Sir John Fortescue, Knight, Chief Justice of England and Lord Chancellor to King Henry the Sixth, Now First Collected and Arranged by Thomas (Fortescue) Lord Clermont* (London: privately printed, 1869), 215.

171 The *Great Chronicle of London* refers to the informers as "promoters of all yll," and distinguishes Grimaldi as "the most crewell and subtyllest wrecch of theym alle." A. H. Thomas and I. D. Thornley, eds., *The Great Chronicle of London* (London: George W. Jones, 1938; reprint Gloucester: Alan Sutton, 1983), 337.

172 Polydore Vergil, *The Anglica Historia of Polydore Vergil, AD 1485–1537*, ed. and trans. Denys Hay, Camden Society vol. 74 (London: Royal Historical Society, 1950), 129. It is worth noting that this tradition does not appear in contemporary chronicles, but emerges in the 1530s and 1540s.

Though Vergil's account must be treated with caution, there is no doubt that Empson and Dudley were assiduous in the king's service, and that their activities were resented. The *Great Chronicle of London* fulminates against the treatment of Sir William Capell, one time mayor of London, who ended up in prison through the indictment of a jury which was "ffastly boundyn to the gyrdyllis of [D]udley & Empson."[173] We cannot prove or disprove Capell's guilt, but it was well within the parameters of Henry's policy to bring a prominent Londoner to heel, while the chronicle was inclined to presume his innocence. Taxation, in whatever guise, is never popular with the taxed, and taxation which targets the wealthy and powerful is likely to elicit complaints from the most vocal elements of society. This does not prove that Empson and Dudley were corrupt, but simply that they were efficient. As Dietz makes clear, Empson and Dudley's primary targets were those who created disorder, by such activities as keeping retainers or ravishing women, and those who intruded on lands, thus compromising the royal prerogative.[174] There is no doubt that on occasion Empson and Dudley worked on the fringes of the law; in fact while imprisoned in the Tower Dudley himself put together a list of individuals he felt had been wronged by his activities.[175] The brevity of the list is quite remarkable, however, in light of their varied activities, and in general it would be more accurate to say that, rather than working outside the law, they pushed the law to its furthest extent in the service of the king's policies.

This raises a crucial question: what was Henry VII's purpose in seeking to enforce his prerogative rights? Was his aim purely, or even primarily, financial? There can be no doubt that wardship and primer seisin were quite lucrative. Though it is difficult to produce any hard and fast figures, Dietz estimates that the income from wardships was less than £350 in 1487, rose to £1,588 by 1494 and by the fiscal year 1506–07 had jumped to more than £6,000.[176] Wolffe found that the total revenues from crown lands brought Henry about £3,000 a year from 1487 to 1489, rising to £11,000 a year between 1492 and 1495 and reaching £40,000 between 1502

173 Thomas and Thornley, eds., *Great Chronicle of London*, 336.

174 Dietz, *English Government Finance*, 44.

175 C. J. Harrison, "The Petition of Edmund Dudley," *English Historical Review* 87 (1972): 87–90.

176 Dietz, *English Government Finance*, 31.

and 1505.[177] This includes a variety of other kinds of income besides wardships and primer seisin, but there is no doubt that they constituted a welcome addition to royal funds. This was not a great deal of money in absolute terms, however, and the hostility which met this new level of demand prompts the same question raised by Hurstfield in relation to later fiscal feudalism: why provoke so much resentment for so little return?[178]

It appears that the king was using his undisputed feudal rights as a method of acquiring and keeping control of his subjects.[179] Lander argued that Henry used a system of bonds to keep peace among his nobility; this system required troublesome individuals or groups to post bonds for their good behaviour and often caught a group of men in one net by requiring them to guarantee each other's behaviour.[180] Though the sums involved were substantial, the king rarely collected all of the posted amount even when the individual broke the bond, but instead left him in debt to the king. Henry VII had no desire to impoverish his nobility, for that would have diminished their capacity to govern on his behalf. However, he did want to control them. Bonds to keep the peace were one method of achieving this aim; commissions to investigate concealed lands and wardships were another. Both had the advantages of being relatively cheap, peaceful, and legal. No one could dispute the king's right to collect his feudal dues or to collect on a bond when the condition had been broken. The king could always choose to be lenient and remit payment of either, he could suspend payment during pleasure, or he could demand the full weight of the law.

In the first ten years of his reign, Henry VII showed himself to be a determined and resolute king, intent on maintaining his position by subduing foreign and domestic enemies, and on re-establishing the wealth and prestige of the monarchy. It was perfectly clear to Henry that his priority must be to restore royal control over the magnates. It has been demonstrated that, contrary to long-held beliefs, the higher nobility were not destroyed in the conflicts of the fifteenth century. Though some families clearly did suffer as a

177 Wolffe, *Crown Lands 1461–1536*, 69.

178 See Joel Hurstfield, "The Profits of Fiscal Feudalism, 1541–1602," *Economic History Review* 2nd ser. 8 (1955): 53–61.

179 See Elton, "Henry VII: Rapacity and Remorse," 57; Dietz, *English Government Finance*, 44.

180 Lander, "Bonds, Coercion and Fear," 293.

result of their political activities, their decline in the late fifteenth century was not significantly greater than would have been caused by natural factors.[181] They did appear to be somewhat demoralized by the recent conflicts, but without strong royal leadership there was no guarantee that they would remain quiescent. Henry VII's challenge was to develop a style of government which would allow him to keep the nobility firmly in their place, without depriving them of the wealth and authority which made them useful servants of the crown. Christine Carpenter has criticized Henry's approach to the nobility, arguing that he essentially misunderstood the relationship between king and nobility in seeking to control and intimidate the magnates, rather than working with them.[182] She considers his emphasis on financial solvency to be misguided, particularly as it caused resentment among those whose support the king most needed.[183] Carpenter's emphasis on trust between king and magnates, though it may be good political theory, seems rather unrealistic for a king who grew up in exile and came to the throne as the third usurper in less than thirty years. For Henry, it was far more important to be feared than loved.

The stability of the throne was obviously of paramount importance to the first Tudor. One pretender to the throne had already been disposed of, but in 1491 Perkin Warbeck appeared to worry Henry again. By 1493, Henry had determined the truth of Warbeck's background and he gathered enough information about his supporters within England to pass a number of attainders in the parliament of 1495.[184] Though Warbeck was not arrested until 1498, the attainders of 1495 broke the conspiracy within England, and the failure of his attempted invasion from Scotland in September 1496 was the final proof that Warbeck was no real threat to Henry's security. The whole incident was disturbing, however,

[181] K. B. McFarlane, *England in the Fifteenth Century: Collected Essays* (London: Hambledon, 1981), 257, argues that approximately 25 percent of noble families failed in the male line every twenty-five years. See also J. P. Cooper, "The Counting of Manors," in *Land, Men and Beliefs: Studies in Early-Modern History*, ed. J. P. Cooper (London: Hambledon, 1983), 2.

[182] Christine Carpenter, *Locality and Polity: A Study of Warwickshire Landed Society 1401–1499* (Cambridge: Cambridge University Press, 1992), 560–96. S. J. Gunn's review of *Locality and Polity* in *Historical Journal* 35 (1992): 1002–03 provides a brief but insightful response to some of Dr. Carpenter's points.

[183] Christine Carpenter, "Henry VII and the English Polity," in *The Reign of Henry VII: Proceedings of the 1993 Harlaxton Symposium*, ed. Benjamin Thompson, Harlaxton Medieval Studies V (Stamford: Paul Watkins, 1995), 26–28.

[184] Chrimes, *Henry VII*, 84–85.

especially with the revelation that Sir William Stanley, Henry's step-uncle, was deeply involved. It is not coincidental that immediately after Bacon describes the king's profitable excursion to France and the threat from Perkin Warbeck, he notes that:

> about this time [1495] began to be discovered in the King that disposition, which afterwards nourished and whet on by bad counsellors and ministers proved the blot of his times: which was the course he took to crush treasure out of his subjects' purses . . . At this men did startle the more (at this time), because it appeared plainly to be in the King's nature, and not out of his necessity; he being now in float for treasure.[185]

For Bacon, then, the beginning of the king's fiscal drive was obvious, intimately associated with his success abroad, with a political threat at home, and clearly not based on financial need.

It is obvious that Henry understood clearly the advantages which could be derived from exploiting the relationship between political support and security of tenure. Luckett argues that Henry assumed that his tenants should be directly loyal to him, and thus saw grants of land "as initiating an ongoing relationship with the recipient."[186] Once the land was granted, good service was assumed, and continuous good service was necessary to retain the land given, before there was any possibility of further gifts.[187] Luckett argues that this attitude developed as a result of Henry's experiences with Stanley and Daubeney, when he realized that extensive gifts of land were no guarantee of loyalty, and in fact might lead to disaffection.[188] Thus he recognized a clear and intimate connection between the holding of royal land and the need for political loyalty, and made a policy choice to emphasize that connection in his limited and careful grants of land.

The greater nobility were not only faced with a resurgent monarchy, they were also losing some of their influence in the localities. Carpenter suggests that during the course of the wars the gentry began to move away from dependence on the greater lords, as such dependence seemed too likely to involve them in war. She argues that they began to take care of their own affairs and form their

[185] Francis Bacon, *The History of the Reign of King Henry the Seventh*, ed. Jerry Weinberger (Ithaca: Cornell University Press, 1996), 131.

[186] Luckett, "Crown Patronage and Local Administration," 37. [187] *Ibid.*, 209.

[188] D. A. Luckett, "Crown Patronage and Political Morality in Early Tudor England: The Case of Giles, Lord Daubeney." *English Historical Review* 110 (1995): 594.

own connections without relying on patronage from above. Having established this new pattern, they did not return to reliance on the nobility with the return of peace.[189] Though any report of the demise of the greater nobility is likely to be exaggerated, these trends do suggest that they were weakened by the end of the fifteenth century. The landed gentry could never replace the nobility, but they could temper their influence. With a strong monarch and a more independent gentry, the nobility were sandwiched in between, returned to their position as great lords, but no longer over-mighty subjects.

On the basis of these developments, Henry VII could re-establish the hierarchy of an earlier period, a hierarchy that had been severely shaken. The resuscitation of fiscal feudalism was quite appropriate for Henry VII, for he sought to re-establish the feudal hierarchy, adapted to his purposes. In order to achieve his ends, Henry VII believed that he needed a healthy treasury and the means and the will to exploit his financial resources. In turning to the possibilities inherent in the royal prerogative, Henry was looking at a source of income which did not carry the political problems associated with taxation, and which could serve a double function in suppressing his domestic opponents and rebuilding his finances. The king's prosecution of his feudal rights attracted comment even from outsiders: a Venetian observer at the turn of the century, describing the king's regular sources of income, concluded that "the King need never be in need of more money still, should he require it" because of his feudal rights, and estimated his income from "widows and wards" at 50,000 crowns per annum.[190]

Thus from the beginning of his reign Henry paid close attention to his feudal rights. The commissions to investigate were an obvious beginning, a way to establish the size of the problem, but they were only the beginning. The extent of the losses caused by feoffments to use was apparent, and in 1490 the crown introduced its first general

[189] Carpenter, *Locality and Polity*, 602–11 and 635–41. Payling disputes Carpenter's account, arguing that in other parts of England an independent gentry had emerged by the late fourteenth century. Simon Payling, "The Waning of Noble Lordship in Late 15th Century England," *Parliamentary History* 13 (1994): 329–30.

[190] Charlotte Augusta Sneyd, ed. and trans., *A Relation, or Rather a True Account, of the Island of England; with Sundry Particulars of the Customs of These People, and of the Royal Revenues under King Henry the Seventh, About the Year 1500*, Camden Society vol. 37 (London: John Bowyer Nichols & Son, 1847), 50–51.

statute aimed at dealing with uses.[191] The 1490 statute confirmed the statute of Marlborough's provisions against fraudulent enfeoffments and went on to ordain that, if a tenant enfeoffed his land to use and died leaving an under-age heir without having made a will, the lord could sue a writ of ward to regain both the body of the heir and the land. If the heir was of full age, he must pay relief as though the land was not enfeoffed.[192] The statute was intended to fill a gap in the interpretation of the statute of Marlborough, and it was not conceived as a new assault on uses.[193] Nevertheless, it offers an example of the revitalized royal machinery, for though the statute is framed to deal only with the tenants of mesne lords, rather than tenants-in-chief of the king, the main provision was in fact applied to tenants-in-chief of the crown.[194] If a feoffor of land held of the crown died intestate, the king would claim his heir and land.

Royal administrators quickly realized that their efforts to expand feudal revenues would be useless without bringing uses under control.[195] The statute of 1490 was a small step towards this goal, but it was limited in its application. By this time uses were a fundamental part of the structure of English landholding and the landed classes responded negatively to any attempt to control uses which would affect the property settlements they had made over preceding generations. The crown made no further attempt to deal with the problem by legislation until the 1530s, but it did not give up on the financial possibilities of the prerogative.[196] Bean comments that, having tacitly accepted the continuing employment of uses, the king had to consider other methods of increasing feudal revenue.[197] It seems likely that at this point Henry turned his

[191] A statute of 1484 attempted to deal with the problem of uses in the lands of the duchy of Lancaster, but the 1490 statute was the first attempt to deal with the problem nationally.

[192] 4 Hen. VII, c.17, *Stat. Realm*, vol. 2, 540–41.

[193] J. H. Baker, ed., *The Reports of Sir John Spelman*, 2 vols., Selden Society vols. 93 and 94 (London: Selden Society, 1976 and 1977), vol. 2, 194.

[194] This development is examined in more detail in chapter 2, pp. 105–11 below.

[195] Bean, *Decline of English Feudalism*, 237.

[196] 19 Hen. VII, c.15 (*Stat. Realm*, vol. 2, 660), took some steps to reduce the abuses associated with uses, by making the lands of the *cestui que use* liable to executions on judgments, providing for relief and heriot for lords of socage lands where no will was declared, and giving the *cestui que use* all the advantages of the sole seised at law. While this demonstrates the ways in which the use was being brought into the common law structure, it did little to help the king.

[197] Bean, *Decline of English Feudalism*, 256.

attention to *Prerogativa Regis*. This text remained the foundation of the king's rights, and his servants had to follow its guidelines, but in their desire to extend royal claims as far as possible, they discovered that the general words of the old statute were open to a broad interpretation. Henry had little difficulty in constructing a system to achieve his aims, but he had also to deal with the question of whether such an exploitation of the royal prerogative fell under the provisions of *Prerogativa Regis*.

2

EXPANSION AND DEBATE

Though circumstances seem to have been pushing Henry to focus on his feudal revenue from the early 1490s, 1495 saw the policy begin in earnest. This new drive coincided with the call of serjeants, including Constable and Frowyk, in the autumn of 1495. A feast, paid for by the new serjeants and attended by the members of the Inns and various notable figures, was a regular feature of the celebrations surrounding a call of serjeants. Henry himself attended this feast, held at the bishop of Ely's palace in Holborn, being, as Bacon noted, "a Prince that was ever ready to grace and countenance the professors of the law; having a little of that, that as he governed his subjects by his laws, so he governed his laws by his lawyers."[1] There is no evidence of royal intervention in the choice of text, or in the substance of Constable's or Frowyk's lectures, or indeed of any of the readers' lectures, but Constable and Frowyk's awareness of the significance of their discussion must have been heightened by the king's interest. However, the readers' lectures were not critiques of contemporary policy, but explications of the law. They did not respond directly to the practices of the administrators but they taught their students about the duties and obligations of the king and his tenants-in-chief.

These men could not expect to find much coherent or comprehensive information on the working of the king's prerogative outside the Inns; indeed, we face many of the same problems that

[1] Francis Bacon, *The History of the Reign of King Henry the Seventh*, ed. Jerry Weinberger (Ithaca: Cornell University Press, 1996), 133. Weinberger points out that this comment is not in any of Bacon's sources. C. L. Kingsford, ed., *Chronicles of London* (Oxford: Clarendon Press, 1905), 207–08. It is not clear whether there was any significance to the king's attendance. Henry VII missed the serjeants' feast in 1486, but he was present in 1503. Henry VIII's attendance record was not as good as his father's: he attended only two out of six serjeants' feasts in his reign, those of 1521 and 1531.

they did. Although Henry VII had been sending out commissions to investigate lands held by tenants-in-chief from the early years of his reign, there is little evidence of the activities of the commissions in the records of the courts in the years before the readings. Information on the administration of the prerogative is scattered, for several institutions had jurisdiction over the various processes involved in seizing lands and wardship, suing livery, seeking dower, and so on. The chancery and exchequer are the most obvious sources of information, for chancery dealt with all kinds of inquisitions and exchequer was the central financial office. Wronged tenants could traverse inquisitions in the common law side of chancery. The chancellor dealt with some of the traverses himself, but where the case required a fresh examination of the facts he had to send it into the court of king's bench so that a jury could be called. Unfortunately, only a small amount of the chancery material has survived for the reign of Henry VII, and these cases are clustered around the years 21 and 22 Hen. VII.[2] The king's bench rolls, by contrast, have survived largely intact. Though they only provide information for cases which required a jury, they have the advantage of recording the entire course of the case: the inquisition, the chancery traverse, the presentation of the case in king's bench, the calling of the jury, and the judgment when one is found. They are limited in number, with only fifteen cases involving the prerogative in the king's bench rolls for the first ten years of Henry's reign.[3] Some of them involve wardship, but they usually turn on the issue of seisin of land held in chief. The plaintiff argues, for example, that the deceased did not hold the land, or that the land was not held of the king, and there is little in them to give us any insight into the state of the law. The king's bench cases simply tried issues of fact; any issue of law was discussed and settled in court before the jury was called and had no place in the official record.

[2] They comprise about fifty cases, and we will return to their significance below.

[3] In fact, there is no appreciable growth in the number of cases dealing with the prerogative which reach the court of king's bench until the early years of the sixteenth century. In the first fifteen years of Henry VII, three years see no cases dealing with the prerogative, seven years have one, three years have two and only two have more (3 Hen. VII sees five and 11 Hen. VII sees six). I have treated records in the same year dealing with the same person as one case. From 16 Hen. VII, the number grows steadily, with three in that year, followed by six, four, five, three, five, and twelve to a high of twenty-five in 23 Hen. VII.

The year books are generally a more fruitful source for issues of law, but even they are largely silent on the question of wardship in the years before 1495. The few cases which do merit a mention in the year books deal mainly with questions of procedure, an issue of great interest to the lawyers throughout the period. Even when the statute of 4 Hen. VII, c.17 changed the law concerning the wardship of land enfeoffed to uses, the year books show no early discussion of the issue.[4]

Thus it seems that the readings delivered by Frowyk and Constable provided a much-needed systematic exposition of the prerogative, and a recognition of its renewed importance. *Prerogativa Regis* was still a problematic topic for a reader to take on in 1495, and both Frowyk and Constable discuss at some length whether the text is a statute or not. Constable argues that *Prerogativa Regis* is in fact a statute, and he gives four reasons for this belief. He uses the year book case from 1370; he argues that after the statute a tenant alienating land without licence from the king had to pay a fine, that this is more than the common law requires, and that therefore the text must be a statute; he points to the fact that it appears on the exchequer roll of statutes made in the reign of Edward I, and is entered near the end of that king's reign, and he contends that it is "accepted, used and affirmed as a statute," in this latter point re-affirming the idea that practical use was the most important criterion in determining whether a text carried statutory authority.[5]

Frowyk, however, follows Littleton in arguing that *Prerogativa Regis* "is not any statute nor declaration . . . but a treatise made by some men wise in the law, just like *Bracton*, *Visus Franciplegii*, *Modus Calumniandi Essoniorum*, *Hengham* and other similar works."[6] This argument was continued through the later readings; Spelman returns to the earliest reading, arguing that most of the first chapter of the statute was simply declaratory of the common law, but that the statute was made in order to except the lands of the archbishop of Canterbury, the bishop of Durham, and the lords of

[4] The first mention of the new statute in the year books is from Mich. 10 Hen. VII, f.10, pl.24.

[5] Robert Constable, *Prerogativa Regis: Tertia Lectura Roberti Constable de Lincolnis Inne Anno 11 H. 7*, ed. S. E. Thorne (New Haven: Yale University Press, 1949), 2–3.

[6] Frowyk, CUL MS Hh.2.1, f.1.

the Marches from the prerogative. Therefore, in Spelman's view, "all this branch is a statute."[7] Frowyk's side of the argument had its supporters through the period, however, for Danvers said in 1497 that *Prerogativa Regis* was "no statute, but an affirmation of the common law, which was made to make the prerogatives more certain."[8] Caryll, in his report of the same case, agrees and adds that it was made because "before that declaration the king could sometimes use his prerogative according to his pleasure and not in accordance with the common law," suggesting that the text was intended to limit the king.[9] The view of the text as an affirmation of the common law seems to have prevailed, for George Willoughby's reading in 1549 again returns to Littleton. Willoughby considers that *Prerogativa Regis* "is only a treatise and declaration of the prerogative of the king at the common law and not a statute, as it appears in 15 Edw. IV, for if this was a statute it would be observed in every point, but many articles of it are not held as law."[10] He goes on to compare it to Magna Carta before its confirmation in the statute of Marlborough, arguing that since that confirmation Magna Carta had been observed in all its articles, whereas before Marlborough it was only a treatise on the common law, just like the treatises *Dies Communes in Banco* and *Dies Communes in Dote*.[11]

This discussion demonstrates a problem facing the legal profession at the end of the fifteenth century. What Plucknett characterizes as the "more businesslike methods of Parliamentary procedure" meant that by this time parliament considered both the general policy and the actual wording of new statutes, so that, when judges came to apply the statutes, they were more conscious of the precise meaning of the text.[12] This is a very different attitude to statutes than that common in the period in which *Prerogativa Regis* was framed and indeed in most of the Middle Ages. Lawyers were now faced with texts which differed greatly in their precision of wording and intent, all falling into the category of "statute." Furthermore, generations of lawyers and judges over the centuries had treated this body of statutes very differently. The need to reconcile these

[7] Spelman, Gray's Inn MS 25, f.303. [8] YB Mich. 13 Hen. VII, f.11, pl.12.
[9] John Caryll, *Reports of Cases by John Caryll*, ed. J. H. Baker, 2 vols., Selden Society vols. 115 and 116 (London: Selden Society, 1998 and 1999), vol. 1, 364.
[10] BL MS Harl. 1691, f.197. [11] *Ibid.*
[12] T. F. T Plucknett, "Ellesmere on Statutes," in *Studies in English Legal History* (London: Hambledon, 1983), 248.

disparate texts and traditions led to the emergence of the concept known as the equity of a statute. According to this theory, a statute in affirmation of the common law could be extended to include situations similar to those mentioned in the statute, while things which had not been in existence at the time when the statute was made could be encompassed by it under the equity of the statute.[13] For example, when a tenant-in-chief of the king held lands of other lords in socage or burgage and died leaving an under-age heir, it was not clear whether the king should have wardship of the lands held of the other lords as well as the land held of him. In discussing such a case, Staunford notes the argument that "the kynge shal haue prerogatiue in them . . . for this statute is but a confirmacion of the common lawe, and therefore shallbee taken by equities."[14] The financial benefits of such an interpretation are clear. A treatise on the common law could not be extended in this way. It was a declaration of the common law, and was thus open only to interpretation, rather than extension. Frowyk presents the text as a treatise, and even in his hands *Prerogativa Regis* was given a broad scope, but Frowyk generally interprets the text more conservatively than Constable.[15]

In the end, Frowyk's views seem to have prevailed. We have seen that Willoughby, the last confirmed reader on the topic, followed Frowyk, and Staunford, author of the only published treatise on *Prerogativa Regis,* did likewise. Staunford argues that, while parliament set out in writing the extent of the prerogative, it "maketh no part of the kinges prerogatife, but long time before it had his being by thorder of the commen law, as plainlye may appeare by them that haue written before the making of the saide statute of

[13] See S. E. Thorne, ed., *A Discourse upon the Exposicion and Understandinge of Statutes* (San Marino: Huntingdon Library, 1942), 159–61. The corollary of this doctrine is that statutes abridging the common law should be interpreted strictly. The case of William Stonor is an excellent example of the judges considering the meaning and intent of the statute of 4 Hen. VII, c.17, and it is discussed further at pp. 105–11 below. See also J. W. Tubbs, *The Common Law Mind* (Baltimore: Johns Hopkins University Press, 2000), 40–42.

[14] William Staunford, *An Exposicion of the Kinges Prerogatiue, collected out of the great Abridgement of Iustice Fitzherbert, and other olde Writers of the Lawes of Englande* . . . (London, 1567), f.8v.

[15] In discussing chapter two of *Prerogativa Regis*, Frowyk reaches the same conclusions as Constable by arguing that the king's rights were granted by an earlier law and simply repeated in *Prerogativa Regis*. However, in his discussion of chapter three, on primer seisin, this argument leads him to reach a more limited interpretation than Constable.

prerogatife."[16] Staunford follows this idea through his discussion, for he begins chapter two with the statement that:

> all that is contayned in this Chapiter was the kynges prerogatiue by the order of the common lawe, as it maye appeare in the bokes of *Bracton* and *Britton*... and in a boke in the 24 yeare of kyng Edward the thyrde where it is sayde that no lorde can be more auncienter than the kynge, for all was in hym and came from hym at the begynninge.[17]

He begins chapter three with a similar statement. Furthermore, Staunford concludes his discussion of the king's rights over socage land held by his tenant with a comment on a case from 21 Hen. III "[from] which text if a man will any thing wrest he may make the kinges prerogatiue more lyberall then is made or declared by this statute or any other [previous writers]... but forasmuche as the saide other writers haue written so plainlye in this matter we will stand to them and extende the prerogatiue no further."[18] Thus the lawyers seem to have managed to keep the extension of the royal prerogative within limits.

Constable and Frowyk were obviously taking a controversial path in 1495. Despite the earlier readings, *Prerogativa Regis* was clearly not universally accepted as a statute by the legal profession, and they felt compelled to justify their choice to their peers in the Inns. That this was unusual is clearly demonstrated by the fact that no reading on any other statute has a similar discussion of whether the text under consideration was a statute, while every reading on *Prerogativa Regis* deals with it to some extent.[19] It should also be remembered that both men were serjeants-elect. They had both delivered two readings already, and their third would carry a great deal of weight. Since the readers were chosen because of their practical knowledge and ability, we might expect that their lectures would be directed at conveying an understanding of a field of immediate relevance, and this is indeed the case. Beyond this, a serjeant-elect's

[16] Staunford, *Exposicion*, f.5v. [17] *Ibid.*, f.10. [18] *Ibid.*, f.6.

[19] I have not examined every extant reading, but Professor Baker tells me that this is the case. This would not be an issue for most readings of course: no one was likely to doubt the status of Westminster II, but *Quo Warranto* was commonly read upon, for example, and its status was more questionable. Moreover, the novelty of reading on a disputed text continued to attract attention. The index of the 1679 edition of the year book for Edw. V–Hen. VII, under the heading "*Statut. de Prerogativa Regis*," comments that "it is called a Treatise by Frowicke: Note this, because he read on it." The reference given is to *Stonor's Case*.

reading was an important occasion, and the audience would include a large proportion of the members of the Inn, together with some serjeants and possibly even a judge or two who might return to his old Inn. That two of the four readers in 1495 chose *Prerogativa Regis* in this context suggests that the text was of great interest at the time.

Though the first chapter of *Prerogativa Regis* outlines the king's prerogative in very generous terms, both readers view it as a general statement of the king's rights, which the subsequent chapters then describe in more precise detail. Thus they do not discuss the broad implications of the chapter, but rather they examine the words used in it closely, in order to outline the ways in which lands could be held of the king. The lecture on chapter one is thus an introduction to forms of landholding and their consequences. The readers clearly intend their lecture to be understood by the younger students in their audience, for they open their exposition at a basic level, in fact a much more basic level than either of their predecessors. They begin by dividing the services due for land held of the king into two categories, knight service and socage, and provide a description of each.

Knight service was essentially military service, usually the actual provision of knights for the king's army. It also included other kinds of service, however, such as scutage, which in most cases quickly replaced the obligation to provide knights. Scutage was a monetary sum assessed towards the cost of providing an army, and Constable concludes that it is "a clear payment for war."[20] There is also another element beyond the purely military in determining if a particular service is knight service, for if the tenant holding by scutage pays a set amount of money, such as 10s, regardless of the amount assessed, this is not knight service, whereas if he pays a proportional amount, for example 10s when scutage is assessed at 15s per knight's fee, then it is uncertain scutage, and this is knight service.[21] Castle ward, the duty of guarding a castle such as Dover in the event of a possible invasion, is similarly an uncertain duty and is also knight service. Thus knight service is, in essence, a military service that can be demanded at any time without warning.

The lowest form of tenure was socage tenure and this was simply the payment of a set sum. Though the sum was often a simple

[20] Constable, 3. [21] *Ibid.*

money payment, it could be something more complex, such as the provision of a single red rose or a pound of white pepper.[22]

Other tenures occupy a middle ground. Grand serjeanty, for example, is akin to knight service, for a tenant who holds by grand serjeanty is usually required to perform some particular personal service for the king, for example to carry his banner or to buckle on his armour. At the same time, grand serjeanty did not carry all the burdens of knight service, for the tenant by grand serjeanty did not have to pay the feudal aids granted to the king to marry his daughter and knight his son,[23] nor did he pay as heavy a burden of relief as the tenant of land held in knight service.[24] Cornage also occupies a middle ground. This was the duty to blow a horn or light a fire to warn of an invasion, and, if land was held of the king by cornage, that was knight service, but if it was held of an ordinary lord in cornage, it was not.[25] Land could also be held in petty serjeanty, which was akin to socage tenure. Like grand serjeanty, it involved the provision of something for the king, often something military in form, such as a bow or an arrow. It did not, however, require the personal service of the tenant in war, as grand serjeanty did.

The type of service due was established at the time the king granted land to his tenant. It was not possible for the king to grant land without requiring some service, however minor, in return. Thus, if he made a grant of land without specifying service, the law assumed that it was given in knight service, since that was the best for the king. The assumption in the king's favour was a long-established element of the royal prerogative, given "because he is the conservator of the common weal, that is, the law, and for this reason he will be more favoured than any stranger who is only a private person."[26] Similarly, even if the grant specifically stated that

[22] Although these tenures might sound rather obsolete, even in the fifteenth century, see A. J. Pollard, *North-Eastern England During the Wars of the Roses: Lay Society, War and Politics 1450–1500* (Oxford: Clarendon Press, 1990), 97–98 for services of castleguard at Richmond, as well as rents of a barbed arrow and a pound of cinnamon.

[23] Frowyk, f.1v.

[24] Constable, 4. Relief will be considered in more detail later.

[25] *Ibid*. This point is queried in the text, so it may have been considered knight service in either case. See M. L. Bush, "Tenant Right under the Tudors: A Revision Revised," *Bulletin of the John Rylands University Library of Manchester* 77 (1995): 162 for cornage in the north of England. F. M. Nichols, "Observations upon the Nature of the Tenure or Service of Cornage," *Archaeologia* 39 (1863): 349–56 has a further discussion of the origin of cornage.

[26] YB Trin. 8 Hen. VII, f.2, pl.1.

the land was given *absque aliquo reddendo* or if it ordained that the tenant was to pay 12d rent and render fealty (a socage tenure), but did not add that this was *pro omnibus serviciis*, then the land was held in knight service.[27] Thus the king was free to grant land with whatever services he wanted, and he could reward friends or followers by granting lands at a nominal rent, such as a single red rose each year, but he was restricted by law from granting it without any services at all, because such a grant was completely outside the understanding of the law.

This point was of practical importance to the audience at the reading, because, while it was unusual for the king to grant land without specifying service, by the late fifteenth century it was fairly common to find inquisitions returned in which the jury was unsure how the land was held. In this case, the law would again presume the tenure most favourable for the king (knight service), and the escheator would seize the land in question. If the land was in fact held in socage, it was up to the tenant to come to chancery and traverse the inquisition. The chancellor would then pass the case to the court of king's bench to be put before a jury. While the king's bench records can tell us whether the land was returned to the plaintiff or not in any particular case, they give us virtually no idea of the legal arguments involved. However, *Stonor's Case*, discussed before the justices in the exchequer chamber in 1497,[28] dealt with the question of what was to be presumed when the inquisition jury was ignorant of the tenure of land, and provides some insight into the issues involved.[29] Sir William Stonor died seised of an advowson held in chief of the king, and of the use of land held of another lord, service unknown. Serjeant Kingsmill accepts that the tenure should be presumed to be knight service, though he argues that this is not

[27] Frowyk, f.1v.

[28] A meeting in the exchequer chamber had nothing to do with the regular functioning of the exchequer. Cases were adjourned to the exchequer chamber when they raised difficult points of law and they were discussed there in a meeting of all the judges of England, from king's bench, common pleas, and exchequer. The serjeants were, of course, also present. Cases adjourned to exchequer chamber were of particular interest to the reporters, both because they usually involved important issues, and because a statement by all the judges in the exchequer chamber was of particular value.

[29] YB Mich. 13 Hen. VII, ff.4–9, pl.3, also printed, with translation, in M. Hemmant, ed., *Select Cases in the Exchequer Chamber before All the Justices of England*, vol. 2, 1461–1509, Selden Society vol. 64 (London: Bernard Quaritch, 1948), 164. The case first appears in the previous term, Trin. 12 Hen. VII, ff.19–22, pl.1.

because that is the most favourable for the king, as some say, but because it is the most common tenure of all.[30] Sedgwick and Boteler, however, contend that the land should be presumed to be held in socage, Sedgwick arguing that fealty is incidental to every tenure, and land held by fealty is socage tenure,[31] with which Boteler agrees, adding that socage is the tenure most favourable to the tenant.[32] Boteler's point is quite a departure from the regular tenor of such a discussion, for it was understood that, when there were two possible interpretations, the law was to be interpreted in the king's favour. No one else picks up this thread in the argument though, and we can assume that Boteler's view was not representative. Though the lawyers often disagreed about the extent of the prerogative, there was never any dispute about the king's basic rights, including his favoured status under the law.

Frowyk took part in the discussion in *Stonor's Case*, and he too believes that the land should be presumed to be socage tenure, though for different reasons. He agrees that the tenure should be presumed to be whatever is most favourable for the lord, who in this case is the prior of St. Swithin's. According to Frowyk, "each tenant shall hold of his lord according to the common law, just as his lord holds above: hence it shall be commonly understood that the prior holds in frankalmoin, therefore it shall be said that the tenant holds of him in socage, because this is the most favourable service there can be."[33] There is no final agreement in the discussion, but three of the five who give an opinion on this question believe that socage tenure should be presumed.

The issue was relevant to more than this single case, for a large number of the king's bench cases hinge on the fact that the jury was ignorant of the tenure.[34] It was also common for a plaintiff to traverse an inquisition which returned that the land in question was held of the king, by arguing that it was in fact held of another lord, and often the lord was a prior, abbot, or some other ecclesiastical foundation.[35] Frowyk's opinion is particularly relevant for these cases, for the burden of holding land of a prior in socage was considerably lighter than holding of the king in knight service. Caryll's report of *Stonor's Case* is instructive, however, for he abridges the

[30] Hemmant, *Select Cases in Exchequer Chamber*, vol. 2, 164.
[31] *Ibid.*, 162. [32] *Ibid.*, 167. [33] *Ibid.*, 165.
[34] See, for example, KB 27/926 m.vii; KB 27/933 m.ix; KB 27/972 m.vii.
[35] See, for example, KB 27/906 m.v; KB 27/926 m.vii; KB 27/932 m.v.

discussion considerably and concludes simply that when the inquisition was returned with the jury unsure of the tenure "if it refers solely to land held of other common persons, some hold the office to be void, because it expresses no certainty," but that "in the present case . . . because it is found by the said office that the advowson is held of the king in chief by knight-service, it shall be taken more strongly in favour of the king, namely, that the other land is held by knight-service; in the same way as where it is found that someone holds of the king, 'but by what services they know not'."[36] Thus, according to Caryll, it was concluded that the king's prerogative was broad enough to extend to the service due on lands which his tenants held of other lords. Though this year book discussion goes beyond the material covered in the reading, it reflects the basic principles being presented by the readers, and demonstates how important an understanding of these ideas was. Year book discussions such as this rarely relied on a memorization of cases, but instead on an adaptation of the kind of principles covered in the readings.

The king not only granted land to his tenants, he could also grant other rights, such as the right to hold courts, to have the profits of courts, or to hold fairs or markets. All of these could be held in knight service in chief, though the king could grant them under any service he wished.[37] However, unlike land, if the king did not state how fairs, markets, fee farms, and so on were to be held, he did not have any special privileges with them.[38] *Skrene's Case*, in considering various kinds of tenure, raised this issue and suggested that holders of such rights were subject to the prerogative, though Nedham believed that markets were not held of anyone.[39] This vacuum was apparently filled by 1495, and Constable asserts that these rights could only be held of the king, for no one else was able to grant rights to such things as fairs and markets.[40] They also confirm that all of these grants carried the prerogative with them in the same way as a grant of lands; thus, if one died seised of a market held in chief of the king and lands held of other lords, the king would have his full prerogative in those lands.

The readers thus distinguish the various services by which land could be held and the various things which could be held of the king, but they make a further distinction, between land held in

[36] *Caryll's Reports*, vol. 1, 365. [37] Constable, 5–6. [38] Constable, 6.
[39] YB Mich. 15 Edw. IV, f.14, pl.17. [40] Constable, 6.

chief and in common tenure. The earlier readers mentioned this, but their discussion was brief. Land in chief was originally held directly of the king *ab antiquo*. This was land that had been held of William I, together with some manors that escheated to the king at such an early date that they are generally held to be part of the ancient demesne.[41] The king had his full prerogative in the land held *ab antiquo* and in the ancient escheats.[42] Much of the land held of the king was held in common tenure, that is, as of a manor which had escheated. The king got the same profit from such a manor as its lord had done before the escheat and he was entitled only to the same prerogative in the land as its lord would have had.[43] This principle was established by chapter 31 of Magna Carta, and it continued to apply to lands which escheated to the crown in later years.[44] The turmoil of the fifteenth century led to the extinction of many noble houses through death or forfeiture. The principle established in Magna Carta ensured that tenants were not exposed to the heaviest claims of the royal prerogative when their lords suffered misfortunes.

Lands escheated for various reasons, including failure of heirs, treason, and felony. Escheat for failure of heirs was fairly straightforward, for the land returned to the king because it was originally his land, granted to his tenant and his tenant's heirs. The numbers involved indicate that this was a profitable prerogative for the king. According to Cooper, "33 per cent of the families that held peerages in 1485 had come to an end for lack of male heirs by 1547; during the same period 31 per cent of the families given new peerages died out

[41] B. P. Wolffe, *The Royal Demesne in English History: The Crown Estates in the Governance of the Realm from the Conquest to 1509* (London: George Allen & Unwin, 1971), 26. Wolffe points out that it was only in the twelfth and thirteenth centuries that this land became known as tenure in ancient demesne, and that the term does not date from the period of the Conquest. See A. W. B. Simpson, *A History of the Land Law* (Oxford: Clarendon Press, 1986), 165–66, for an introduction to the ancient demesne; and Robert S. Hoyt, "The Nature and Origins of the Ancient Demesne," *English Historical Review* 65 (1950): 145–74, for a more detailed historical exposition.

[42] Constable, 10.

[43] Constable, 1, 10. Caryll reports that the honour of Wallingford was not bound by the prerogative, but notes that there was some disagreement as to whether that was the law or not; *Caryll's Reports*, vol. 2, 672.

[44] Caryll notes that similarly, when the king purchases a manor, the tenant holding of the previous lord in chief will owe the king the same services as he owed his lord "because the king shall not by this purchase cause the tenant paravail to change his tenure." *Caryll's Reports*, vol. 2, 671.

in the male line."[45] Escheat for treason or felony was more complex, and there is some dispute in the readings on this question. Constable presents various views on the question, in a manner typical of the readings. He says that some argue that, if land comes to the king for treason, then the tenants of this land hold of the king in chief, for only the king can have escheats for treason.[46] Others argue that, whether the forfeiture is for felony or treason, if the land was held in chief of the king before the forfeiture, it will be held in chief of the king, by the tenant, after the forfeiture. After rehearsing various opinions on the question, Constable gives his own. He concludes that, if a tenant-in-chief forfeits his land for felony or treason by order of the common law, or if it escheats for failure of heirs, then the tenant holds in chief as the lord did.[47] Thus any forfeiture given to the king by the common law will bring the prerogative with it, whether it is tenurial or not. Therefore, in Constable's view, though *Prerogativa Regis* is a statute, it operates through the means of the common law.

Frowyk takes the opposite view on escheat for treason, but he gives almost the same reason as Constable. Where Constable argues that land which escheats to the king for treason is held of the king in chief because only the king can have such escheats, Frowyk argues that escheat for treason does not cause the tenant to hold in chief, for land will always escheat to the king in this case, even when it is held of someone else. Thus he believes that the tenant should not suffer for the misdeeds of his lord. If land escheats for felony, on the other hand, the tenant will bear the weight of the prerogative.[48] This difference of opinion between the two readers is typical of their respective approaches, with Constable seeking the best position for the king, while Frowyk tries to balance the rights of king and tenant.

[45] J. P. Cooper, "The Counting of Manors," in *Land, Men and Beliefs: Studies in Early-Modern History*, ed. J. P. Cooper (London: Hambledon, 1983), 2.

[46] Constable, 11. The readers often set up the "some say . . . , others say . . . , but I say . . ." paradigm.

[47] If, however, there are three or four lords between the king and the manor, though these lordships are extinct by the forfeiture, the king will not have his prerogative of those tenants. Thus, if A held land of the king, and B held land of A, and C held land of B, and D held land of C, and D's land is forfeited to the king, A, B, and C's lordship over the land is extinguished, but the king gains no extra rights over these men.

[48] Frowyk, f.1. He is discussing a mesnalty here; if a barony or honour escheats for felony, the tenant will hold as he held before.

When the readers turn to discuss the re-granting of forfeited land, Frowyk, as we might expect, aims to preserve the pre-forfeit tenures as much as possible. He argues that, if a man forfeits by parliamentary attainder and the attainder contains a proviso that the other lords of whom the attainted man held land should continue to receive the services from their land as they did before the attainder, and the king then grants the forfeited land to another, the new tenant holds his land from the other lords as well as from the king. Similarly, he believes that, if lands come into the king's hand by forfeiture under the statute *de Religiosis*,[49] they must be returned to the lord who granted them to the religious institution in the first instance. The king could thus compel the original lord to return the services which were due from the land, but he could not grant the land to a stranger.[50] Frowyk's arguments reflect an older practice: it had been customary to return confiscated lands to the families who had lost them after the passage of an appropriate amount of time and/or service. Edward IV had tended to use such confiscations for his own purposes, often to settle loyal men in the shires, and Henry VII, in this as in many other things, had followed his example.[51] Although the value of establishing servants loyal to the king throughout the country might seem self-evident, the disruption to local society caused by such interpolation could outweigh the benefits. Frowyk's arguments suggest an inclination within the law to preserve the inheritance lines, and thus the stability of local communities.

Though it quickly becomes apparent that Constable is more likely to stretch the law in the king's favour, while Frowyk is more likely to restrict it, it is important to note that the readers' positions cannot always be predicted, and their obligation to interpret the law faithfully could lead to conclusions inconsistent with their inclinations. We can see this in the confusion which arose when they came to consider what would happen when land held of the crown in chief *ab antiquo* was forfeit to the king and he re-granted it. Constable argues that, though the king could grant the land to be held in chief,

[49] If lands were alienated into mortmain without a licence from the king, the king could seize them. Alienation into mortmain deprived the king of many of his prerogatives, for the church was never under age, never died, and never committed treason or felony.

[50] Frowyk, f.1v.

[51] Christine Carpenter, *Locality and Polity: A Study of Warwickshire Landed Society, 1401–1499* (Cambridge: Cambridge University Press, 1992), 634.

it was no longer held of the crown *ab antiquo*, and thus the king would not have his prerogative in the lands the tenant held of other lords.[52] Frowyk, on the other hand, notes that "I have not seen any issue taken on this question, that is, whether it was held *ab antiquo de corona* or not, but whether it was held in chief or not."[53] Thus, according to Frowyk, *ab antiquo* effectively meant "in chief of the crown" and, as long as the land was so held, the full prerogative would apply, while Constable limits it to those cases where the land was held in chief *ab antiquo*. Frowyk is in closer agreement with the earlier readers, who argued that land given to be held of the king in chief at any time brought the prerogative. Even according to Constable's own interpretation, the point is quite meaningless, for he gives the king as wide, or wider, rights in the two most profitable areas of the prerogative, wardship and primer seisin, as Frowyk does.[54] Thus his interpretation of the phrase *ab antiquo* in the opening chapter does not affect the rights he accords to the king in the later chapters.

The same kind of rules governed the granting of lands by the king which he had acquired in other ways. The readers agree that, if the king buys a lordship, the tenant does not hold in chief.[55] The readers also agree that, if a lordship descends to the king through a collateral ancestor, the tenant does not hold in chief.[56] The prerogative is also limited when land is in the king's hands temporarily, such as by wardship, by lease for term of years or life, or by forfeiture for outlawry by a tenant for term of years or life.[57] Constable sums this up by concluding that the king "shall never have any prerogative except where the ancestor held in chief and the king is seised of the lordship in chief by as high an estate as he is seised of his crown."[58]

[52] Constable, 12. [53] Frowyk, f.1.

[54] The text itself specifically states that the king has the right to wardship of his tenant's heir, no matter how he held his land of the king, while Constable interprets the king's rights to primer seisin to apply to land held in escheat as well as land held in chief. Both points are covered in more detail below.

[55] Frowyk, f.1; Constable, 24. Frowyk later adds that, if the king buys land and gives it to hold of him, it is in chief, but not *ab antiquo*. This seems to contradict his earlier point, and may be an interjection. Frowyk, f.1.

[56] *Ibid.* If the prince buys land and gives it to hold of him and he then becomes king, the lands are not held in chief. On the other hand, if the prince gives lands in tail, becomes king and releases full rights in the land to the tenant, the tenant holds the land in chief.

[57] Constable, 24. Constable returns to this point at more length later in the reading.

[58] Constable, 25.

In their treatment of the first chapter, therefore, the readers establish what the king can grant, how such grants can be held, and whether they open the holder to the burden of the prerogative in general terms. They build on this foundation in addressing chapter two of the statute, which gives the king rights to the marriage of under-age heirs in his custody. Constable and Frowyk disagree over whether this chapter gives the king any new rights. Constable argues that the king always had the right to the wardship of the heir of his tenant-in-chief by the common law, but *Prerogativa Regis* adds to this by giving him something new, namely, the same right over heirs of tenants holding of the king as of an escheat or of the duchy of Lancaster "in which King Henry III had abridged his power by Magna Carta, that is, to have no other prerogative except what the lord of that honour would have had if it was in his hands." The rights given up by Henry III were partly restored by *Prerogativa Regis*, which "grants to the king the wardship of the body of any heir of a tenant who holds of the king as of these escheats or others, and the king shall have the prerogative of the body of this heir even if he [the tenant] holds of another by priority."[59] Frowyk agrees that the king has the right to this broad prerogative, but he claims that *Prerogativa Regis* is not giving the king anything new here. He holds that the king always had this right, and, when Magna Carta restricted the king's rights in the lands held of an escheat, it had no effect on the king's rights over the body of the heir.[60] Thus, in order to maintain his view that *Prerogativa Regis* is not a statute, he must argue that the king's rights had been too narrowly interpreted, but that they had always been the same.

The actual patterns of landholding in early Tudor England were far more complicated than the provisions of the text might imply, and the readers recognize this by considering some situations likely to arise in practice, and explaining how the prerogative would work in these cases. These examples do not simply provide illustrations

[59] Constable, 27. Constable points out later that, though this principle applied to land held of the king as of the duchy of Lancaster, land held of the duchy was handled by the offices of the duchy and not by the chancery. However, if it was found that a tenant of the king held land of another lord by priority and land of the duchy by posteriority, as duke, the king lost the wardship, but as king he gained it. In this case, and only in this case, the ward had to sue livery of the king in the chancery and not in the duchy. Constable, 29.

[60] Frowyk, f.2v.

for their points; rather they allow the readers to develop their interpretation of the law and to construct a more complex, but still logical, framework of rights and obligations.

In their explanations, the readers again begin with some of the more basic points of the prerogative. For example, they make it clear that the prerogative applied to land which passed by descent, but only when land passed by direct descent from the tenant-in-chief to his heir, whether an heir to land held in fee tail or fee simple. They give the same kinds of examples as the earlier readers, of the descent of lands to sons and daughters in various combinations of fee simple and fee tail.[61] However, these readings extend the discussion to more complex cases. For example, Constable argues that, if a tenant held land in fee simple and land in tail with a remainder over and died without issue, leaving his under-age brother as his heir, the king would have the wardship of the land in fee simple which descended from the tenant to his brother, but he would have no rights in the land held in tail, which would go to the remainderman.[62] Thus the king had his prerogative in the land which passed from his deceased tenant-in-chief to the heir of the land held in chief, but, despite the words of the statute, he did not always have his prerogative in all the land of which his tenant died seised.

Frowyk agrees in substance with Constable's assessment, though he presents it in slightly different terms. He gives the example of a tenant who held a mesnalty of the king in general tail and bought the tenancy in special tail to him and his heirs female and died leaving a son and a daughter. The king will have the mesnalty, which descends to the son, and not the tenancy, for it is not held of the king and it does not descend to the son, but to the daughter.[63] He also argues that, if the tenant holds a mesnalty of the king in tail and buys the tenancy in fee and has a son and daughter by one wife and a son by his second wife and dies, and then the elder son dies without issue, the king will have the mesnalty which descends to

[61] See chapter 1, pp. 35–36 and 49 above. Constable, 13–14; Frowyk, f.2.

[62] Constable, 14. Frowyk makes the point that, if the king's tenant gives lands in tail, remainder in fee, and the remainder escheats to the king, the tenant in tail will hold of the king in chief and the king will have the ward of the land. Frowyk, f.1v. This point seems to have come up for discussion after the reading, for the note-taker has recorded further comments on the topic which Frowyk "dit apres" at the end of the lecture. Frowyk, f.2v.

[63] Frowyk, f.2.

the younger son, but not the tenancy which descends to the daughter.[64]

Similarly, Constable argues that, if land descended to the heir from another source than the tenant-in-chief of the king, the king would not have his prerogative in that. For example, if the heir of a tenant-in-chief of the king had land held of the king by descent from his father and land held of someone else by descent from his mother, the king would only have rights in the land which descended through the father and not in the land which descended through the mother.[65] Constable concludes that "the prerogative holds for the king to have all the lands in tail and fee simple which descend to the heir only through the tenant who has died, and not of those to which he has no title."[66]

Thus Frowyk focuses on tenants who hold of the king in tail, while Constable considers those who hold in fee, but the basic principle enunciated by both readers is the same. The king will only have his prerogative in lands which pass through the tenant-in-chief to the heir of the lands held in chief. Thus, if the tenant-in-chief simply serves as a channel for lands held of another lord to pass to another heir, the king has no prerogative in these lands.[67] Similarly, if the heir of the lands held in chief receives lands from a source other than the tenant-in-chief, the king has no rights in these lands. Lands of any kind, held of any lord, in any kind of service, which pass through the tenant-in-chief to the heir of the lands held in chief are, however, subject to the royal prerogative. This principle can be seen more clearly in the figures below.

64 Frowyk, f.2. The question of descent was complicated by issue of different marriages. In this case, the sister is the heir of her brother, in preference to their half-brother, because they were born of the same parents. The half-brother shares only one parent and so is more distant in blood (the relationship was called half-blood, *demi-sanke*). If there was no sister in this case, the land in fee simple would have gone to the nearest heir of the full blood, for example the uncle of the deceased. The land in fee tail, on the other hand, descends to the issue of the body of the tenant, and, with the death of the elder son, the younger son is the nearest male heir of his body. If the land was in fee tail special which restricted it to the issue of the body of the tenant begotten on the body of his first wife, it would not have gone to the half-brother, but to the sister. See Littleton, *Tenures*, §§ 6–8. Constable, 29 makes the same point more briefly. This situation is discussed in the context of London customs in YB Pas. 24 Edw. III, f.24, pl.4. In *De Laudibus Legum Anglie*, ed. S. B. Chrimes (Cambridge: Cambridge University Press, 1942), 14, Sir John Fortescue gives this example of a sister of the whole blood being preferred to a half-brother as something that might bewilder those not learned in the laws of England.

65 Constable, 14. 66 Constable, 14.

67 Cf. Kebell, YB Pas. 11 Hen. VII, f.19, pl.2.

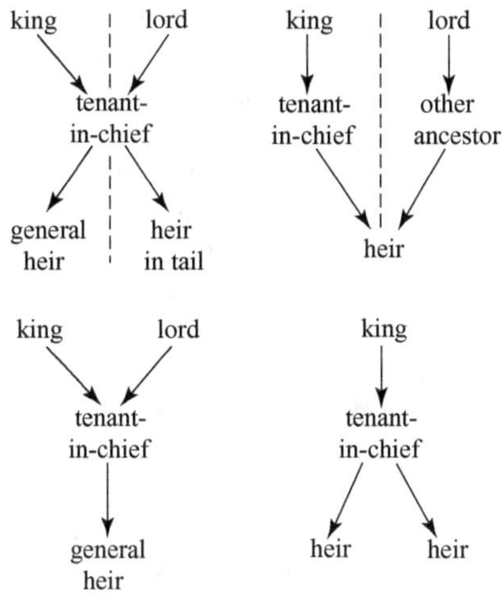

Figure 1

In the first two examples, the king will not have the wardship of the lands on the right-hand side of the figure, but he has all the lands in the other two examples. This principle was well-established by 1495; in *Skrene's Case*, Jenney argued that "if a man had issue two sons and died seised of a manor which is held of the king and the king seised the body of the elder son, and the manor, and then the younger son died seised of another manor held of a stranger by knight service, so that the brother is his heir and he [the brother] enters into the manor, and the king in this case shall never have the wardship of this manor, because this manor came to the heir by another ancestor, and note that this case was granted by the Court."[68]

Though the king's prerogative was limited quite severely in this way, Constable extends it in other areas. He argues that, if a tenant of the king alienated his land in fee tail, the tenant in tail then held the land of the king but the donor and his heirs also remained tenants of the king, since, as Bryan pointed out, "when the reversion was in him [the ancestor], he was a tenant of the king, and he died seised of a tenement."[69] In this situation, Constable argues that both the

[68] YB Mich. 15 Edw. IV, f.11, pl.17.

[69] YB Pas. 11 Hen. VII, f.19, pl.2. The reporter notes that all the judges agreed with this, though Kebell appears to have had some reservations.

tenant in tail and the reversioner hold of the king.[70] If the tenant in tail holds of another by priority and dies leaving an heir under age, the king will have the wardship of the body.[71] Similarly, when the reversioner dies, the king will have the wardship of the body of his heir and the reversion, even if the tenant held of another by priority.[72] Thus, although only the tenant in tail actually derives any benefit from the land, both he and the reversioner are considered to be tenants of the king and subject to the prerogative. This is a departure from the earlier readers, who argued that the reversioner remained the king's tenant throughout.

Having demonstrated ways in which the law both limited and extended the prerogative, the readers go on to discuss the ways in which the rules of inheritance might give the king wardship of several children of any one tenant-in-chief. If the tenant leaves four or five daughters and no sons, the king will have his prerogative of them all if they are under age, even where their ancestor held of another by priority.[73] Similarly, if a tenant who holds land of the king in gavelkind by knight service holds of others by priority and dies, leaving several sons under age, the king will have the wardship of all.[74] In both of these cases, the sons and daughters are co-heirs and thus the king has a right to the wardship of each heir. If a tenant holding land in borough English dies, the king will have only the younger son in ward, for the younger son inherits the land under this custom.[75]

The heir in the king's wardship might also change according to circumstances. The most likely situation in which this might happen was if a tenant of the king died leaving his wife pregnant and his heir a daughter under age. Constable argues that the king would seize the wardship and marriage of the girl, but, if the widow then bore a son, the king would seize him also. If the daughter was still unmarried when her brother was born, she would be released from the king's wardship, but if she was already married she had

[70] Similarly, if a tenant of the king leases land for term of life, he holds the reversion of the land.

[71] Constable, 30.

[72] Constable, 32. Cf. YB Pas. 11 Hen. VII, f.19, pl.2.

[73] Constable, 29. If one or two of them are under age and the others of full age, the king will have his prerogative in those still under age.

[74] Constable, 29. As in the previous case, if some of the sons are of full age, the king will only have the ward of those under age. Constable also describes how land in gavelkind might come into the king's hands.

[75] Constable, 30.

no remedy.[76] Frowyk considers what would happen if the tenant held lands only of a mesne lord and died in the same situation, when the lands and the daughter would go to the lord of whom the lands were held. If lands held of the king then descended to the daughter and a son was born, the king would have the wardship of the son.[77]

The ward in the king's hands might also change on entry into or departure from religion, which was similar in effect to death or birth.[78] If a tenant of the king entered into religion seised of his lands, the king would have his prerogative as though the tenant had died naturally.[79] Constable argues that, if an elder son entered religion in his father's lifetime and his father died seised of lands held of the king in knight service as of an escheat and other lands held of others by priority, leaving either a daughter or a younger son under age as heir, the king would have the wardship of the heir. If the elder son then left religion, still under age, the king would seize him and the other son, or daughter, would be out of wardship. If the younger son or daughter was married, he or she would have no remedy, for "il est heire all temps."[80] Frowyk also addresses this question, but again he presents the situation where the father dies seised only of land held of another lord. The lord has the wardship of the heir and then land held of the king descends to the heir. If the elder son then leaves religion, the king will have the wardship of the elder son and will oust the lord from the land. If the elder son then dies, the younger son will be back in wardship.[81] Once again, the readers were not merely indulging in academic speculations on this issue, for Caryll reports a similar situation. He presents it as follows: a man has two sons and the elder enters religion in his father's lifetime. The father dies seised of land held in chief of a lord and the

[76] Constable, 31.

[77] Frowyk, ff.3–3v. If the same situation obtained but the child born was a girl, the king would have the ward of the second girl.

[78] This was not always the case. Caryll notes that, if a tenant in tail aliens land and enters into religion, the heir will not have any remedy during the donor's natural life. Robert Keilway, *Relationes quorundam Casuum selectorum ex Libris Roberti Keilway Armiger* (London: 1602), Casus incerti temporis, f.104, pl.10.

[79] Constable, 30. [80] Constable, 31.

[81] Frowyk, f.3. Frowyk's argument that the king will oust the lord is marked with a query in the text. It seems likely that the argument was that the lord would hold the land which had vested legally in him (see pp. 97–98 below) and the king would only have the body of the elder brother and the land held of him, but with the change in heir the lord would lose his land.

body of the younger son is seized by another. The lord brings a writ of ravishment of ward and then the elder son leaves religion. The issue was whether the writ would then abate.[82] Caryll's case is presented as an issue of procedure, while the readers' cases are more substantive, but both are dealing with elements of the same problem.

There were some areas in which both readers allowed an extension of the words of *Prerogativa Regis*. The statute stated that the king had his prerogative only in the lands of which his tenant died seised, but the readers ameliorated that provision in the cases where the tenant had been disseised of particular land, but remained a tenant of the king. Thus Constable argues that, if a tenant is disseised and dies leaving an heir under age and this is found in the inquisition, the king will have his land as if the disseisin had not taken place. Similarly, if the grandfather was disseised of land held of the king in chief and died seised of other land and the father died leaving an heir under age and this is found by an inquisition, the king will have it all, both that remaining in the hands of the tenant and that held by the disseisor.[83] If the disseisor dies while the disseisee is still living and the disseisor's heir is under age, the king will have the heir and his prerogative. If the disseisee dies while the king has the heir of the disseisor, and his heir is also under age, and it is found that the heir of the disseisee should enter, then the king will have the wardship of the disseisee as the heir of the tenant by right.[84] This happens because "the king is judged rightful guardian of his ancient tenant etc. and he [the tenant] cannot decide from whom to hold, but the law judges right etc."[85] The earliest reader did not deal with this point directly, but Grantham argued that the king would not have the wardship of the heir of the tenant in tail, since he was only the king's tenant in possession and not in right. When the argument in favour of the lord was made explicitly by Philpot

[82] J. H. Baker, ed., *Readings and Moots at the Inns of Court in the Fifteenth Century*, vol. 2, Selden Society vol. 105 (London: Selden Society, 1989), 97.

[83] Constable, 14–15.

[84] Constable, 15. Constable is here a little confused about the timing necessary in order for the double seizure to take place. Frowyk's account makes more sense, for his version is: "The king's tenant is disseised and dies with his heir under age and before the inquisition the disseisor dies, his heir also under age and this is found by various inquisitions; the king will have his prerogative of both." Frowyk, f.2v.

[85] Constable, 16.

in *Skrene's Case*, "fuit ei negatum,"[86] but the law was obviously evolving in that direction.

Allowing the king the right to land of which his tenants had been disseised was one way of combating the more unorthodox transfers of land in the fifteenth century, but it did little to hinder the activities of those who took more proactive measures to avoid the king's grasp. The most common method of evasion was to place lands in use, an action which could be considered alienation by collusion. Though uses were the most topical method of alienation by collusion, the readers do not address them immediately, but deal with the general principle first. Constable argues that, if the tenant alienates land held in chief and this matter is found by inquisition, then the king will have all the alienated land as well as all the land which passed from the tenant to his heir. If the tenant alienated not only land held in chief but also land held of other lords, the king will have it all, for the principle is the same as above: the king would have had everything if there had been no collusion so he has everything when the collusion is discovered.[87] Frowyk agrees with Constable concerning land held of the king in chief alienated by collusion.[88] When it comes to land held of others, however, he argues that the king will not have the land. He claims that the king would have to aver covin by the statute of Marlborough, but he cannot do this, because the statute was made for the advantage of the lords and it cannot be used by the king. Awkwardly enough, the lords of whom the land was held have no remedy under Marlborough either. If they did recover the land alienated by collusion by the tenant-in-chief, it would go to the king with the wardship of the other lands. Thus the recovery would do them no good.[89] Frowyk also argues that, when the king's tenant alienates by collusion and dies with an

[86] YB Mich. 15 Edw. IV, f.11, pl.17. Philpot was speaking in general terms of a lord's rights, however, and not of the king's.

[87] Constable, 18–19. Constable argues that a licence to alienate does not protect a tenant against this charge, for even alienation by licence can be collusive. In *Stonor's Case*, however, Danvers thought that "the King cannot aver collusion contrary to his own licence, for if the tenant aliens, the King shall seize the land for the fine, and not because of collusion; and if he aliens by licence, the King cannot say that the feoffment was made to defraud him of the wardship where he himself is a party to the feoffment." Hemmant, *Select Cases in Exchequer Chamber*, vol. 2, 172.

[88] Frowyk, f.2. [89] Frowyk, f.2.

under-age heir and his feoffee also dies leaving an under-age heir, the king will have his prerogative of both.[90] He points out that this is the same result as in the case discussed above, where the king's tenant is disseised and dies leaving an under-age heir, for in both cases the original tenant held of the king by right and the disseisor or the feoffee holds of the king in fact.

After dealing with the topic in general, Constable and Frowyk move on to the issue of uses, and the statute of 1490 which attempted to deal with the problem. This new statute confirmed Marlborough and enacted further provisions dealing with enfeoffment to uses. From this point on, if a tenant conveyed land to his use and did not declare a will, the lord had the same rights over the land as he would have had if the feoffment had not been made.[91] Constable argues that, if a will was declared, this exempted the land from wardship, but did not apply to the body of the heir.[92] If, in the will, the land was enfeoffed to use for the purpose of paying debts or providing a marriage portion for children after the death of the tenant, the executors could retain the land until this purpose was fulfilled.[93] If the heir was still under age at the fulfilment of the will, the land would then pass into the king's hands. If the will simply stated that the land was enfeoffed to the use of the heir, then it was as if no will was declared and the land was immediately in the hands of the king.[94] Thus, though the king is not mentioned in the statute, Constable argues that he had the same rights as the lords and could seize or recover land alienated in this way at his pleasure. He would also have his prerogative in the recovered land.[95] If the tenant had only land held of the king as of escheat and of another by priority, still the king had the wardship of the heir and his prerogative.[96]

Frowyk, however, equates the new statute with the statute of Marlborough, and argues that the same reasons which prevent the king from using Marlborough also limit his use of the new statute. Thus, if the king's tenant makes a feoffment to use of land held

[90] Frowyk, f.2v.
[91] 4 Hen. VII, c.17, *Statutes of the Realm*, 11 vols. (London, 1810–1822), vol. 2, 541.
[92] Constable, 36.
[93] Constable, 20–21. It must be found by inquisition that such debts exist.
[94] Constable, 21.
[95] Constable, 37. He says that this also applied to collusive feoffments.
[96] Constable, 32.

of another lord, neither the king nor his lords have a remedy under the new statute for that land.[97] Frowyk's brief mention of the most recent statute relating to the question under consideration is striking, and the only explanation for his off-hand treatment is his obvious belief that the statute simply did not have any relevance for the king's prerogative, since the king was not mentioned in it. As Constable was equally obviously of the opinion that the king could use the statute, and neither reader mentioned a different interpretation of the law than his own, the stage was set for a new round in the struggle over the prerogative.

Thus far, we have been considering individual landholders, but it was also common for land to be held in joint tenancy, and this brought its own complexity. While alienation could prevent the king from claiming his prerogative, the existence of a joint tenant could delay descent and thus delay wardship. Frowyk points out that, if the king's tenant, A, and another, B, hold lands together and A dies, the king will have no right in the land, because B will hold it as survivor, with sole rights in the land.[98] If, however, the land was given to A and B and the heirs of A, the situation is changed. Here A is the tenant in fee and B is simply a tenant for term of life. When A dies, B continues to hold as survivor, but, when B dies, the king will have rights in the land.[99] The kind of rights the king has will vary depending on what other lands A held and of whom. As we have seen, when A dies, the king will not have his land, for it goes to the survivor. Neither will he have his heir, for, if A held land in socage of another lord which descended to his heir under age, the heir is in the wardship of his *prochein amy*, usually a close relative such as his mother or uncle. When B dies, and the land held in chief descends to the heir, the king will have the land held of him, together with the land held in socage and the body of the heir, if the heir is still under age.[100] If, however, the land which descended previously from A to his heir was held of another lord in knight service, rather than in socage, the lord will have the wardship of the heir and the land held of him, and he will retain the wardship of both body and land, even when the lands held by B descend to the heir. The king in this case has the wardship of the lands held of him and the wardship of

97 Frowyk, f.2. The implication is that the restriction works in the same way and for the same reasons.

98 Frowyk, f.2. 99 Frowyk, f.2; Constable, 35.

100 Frowyk, f.2; Constable, 35.

those things which no other lord can have, but not the land which has legally vested in the lord.[101]

The king's access to his rights might also be delayed by a lease for term of life made by the tenant-in-chief. This issue appeared in both the earlier readings, where the readers agreed that the king could not re-enter, but disagreed over his rights to the heir and any reserved rent. The earliest reader argued that the king would have the heir and the rent from the land. Grantham said that the lease would delay the wardship of both land and heir, but in the same reading Brown disagreed, and accepted the earlier reader's point that the king would get the wardship of the heir. Constable agrees with the first reader, arguing that the king will seize the body of the heir, the reversion of the land held of him, and the reserved rent, while Frowyk follows Grantham's view that the king would only have his prerogative in the land when the tenant for term of life died, without specifying any exception.[102] This seems to follow the readers' usual inclinations, with Constable supporting the broader right, and Frowyk taking the more limited interpretation. However, Constable goes on to argue that, when the tenant-in-chief leased his land held of the king for term of years and died seised of other lands held of other lords in knight service, those other lords will have the wardship of their lands, for the tenure in chief is in suspense until the term of years ends. When the term is finished the king will have the leased land, if the heir is still under age.[103] Thus Constable, like Brown, is inclined to protect the right of the termor, not by breaking up the term, but by asserting the right of the tenant for term of years to retain the land against the king in the same way as the tenant for term of life. Any argument in favour of the termor was still relatively new, for, though Baker notes that some doubt had been cast on the king's rights in 1490,[104] the old opinion still had its supporters: in 1499 Higham believed that "the guardian shall put the termor out, for

[101] Constable, 21–22. Frowyk adds that a father will have the wardship of his son or daughter unless he is attainted of felony. He also equates villeins to children here, pointing out that if lands held of the king descend to a villein the king will not have the body, but if he is manumitted the king may seize him. If the heir is still under age when the father dies, the king may then seize the wardship. Frowyk, f.3.

[102] Constable, 23; Frowyk, f.2.

[103] Constable, 24. Presumably, the king will not have the body of the heir, which has vested in the lord.

[104] YB Trin. 5 Hen. VII, f.37, pl.3.

his title is the older."[105] However, early in Henry VIII's reign, the termor's right to retain the land was confirmed by Fyneux.[106]

While the king might lose a wardship, or at least be delayed by such circumstances, he might also get a wardship when the circumstances changed. Frowyk gives an example where the heir's body had vested in another lord, but then the lord lost the land by which he held the wardship. In this instance, the king could seize the wardship of the body, even when there was another lord whose title was older than the king's title.[107] If the lord had already married the ward or if the ward had satisfied the lord for his marriage, the king would not have the ward when the lord lost his land. If, however, the lord had only granted the marriage of the ward to another before he lost the land, the king could seize it back.[108] Similarly, if a tenant sold his heir's marriage and then died before the marriage was carried out, the lord would still have the wardship, despite the sale. If the tenant had made a will which left the custody of the heir to someone other than the lord, this too was void, for the lord had the wardship by reason of the tenure in knight service.[109]

Provisions such as these in the law envisage a close monitoring of the king's tenants and suggest the existence of an active and organized system which enquired into the status of land throughout the country on a constant basis and protected the king's rights whenever and wherever they fell due. Though in theory the commissions and the regular work of the escheators provided this system, it is not at all clear that Tudor England had the resources to bring it to fruition. However, there is no doubt that Henry VII was determined to make the system as effective as possible; Luckett argues that from the mid-1490s inquisitions *virtute officii* became increasingly common, and were not in default of inquisitions based on a chancery writ, but were mainly intended to supplement such writs and to enquire more closely into the holdings of tenants-in-chief, often years after the death of the tenant in

105 YB Pas. 14 Hen. VII, f.22, pl.4.

106 Baker, *Spelman's Reports*, vol. 2, 182; *gardes*, vol. 1, 142. The date of Fyneux's decision is unclear: Baker gives it as 1513 or 1523.

107 Frowyk, f.3v. If the lord then recovered his land, he would also recover the wardship out of the hands of the king.

108 Frowyk, f.3v.

109 *Caryll's Reports*, vol. 2, 692. Caryll notes that it was unclear whether a will would bar the guardian in socage.

question.[110] Although these inquisitions seem to have been quite fruitful, it is impossible to tell how much they missed. The intention, nevertheless, was clear, and there is no doubt that the law allowed the king to claim his full due whenever the system did bring such tenants to the fore.

We have already seen that Frowyk and Constable disagreed on their interpretation of the king's rights over lands seized for treason or felony. This disagreement extends into their discussion of his rights over the heirs to such lands. Frowyk argues that the king will not have wardship of the heir of land in his hands by forfeiture for felony or treason. Thus, if a man dies seised of two acres held of two lords, one by priority and one by posteriority, and the lord by posteriority is an outlaw in a personal action so that his land is in the king's hands, the king will not have the body of the ward, because the ancestor did not hold the land of the king.[111] Similarly, if the lord by posteriority is attainted of treason and before the inquisition the tenant dies, his heir under age, the lord by priority will have the wardship.[112] Constable, however, holds the exactly opposite view. He argues that the king will have his prerogative in the body and marriage of any heir who holds of any manor in the hands of the king as king. Thus, if the king has the land of an idiot or land forfeit for felony by a tenant in tail or a tenant for term of life, and then one who holds land of such a manor in the hands of the king by posteriority and land of another by priority dies, the king will have the body of the heir "by the equity of this statute or implication, for they [the statutes] cannot express each case etc."[113] The same is true of land in the king's hands for term of years or for other reasons, such as the vacancy of a bishopric, year, day, and waste, alienation without licence, or primer seisin.[114] Even if the manor was not held of the king, as was perfectly possible in many of these cases, he was to have his prerogative "for the king has all these as king and no other person can have them by forfeiture by common

[110] D. A. Luckett, "Crown Patronage and Local Administration in Berkshire, Dorset, Hampshire, Oxfordshire, Somerset and Wiltshire, 1485–1509" (PhD diss., Oxford University, 1992), 302.

[111] Frowyk, f.3v. [112] Frowyk, f.3v. [113] Constable, 39.

[114] Frowyk argues that, if the king's villein has a lordship by posteriority and before office found the tenant dies, his heir under age, the lord by priority will seize the body. The king will seize the lordship of the villein, but he will not have the body of the heir, which has already vested. Frowyk, f.3v. Constable, on the other hand, argues that the king is seised of the villein "en droit de son coron" and as a result will have the ward of the heir and his prerogative in the body. Constable, 40.

law."[115] Constable's extension of the prerogative by the equity of the statute here vastly increases the wardships which would accrue to the crown, if the principle were accepted by the profession. It is also linked to his earlier argument that forfeitures to the king for treason or felony should be held in chief. Both rely on the idea that the king has his prerogative in those things which come to him as king, rather than simply through tenure.

Constable's position is the more obviously royalist of the two readers, and it is tempting to see in his interpretation a new conception of the prerogative, one which seeks to give broader rights to the king as king. Though this might have been the final result of Constable's argument, it is important to remember that his arguments are based on the principle that *Prerogativa Regis* is a statute, and thus can be extended by the equity of the statute to incorporate situations not explicitly mentioned therein. Constable has no new conception of the prerogative, but he is interpreting widely accepted ideas to broaden the king's rights. Frowyk, on the other hand, by rejecting the idea that *Prerogativa Regis* is a statute, rejects the kinds of extensions that Constable is making. He does not deny the king's legitimate rights, and in some areas he is willing to extend them beyond the explicit words of the text, but in general he believes that any further expansion is beyond the limits of the law as it stands. Thus, although the readers differ from each other in their interpretation of the law, they do not differ on their essential understanding of the prerogative as the king's legal rights as sovereign lord.

This basic disagreement over the foundation of *Prerogativa Regis* also permeates the readers' treatment of the recovery of land by an heir. Constable argues that, if the heir recovers the land through formedon or mort d'ancestor, he holds the land by descent (since that was the basis of the action) and if he recovers while he is under age he will be in ward to the king. If part of the recovered land was held of the king and part was not, the king will have all and he will oust the other lords of the wardship of their lands, for with the recovery it is as though the alienation had never happened.[116] After such a recovery, even if the heir does not enter on the land, but the matter is found by inquisition, the king may seize the body, but not before either the inquisition or the entry.[117] If, however, the heir had

[115] Constable, 39–40. [116] Constable, 17–18.

[117] Constable, 36. Caryll agrees with Constable that the king can enter in right of the heir, even when the heir has not entered himself. *Caryll's Reports*, vol. 1, 364.

possession of land held of another by which he is in ward to another lord, and recovers land by formedon, the king will not be able to seize the body, but only the wardship of the land held of him, for the heir's body was legally vested in the other lord.[118] Recovery made when a condition of feoffment was broken was a parallel to recovery for disseisin. Such a recovery would be possible if a tenant of the king who held of him as of escheat and of another by priority alienated land in fee on condition of payment and the payment was not made, or for a certain rent and the rent was not paid. Constable argues that, if the tenant dies leaving an heir under age and there is such cause for re-entry, the king will not have the wardship of the heir until the cause is found by inquisition or the heir himself enters. Without such an inquisition or entry the king has no title to the land, and thus no right to the heir, for the feoffee's title was good before the default.[119] Once the inquisition is found or the heir enters, the king has the right to wardship. If the cause for re-entry occurs after the death of the tenant, and the heir is already in ward to another lord, the king will not have the body, but simply the land held of him.[120]

Frowyk argues rather differently. He argues that, when an infant in ward to another recovers land by an ancestral action, or for a broken condition, the king will not have the wardship, because it had vested in the lord.[121] However, if the infant enters on a disseisor, the king will have the wardship of all.[122] In *Stonor's Case*, he will argue that the king will not have land recovered because of a broken condition for the same reason that he will not have land recovered by an ancestral action, namely, that the tenant did not die seised of the land.[123] He appears to have developed his ideas somewhat since the reading, however, for he rejects the king's right to wardship even if the heir enters on the land.[124] Thus the essential condition of wardship for Frowyk is possession, rather than simply right to the land. Constable, on the other hand, is willing to

118 Constable, 37.

119 If the feoffment was made by an infant or a lunatic, the feoffee's title was voidable from the beginning. Constable, 35–36.

120 Constable, 37. 121 Frowyk, f.3. 122 Frowyk, f.3.

123 YB Trin. 12 Hen. VII, ff.20–21, pl.1. See p. 107 below.

124 *Ibid.* Kebell argues that, if the heir entered on a stranger after the death of his father for a condition broken, following recovery by an ancestral action, the king was able to enter on him, even though the father did not die seised. Frowyk's reply is a direct answer to this.

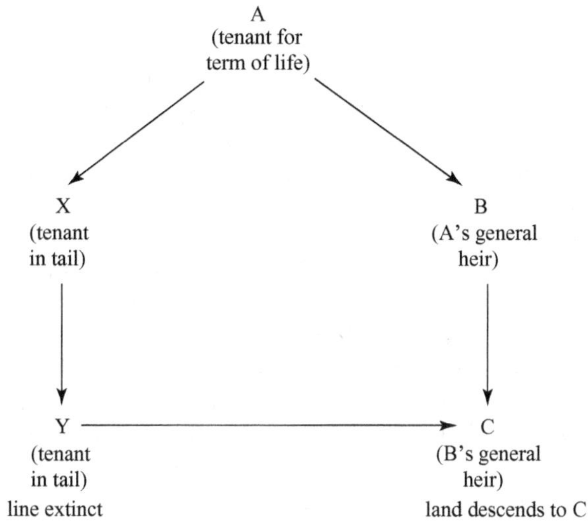

Figure 2

allow the king his prerogative once the heir's right to the land is established.

This is the same issue which had caused the earlier readers so much difficulty, though it emerges in a different context in 1495. However, the issues of right and possession that Frowyk and Constable are discussing are the same issues that perplexed Grantham and the justices in *Skrene's Case*. Then it was argued by Choke that "the king will have nothing by the death of his tenant where he had nothing but a right."[125] The point was hotly disputed, and several of the lawyers responded that the king often had his prerogative where the tenant did not die seised of land held of the king. Brygges instances a case very much like one posited by Constable in which there is a tenant for term of life of any lord with a remainder over in tail, remainder to the right heirs of the tenant for term of life. In this case, when the tenant for term of life, A, dies, his general heir, B, has a fee simple. B does not inherit the land directly from his ancestor, but he inherits a right in the land, which will come to him, or to his heir, when the tail is extinct. If the tenant in tail dies without issue while the general heir is still under age, Constable argues that he (in this example, C) will be in ward.

[125] YB Mich. 15 Edw. IV, f.13, pl.17.

Constable admits that others say that the heir will only be in ward when both the fee simple and the freehold are in the ancestor and descend together to the heir; thus in this case the heir would not be in ward.[126] This is a variation on Bryan's argument in 1475, that right and possession did not have to descend together: as long as they were joined at some point, the king would have his claim.[127] This is the position that Frowyk held in his reading, though he later came to reject it in favour of the more stringent view.

Having looked at the impact of a recovery on the heir of a feoffor, Constable also considers how a recovery for a broken condition affects the heir of the feoffee. He argues that the feoffee holds his land of the king, since the feoffor can only alienate land by substitution. If the feoffee dies with his rent in arrears and the feoffor enters, the king will still have the wardship of the body of the feoffee's heir. When the inquisition finds that the feoffee held of the king, the escheator will seize the land out of the hands of the feoffor, "since land to which the king has title shall never be lost because of a charge due on it."[128] If, however, the feoffor had given the land in fee until his heir was of age, or until he had married into a certain family, these would be good conditions. If the feoffee then died holding this land of the king as of an escheat and land of another by priority, the king would have the body of his heir until the land was legally out of his hands by suit, and the feoffor would have the land back.[129]

Though the king's rights to wardship were limited in several cases, usually where the body of the heir had already vested in another lord, they were extended in his ability to claim wardship by reason of wardship. The readers argued that since the king's right was infinite, if a tenant of the second ward died leaving an heir under age, the king would seize that wardship also, and so on. Wardship by reason of wardship could also accrue within one family. Frowyk gives the example of a lord and tenant who both hold by knight service, and the lord has a son and daughter and buys the tenancy to him and the heirs female of his body and dies seised of an acre held of the king. In this case, the king will have the wardship of both infants, since the lordship descends to the son and the tenancy to the daughter. Thus the son holds of the king and the daughter

[126] Constable, 34. [127] YB Mich. 15 Edw. IV, f.14, pl.17. [128] Constable, 38.

[129] Constable, 38. This was supported by Ursewike, chief baron of the exchequer, in *Skrene's Case*, though the condition he suggests sounds like an ingenious way of avoiding wardship.

holds of her brother. If both are under age the king will have the wardship of the son as heir of his tenant and of the daughter by reason of wardship.[130] The king's right, however, lasted only as long as the first heir was in ward. When the first heir sued his livery out of the hands of the king, the ward by reason of wardship would remain in the hands of the king, for her body had vested there. However, if this second heir died leaving an heir under age, the wardship would go, not to the king, but to the first heir who had sued livery and who held the land which the second heir was to inherit.[131]

The primary purpose of the readings was pedagogical, and the readers were careful to build their arguments slowly in order to convey the reasoning behind them to their audience. The principles they are using thus emerge through their examples rather than being explicitly stated. The law concerning wardship evolved over a long period, and a core of accepted rules had developed in order to allow it to function. Once they moved beyond these basics, there were many points on which the two readers differed, however.

We can get some idea of the representativeness of the readers' opinions by looking at *Stonor's Case*, argued in the courts just two years after the readings given by Constable and Frowyk. The case raised many of the issues covered by the readers, and demonstrated how necessary an understanding of the rules governing both inheritance and the prerogative was to a practitioner of the law. Sir William Stonor died seised of an advowson held of the king in chief. He and Ralph Vyne were also enfeoffed of two manors, one held of the king in socage and the other held of the prior of St. Swithin's, service unknown, to the use of Stonor and of his heir, who was under age at the time of his death. Following Stonor's death, the escheators seized his land for the king, and the case came before the judges. The issues involved were important enough to merit a discussion before all the judges in the exchequer chamber in the autumn of 1497, but the first report of the case is in the summer of that year. At that stage, the main argument in the court was whether the king should have the benefit of the statute at all. Marow points out that the enfeoffed land was held of another lord, and only the

130 Frowyk, f.4.

131 Frowyk, f.3v. Similarly, if the king had a ward by reason of a lordship which was parcel of the principality of Wales and then a prince of Wales was created and restored to the principality and the ward died, the prince, and not the king, would have his heir in ward. Frowyk, f.4.

lord could have the benefit of the statute. He adds further that "this [statute] gives the king no prerogative . . . therefore the king's prerogative does not hold there; for to my understanding the king can have no prerogative except of things which have always been given to him by the prerogative, for a prerogative cannot begin at this time."[132] He comes to the same conclusion as Frowyk's reading, that under common law, if the tenant of the king makes an enfeoffment of land which he holds of another lord, and then dies with an heir under age, the king will not have the land out of the hands of the feoffee; this statute "is a special law which gives advantage to the lord, and not to the king" and therefore the king will still have nothing.[133]

Hobart, the king's attorney, disagrees with Marow. He believes that the king will have his prerogative, arguing that the intent of the makers of the statute must be taken into consideration, and their intent was clearly that "the Lords should be in the same condition, when their tenants make a feoffment to their [the tenant's] use and declare no will, as if they had died seised in their demesne as of fee with no feoffment made."[134] The idea that statutes should be interpreted according to the intent of their makers was an old one, but it was usually used to cover flaws in drafting when the meaning was fairly obvious; it is not at all clear that this was in fact the intention of the makers of the statute.[135] Hobart also makes the point that the king is included in the statute because all land is held of him, either immediately or mediately, and so he is lord to everyone.

Sedgwick disagrees with Hobart. He argues that there is a distinction between a prerogative which the king has at common law, which is then enlarged by statute, and something which is granted by statute. He uses the example of the king's right to year, day, and waste in the goods of felons. If a statute declared that it was a felony to forge deeds, then the king would acquire the right to year, day, and waste in the land of convicted forgers, for the statute simply extended a prerogative he already had by adding to the list of felonies. If, on the other hand, the statute ordained that the lands of a convicted forger should escheat to his lord, the king would have no prerogative, because the statute was enacting something new.

132 YB Trin. 12 Hen. VII, f.19, pl.1. 133 *Ibid.* 134 *Ibid.*
135 Baker, *Spelman's Reports*, vol. 2, 194. See chapter 1, p. 71 above.

Sedgwick believes that the same thing is true of this new statute, for under common law the lord had no rights to the heir when the land was in use, but by the statute, where no will is declared the heir will be in ward and this "does not extend to the King and his prerogative, for there was never anything like this at common law, that any heir will be in ward in such case, nor the land of the feoffee; for which reason it seems to me that the king will not have his prerogative."[136]

Mordant next enters the argument on the king's side, and he returns to the principles of statutory interpretation for his case. He again notes that the statute should be construed according to the intentions of the makers, and argues that, if the king were excluded from the working of the statute, he would be in a worse position than a common person, which does not make sense. If a statute is made which restricts liberty, the king is not bound by it unless he is specifically named in it; on the other hand, if a statute is made which is beneficial to the king, he will have the use of it even if he is not named. He concludes by referring to the general point made by Hobart, that the makers of the statute clearly intended to restore the pre-enfeoffment position.[137] Kebell agrees with Mordant, using the same point as Hobart.[138]

Frowyk is the final commentator in the report, and he believes, as we might expect, that the king should not have his prerogative. His point here differs from that of his reading, however. In the reading, he based his argument on the similar restrictions in the use of the statute of Marlborough and the new statute. Here, he simply points out that the words of *Prerogativa Regis* give the king his prerogative where the tenant dies seised, and the tenant did not die seised in this case. As well as this, he argues that the statute "gives the ward solely by express words of the statute to the lord; thus if he recovers by force of the said statute, it is not reasonable that the king should take this from him by his prerogative."[139] Thus Frowyk now believes that, where the words of the statute give the lords a remedy, they should be able to keep it against the king. He is also reiterating his stand that, since *Prerogativa Regis* gives the king his prerogative only where his tenant dies seised, the king should only have it in that case.

136 YB Trin. 12 Hen. VII, ff.19–20, pl.1.
137 *Ibid.*, f.20. 138 *Ibid.* 139 *Ibid.*, f.21.

The report of the case is inconclusive, and it was removed to the exchequer chamber for further discussion. Sedgwick opens the report this time, and he makes the same argument as before. Kingsmill responds with the argument that the makers of the statute intended the king to have the benefit of the statute. Frowyk is the third speaker, and he has developed his view of the case. His opening point is one not raised before. He reminds the court that Stonor and Vyne were enfeoffed with the land to the use of Stonor and his heirs, and argues that this means that Vyne holds the land as survivor. Therefore, the case is completely outside the statute and the king cannot have his prerogative. He goes on to argue that, even if the case was within the statute, the king would still not have wardship, for any right to wardship is given by the statute, and the statute only speaks of lands held in knight service and says nothing about lands held in socage.[140]

Mordant replies to Frowyk's argument, and he is quick to bring the discussion back to safer ground. He opens with a return to the bastion of statutory interpretation as he points out that the statute is an affirmation of the common law and thus should be interpreted "as widely as possible."[141] He continues by pointing out that under the common law the king would have the wardship, but that the deceit of the use kept it from him. Since the statute was designed to restore the common law, the king should have the wardship. He replies to Frowyk's point about the joint tenure by arguing that "this is not material, for the land in this case descends in conscience to the heir, just as though he alone had purchased the land and had made feoffment in fee to his use, for it is all one and a mischief to the lord."[142] Mordant is followed by Boteler, who argues against the prerogative on the grounds that the king is not mentioned in the statute and is not immediate lord.[143] Kebell then argues for the prerogative, using exactly the same argument as before,[144] and Wode agrees with Kebell on the grounds that the king will have the benefit of the statute even though he is not mentioned in it, and that the statute provides that the heir will be in ward as if his father had died seised, which would place him in the king's hands.[145] The lines of argument were thus clearly established, and for the most

[140] YB Mich. 13 Hen. VII, f.5, pl.3. Also printed, with translation, in Hemmant, *Select Cases in Exchequer Chamber*, vol. 2, 164.

[141] Hemmant, *Select Cases in Exchequer Chamber*, vol. 2, 165.

[142] *Ibid.*, 166. [143] *Ibid.* [144] *Ibid.*, 168. [145] *Ibid.*, 169–70.

part followed those given in the earlier rehearsal of the case. Vavasour, however, enters the fray at this point and takes a different position. He believes that the king should not have his prerogative and considers that this was not the reason behind the statute, "for no mention was made of this at the time of the making of the statute."[146] He goes on to agree that, if the tenant had died seised, the land would have been in wardship, but points out that that is irrelevant, because "this statute declares which lord will have the wardship and to which lord the heir shall be in ward, to wit, the immediate lord shall have the wardship of the lands held by knight's service and of no other lands, for the lord shall have no benefit by this statute of lands held in socage."[147] He argues that, since tenure in socage brings no wardship with it, it cannot be argued that a feoffment to use of such land was intended to defraud, and so the king cannot claim wardship on the grounds of collusion. Nor can he claim any such right by arguing that he is the lord, mediate or immediate, of such land, since the lord has no right to wardship.[148] Fyneux takes up Vavasour's point, accepting that the king has no right to socage land by the statute, but he believes that the king will still have his prerogative in land held in knight service, for he argues that the statute expressly gives the lords the right to wardship because of their seigniory over the land. Thus, he argues, it is the tenure by which the land is held that conveys the right to wardship, even under the statute, and so the king will retain his prerogative by right of tenure.[149] Danvers speaks against any restriction of the king's right to wardship of land held in socage, arguing that it should be given by the equity of the statute. He considers that, if the king is excluded from the statute, his prerogative will be completely defeated, and, if land held in socage is excluded, it will be restricted beyond reason.[150]

By this point the discussion has wandered from the case in question, and the justices appear to be no closer to agreement. Two distinct trends are clear in the protracted argument and they are of

146 *Ibid.*, 170. 147 *Ibid.*, 171. 148 *Ibid.*

149 *Ibid.*, 173–74. Danvers and Bryan spoke between Vavasour and Fyneux, but they introduced nothing of relevance to this discussion. Bryan raised some doubts about the validity of the inquisition which were taken up by Fyneux, but this is discussed in chapter 3, p. 137 below.

150 YB Mich. 13 Hen. VII, f.11, pl.12. This is a continuation of the discussion, printed separately in the year book. It contains Danvers' views and a further section attributed to Sedgwick which mirrors Boteler's contribution.

equal strength. Half of the disputants argued, essentially, that the statute should be interpreted according to the intention of its makers, keeping in mind that statutes were generally to be interpreted in favour of the king. The other party argued for a strict interpretation of the statute, keeping in mind the rules already established for wardship, especially the claims based on tenure. Fyneux was the only justice to concede a point to the opposition. Frowyk was a prominent member of the second party, but his arguments were different from all the others, and they continued to develop over the course of the discussion, suggesting that, though the statute of 1490 did not bulk large in his reading, for the simple reason that he did not believe that it was relevant, its implications and the continuing development of the prerogative remained a topic of great interest to him. Frowyk's arguments are also given at length by the reporter, suggesting that his special knowledge of the topic was recognized.

The year book gives no conclusion to the case, but in his abbreviated report of *Stonor's Case* Caryll suggests that the king will have his prerogative in the land.[151] The issue was clearly one which divided the legal profession, however, and, whether Caryll is right in his conclusion or not, the position continued to shift, in the king's favour, for some years after. Caryll reports a citation of *Stonor's Case*, probably in the Inner Temple, in 1506, according to which it had been decided by all the judges of England that the king should have the wardship of the land held of him and the land held of the other lord in knight service, but not of the land held in socage.[152] Thus Frowyk's and Vavasour's point about the king's rights to socage land was accepted by the profession, but they were overruled in their contention that the king should not be included in the statute. Since the land in use in this case was held of the king, this case does not throw any light on the king's rights when his tenant enfeoffed lands held of others to his use. Caryll notes, however, in 1514, "the common experience is that the king shall have prerogative wardship both of the lands whereof the ancestor was seised in use and in possession, whether the land was held in socage or in knight service."[153] His report of the case of *Conyngesby* v. *Throgmorton* in 7 Hen. VIII states that, where "the king's tenant dies seised of land in chief and of lands in socage in use, the prerogative

[151] *Caryll's Reports*, vol. 1, 366.
[152] *Caryll's Reports*, vol. 2, 530.
[153] *Caryll's Reports*, vol. 2, 531.

shall hold place of the lands in use [and] in socage: by ALL THE JUSTICES OF ENGLAND in the Exchequer Chamber."[154] This case perfectly answers the situation found in *Stonor's Case*, and Caryll's confusion over the dating of the shift, connecting it with a case of 1506, reporting it as common experience by 1514, and reiterating it in a case from 1516, suggests the process by which it became accepted. In any case, it is clear that half of the justices in 1497 had attempted to restrict the extension of the king's prerogative under this new statute which made no mention of the king or of his prerogative. The weight of tradition in both statutory interpretation and the king's procedural prerogative seems to have been too much for them. The most Caryll could say to restrict the use of the new statute was that "the king shall not have primer seisin of the lands whereof the ancestor died seised in use, because the statute only remedies wardship."[155] Primer seisin was another burning issue at the end of the fifteenth century, and we will turn to this in the next chapter.

The questions surrounding the statute of 4 Hen. VII, c.17 provide a useful illustration of the role of the readings. The discussion between the judges in court was generally unrehearsed and undirected. Even when a case was adjourned to exchequer chamber, giving the judges some opportunity to consider their positions, they were forced to respond to the statements made by their colleagues, rather than being able to control the direction of the discussion. Although interesting and useful points of law were raised in the course of these wide-ranging arguments, they did not even approach a systematic exposition of the topic. The confusion in the year books, and particularly in *Caryll's Reports*, over the later interpretations of the statute, also demonstrates why regular coverage of the law continued to be necessary. A student, left to find his way through the conflicting reports of the law and to derive the logic behind individual decisions from the statements of the justices, would be in difficult straits indeed without the framework of the readings.

[154] *Caryll's Reports*, vol. 2, 664. [155] *Caryll's Reports*, vol. 2, 531.

3

FROWYK AND CONSTABLE ON PRIMER SEISIN

By the late fifteenth century there was no doubt that the heir of full age would receive his ancestor's lands as a matter of course, but primer seisin remained unpopular with tenants. The immediate loss of income was one concern, both in the loss of issues while the king held the land and in the sum the heir had to pay for livery. Primer seisin also gave the king the opportunity to investigate the titles by which his tenants held their lands, and its reach was wider than wardship, for every parcel of land was open to primer seisin, while wardship could be avoided, either through natural good fortune or evasion. Effective implementation of the king's rights to primer seisin meant that over the course of a generation the king could, in theory, carry out a Domesday-like survey of landholding in England.

Primer seisin was to some extent a more sensitive topic than wardship, but the readers approached it in much the same way that they investigated wardship. Both opened their discussion with a brief history of the topic, accepting that the statute of Marlborough ordained that the king should have primer seisin of land held of him in chief, and that this was a confirmation of the common law.[1] Constable points out that "it is reasonable that the king will grant livery of the land which was held of him to the one who will be his tenant of record and will have the issues in the meantime."[2] Their interpretations of the common law differ, however. Constable argues that *Prerogativa Regis* extended the king's rights over his tenants-in-chief to include all the land of which the tenant died seised, even

[1] Robert Constable, *Prerogativa Regis: Tertia Lectura Roberti Constable de Lincolnis Inne Anno 11 H. 7*, ed. S. E. Thorne (New Haven: Yale University Press, 1949), 41; Frowyk, CUL MS Hh.2.1, f.4.
[2] Constable, 41–42.

when it was held of other lords.[3] Having thus extended the king's rights when the tenant holds land of him in chief, Constable then treats of land held of the king as of an escheat. He argues that under common law the king had the right to primer seisin and the issues of all the lands of which his tenant died seised. Magna Carta c.31 then restricted the king's rights when his tenant held of him as of an escheat, so that he would have only the same as the lord would have had. This meant that he could not have the issues of the lands his tenant held of others. He did, however, retain the right to seize the land and to grant livery of it, since this was his at common law.[4] Thus, according to Constable's reading, the king could seize all the land of which his tenant died seised: if the tenant held in chief he could hold all the land until livery was sued, with issues; if the tenant held as of an escheat, he could retain the issues of the land held of him but had to concede the issues of the land held of others.

Frowyk once again argues that *Prerogativa Regis* simply confirms the common law. According to common law and the statute of Marlborough, the king had the right to primer seisin of all his tenant's land when the tenant held of him in chief and the heir had the obligation to sue livery, and *Prerogativa Regis* did nothing to change that.[5] Frowyk is quite explicit that the tenant must hold his lands in chief in order for the king to claim primer seisin, and so we can presume that he thought the king had only the same rights of seizure over the lands of a tenant who held as of an escheat as the lord would have had. The difference in opinion between the readers, though small, was significant. In effect, Constable allowed the king more room to seize lands, though he recognized that the king did not have the right to the profits of all the lands thus seized. Frowyk, on the other hand, believed that the king had no right to seize lands when he could not retain the profits. Thorne points out that "both were in substantial agreement as to the lands whose issues and profits came properly to the king, and thus Constable's analysis, which allowed the seizure of other lands but permitted their owner or owners to sue them out of the king's hands *cum exitibus*,

[3] Constable, 42. [4] Constable, 42.

[5] Frowyk says that "the king will have primer seisin of all lands and tenements which his tenant held of him, and of which he died seised, as long as he held of him in chief, which the common law affirms." Frowyk, f.4. He reiterates this latter point at f.6.

with the accrued issues, led to no greater financial loss than Frowyk contemplated."[6]

Though this is true in the short term, when Constable's and Frowyk's arguments are placed in the context of Henry VII's policies at the time, it quickly becomes apparent that more is at stake here than a difference in administrative procedure. Thorne accepts that Constable's reading provides a more accurate representation of contemporary practice, for the king's escheators were in fact seizing all the lands of tenants who held of the king as of an escheat.[7] Thus, he presents Constable's reading as "an attempt to rationalize current practice as a whole without dismissing, as Frowyk did, some instances of the application of the prerogative as merely incorrect or unjustified."[8] It seems unlikely that Constable was performing an academic exercise in attempting to provide a justification for current practices, but rather was attempting to rationalize the king's rights to seize as much land as possible into his hands in an attempt to track down his tenants-in-chief and establish what they held of him and how it was held. Once the king had seized land, the rightful owners had to come to chancery to display their title and claim the land back from the king, with the accrued issues. They lost no money, at least in the short term, but they were forced to make their title known and have it become a matter of record in chancery. By seizing all the land of which his tenants by escheat died seised, the king was greatly increasing the amount of land that could be investigated following any particular death. Constable was here drawing on the principle that Grantham laid out, that the king had the right to know every time land held of him changed hands. However, both of the earlier readers had a much more limited view of the king's right to primer seisin: the earliest reader gave the king only the lands held of him; and, while Grantham gave him the right to seize lands his tenant held of other lords, there is no indication that he expected the king to exercise this right so broadly. The development of the administrative structure under Henry VII meant that the principle accepted by the earlier readers had very different implications in Constable's hands.

Constable sets about dealing with the question in a very clear, logical manner. He first establishes the king's general rights to primer seisin, and then discusses when the king will have primer seisin of

[6] Thorne, ed., Constable, xxii. [7] *Ibid.* [8] *Ibid.*, xxiii.

land held as of an escheat, pointing out that the king will seize all the lands of which his tenant died seised, even lands which do not bring primer seisin by themselves, such as burgage lands. Having covered what the king can seize, he turns to what issues the king can keep. He discusses this in terms of suing livery, since the tenure by which the lands are held determines both the king's rights to issues and the form of the heir's livery. This leads him naturally into a discussion of the procedure to be followed in suing livery, and he covers this in some detail.

Frowyk's treatment differs considerably from Constable's. As we have seen, Frowyk assumes that the king has no prerogative in lands held of him as of escheat, and this means that he does not have to discuss the king's rights in this case. Instead, Frowyk focuses on the other major issue connected with primer seisin. Wardship provided a natural parallel to primer seisin, for the former applied to lands where the heir was under age, while the latter applied to lands where the heir was of full age. There was a temptation to assume that the king's rights would be the same in the two cases, but Frowyk argues that this was not in fact the case. He thus directs his reading to this question and highlights the differences between the king's rights to primer seisin and his rights to wardship.

Constable deals with many of the same issues as Frowyk, but he does not highlight the comparison with wardship. It is thus possible to compare the readers' expositions, but only in a limited way. In essence, the readers are giving lectures on different things. Frowyk concentrates his energies on showing that the king's rights to primer seisin arc quite different from his rights to wardship. Constable accepts this and shows little interest in any further consideration of the question, but focuses instead on proving that the king had rights to land held as of an escheat. The simple fact that their lectures differed so much provides a further indication of the confusion surrounding primer seisin and the lack of any established learning in the field.[9] Though the theoretical questions they address differ considerably, both readers devote a considerable amount of time to discussing the procedure involved in primer seisin and livery, the most practically useful element of the reading for their audience,

[9] In the readings of the sixteenth century, these two issues are accepted as the topics to be discussed under primer seisin, and the views of both Constable and Frowyk undergo some modification.

and one intimately connected with the development of both the administrative structures and the substantive law.

The readers open their discussions with the principle that the king will have primer seisin of all the lands held by his tenant, when the tenant held any land of him in chief and died leaving an heir of full age. The king's rights to primer seisin were more extensive than his rights to wardship, for he had primer seisin when land was held of him in socage in chief as well as in knight service.[10] Constable is concerned to establish the breadth of the king's rights to primer seisin, arguing that he can seize the lands of tenants who held of him in chief whether they held in fee simple or fee tail and whether there are many heirs or one.[11] The king will thus have primer seisin of all, whether the deceased tenant was a sole tenant, joint tenant, or tenant by right of his wife, as long as he held land in chief of the king and other land by estate of inheritance.

Constable goes on to give the example of two joint tenants who held land in chief. If the land was held by the joint tenants and to the heirs of the deceased, then the king would seize all the joint tenancy and the rest of the land held by the deceased, for in this case the deceased joint tenant held the fee simple.[12] Frowyk admits that this is the current practice and that when a joint tenant dies the other tenant, often the spouse, must sue livery, which he considers to be unreasonable.[13] Thus, while Frowyk presents the same picture of reality as Constable, he differs from him in his view of what should be done. Frowyk's view is more consistent with the readers' discussion of chapter two of the text. In their discussion of wardship, the readers agreed that the second joint tenant should retain the land as survivor, thus effectively becoming a tenant for term of life. The king's right to the wardship of an under-age heir was not activated

[10] Constable, 47–48; Frowyk, f.4. In his attempt to preserve his argument that *Prerogativa Regis* does not give the king anything new, Frowyk has to stretch this point. Marlborough does not say anything about socage tenure in chief in this context and so Frowyk comments that "this statute mistakes one thing" in talking only about knight service. Thus he argues that primer seisin always applied to land held in socage in chief, but Marlborough omitted to mention it, rather than trying to suggest that *Prerogativa Regis* altered the situation.

[11] Constable, 49. I have elected to follow the structure established by Constable, since his reading is the more clearly organized of the two.

[12] Constable, 49.

[13] Frowyk, f.5v. It was accepted that the survivor would have the profits of the land in the meantime, which mitigated the burden somewhat, but the tenant was still put to the inconvenience and expense of suing livery.

until the death of the survivor, but, according to the description given by the readers, when the heir was of full age the king had an immediate right to primer seisin.

In general, the readers agree that the king's right to primer seisin is broader than his right to wardship, though they emphasize different elements of the extension. Frowyk argues that, if the king's tenant gives land to another in tail and dies, having reserved certain rent from the land, the king will have primer seisin of the rent.[14] If the tenant in tail dies without issue, even after the donor's heir (who holds the reversion) has sued livery, the king will have primer seisin of the land, because at this point the land changes hands again.[15] In this way, the king has primer seisin when his tenant is the donor of a gift in tail, but he also receives the benefits of primer seisin when his tenant receives land in tail. Thus, if lands are given to a tenant of the king and the heirs male of his body and he dies without male issue, the king will have primer seisin of all, and the donor will have to come and sue *ouster le main* for the land.[16] Frowyk also points out that, if the king's tenant holds lands in borough English of another lord, and dies leaving two sons of full age, the king will have primer seisin of all, though if the sons were under age he would only have the wardship of the elder son's land, since the younger son did not inherit land held of the king.[17] Constable deals with a similar issue connected to descent, pointing out that it is irrelevant for the purposes of primer seisin whether the heir inherits the land from different ancestors. With wardship, if the heir had land from his mother held of the king and land from his father not held of the king, the other lords would have wardship of the land held of them. If the heir in this situation is of full age, the king will have primer seisin of all the land.[18]

Though some of the king's rights to primer seisin were wider than those he had with wardship, some were more limited. Constable argues that, if the king's tenant died disseised of land held of the king in chief, then the king would not have primer seisin, for the heir was old enough to enter, though he gave the king the right to seize in this situation when the heir was under age.[19] Frowyk agrees that the king will not have primer seisin "for a right only without possession," thus reinforcing the point that he made concerning

[14] Frowyk, f.4. [15] Frowyk, f.4. [16] Frowyk, f.4. [17] Frowyk, f.4.
[18] Constable, 50. [19] Constable, 52–53.

wardship.[20] Thus, although the deceased tenant had the right to the land, the king could not claim primer seisin, because the tenant did not actually die in possession of it.[21]

While disseisin eliminates the king's rights to primer seisin, Frowyk argues that, if the tenant leases land for term of life, this should postpone the king's rights. Thus, if a tenant of the king leases land for term of life and dies, having reserved certain rent, the king will not have primer seisin of the reversion or of the rent until after the death of the tenant for term of life.[22] If, on the other hand, the tenant leases lands held of the king, but retains lands held of another lord, the king will have no access to the lands held of him, but he will have primer seisin of the lands held of the other lords.[23] Thus, while the king did not have the right to primer seisin when his tenant had been disseised, he could claim the right through lands which were temporarily and voluntarily out of the hands of his tenant. Frowyk warns, however, that if the king's tenant leases land to someone for term of life with the remainder over to another, and the remainderman dies, the king will not have primer seisin of the remainderman's lands, for the remainderman has as yet no rights in the land held of the king.[24]

Constable does not accept that a lease delays primer seisin and in fact emphasizes the ways in which a lease extends the king's rights to primer seisin. Thus he argues that, if there is a tenant for term of life of lands held in chief of the king,[25] who also holds lands in fee of other lords, and he dies, the king will seize all the lands, "even though they are not held of the king, viz. to have notice if the tenure was properly found and also to know who should hold the land."

20 Frowyk, f.4v.

21 The readers apply the same principle to cases where the king's tenant was not disseised, but conveyed his land to another for a particular purpose, for example by making a collusive feoffment or a feoffment to use.

22 Frowyk, f.4. Frowyk made the same argument about wardship though Constable disagreed.

23 Frowyk, f.4. This differs from Constable's argument on wardship, where a lease of lands held of the king delayed the king's right to claim the lands his tenant held of other lords. See p. 98 above.

24 Frowyk, f.4v. Frowyk's account of this issue is very short and it does not really explore the complexities involved. The distinction between the king's rights to wardship with reversion and remainder are quite clear, but here they are more blurred.

25 Constable, 51. Lands held for term of life here include dower lands and land held by curtesy.

In this case, however, "whether other lands are seized or not, those who will have them . . . will not lose the issues from them."[26]

Constable's interpretation again increases the king's ability to investigate land tenure, but he further argues that whenever land held of the king changes hands the new tenant will sue livery, according to the common law, for "the king's tenant will have the land from his hands at each change of tenant."[27] He is effectively arguing that the king should have primer seisin every time land held of him changes hands, whether permanently or temporarily, rather than simply when it descends from ancestor to heir. This would explain why he believes that the survivor should sue livery on the death of a joint tenant.[28] Besides increasing the income from crown lands, such a policy would allow the king to keep track of every land transaction concerning land held of him, but would probably have been beyond the administrative abilities, if not the appetite, of the system. Frowyk does not approve of any move in this direction. He recognizes that it is becoming common practice, but argues that it "is not warranted by the law, but only by their fees in chancery."[29] Though this practice would have increased processing fees, it is likely that the government was encouraging it more for its political than economic value, and Frowyk is reacting against it for the same reason. Frowyk's argument also suggests that, while it was acceptable to argue in favour of the king's rights to review his tenants' holdings while the system was fairly primitive, the development of the machinery under Henry VII had changed the balance between the king's and the tenants' rights.

Having established his right to primer seisin, the king could then seize all the land held by the deceased tenant-in-chief, as long as the tenant held it by an estate of inheritance, even land held in burgage which was otherwise exempt from primer seisin. If the tenant had land for term of years or in wardship, however, the king could not seize it, for he could not grant livery of it.[30]

The readers agree that primer seisin is occasioned by any land held in chief, but Constable argues that it is also caused by lands

[26] Constable, 52. [27] Constable, 61. [28] See p. 116 above.

[29] Frowyk, f.5v. Frowyk expands on the issue somewhat in a case of 1506, but there he is not referring specifically to the king, but to any lord. John Caryll, *Reports of Cases by John Caryll*, ed. J. H. Baker, 2 vols., Selden Society vols. 115 and 116 (London: Selden Society, 1998 and 1999), vol. 2, 519.

[30] Constable, 51.

held of the king as of an escheat. Thus, when a tenant of the king as of the duchy of Cornwall, the honours of Nottingham, Windsor, or any other escheat, except the duchy of Lancaster, dies with an heir of full age, the land will be seized by primer seisin so that the "heir will sue livery and make his services to the king and receive this land from the king's hands, and all the other lands will be seized also, that is, to find out if the tenure is well-found and to know who will have them."[31] If such lands were in the hands of a tenant for term of life, or a tenant by curtesy or in dower, the king would seize them after the death of the sitting tenant and the reversioner or remainderman must sue them out of the hands of the king by livery and he will then become "tenant of record as is reason if no statute was ever made concerning this."[32] If there are joint tenants who hold of the king as of an escheat and not in chief, when one dies the king will seize all. If they are tenants in common, the king will only seize half, except of those things which cannot be divided, such as a horse, or an advowson, and in this case he will have all.[33]

Thus Constable argues that the king will have primer seisin when his tenant died seised of land held of him in chief or as of an escheat which he held by inheritance. However, if the tenant held of the king as of land in the king's hands temporarily, such as by the forfeiture of a tenant for term of life, by seizure for alienation without licence, or by wardship of the lands of an idiot, and this was found by inquisition, then the king would not have primer seisin, though he would have wardship in that situation.[34] Constable does make one exception to this rule, for when a tenant holding of a ward in the king's hands died, all his land would be seized and livery would be sued of the land held of the ward and *ouster le main* of the other land, even though this land is only in the king's

[31] Constable, 55. The king will not have primer seisin of land held of the duchy of Lancaster when the tenant holds nothing else of the king, for it is separate from the crown. Constable, 56. Frowyk agrees and adds that the heir in this case will enter without suing livery. Frowyk, f.4v.

[32] Constable, 55.

[33] Constable, 55. It is not clear whether the king can seize the lands such a tenant by escheat held of others. At one point, the reading says that "by such a primer seisin the king will not seize any other lands except those held in such a way," but it later concludes that "the king will seize all the other lands held and not held." Thorne speculates that the first comment is an interpolation and this is likely, for Constable generally gives the king the broader right.

[34] Constable, 56.

hands temporarily.[35] Frowyk thinks that this is "conter reason," but admits that such a precedent was set in 28 Hen. VI.[36] The tide of opinion seems to have moved in Frowyk's direction in the following years, for in 1516 it was agreed that the king would not have primer seisin by reason of wardship, just as he would not have primer seisin where the tenant's land was enfeoffed to his use.[37]

In general then, the king's rights to primer seisin more closely follow the idea that he should have everything of which his tenant died seised than do his rights to wardship. The readers agree that the king can seize everything of which his tenant died seised, though they disagree on whether that should apply to tenants by escheat, and they agree that the tenant must die seised for the king to have his right. The only major restriction the readers place on primer seisin is where lands are in the king's hands temporarily, such as forfeiture for alienation without licence.

Having established when the king will have primer seisin, Constable goes on to consider when he will have all the issues and profits of the land he has seized, when he will have part, and when none. He argues that this question can best be answered in conjunction with an examination of how land in the king's hands will be retrieved by the heir, since both the king's rights and the heir's process are determined by the manner in which the land is held. Both readers agree that, when the king has land by primer seisin and the inquisition which gives the king title is true, the heir will have the land from the king by writ of livery or *ouster le main*. If the king has the land by an inquisition held *virtute officii* or by an enquiry out of the exchequer, then the heir cannot have livery on the basis of such a title, even if it is true, but must

[35] Constable, 56. Constable later explains that this is because the king holds the land as guardian and so the second heir must sue livery and swear fealty. If the first heir sues livery before the second heir, the second heir must still sue from the king, for at the time of the death of his ancestor, the lands were held of the king. In this case, he does not have to swear fealty to the king.

[36] Frowyk, f.4v, f.8. The case is YB Trin. 28 Hen. VI, f.11, pl.23. He points out that there are some occasions where a ward in the king's hands will not sue livery. If the king holds the ward because of a forfeiture or a grant, the heir does not have to sue livery. Thus, if a guardian is outlawed in a personal action, the heir will not sue livery at full age, because the king does not hold the wardship by reason of any lordship. If the king grants a lordship for term of years and a wardship falls during the term and the heir is not of full age by the expiration of the term, the ward will not sue livery of the king. Frowyk, f.8.

[37] *Caryll's Reports*, vol. 2, 669.

sue a writ of *diem clausit extremum*, *mandamus*, or whichever writ is appropriate.[38]

Livery could be with or without the issues of the land during the time it was in the king's hands, while *ouster le main* was always with issues. The heir sued the land out of the king's hands according to the tenure by which his ancestor held it; thus he could have livery of part of the land seized, with or without issues, and *ouster le main* of the rest.[39] The simplest situation is when a tenant-in-chief of the king held land in fee or in tail or for term of life and died leaving an heir of full age, who inherited all the land of which his ancestor died seised. In this case, the heir will sue livery and lose the issues of the land, and the livery will be of the land held of other lords as well as of land held of the king.[40] If there are heirs in gavelkind of full age, or heirs female of full age, of land held in chief of the king, they will sue livery of all the land, but there they must each sue livery separately, for the land will have to be divided among them and divided in such a way that each holds land of the king, even if it is only an acre.[41] In this way each co-heir becomes a tenant of the king and open to the charges of the prerogative on all of his or her land, whereas, if the land held of the king had gone to only one heir, the others would have been free of the prerogative.

The deceased tenant might have different heirs to different parts of his land, but, as long as the land was held in chief, all his heirs would have to sue livery. Thus, if a tenant held land in fee simple in chief and land in fee tail to his heirs male in chief and the daughter of his elder son is the general heir and his younger son is the special heir, then each will lose the issues of the land and sue livery. If the land in fee simple was not held of the king, then the son would still sue livery of the king for the land in tail, but the grand-daughter would only sue *ouster le main* with the issues, for she is not inheriting any land held of the king, and, if she does not hold any land of the king, then he cannot grant livery.[42] Similarly, if a tenant held land descended from his father and land descended from his mother, and parts of both were held in chief of the king, and he died without issue, both heirs would sue livery of the king. If all the land held

[38] Constable, 57. Frowyk suggests that a special commission also gives the heir the right to sue livery, but Constable disagrees. Frowyk, f.6; Constable, 57.
[39] Constable, 57. [40] Constable, 57. [41] Constable, 58. [42] Constable, 58.

in chief of the king was in one inheritance, for example the land descended from the mother, then the mother's heir would sue livery and the father's heir would sue *ouster le main.*[43] Thus Constable concludes that where land is held in chief of the king the heir will sue livery, but where land is not held of the king and the heir holds no land of the king, the heir will sue *ouster le main.*[44] Frowyk agrees with Constable on this issue, though he gives different examples.[45] Frowyk goes on to argue that, in all cases where the king's tenant died seised of lands held of another lord and a stranger inherits this land, the stranger will have *ouster le main*, and he can have this on an inquisition held *virtute officii*.[46] Thus the correct procedure ensures that the tenant pays relief only on the land held of the king and that the king will grant livery only when there is land held of him, and thus protects the heir against any financial depredations, but it is the original seizure which allows the king the right to investigate the lands.

When there are others besides the heirs who have a right to land seized by the king, they too will have livery of the land held of the king, whether it is held in chief or as of an escheat, and *ouster le main* of land held of other lords.[47] Thus, if the deceased was a joint tenant in land held of the king, and the alienation to them had been by licence of the king, or they had received a pardon for the alienation before the inquisition, the survivor would have livery with issues. If they had neither licence nor pardon, the survivor would not have livery until he had a pardon from chancery, but he would lose the issues of the land. This loss, however, is "because of alienation without licence and not because of primer seisin."[48] Frowyk agrees with Constable on the principle involved, but argues that the king does not have the right to the issues, but only to a fine for the alienation.[49] He seems to have moderated this view in later years, according to a case reported in Caryll. Caryll notes that, when the king's tenant alienates without licence and this is found by inquisition, the king will have the issues of the land only from the time of the inquisition and not from the time of the alienation, and says that this was "clearly agreed by FROWYK CJ and THE WHOLE

43 Constable, 58.
44 Constable, 58. The only exception Constable makes is when the king claims primer seisin of land held of a ward in his hands.
45 Frowyk, f.7. 46 Frowyk, f.7. 47 Constable, 58.
48 Constable, 59; Frowyk, f.5v. 49 Frowyk, f.5v.

COURT."[50] Thus Frowyk apparently came to accept that the king did have some rights to the issues of these lands, but retained the principle that this was only because of the alienation without licence and not because of primer seisin.

The readers agree that, if a lease for term of life of land held in chief is made by licence, the remainder over in fee, tail, or for term of life, the remainderman will have livery with issues, for the king has effectively licensed him to enter already by licensing the lease. If the alienation was made without a licence but with a later pardon, there will be livery without issues of the land held of the king. Thus the remainderman sues livery of the land held of the king and *ouster le main* of the land held of other lords. If the tenant held land of the king which descended to the heir and land of others which descended to another as a remainder, then the heir sues livery of the land held of the king and the remainderman has *ouster le main* of the land held of the other lords.[51] If the remainderman also inherits land held of the king, he will sue livery for that land. Thus, even though the king seizes all the land of which his tenant died seised, he will only have the issues of the lands held of him, and he will not always have those.

It is apparent that, though the readers agree that the king's rights to primer seisin are wider than his rights to wardship, his rights to the issues and profits of the lands thus seized more closely approximate those of wardship. Though he can seize all the land of which his tenant died seised, regardless of whether it comes from a different ancestor or descends to a different heir, he cannot keep the profits of the lands in those cases. The burden of recovery, however, lies on the tenant or lord of the land seized. The prerogative right to primer seisin ensured that a large amount of land would pass through the king's hands and would be allowed to leave only when the king's officials had securely established the plaintiff's title to it.

Thus far, the readers have dealt only with the issues of land held in chief of the king. Constable goes on to cover the issues of land

50 *Caryll's Reports*, vol. 2, 424.

51 Constable, 60; Frowyk, f.7v. Frowyk adds the point that, if the king's tenant leases land for term of life, remainder in fee and the remainderman dies, his heir of full age, the heir must have an inquisition by writ which finds his title. When the tenant for term of life dies, the heir must then have an inquisition *virtute officii* proving the death.

held as of escheat and he admits that, while the king can seize all the lands of which his tenant as of an escheat died seised, the other lords of whom the tenant held can sue to have their lands out of the king's hands. Constable explains that this is because according to *Prerogativa Regis* the king will only have the issues of the land where the heir will have livery of all from the king, and against all other claimants the king is bound by the common law. He justifies this according to the construct he gave at the beginning of the discussion of this chapter, in which common law gives the king the right to seize all his tenants' lands, but no right to their issues. *Prerogativa Regis* gave him the issues of lands held of him, but had no impact on the lands held of other lords. If the land held of the king is not held in chief, the heir is bound by common law regarding the issues of all the other lands he holds. Thus, although the king will seize everything, he will have no rights to the issues.[52]

The king's rights were also restricted by the common law in other ways. If the king's tenant died disseised and this is found, the king cannot seize the land, but, if the heir is of full age and it is found in the inquisition that he has re-entered upon the land, the king can seize the recovered land held of him. Constable points out that this is not based on the statute, but on common law, for the heir is the king's tenant in right and must sue livery and perform his services.[53] If the heir recovers the land his ancestor held of others, however, the king has no right to seize it, for his tenant did not die seised. If the tenant did die seised of land held of others, but not of the land held of the king, the king still has no right to seize those lands following the re-entry of the heir, for his tenant did not die seised of land held of him.[54] The same rule applies where the heir entered because of a broken condition or by recovery by formedon or mort d'ancestor.[55] Thus Constable is willing to concede that the king's rights are somewhat limited in land held as of escheat, where the tenant did not die seised.

This limitation is hardly restrictive, however, given the breadth of the king's rights, especially as defined by Constable. Constable gives the king the right to primer seisin of all the lands of which his tenant-in-chief died seised, even when they descend to someone

52 Constable, 61–62. 53 Constable, 62.
54 Constable, 62. 55 Constable, 62.

other than the heir, and the right to primer seisin again when they finally pass to the heir. He also gives the king the right to primer seisin of lands held of him as of escheat, though he concedes that the king can only take advantage of this right when the deceased tenant's title was secure. Though Constable is willing to admit that the king has no right to the income from much of the land seized in this way, the simple right to seizure was onerous and intrusive. Frowyk recognizes this and emphasizes the fact that these newly extended rights are not reasonable, but simply increase profits. He freely admits that the king has the right to seize lands held of him in chief, but makes no attempt to extend his rights beyond this. Frowyk and Constable were, of course, not lecturing in opposition to each other, and we cannot expect to find each responding directly to the argument of the other. Constable is more forward in advocating the extension of the king's rights than Frowyk is in denying it. This may be partly because it was more likely to be profitable to speak loudly in favour of the king's coffers than against them, but it is also striking that Constable was following the arguments of the earlier readers more closely, though the context in which he was using those arguments had changed. Frowyk was reacting against the letter of Grantham's reading, though he was probably arguing in the spirit of the earlier reader. This was a more difficult balance to achieve, however.

Though the readers obviously have significant differences of opinion concerning the extent of the king's right to primer seisin, the discussion of this issue takes up only a small part of their lectures on chapter three of the text. Unlike their predecessors, they devote the majority of their time to a consideration of the process to be followed in suing livery or in disputing the king's right to seize the land. This leads them into a lengthy discussion of the process involved in holding inquisitions, and the implications of the various methods by which inquisitions were held.

Although it may not seem worthwhile to pursue the details of process, it is in fact central to the working of the system, and to the development of the readers' ideas. It is also striking that many points of process remained unclear, and they were discussed in the year books with some regularity. They were not just of administrative importance, however, for a quick glance at any of the year book cases dealing with these issues demonstrates how intimately process and substance were connected. Both the readings and the year books make clear the law's desire to find and uphold clear titles, though even the briefest glance at the cases passing through the courts makes it clear that this was often no more than a pious hope. The profession obviously relied upon a strict adherence to the correct procedure to protect titles, and for this reason a thorough understanding of the subject was necessary for practitioners. This part of the readers' lectures covers material of relevance to both wardship and primer seisin, for the ward who comes of age must follow a similar process to the heir of full age, though he has the added step of proving age.

The king's right to primer seisin was based on the information given in the inquisition, as with wardship, though here it relied on the heir being found of full age. The king could seize the land following an inquisition, no matter how the inquisition was called.[56] However, Constable argues that the escheator was able to seize the land of a tenant-in-chief before an inquisition was held. He presents two arguments to support this position: the escheator was allowed to seize the body before the inquisition; and, since there was need for a rule that the king could not grant land away before inquisition, it was implied that the king was seizing the land before the inquisition.[57] Frowyk takes the opposite view. He argues that the king cannot seize the land, for the king can only seize land by matter of record. If the king seizes before an inquisition is held, any party wronged would be without remedy, for the king's title must appear as a matter of record to which the party can respond.[58] Frowyk agrees with Constable that the statute of 18 Hen. VI ordained that the king could not grant a ward before the inquisition, but he interprets this to mean that the king cannot seize the heir before the inquisition, even though at common law the king could seize the body of the heir as he would seize any other chattel. Frowyk does accept that there are some cases in which the king can seize without inquisition, as where one seised of a wardship is outlawed in a personal action. In

[56] Frowyk, f.6; Constable, 57. [57] Constable, 46.

[58] Frowyk, f.4v. He reiterates in f.5 that "in no case will the king have primer seisin of tenants who hold of him in chief without an inquisition, for he has this as king." Luckett records instances of the crown arranging wardships before the inquisition was held but attributes this to the crown's confidence in its information rather than its legal right to dispose of the body of the heir. D. A. Luckett, "Henry VII and the South-Western Escheators," in *The Reign of Henry VII: Proceedings of the 1993 Harlaxton Symposium*, ed. Benjamin Thompson, Harlaxton Medieval Studies V (Stamford: Paul Watkins, 1995), 59–60.

such a case, the king can seize the ward without an inquisition, but not the lordship.[59] Similarly, if it is a matter of record elsewhere, for example in the records of parliament, that the tenant held the land of the king, the king can seize without an inquisition.[60] In no case, however, he argues, can the king have primer seisin of land held of him in chief without an inquisition.[61]

If there are ambiguities in the title found by the inquisition, the king will get the benefit of the doubt, as part of his procedural prerogative. We have already seen that, if the inquisition finds that the tenant held of the king but does not expressly say that the tenure was in chief, the king will seize the land. Similarly, if the inquisition does not find of whom and how the land was held, or by what services, the king will seize.[62] If an inquisition in one county found that a tenant died with his heir of full age, and an inquisition in another county found that the same tenant died seised of land held of the king, but did not specify an heir, the king could seize the land in the second inquisition, based on the information in the first.[63] It was possible that the inquisition would return a finding which was at odds with other records. In this case, the record would take precedence over the inquisition. Thus, if the inquisition found that land was held of a certain lord, but it was recorded in chancery that the land was held of the king, the king got primer seisin.[64] If the inquisition found that the king's tenant was attainted of treason or felony and there was no such attainder, the inquisition was void.[65] It was also possible that the inquisition would not prove enough of a title for the king to seize the lands.[66]

[59] Again, this is because the wardship is a chattel, while the lordship is not. Frowyk, f.5.

[60] Frowyk, f.5. Frowyk gives various other examples which are mainly variations on this theme. He also argues that, where the king seizes land before an inquisition the heir does not have to sue livery at all, but can just enter on the land.

[61] Frowyk, f.5.

[62] Frowyk, f.5. If no tenure is found, the king will seize, but Frowyk argues that this is "a bare and single title for the king." This kind of seizure was fairly common: see, for example, C/43/1/48 (21 Hen. VII), where the king seized the land of which John Bromyche died seised. The inquisition found that he died in January 1485 and that his land was worth £8, but they did not know of whom or how it was held. His son John came to chancery arguing that the land was held of George, duke of Clarence, in socage.

[63] Frowyk, f.5. [64] Frowyk, f.5. [65] Frowyk, f.5.

[66] In this case, the king had to sue *scire facias*. This is dealt with at pp. 135–37 below.

If the inquisition was mistaken, plaintiffs were given a month after the inquisition in which to traverse it.[67] The king was unable to grant land away before the inquisition, or during that month. If a decision was found for the plaintiff, he would have the land out of the king's hands. There were many different reasons for traversing an inquisition, and the handling of the traverse varied depending on which part of the inquisition the plaintiff was challenging. If the inquisition was true in everything except in naming the heir, then the claimants to the land would interplead.[68] If it was found by the inquisition that the heir was under age when he was in fact of full age, he could not traverse the office, for the office did not deny his title to the land.[69]

If it was found that A was seised of land which was actually held by B, and B did not hold the land of the king, B would go to chancery and traverse the inquisition. In his traverse, he would recite the inquisition and demonstrate that such a person had enfeoffed him of the land, that it was not held of the king, and that A did not die seised of any part of it.[70] If B was successful, he would have a writ of *ouster le main* with issues. The law was the same if the inquisition found that the tenant died seised of land held of the king when in fact he held it of another lord, and his heir traversed the inquisition.[71] All of these actions lie on an inquisition taken either *virtute officii* or *virtute brevis*. If, however, the person traversing

[67] By the statute of 18 Hen. VI, c. 6, *Statutes of the Realm* 11 vols. (London, 1810–1822), vol. 2, 306–07. In 1509, this was extended to three months because, according to Caryll, escheators were waiting until the law courts were on vacation to return their inquisitions so that plaintiffs could not bring their traverse within the specified month. *Caryll's Reports*, vol. 2, 677.

[68] Constable, 70. In interpleader, the claimants would accept the finding of the inquisition concerning the tenure of the land and plead between them to find which of them was the correct heir. This applied when different inquisitions found an elder and a younger brother to be heir. (Frowyk, f.8). The claimants had to wait until they were of full age to interplead. YB Pas. 1 Hen. VII, f.14, pl.1; *Caryll's Reports*, vol. 2, 671. It was thought that the successful claimant would need a commission to find him heir in the counties where his opponent had previously been found heir, for "he will not have livery without an inquisition found for him" (YB Pas. 1 Hen. VII, f.14, pl.1). Interpleader was only to try nearness of blood, so if two inquisitions returned different verdicts on tenure, with one finding that land was held in general tail, so that a daughter was heir, while another returned that the land was held in tail male, so that a nephew was heir, the claimants would not interplead. *Caryll's Reports*, vol. 2, 565–66.

[69] Constable, 73. The heir had no remedy in this situation and he would have to wait until he was of full age according to the inquisition.

[70] Constable, 70. [71] Constable, 71.

wished to sue as heir and the land was held of the king, he must still have an inquisition found for him *virtute brevis* before he could sue livery.[72]

If the inquisition found that the land was held by a greater tenure than was the case, or by a higher rent, or in fee simple when it was actually fee tail, the tenant would traverse and have a writ of *melius inquirendum* to establish the truth. If, for example, it was found that the heir held by knight service, then he could traverse that in fact he held only by homage and fealty and not by knight service. If the court found for him, then he would have his lands and the issues and he would not have to start again from the beginning with a new writ of *diem clausit extremum.*[73] If the case was not found for the plaintiff, then there was nothing more he could do, and he had to sue livery on the original inquisition.[74]

According to Frowyk, when the king and the plaintiff were at issue on the traverse, the record was sent into king's bench and the issue was tried there.[75] Constable agrees with this, and notes that the judgment will be given in king's bench rather than sending the case back to chancery for judgment.[76] The judges in king's bench were unable to grant livery, however, and so they would have to send the record back to chancery with the judgment so that the heir could have his livery there.[77] Frowyk notes that a traverse on an inquisition found *virtute officii* did not need to be sent to king's bench, but could be tried in the exchequer by the barons.[78]

There were limits to the range of the traverse, for it could only be used where the inquisition was mistaken on facts. If the facts were right, but the king's title was unjustified, the tenant had to go either to a *monstrans de droit* or a petition. In 1488, Kebell argued in exchequer chamber that in effect "every traverse is a *monstrans de droit* and more than that, for he shows his title and traverses the king's title, and in a *monstrans* he confesses the office and shows his right over."[79] Some discussion seems to have ensued, in which it was argued that a *monstrans de droit* lay when the king was entitled

[72] Constable, 70.

[73] Constable, 71. The same applies if the court finds that the land is held in serjeanty or barony, or in any other tenure which implies homage and fealty or just homage.

[74] Constable, 73. [75] Frowyk, f.9. [76] Constable, 84.

[77] *Caryll's Reports*, vol. 2, 567. [78] Frowyk, f.9.

[79] M. Hemmant, ed., *Select Cases in the Exchequer Chamber before All the Justices of England*, vol. 2, 1461–1509, Selden Society vol. 64 (London: Bernard Quaritch, 1948), 133.

by matter in fact and the party had a right to the land, while petition lay when the king was entitled by matter of record, but the discussion was not conclusive.[80] In the following year, the judges were back in the exchequer chamber to discuss the case of James Ormond. He was attainted during the reign of Richard III and lost his lands, but his heir claimed that the attainder was reversed by act of parliament and James was restored to his lands. All the serjeants believed that the heir should have petition and not *monstrans de droit*, because the king was entitled by matter of record. The judges agreed in principle, but argued that, because in this case the heir's claim was by an act of parliament, a record as high as the king's, the plaintiff would not have petition, but neither would he have traverse.[81]

Frowyk does not have a great deal to say about the *monstrans de droit*. He notes that, if a plaintiff wishes to use the *monstrans de droit*, he must have been expelled from the land as a result of the inquisition. Thus, if the plaintiff had a title to the land but was not on the land at the time of the inquisition, his only remedy was by petition.[82] If the king's tenant was disseised of land held of the king, and the inquisition finds that the disseisor died seised, the disseisee has no remedy until the heir sues livery, for a writ of right does not lie against the guardian. If, however, the heir had entered before the inquisition, then the disseisee could have *monstrans de droit* against the guardian.[83] Constable does not deal with the *monstrans de droit* at all, but focuses on petitions.

Both readers break petitions into petitions of right and petitions of grace. The former are applicable for land in the king's hands, while the latter are used for chattels.[84] Both are used in situations where the king has land by matter of record and the tenant is out of possession. Thus, if it happened that B was disseised of land held of the king and the disseisor died without an heir, B could not traverse, because the inquisition was true in its finding that the disseisor was a tenant of the king and that he died without an heir. In this case, B must resort to a petition.[85] The petition is brought to chancery, where the plaintiff presents his title and asks that right be done, and the king endorses the bill. It then goes to a commission in the

80 *Ibid.* 81 YB Pas. 4 Hen. VII, f.7, pl.6.
82 Frowyk, f.9v. 83 Frowyk, f.9v.
84 For petitions of grace, see Frowyk, f.9v; Constable, 82–84.
85 Constable, 74.

county to investigate. If the party is successful, he will have his lands, but not the issues in the meantime.[86]

Thus the readers made some attempt to address the question of process, but the rules were obviously still unclear. The state of knowledge of the profession was tested by a case in the first year of Henry VIII. An inquisition found that William Oldale was attainted of treason in 31 Hen. VI and that by force of the attainder Henry VI seized his manor of Dytton Valence and granted it to Jasper, earl of Pembroke, his uterine half-brother. The inquisition further found that all the grants made to Jasper were confirmed by his nephew, Henry VII, in his first parliament. A further act in the parliament of 11 Hen. VII ordained that when Jasper died all his lands should go to Prince Henry, who was then duke of York, and, if Prince Arthur died, so that Henry became prince of Wales, that the land should then go to Henry VII. Arthur died, so when Jasper died the land descended to Henry VII, but the inquisition found that Sir William Capell intruded on his possession.[87] Humphrey Conyngesby and William Mallom came to chancery and "commenced pleading according to the manner of a traverse."[88] They argued that it was true that Oldale was attainted in 31 Hen. VI, and that the land was granted to Jasper, but they added that the attainder was reversed in 33 Hen. VI and Oldale was restored to his lands by another act of parliament "by virtue whereof he entered and was seised of the said manor as in his old right."[89] Oldale then died and the land descended to one Gorge and he entered and was seised, until Jasper put him out by virtue of the act of 1 Hen. VII. By another act of 4 Hen. VII, that act was reversed, and Gorge entered the land again. The plaintiffs accept that the act of 11 Hen. VII gave the remainder of all the land held by Jasper to Henry VII, but argue that there was a proviso which excepted this parcel of land from the act. They protested that "everything which would serve the said King Henry VII, namely the attainder of William Oldale, the grant made to the earl of Pembroke by the said King Henry VI, and also the confirmation of the same grant in the first year of Henry VII, and also the conveyance of the said manor from [*sic*] the said late King Henry VII by the said act of the eleventh year, were found by

[86] Constable, 80. [87] *Caryll's Reports*, vol. 2, 595–96.
[88] *Ibid.*, 596. The record of the case in the chancery is C43/2/35, 37.
[89] *Caryll's Reports*, vol. 2, 596.

the office. On the other hand, everything which would have helped the said Conyngesby and Mallom were omitted."[90] They concluded that Gorge had conveyed the land to Conyngesby and Mallom and others and they were the only survivors and they prayed that they would be restored with issues.

The case provided the judges with much food for thought. Boteler concluded that the inquisition relies on the act of 11 Hen. VII, but, since it does not mention the proviso in that act, the inquisition is flawed and is not enough to entitle the king. He also believed that the plaintiffs should have *monstrans de droit*, because "where someone is put out of possession by reason of an act of parliament for attainder of treason, and by reason of an office found accordingly, and then this attainder is repealed by another act and also the party is restored, in this case he shall be helped by way of *monstrans de droit*, because the act of restitution is of as high a nature as the act of attainder."[91] Fisher and Grevill agreed with Boteler and rehearsed various other cases in which the plaintiff would have *monstrans de droit*, concluding that it lay in those cases where the plaintiff was in the land by an ancient right and actually in possession before the inquisition which entitled the king.[92]

Not all of the justices agreed, however. Brudenell argued that the plaintiffs should be put to their petition, because they were not mentioned in the inquisition and so could not sue *monstrans de droit*. The other justices were quick to deny this and pointed out that Conyngesby and Mallom were the freeholders of the manor and were harmed by the inquisition, and this was enough to admit them to the *monstrans de droit*.[93] Brudenell was unwilling to let the point go, and he reiterated his belief that the plaintiffs could only have a petition because the inquisition did not find anything which would support their claim.[94] Rede entered into the discussion to support Brudenell. He made what is probably the clearest statement about the difference between the various actions in the whole discussion. It begins by asserting what was commonly accepted: the king cannot have possession of any land except by matter of record. Therefore, "if a common person in this case has title to this land, or to have a

[90] *Ibid.*, 596–97. [91] *Ibid.*, 598. [92] *Ibid.*, 598–99. [93] *Ibid.*, 599.

[94] *Ibid.* Brudenell entered a long digression which culminated in a review of the case of the earl of Kent and the attainder of his younger brother. He covered it in hypothetical terms, but the other justices recognized the case and joined the discussion.

rent out of this land, and has no matter of record proving his title, he shall never have a *monstrans de droit*... but is put to his petition of right... If, however, his title is of record, as well as the king's title, then he shall have his *monstrans de droit*."[95] He concludes, however, with Brudenell, that in this case the plaintiff must sue a petition and he gives the same reason.[96] Fyneux also agrees, pointing out that the proviso in the statute of 11 Hen. VII is the central point of their plea, and "because this clause is in general terms, and is in no way helped or amended by the office, the *monstrans de droit*... will not lie. Therefore they have no other remedy but only by way of petition of right."[97] Fyneux also points out the biggest difference between a petition and a *monstrans de droit* or traverse. He notes that if the king grants a petition the party does not need any kind of judgment, because he did not choose to pursue the course of the common law, but turned to the king's authority. For the same reason, if the king denies his request, he has no remedy.[98] Fyneux, along with the other justices, wanders widely over the course of his discussion, and concludes with the admission that "these cases are not very relevant to the matter in hand, but I have shown them for the sake of learning. As to the principal case, I am clear in my opinion that the parties are put to their petition of right."[99] Thus the justices reached agreement on the case at hand, and on the use of the *monstrans de droit* and petition. *Monstrans de droit* lay where the plaintiff had title by as high a record as the king, while petition was for those whose title was "a bare surmise or upon bare matter in fact, which is a long and tedious suit."[100] Unfavourable as this was for their case, Conyngesby and Mallom were fortunate in bringing their complaint in 1509. Rather than being put to the uncertainty of petition, Caryll notes that the chancellor, who had been present during all the discussion, "later gave judgment in the Chancery – without the advice of any justice, and without making any of the king's counsel privy – that the king's hands should be removed [from the land]. This was against the law, as was said. However, it was said that he did it because the office had been found through the falseness and trickery of Sir Richard Empson and [Edmond]

95 *Ibid.*, 601. 96 *Ibid.*, 603. 97 *Ibid.* 98 *Ibid.*, 604.

99 *Ibid.* Caryll reports on the use of the *monstrans de droit* again in *ibid.*, 673, but the comments there are simply a recapitulation of Rede's arguments in this case.

100 *Ibid.*, 674. This also is a recapitulation of the earlier case.

Dudley in the time of the previous king, who were his haughty and cruel approvers."[101]

In addition to all the actions that could be brought to challenge the king's title to the land, there was a further action called *scire facias*. This was a writ based on a record, sent to the sheriff. It required him to warn the party to whom it was directed to show cause why the person bringing it should not have the benefit of the record. It could be used in a variety of circumstances, such as when an inquisition gave the king a reason to seize land which was held by someone other than the deceased tenant. Frowyk argues that, in every case where a common person would have to sue an action to regain his land, the king could not seize simply on the basis of an inquisition, but must have a *scire facias*.[102] Thus he points out that the statute of Lincoln provided that, when the heir had already sued land out of the hands of the king and a new title was found for the king, the king could not simply re-seize the land, but had to sue a *scire facias*.[103] Similarly, one who tendered a traverse must traverse all the inquisitions found before his tender, but not one found during it, for that would cause infinite delay. If the traverser was successful, then *scire facias* would issue for the king on the inquisition found during the traverse.[104] *Scire facias* was not only available to the king, however, for in cases of petition or traverse, if the king had granted out the lands before the petition or traverse, the plaintiff had to sue *scire facias* against the grantee or patentee.[105]

It was not always clear when the king was obliged to sue this writ, however, for his rights and obligations varied from case to case and the profession did not always agree on which circumstances obliged the king in which way. The question of the rules governing *scire facias* arose in *Stonor's Case*, and most of the viewpoints surrounding the question were presented in the course of the discussion. Stonor had died seised of an advowson held of the king in chief and the use of lands held of the king and of the prior of St. Swithin's in socage.[106] It was questioned whether, if the king had the right to the wardship of Stonor's heir, he could simply seize the land enfeoffed to use and the body, or whether he had to

[101] *Ibid.*, 605. [102] Frowyk, f.5v. [103] Frowyk, f.4v.
[104] Frowyk, f.9. [105] Frowyk, f.9.
[106] See chapter 2, pp. 105–11, for a fuller description of the case.

sue *scire facias* against the feoffee. Frowyk raised this issue at an early point, making the same argument as in his reading, that the king could not simply enter in a situation where a common person would have to sue.[107] Though, as we have seen, Frowyk did not believe that the king was entitled to the wardship in this case, he argued that, even if he did have the benefit of the statute of 1490, the only remedy ordained by the statute was a writ of ward; thus, if the king wanted to have the benefit of the statute, he should follow its rule and sue either writ of ward or *scire facias*.[108] In the longer discussion of the case, Vavasour, Danvers, and Sedgwick agreed with Frowyk, the latter adding that "it will be against reason to oust without process the feoffees who have freehold and inheritance in the land."[109] Boteler also took this side, citing the provisions of the text and the right of the feoffees to challenge the king's seizure.[110]

There was substantial opposition to this position, however, and a number of the justices felt that the king could seize in this instance without a *scire facias*, most of them arguing that the king was not defeating the tenant's right forever. Kingsmill and Wode believed that the king should seize the land, because, as Kingsmill put it, "by this seizure no freehold is vested out of the feoffee's hand, for the king only obtains a chattel."[111] Mordant, the king's serjeant, agreed with Kingsmill, pointing out that "the feoffees shall be put to their petition or to traverse the office; for it is not like the case of waste or *cessavit*, for there the king is defeating the interest of the tenant forever."[112] Kebell joined in on their side, and he pointed out that the feoffee was in fact in a better position against the king than he would be against another lord, for he could not traverse a seizure by a lord. Kebell also challenged the idea that the king must sue *scire facias* in those instances where a common person would be put to his action, and cited examples where the rule did not hold.[113] Rede joined in to argue for seizure also, presenting much the same

[107] YB Trin. 12 Hen. VII, f.21, pl.1. [108] *Ibid.*

[109] Hemmant, *Select Cases in Exchequer Chamber*, vol. 2, 163.

[110] *Ibid.* [111] *Ibid.*, 164.

[112] *Ibid.*, 166. The two most common examples given in the course of this discussion were when a tenant of the king made a lease of land and an inquisition found that the tenant had committed waste, and when the tenant had ceased to pay his rent (*cessavit*). In both cases, the king had to sue *scire facias* against the tenant before he could re-seize the land.

[113] *Ibid.*, 169.

argument: the king sought only the wardship of the land, which was merely a chattel, and the feoffee suffers no loss, for, if he can prove that a will was made, he can have the land back.[114]

Bryan then joined the discussion and changed its direction somewhat. He argued that in this case the feoffee could not traverse the inquisition, for everything the inquisition said was true. If the inquisition had specifically said that the tenant did not make a will, when in fact he did, then it would be possible to traverse, but the inquisition did not mention a will at all.[115] Bryan also believed that the inquisition was void because of the amount of information missing from it, however, and so he argued that the king could not sue *scire facias* on a void inquisition. Fyneux was quick to disagree with Bryan on both issues. He did not accept that the inquisition was void, and argued that, while the tenants could not traverse the inquisition in *scire facias*, they could still traverse it in chancery. He also believed that the king could seize the land and agreed with Kebell that there were many situations in which the king could seize when another lord would be put to his action.[116]

The dispute visible in *Stonor's Case* appears several times in the year books, in different guises. The legal profession was divided over who should be given greater consideration when a title was in dispute, whether the dispute was between two tenants, or between a tenant and the king. Disputes between two tenants appear in the year books early in Henry VII's reign. Thus in 1 Hen. VII a plaintiff came to traverse an inquisition and, after he had tendered his traverse but before any judgment, the king granted livery to the heir. It was asked whether such livery was good or not, and the answer was that it was good, because "the one who has right can sue against the heir: and if the land is re-seized [pending the traverse], the king will have the rent, and the issues etc. and if the traverse was found against him who tendered the traverse, this is a wrong against the heir."[117] The same point arose in another case in the same year, and though Catesby and Suliard objected that the traverser had the

114 *Ibid.*, 172. 115 *Ibid.*, 173.

116 *Ibid.*, 175. In *Conyngesby and Mallom* v. *Regem*, however, Fyneux stated that, whenever a common person was put to his action, the king must sue *scire facias*. *Caryll's Reports*, vol. 2, 604.

117 Because the heir had lost the issues to the king. YB Hil. 1 Hen. VII, f.12, pl.24.

right to have his case heard, the other justices all agreed that, if the heir sought livery, the king had no right to deny it. Again, they pointed out that the plaintiff could still sue the heir for his right.[118] The same principle can be seen in Hussey's argument concerning interpleading.[119] He believed that, though the claimants cannot interplead until both are of full age, the first claimant to reach his majority may sue livery of his land rather than having to wait for the younger.[120] Thus the general feeling was that the heir found by the regular course of the law should be allowed to sue livery of his land, whatever the claim against him. Any plaintiff coming to dispute the heir's claim was immediately at a disadvantage, but it was believed that, if he had a genuine title to the land, he could prove his suit through the courts.

On occasion, the plaintiff might be the king. Thus in the chancery in 4 Hen. VII it was found that land had been alienated without licence of the king, and the feoffee came and wanted to pay his fine and have livery of the land. The king's attorney asserted that the land was enfeoffed to the use of the king, and asked that it should remain in his hands. It was felt that the king could not have remedy in this way, and the chancellor directed that the feoffee should have his livery, because the claim made for the king was only "a bare surmise," which would not delay the tenant in his right.[121] It was generally accepted that, if there was matter of record in the court which entitled the king, then the decision would be otherwise, and the serjeants took the opportunity to note that if the king had twenty titles the plaintiff would have to traverse every one of them, but since that was not the case, he had his livery.

That this whole question was of concern to the legal community at the time is clear from the chancellor's comment that "this matter is a matter which touches the Community of the Realm in time to come," as he made a stand for the tenant's title against the king's challenge.[122] Any development which threatened an heir's right to livery of his lands would shake the entire landholding system. The suggestion that the king should continue to hold lands which were

[118] YB Trin. 1 Hen. VII, ff.27–28, pl.5. It was agreed that, if the heir delayed in suing livery, the king had the right to the issues in the meantime, for such delay was the fault of the heir, but, as soon as the heir who had proved age came to seek his land, the king had to give livery.

[119] See n. 68, p. 129 above. [120] YB Pas. 8 Hen. VII, f.11, pl.2.

[121] YB Hil. 4 Hen. VII, f.5, pl.10. [122] *Ibid.*

in any kind of dispute until that dispute was resolved clearly did not appeal to the majority of the legal profession. Its appeal for the king was obvious: he would retain the income from the land until the dispute was settled, and he could require a thorough examination of the claims of both parties and their alleged titles to the land. Once the land was out of his hands, not only did he lose the immediate financial benefit, but it was always possible that the claimants would settle their dispute through arbitration and would thus keep their landholding arrangements obscure. The lawyers, however, clearly felt that the king could not refuse livery of his land to the heir named by the due process of law, regardless of any other claims on the land. Though their attitude put any particular claimant at a disadvantage, in general terms it upheld the tenant's right to his land against the king's interest in retaining it.

The number of reported cases which deal with this question in the early years of Henry VII's reign suggests that there was more seizing and traversing going on than usual. This was probably the result of Henry's more active fiscal policy, and it forced the courts to deal with a basic issue involved in both processes. The simple fact that the cases were reported indicates that the legal profession was not quite sure how to balance the rights of the respective parties, but the point seems to have been settled quite quickly. The case of 4 Hen. VII is the last to deal with the issue directly, while Hussey's argument in 8 Hen. VII assumes the heir's right to sue livery. The decision was overwhelmingly in favour of following the natural course of the law, both in assuming that the law had found the correct heir unless otherwise proved and in assuming that the law would prove otherwise if it had been mistaken.

The king was in a different position from any other plaintiff. He had no right to traverse an inquisition if it found against him. Where the king had a better title than was found for him in the inquisition, he could have a *melius inquirendum*, but only when he could produce a matter of record which displayed his better title.[123] If the *melius inquirendum* found against the king he had no further recourse, but was bound to recognize its findings.[124] The king,

[123] This was agreed in YB Mich. 4 Hen. VII, f.16, pl.1. Thus, if the inquisition found a title for the king by matter in fact, when in reality he had a right by matter of record, the king could seek *melius inquirendum*.

[124] Sir James Ley, *A Learned Treatise Concerning Wards and Liveries* (London, 1642), 71.

however, had enormous advantages in pleading and procedure and he had the whole machinery of the exchequer and chancery working to protect his rights. His escheators seized not only the large amounts of land to which he was entitled under the prerogative, but also those whose title appeared ambiguous in the inquisition. A determined exploitation of the king's procedural prerogatives as well as his substantive rights meant that the royal officials could seize large amounts of land to which the king had no rights, as well as those which were properly his.

The new concern in the year books and in the readings for the niceties of procedure suggests that this was the focus of Henry's attack. Most of the substantive rights he was claiming were known under his predecessor, but he was innovating in his exploitation of procedure. It seems that the profession was caught by surprise by this new tactic, and they had a two-fold response. First, as we have seen, they agreed that the rights of the heir by law were protected and that the ultimate decision regarding title was to be made according to the rules of the law. They then moved to elucidate the rules of procedure, to clear away confusion and ambiguity and ensure that both sides would follow the same rules. It took some time to achieve that end, and in the meantime the escheators were seizing land to which the king did not have title. These seizures relied on the findings of the inquisition juries, and one of the charges most commonly brought against Empson and Dudley was that of intimidating juries to find in the king's favour.[125] There is no doubt that the king's "haughty and cruel approvers"[126] were over-zealous on occasion, and that this was recognized by their contemporaries, as Conyngesby and Mallom discovered to their benefit.[127] As Elton points out, however, it seems just as likely that juries were often simply confused by the bewildering ways in which the landed classes settled their property.[128] The simple fact that men intimately involved with the king's policy, such as Dudley and Bray, could fall foul of the commissions strongly indicates that the commissions had no individual bias; they simply swept through an area seizing whatever land they could for the king. As Guy

125 John Guy, *Tudor England* (Oxford: Oxford University Press, 1988), 68.

126 *Caryll's Reports*, vol. 2, 605. 127 *Ibid.* See pp. 132–35, above.

128 G. R. Elton, "Henry VII: A Restatement," *Studies in Tudor and Stuart Politics and Government, Papers and Reviews 1946–1972*, vol. I, *Tudor Politics/Tudor Government* (London: Cambridge University Press, 1974), 76.

puts it, "Henry's technique was to shoot first and ask questions afterwards."[129]

That the king's aim was not simply to grab as much land as possible is apparent from the fact that Henry did in fact stop to ask questions. The first step in opposing a seizure was a traverse in chancery, as we have seen. Only about seventy chancery traverses have survived for Henry's reign, and over sixty of these are clustered around the years 19–23 Hen. VII (1503–07).[130] Many of these traverses were probably a response to the proclamation of 19 August 1504, in which Henry stated that he had "a speciall regard, mynde and desire in noo maner wyse to doo any wronge or to be indebted to any personne . . . ner to haue any mannys landes, goodes ner catalles otherwyse than good reason and conscience woll require, or that by the due order and cours of his lawes hath be adiuged."[131] Anyone who felt that he had a claim on the king, either over a debt or a wrongful invasion of property rights, was to present his complaint within the next two years.[132] Such complaints were taken seriously and "in twenty one cases the Crown conceded the truth of the traverse without delay, and in five cases it admitted, without equivocation, that the inquest was 'feigned'."[133] The king's proclamation makes it clear that there had been some injustice, while the response to the proclamation suggests that tenants were unwilling to turn to the law without explicit encouragement from above, probably because they were intimidated by the activities of the commissioners. Nevertheless, it appears that plaintiffs who did bring a traverse to chancery could have a reasonable expectation that they would recover their lands.

It is possible that these plaintiffs were successful because they acted under the auspices of the king's proclamation and thus at a

[129] Guy, *Tudor England*, 69. The impersonal nature of the commissions is also reflected in the exchequer procedure against those who had not taken up knighthood. In 1500, James Hobart and Richard Empson were among those summoned to appear. H. H. Leonard, "Knights and Knighthood in Tudor England" (PhD diss., London University, 1970), 51.

[130] See *Chancery Common Law Pleadings (C43, C44)*, List and Index Society vol. 67 (London: private distribution, 1971), 3, for a brief description.

[131] C66/594 m.27d, quoted in Elton, "Henry VII: A Restatement," 70.

[132] *Ibid.*, 70–71. Elton presents this proclamation as proof against the argument that Henry's will, which required that his executors should recompense anyone who had suffered from his financial exactions, is evidence of remorse on Henry's part over the harshness of his fiscal policies.

[133] Guy, *Tudor England*, 68.

time when the king was looking to be merciful. The cases concerning the prerogative coming to the court of king's bench suggest that this is not true. In all the cases in the reign of Henry VII, it is rare to find one where the plaintiff failed to recover his lands. Since almost every tenant who challenged the king's seizure of his land in the court of king's bench succeeded, it seems that either the court was heavily biased in favour of the plaintiffs, which is unlikely, or that the king was regularly seizing land to which he was not entitled, most likely because of confusion over title. It is probable that the king did not expect to be able to retain land seized in such a way, but the tenant's recovery in king's bench or in chancery meant that the tenure of the land was then made a matter of record. The king could not lose in this situation: either the tenant sought the return of his lands and produced evidence of his claim, in which case the king got the information on tenure that he was seeking, or the tenant did not come forward and the king continued to hold the land. The seizure of lands was not his primary aim, but, for those whose titles were dubious, the prospect of challenging the king in court must have been intimidating, and the strict legality of his procedure of little comfort. Dudley's advice in the *Tree of Commonwealth* that "subiectes neuer be lettyd or interruptyd by [the king's] . . . commaundymentes to his iudges or other officers, to haue the straighte course of his lawes, Beit traverse, tryall, processe, iudgement, sewing of lyuery or oyerwise," seems to have been a reflection of Henry VII's practice rather than an indictment against it.[134]

When the inquisition was carried out and no plaintiff came to traverse its findings, the king held the land of which his tenant had died seised until the heir came to sue livery. The heir had to make his homage before he could have livery, or have a licence to free him from this obligation, and until he had one or the other he would not have livery.[135] When he did sue livery, he had to ensure that it was done properly, or it would be void. Thus the inquisition must have been held on a writ or commission and it must have found correctly, for there were many rules governing the holding of inquisitions. The penalty for a mistake could be high if, for example,

[134] Edmund Dudley, *The Tree of Commonwealth*, ed. D. M. Brodie (Cambridge: Cambridge University Press, 1948), 36–37.

[135] Constable, 63. Constable goes on to describe the process involved in doing homage and the various administrative stages: Constable, 63–64. Frowyk, f.6v, gives a similar description.

the heir sued livery and it was later discovered that his ancestor died seised of more than was named in the inquisition.[136] The king could then re-seize the land and the heir would be left without remedy.[137] The inquisition must also have been held on the correct writ, not *devenerunt* when it should have been *mandamus*, for example. If that happened, the heir had to sue a new writ explaining the misuse of the first writ and enquiring as though the first writ had not been issued.[138]

Assuming that the tenant had sued the correct writ, the inquisition could only deal with the issues authorized by its writ. For example, the writ of *diem clausit extremum* allowed the inquisition to find the date of death of the tenant, what lands and tenements he held of the king, by what services, how much they were worth, who the heir was, and how old he or she was at the time of death. If it returned any more information than that, it was void.[139] If there was information missing from the inquisition, it was possible to have a commission to enquire further, but only if the new information agreed with that found in the inquisition. Thus, in 2 Hen. VII, William Highford sought a commission to enquire further after the inquisition on his brother's lands. The inquisition found that his brother died seised of land in chief held of the king and that he had three daughters. William asserted that part of the lands were actually held in fee tail and that he was the heir to those lands and sought a commission to prove his title. The court was unanimous that he could not have such a commission, for "he had his opportunity to show his title and interest before the Escheator when he was sitting upon the inquisition, whereby it was possible to find both the title for his heirs male and the other manors for his nieces."[140] Thus, once again, the judges seem to oppose any procedural tactics

[136] Constable, 64.

[137] Frowyk, f.6, f.7v. He refers to a case of Edward III, where the heir omitted an advowson in gross from his livery and the king re-seized. Frowyk, f.7v.

[138] Constable, 64–65. See introduction for a description of the main writs concerned. If the escheator held the inquisition on the wrong writ, then the inquisition was considered to be *virtute officii*, for the escheator had the right to hold an inquisition on his own authority. The heir would still have to have an inquisition *virtute brevis* before he could have livery. YB Mich. 9 Hen. VII, ff.8–9, pl.5. Cf. *Caryll's Reports*, vol. 2, 724. This section has an extended discussion of inquisition procedure: *ibid*., 724–28.

[139] YB Mich. 15 Edw. IV, f.13, pl.17.

[140] Hemmant, *Select Cases in Exchequer Chamber*, vol. 2, 128. Kebell also refers to this decision in YB Mich. 4 Hen. VII, f.16, pl.1.

that would delay the granting of livery to the heirs established by law.

The judges were generally reluctant to grant a new commission in such situations, but they recognized that on occasion that might mean that the king lost his right.[141] Vavasour raised this issue in 4 Hen. VII, and asked the other justices how the king would have remedy, if, for example, an inquisition returned that the deceased did not die seised, when in fact he did. Fairfax promptly responded that the king would enter and the heir would have no remedy. His answer seems to have revealed the division among the justices. Vavasour simply commented that "that seems amazing," but Kebell was more direct, remarking that "you and your company will say anything for your fee from the king."[142]

The readers agree that the heir must also sue livery of all his land at once and not in pieces, even if the land was scattered through various counties, and, if he did not do this, or if he omitted any piece of land, the livery was void.[143] If, however, the heir had part of his inheritance through his mother and part through his father by different inquisitions, he could sue livery as heir to his mother and heir to his father separately on those inquisitions.[144] Constable argues that, if the heir's father was tenant by curtesy of his mother's land and following the death of the father all the land descended to the heir, the heir had to sue livery of all the land at the same time.[145] If the heir sued livery of all his lands when dower was due from those

141 Of course, the plaintiff could traverse the inquisition, or use one of the other methods outlined above.

142 YB Mich. 4 Hen. VII, f.16, pl.1. It is not clear what Kebell meant by this gibe. Fairfax had been king's serjeant from 1467 to 1478 and he was a justice of the king's bench at the time of the case. He might therefore be expected to protect the king's rights, but Kebell's remark suggests something more than professional care.

143 Constable, 65; Frowyk, f.7v.

144 Constable, 65. According to Frowyk, the same applied when he inherited land from any assortment of ancestors. If the king granted the heir special livery of the land inherited from one ancestor, he would have to sue livery separately of the land inherited from another ancestor. Frowyk, f.7v.

145 Constable, 66. Frowyk disagrees, arguing that he should have one writ as heir to his mother and another as heir to his father, but he does accept that "the course in chancery is the contrary." Frowyk, f.7v. There was also some dispute in the year books on this question. It was agreed that an inquisition following the death of the father which found that he held land as a tenant by the curtesy was enough to entitle the king to seize both the mother's and the father's land, but it was not clear that this allowed the heir to sue livery of both. Hemmant, *Select Cases in Exchequer Chamber*, vol. 2, 129–30; *Caryll's Reports*, vol. 2, 727. There were

lands the livery would also be void, whether the dower was due by the same inquisition or another.[146] In this case, however, the heir could sue livery again when the claim to dower was settled.[147] If the land was to be divided among co-heirs, then each would sue livery separately of the part that was to descend to him.[148]

If the inquisition did not accurately find the tenure by which the land was held, the heir's livery might also be void. Frowyk instances a case where a husband and wife held land of the king in tail to the heirs of the husband begotten on the wife, and had a daughter, and the wife died. The husband then married again and had a daughter by his second wife and died. The inquisition following his death found that he died seised of this land in fee and that the elder daughter was daughter and heir and she had livery on this basis. Another inquisition found that the father had another daughter and, because of this, a *scire facias* issued against the elder sister. According to the findings of the second inquisition, the younger sister had a claim on the land as co-heir, and, because the first inquisition did not report that the land was held in tail, the king could re-seize the land.[149] If, however, the tenant had had only one daughter and the inquisition had reported the tenure incorrectly, the king could not re-seize, even if the truth later emerged, because the daughter was sole heir in both cases.[150] Frowyk also relates a similar case where the king's tenant had land in another county held in borough English, and had two sons, and died. An inquisition found the younger son to be heir in the county where the land in borough English was and another inquisition found the elder son to be heir in another county. In this case also, the king has the right to re-seize, for the first inquisition did not cite the fact that the land was held in borough English. Thus the inquisition was incorrect, for the younger son was not heir by blood. Again, if there had been only one son and the inquisition had not mentioned the custom,

cases where it was difficult to be sure whether the heir should sue livery on one or two writs. Frowyk gives an example where the king's tenant had other lands held of the king for term of life and the reversion of this land descended to his heir through another ancestor. He believes that, when the tenant dies, his heir will have to sue two writs of *diem clausit extremum*, but notes that the judicial register allows the heir to have one writ for both lands. Frowyk, f.7v.

146 Frowyk, ff.7v–8. If the dower due did not appear in any inquisition, the widow could sue for it in chancery, and in this case the livery also would be void.

147 Frowyk, ff.7v–8.

148 Constable, 66.

149 Frowyk, f.7v.

150 Frowyk, f.7v.

the king would not have the right to re-seize.[151] If, however, both inquisitions had found the elder son to be heir and he had sued livery and the truth later emerged, his livery of the lands held by common law would remain good, but the king would re-seize the lands in borough English.[152]

If the heir died before livery was sued, leaving an heir of full age, and this heir sued livery as heir of his father, without mentioning the first inquisition taken on the land after the death of his grandfather, then this livery was also void, for the land should remain in the king's hands by the first inquisition.[153] In this case, the livery was faulty from the beginning and the land never really left the king's hands. There were some cases where the livery was good at the time, but later information made it invalid, as where another was found to be a co-heir after the first heir had sued livery. In this situation, the king would re-seize the land and the heirs would sue again.[154] If the livery was insufficient from the beginning, the king could re-seize without a writ of *scire facias*, but if the heir sued livery and a later inquisition defeated the heir's livery the king needed a *scire facias*.[155] The king could use the technicalities of such a situation to his own advantage. Frowyk argues that, if the heir is found to be a bastard before he sues livery, but after the inquisition, the king can re-seize the land. If another writ finds that another is heir, the king can maintain against him that the bastard is heir, based on the first inquisition, and he can refuse livery to the bastard on the grounds of bastardy, and thus neither will have livery. Thus the technicalities of procedure could be used either to maintain strict justice or to manipulate it, and the readings emphasized the importance of a thorough knowledge of the subject for any practitioner.

With the complexity of these rules there was always the fear that any slip would invalidate the whole process, in which case the heir would have to start from the beginning again. Frowyk points out that, if the heir entered on his land following the death of his ancestor and received a pardon for all intrusions from the king before the

[151] Frowyk, f.7v.

[152] Frowyk, f.8. This differed from the case above concerning dower due on the lands, because here the younger brother had the right only to the land in borough English, while the widow had title in each part of the land.

[153] Constable, 65.

[154] Constable, 65. The same rules applied to lands sued by *ouster le main*.

[155] Frowyk, f.8.

inquisition was held, he could avoid the whole process of holding an inquisition and suing livery.[156] If the inquisition was held before the pardon was granted, however, the pardon would only apply to the profits taken by the heir before the inquisition.[157] This was not uncommon, but it was more usual to avoid general livery through suing special livery by letters patent. By this method, the king granted the heir the right to enter into his entire heritage at once, without further enquiry, and it carried the same weight as livery sued through chancery.[158] Special livery also allowed the king to pardon or grant issues and it could be sued before or after the inquisition was held. The advantages of such a livery for the heir were clear, particularly for the heir of a large and scattered estate: it gave him a secure title to all his land and saved him from the time and worry of suing general livery. Special livery reduced the king's ability to establish the tenure of the land held by his tenant, however, and he charged a heavy price for the privilege. There were some risks attached to special livery for the heir also, as the duke of Buckingham found. He appealed to the executors of Henry VII's will to restore the £3,000 that he had paid to Henry for his special livery, claiming that it was extortionate. The assembled company had little sympathy for the duke and told him that "this special livery was solely at the suit of the duke and his own act, and it was nothing like a general livery. For every general livery is a thing of common course in the Chancery, and the party need not make any other suit, but only in the Chancery; and if the king or the chancellor were to deny any man his general livery they would deny justice."[159] Special livery, however, was outside the common law, and when the duke sought it "the king could rightfully have denied it to him, and despite that the king of his grace and in return for the said sum granted the duke his desire, the money was well and lawfully paid; and if that is so, the duke has no cause to have restitution."[160] The fact that the king's tenants were willing both to pay the high financial price of special livery, and to step outside the protection of the common law, suggests that the price of the king's feudal rights was far higher.

[156] Frowyk, f.6. [157] Frowyk, f.6.

[158] Special livery could also be granted to an heir under age, relieving him of the necessity to prove age.

[159] *Caryll's Reports*, vol. 2, 670.

[160] *Ibid.* The justices agreed with this, but the duke was finally allowed £1,000.

The readers consider briefly such questions as how the issues due to the king will be calculated and what happens when rent does not fall due between the date of the tenant's death and the date of the livery.[161] Having dealt with such basic problems, the readers continue with a discussion of the process involved in proving age. This is not directly relevant to primer seisin, but Constable makes a connection by pointing out that everything he has said about suing livery is equally relevant for heirs who were in wardship, but they will have one extra stage to complete first. When it appears from the information in the inquisition that the heir is now of full age, he must sue a writ of *etate probanda* directed to the escheator of the county where the child was born.[162] If there were a number of inquisitions which found the heir of different ages, he cannot sue *etate probanda* until he is of full age according to all the inquisitions.[163]

The heir must find twelve people who will swear that he is now of full age and who will give a reason why they know this, for example that their own son was born at the same time, that they were present at the birth or baptism, or that they broke their leg that day. Each of the twelve witnesses must be aged at least forty-two if the heir is a boy or at least thirty-seven if the heir is a girl, that is, they must have been at least twenty-one when the child was born, so that they could be expected to have clear knowledge of the time of the child's birth.[164] If the heir is not found of full age at this time, he must put off suing livery until this is found and he must then sue another writ. If he is found of age according to one inquisition but is found under age by an inquisition in another county, he must also wait. If he does sue livery under these circumstances, the escheator will be ordered to re-seize the land until the king commands otherwise. If the king

161 Constable, 67; Frowyk, f.5v. Frowyk also makes the point that, if the king's tenant dies seised of land in fee simple leaving an heir of full age and the heir dies seised before an inquisition is held, his heir will be responsible for the issues of the land since the death of his grandfather. If, however, the land was held in fee tail, the heir is responsible only for the issues since his father's death and his father's executors are responsible for the issues due from his father. Frowyk, f.5v.

162 Constable, 68.

163 Frowyk, f.6v. If another inquisition finds the heir under age after he has purchased the writ but before his age is proved, a writ of *supersedeas* will issue to the escheator to halt the process. If the heir's age is proved before the new inquisition is returned, then it will stand, for it is "a perfect trial between the king and him." Frowyk, f.6v.

164 Constable, 68–69; Frowyk, f.6v. Frowyk goes into what will happen if there is a difference of opinion between witnesses or between witnesses and jury.

had granted the ward to another, then the guardian would receive a *scire facias* to come to the enquiry to show proof if the heir was not of full age. The guardian did not have to offer any proof against the heir, but if the guardian did not receive the *scire facias* the heir could not have livery and if he did sue livery under those circumstances it was void.[165]

The lectures delivered by Constable and Frowyk thus outline the king's substantive rights and cover the process to be followed both by the king in seizing those rights and by the heir in reclaiming his land. The readers disagree on both counts, with Constable consistently allowing the king greater latitude both to seize and to retain land, while Frowyk champions the rights of the heir. The differences in their views, together with the year book interest in the issues they cover, indicate that there was little settled learning on the subject, largely because little attention had been given to it. Though the king's rights had not changed dramatically, the prominence accorded to them had, and increased enforcement rather than substantive change made primer seisin a topic of interest.

The particular views expressed by Frowyk and Constable express, in legal terms, an ongoing tension between the king's rights and the rights of his tenants. The complexity of the readings can seem somewhat intimidating, but it is simply indicative of the complexity of land relationships in early Tudor England. Part of the web of enfeoffment was a result of the attempts of landowners to evade feudal dues, but part was simply the result of their attempts to improve their position vis-à-vis their neighbours. As Harriss has pointed out, "as well as inbuilt stability landed society had an inbuilt fluidity; clinging to and competing for land was at the heart of its politics."[166] In order to be of any practical use, the readings had to address the variety of English methods of landholding so that both lawyers and landholders would have a clear picture of the obligations which bound their lands. The readers' exposition of the feudal burdens on the various kinds of lands and the ways in which such burdens might be evaded or delayed also gave the lawyers and landowners some insight into potential loopholes. If

165 Constable, 69. The same applied to a ward by reason of ward.

166 G. L. Harriss, "The Dimensions of Politics," in *The McFarlane Legacy: Studies in Late Medieval Politics and Society,* ed. R. H. Britnell and A. J. Pollard, The Fifteenth Century Series No. 1 (Stroud: Alan Sutton, 1995), 3.

the king was going to establish any real claim to his feudal dues, he needed a strong and active programme of commissions and a system which would guard his rights as they arose. Part of the interest of the prerogative is that the king's revitalization of its administrative machinery hit landed society where it was most sensitive, in its titles to land. The activity of the king's agents was bound to cause protest, though Elton's comment that "the outraged protests read ... like those of men who know that they are guilty of practices in which 'everybody' indulges and who do not see why the law should pick on them" also suggests that the tenants' opposition needs to be placed in a wider context.[167] The tenants-in-chief who were baulking at the burden of Henry's exactions were also lords, with many of the same rights as the king, albeit on a lesser scale. How did these men administer their own lands?

According to McFarlane, "if a general charge had to be preferred [against the nobility], it would ... be one of harsh efficiency; the commonest impulse detectable was to exploit every imagined right, to push every promising advantage to its limit."[168] He points to evidence among the duke of Buckingham's papers, most notably a book of informations (based mainly on an enquiry on the duke's estates in May 1516) and a notebook compiled by the duke's receiver-general in 1518–19. He argues that:

> both books were intended for Buckingham's own perusal and both have marginal evidence that he had read and considered them before referring particular items to his council for legal action. Their purpose was to keep a better check upon local officials, to make it more difficult for them, the tenants, and their neighbours to profit at the lord's expense and to exploit every available source of revenue. The duke's ministers were encouraged to spy upon one another, to report any instances where bribes had been taken or collusive bargains made. Entry fines were to be pushed as high as possible, tenants forced to maintain their buildings in repair, prosperous bondmen were to be detected and squeezed, and every waste of lord's timber, every evasion of his right of wreck, every poaching of his woods and warrens to be smartly punished.[169]

[167] G. R. Elton, "Henry VII: Rapacity and Remorse," in *Studies in Tudor and Stuart Politics and Government, Papers and Reviews 1946–1972* (London: Cambridge University Press, 1974), vol. 1, 55. Originally printed in *Historical Journal* 1 (1958): 21–39, this paper is part of the exchange between Elton and J. P. Cooper on the extent of and reasons for Henry's rapacity. See also J. P. Cooper, "Henry VII's Last Years Reconsidered," *Historical Journal* 2 (1959): 103–29.

[168] K. B. McFarlane, *The Nobility of Later Medieval England: The Ford Lectures for 1953 and Related Studies* (Oxford: Clarendon Press, 1973), 49.

[169] *Ibid.*, 51.

The terms are very familiar, and, if we were to substitute the king's name for the duke's, the description would echo those given by modern opponents of Henry's policies. However, it seems that the king was not indulging in extortion, but simply following standard practices of estate management, although he may have been a little late in entering that arena. McFarlane goes on to comment that "all the evidence suggests that most of the landowners of our period – *all* who have left any records – were well able to take care of their property, and if they got the chance, of their neighbours' also. The indolent, the vacillating, or the feebly good-intentioned would not long have had any estates to enjoy."[170] Henry VII could not have been described as any of those things.

It seems, then, that at least some of the complaints of the landowners cannot be taken as an expression of moral or even financial outrage, for the king was simply using their own methods against them. As expressions of political outrage, the lords' complaints were more justified, for the king was able to use these methods on a far grander scale, and to greater effect, than any other landowner, through his escheators, the chamber machinery, and his procedural advantages in court. However, that was probably the point he was trying to make. Land was the life-blood of the nobility, and Henry's commissions hit them in a vulnerable spot. The commissions which he sent into the shires were a very visible sign of royal authority and created a new awareness of the active presence of the crown in the kingdom.[171] This process was only beginning in earnest when Constable and Frowyk spoke in the autumn of 1495. By the end of the century, the administration of the prerogative had grown to such an extent that the bishop of Carlisle was given jurisdiction over the north, as a general surveyor and receiver of the king's prerogative.[172]

Beyond raising awareness of the power of the crown amongst its wealthier subjects, the commissions could be used to shake the power of the nobility. In 1505, a royal commission of concealments in Northumberland found that over twenty of the tenancies held of

[170] *Ibid.*, 53.

[171] M. E. James, *A Tudor Magnate and the Tudor State: Henry Fifth Earl of Northumberland,* Borthwick Papers No. 30 (York: St. Anthony's Press, 1966), 19. James gives various examples of northerners, including Sir Robert Plumpton and Sir Robert Constable, who discovered that the crown intended to take advantage of its rights, particularly where wardships and marriages were concerned.

[172] W. C. Richardson, *Tudor Chamber Administration 1485–1547* (Baton Rouge: Louisiana State University Press, 1952), 167–68. The exact date at which his jurisdiction began is not clear, but Richardson suggests 1499 at the latest.

the earl of Northumberland were in fact held of the king. The earl's tenants were forced to take their cases to the court of king's bench for resolution.[173] As James points out, "although most of the traverses were upheld, once again in a disquieting kind of way the royal power had made itself felt within a network of traditional ties of dependence, even in the remote backwoods of Northumberland."[174] Some of the Percy tenants took the next available opportunity to become servants of the crown, recognizing that there was a new vibrancy to the royal power in the north. Though the Percies remained strong, there could be no doubt that these royal activities were disconcerting.

The commissions against the earl of Northumberland brought in the biggest haul in terms of concealed lands, but he was not the only northern lord to attract the king's attention. In 1504, the tenth lord Clifford also endured a commission of wardship and concealed lands which found that he had usurped the wardship and marriage of Thomas Blenkinsop of Helbeck and which claimed fifteen Clifford fees. Clifford was fined 1,300 marks. He went on to traverse the findings, and his tenures and offices were later confirmed.[175] He received a general pardon in 1506, but his fine was not remitted.

Henry VII's concern with the northerners extended beyond the major lords. In 1489, he had an early experience of the self-imposed isolation of the inhabitants of Durham and York, when they refused to pay the tax voted for war in Brittany. According to Hall, the king

> commaunded the erle [of Northumberland] in any wyse by distresse or otherwise accordyng to hys discrecion, to exacte the money of the people, and by compulsion to enforce suche to payment as whyned moost at it, least y^{t} it might appere that the decrees, actes and statutes, made and confirmed by him and hys high courte of Parliament, shoulde by hys rude and rusticall people be infringed, despised and vilepended.[176]

The realization that his realm was divided, not only by political faction, but by geographical particularism, must have reinforced the importance of loyalty to the king as a unifying element within the realm.

173 The cases relating to the earl's tenants are by far the largest number of cases concerning the prerogative to go through king's bench in any one year.

174 James, *Tudor Magnate*, 21.

175 The commission also challenged Clifford's right to the hereditary sheriffwick of Westmorland. See C43/1/?(unnumbered).

176 Edward Hall, *Hall's Chronicle*, ed. Henry Ellis (London, 1809), 443.

Support for the king's wars remained the central expression of such loyalty and Henry seems to have sought to encourage the personal involvement of his subjects. In 1492, he recruited an army by indenture with his leading magnates,[177] but in 1495 a statute was passed ordaining that anyone who held offices, fees, or annuities of the king and did not "geve their attendaunce upon hym when he shall fortune to goo in Werres in his persone, in their persones, as their seid dutie bindeth them" would forfeit their office.[178] A further statute of 1504 extended the provision to those who held lands of the king, on the grounds that "they ar more bounden to give ther attendaunce upon the King's moste royall persone in his seid Warres then other rehersed persones havyng but fees offices and annuities for term of lyffe, aswell for the defence of his moste Roiall persone as for the defence of this his Realm."[179] In taking this route, the king was returning to an old ideal of feudal loyalty, and seeking to restate the principle of active service to the king in return for grants of land. However, this principle could be expressed in military terms only in extreme circumstances. Given Henry's unwillingness to engage in continental warfare, he obviously required a more quotidian method of enforcing his lordship, something the regular operation of the prerogative could provide.

The experiences of the northern lords suggest that Henry VII was only beginning to test the efficacy of the commissions as a means of controlling powerful and/or distant lords.[180] Though the traverses brought by the earl of Northumberland's tenants were fairly straightforward, they took some years to work their way through the courts; they reached king's bench in the summer of 1508, but the king's death delayed them and judgment was not recorded until the summer of 1509.[181] The process of traversing the inquisitions was time-consuming and expensive, but that added to their appeal

177 Helen Miller, *Henry VIII and the English Nobility* (Oxford: Basil Blackwell, 1986), 133.

178 11 Hen. VII, c.18, *Stat. Realm*, vol. 2, 582.

179 19 Hen. VII, c.1, *Stat. Realm*, vol. 2, 648.

180 Henry had already tried to control the north through the use of bonds. Cunningham notes that, although all parts of the country were affected, there was a striking focus on the north, and Yorkshire in particular. Sean Cunningham, "Henry VII and Rebellion in North-Eastern England, 1485–1492: Bonds of Allegiance and the Establishment of Tudor Authority," *Northern History* 32 (1996): 48.

181 KB 27/988 mm.v–xv d; and KB 27/992 mm.iii–viii.

from the king's point of view: as long as the case was moving through the system, the king's power was kept firmly in the forefront of the plaintiff's mind and that of his neighbours. Such methods would not break the power of the nobility, but that was not Henry VII's intention, for a strong nobility was necessary for government. The commissions served to remind the nobility of the power of the crown, and that was enough for the king's purposes.

It seems, then, that Henry VII had a wide range of methods at his disposal to enforce his prerogative. Some were very traditional, some were traditional in form but innovative in procedure, and some were pure innovation. Working together, they could ensure that little escaped the feudal net. Maintaining co-operation between these various mechanisms was not easy, however. At first Henry kept the administration of the prerogative under his direct control, but, as the number of commissions in the counties grew and the business became more complex, he began to delegate part of the load. Sir Reginald Bray was one of Henry's most trusted administrators, and he supervised the administration of wardships, operating by word-of-mouth command rather than under any official appointment. Bray died in August 1503, and in December of the same year Sir John Hussey was appointed as Surveyor of the King's Wards, the "chief intermediate officer for overseeing, managing and selling the wardships of all lands which may be in the king's hands."[182] The description of Hussey's role indicates that Henry intended to maintain his personal interest in wardships, but by 1507 it seems that he had ceased to pay much attention to them.[183] Hussey became master of the wards in effect, if not in title, and when in 1508 Edward Belknap became Surveyor of the King's Prerogative, a prerogative administration was in being, separate from the personal interest of the king.[184] The simple fact that these offices were developed is enough to demonstrate that the prerogative had become big business by the end of Henry's reign and that it had grown in profit and complexity. It also suggests that Henry was satisfied with the way in which the commissions of enquiry had succeeded in keeping royal authority before the nobility. By 1507, Henry was secure, both politically and financially, and there was no reason for him

182 Richardson, *Tudor Chamber Administration*, 169. 183 *Ibid.*, 174–75.

184 W. C. Richardson, "The Surveyor of the King's Prerogative," *English Historical Review* 56 (1941): 61, 64.

to continue to give so much personal attention to the administration of his prerogative. He had achieved his immediate ends and he could rely on his trusted officials to keep the machinery running smoothly.

Though the king's interest in the running of the prerogative became less personal, interest in the topic did not fade at the Inns. There was one more reading in the reign of Henry VII, given by John Port, in 1507. This was Port's first reading, and *Prerogativa Regis* was an adventurous choice in this situation. Port seems to have balanced his risk by relying heavily on Frowyk's reading; his references to his predecessor are frequent, but he also refers to other authorities more often than the earlier readers did.[185] His preference for Frowyk over Constable may be an indication of the early reception of the 1495 readers' interpretations, but it is just as likely to be because both Frowyk and Port were from the Inner Temple. Indeed, Port's reading gives us our clearest example of a reader's use of his predecessor's work. In his opening paragraph, he seems to be referring explicitly to a manuscript text, telling his audience to "see on the other side the preceding folio on tenure in chief and then see on the other side this folio in which cases wardship lies on the lands held of another where the ancestor did not die seised &c. and then on the other preceding folio in which cases the wardship does not lie where the ancestor dies seised &c."[186] This suggests that Port was not simply relying on the abstract authority of Frowyk's name, but that he had an actual copy of the reading, which he was referring to as a kind of textbook. It may perhaps have been physically present, or at the very least in a place where the auditors could be expected to have access to it. This impression is reinforced by the fact that his text does not deal with the matters mentioned. Indeed, Port's reading, heavily though it relies on Frowyk, also seems to be trying to develop Frowyk's arguments to the next stage. It does not go into as much detail as Frowyk on some points of law, but it does pause to draw conclusions periodically as it moves through the

185 This reading averages a named authority about every page and a half. Frowyk's name dominates, but after him Port uses Vavasour and Townshend most often. The identification of this as Port's reading is also supported by his reference to "Brygges in lectur," since Port is known to have owned a copy of Brygges' reading on Westminster II. BL MS Hargrave 87, f.153v; cf. Sir John Port, *The Notebook of Sir John Port*, ed. J. H. Baker, Selden Society vol. 102 (London: Selden Society, 1986), xxxi.

186 BL MS Hargrave 87, f.142.

material. Given the similarity between the two readings, a close examination of Port would be redundant, but it is worth considering how he builds on Frowyk, and how and when he chooses to depart from him.

It quickly becomes apparent that this reading is not simply a slavish representation of Frowyk's views, for Port returns to the earliest reader to argue that, when the king's tenant gives land in tail or makes a lease for term of life, the king will have the wardship of the donor, and not of the donee or lessee.[187] He notes that it was adjudged in Edward IV that the king could choose, but he seems to have grave doubts about that argument. From this point, he follows Frowyk closely through a discussion of tenure in chief, again pausing to reiterate the early reader when he emphasizes that the bishops will only have their prerogatives in the lands they held at the time of the statute, and not in lands purchased since.[188] He follows Frowyk's discussion of reversion and remainder through *Skrene's Case*, concluding that there is "no diversity between a remainder and a reversion of lands held of others as for the wardship when they escheat."[189] He goes on to note the difference when the land in question was held of the king, for there "he was the king's tenant by reason of the reversion and not the tenant for term of life, but in the other case the tenant for term of life was the king's tenant and not the remainderman and thus diversity &c."[190] This is the conclusion reached, but not clearly expressed, by Frowyk.

Port follows Frowyk again through discontinuance and recovery, with a quick summary of the king's rights, before he turns briefly to consider collusion. This is an odd section, for he focuses mainly on the king's rights under the statute of Marlborough, as Frowyk had done, and makes only a brief mention of the "novum statutum" which he does not identify. He also makes no reference to *Stonor's Case*.[191] From alienation by collusion he takes a quick sweep through disseisin and tenants by curtesy before returning to sum up the section. Here again he shows his dependence on Frowyk, and prepares for the later section of the lectures by arguing that "There is great diversity between primer seisin of the lands held of others and wardship, for in the case of wardship it is necessary that the land held in chief was held by knight service, but

187 *Ibid.* 188 *Ibid.*, f.142v. 189 *Ibid.*
190 *Ibid.*, f.143. 191 *Ibid.* See pp. 105–11 above.

it is not so for primer seisin." He also concludes that "where the ancestor has a remainder, a reversion, or if he was seised of lands held of others, still wardship, but not primer seisin &c."[192]

This seems to prepare him to move on to the next chapter, but it is followed by a quick statement of the central issue of *Stonor's Case*: "the king's tenant dies seised of an acre of land held of the king in chief and of another acre in use held of another person, his heir under age, the king will have the wardship of both acres."[193] This may suggest that Port was ready to move on when he was halted by his auditors who wanted to discuss the importance of the "novum statutum" and *Stonor's Case*. Port's cavalier treatment of the issue may indicate that he had not thought very deeply about the material, beyond repeating Frowyk, but his attention to the earlier readers, and his desire to sum up the principles behind Frowyk's arguments, suggest that this was unlikely. It is possible that he was simply trying to avoid a difficult issue: Caryll's reports make it clear that the issue was still open for discussion, and Port may have been unwilling to commit himself without a clear authority to follow.

In the second chapter, Port follows a similar process. He expands briefly on Frowyk's introduction, explaining that the king would have the wardship of the heir's body even when he had the lordship by purchase "by the equity" and questioning whether the statute made new law, "for it seems to Frowyk that this is only a rehearsal of the common law."[194] The order of this chapter is significantly different from the order in Frowyk, and Port does cover some material not in the earlier reading. For example, he makes a brief detour into coparceny, which was not covered by either Frowyk or Constable, but which may be a last echo of the Bohun division.[195] From there, he moves on to wardship by reason of wardship.

Much of this is taken from Frowyk, but Port shows an interest in terminology which is largely absent in his model; he considers the implications of a grant of wardship, and notes that a marriage only passes if the grant specifies it.[196] He also pays more attention to the details of the guardian's obligations, pointing out that the guardian must find the infant's marriage and drink, food, and clothing. If the

192 *Ibid.*, f.143v.

193 *Ibid.* The principle is attributed to *Dormer's Case*; Thomas Dormer initiated *Stonor's Case* by traversing the original inquisition on Stonor's land. *Caryll's Reports*, vol. 1, 367.

194 Hargrave 87, f.143v.

195 *Ibid.*, f.144.

196 *Ibid.*, ff.144–44v.

guardian does not do so, the infant can have an action, but, if the guardian is the king, he is put to his petition.[197] He also notes that by the statute of 8 Hen. VI, c. 16 the king cannot grant lands or tenements within the month after the inquisition, but that the grant of the body is good, because it is outside the statute. He sums up this section with a few basic principles: the king will have a wardship by reason of a reversion, but not a remainder, a point he had already made in the previous chapter; if the infant is married in the father's lifetime, the king will not have the wardship of the body; and, if the father is tenant by the curtesy, the king will not have the wardship. These points seem to lie behind his observation that in some cases the king will have the wardship of the body without the land or the land without the body.[198]

Apart from these expansions or clarifications, the chapter in general is an abbreviated but generally straightforward presentation of Frowyk's arguments. Port's treatment of chapter three, however, moves further from Frowyk. Although he still calls on Frowyk's authority regularly, he has changed the shape of the chapter. Frowyk moved through the text clause by clause before moving into a discussion of inquisition writs and the circumstances of their use. Port, on the other hand, moves almost immediately to inquisitions, preceding them only with a brief discussion of the relationship of liber seisin and primer seisin, and the king's prerogative right to primer seisin rather than his tenurial right to wardship.[199] This discussion is again more explicit than Frowyk's, as is his statement that "by primer seisin the king does not have freehold but rather an occupation &c. and the freehold remains in the heir," though he cites Frowyk as his authority.[200]

Port also skips Frowyk's extended discussion of the circumstances in which the king must have an inquisition and its role in his claim to primer seisin. He focuses rather on the general rights to primer seisin, and the ways in which the division of lands determines who will fall into the king's hands. A detailed comparison of Frowyk and Port's versions of chapter three are almost impossible, for Port has clearly decided to leave the structure of his model aside; to give a broad example, while Frowyk moves from a discussion of the inquisition writs, to proving age, to traversing inquisitions,

[197] *Ibid.*, f.144v. [198] *Ibid.*, ff.144v–45.
[199] *Ibid.*, ff.145v–46. [200] *Ibid.*, f.145v.

Port goes from inquisition writs, to traversing, to proving age, back to *ouster le main*, and then on to a discussion of the lesser writs, such as *de terris concelatis*. Port's organization is rather muddled, but he does seem to cover most of the same material as Frowyk, though with a slightly different emphasis. Thus he moves much more quickly through the description of the process for inquisitions, proving age, and suing livery, but spends rather more time on traversing, suggesting, perhaps, that the procedures were more settled by his time, but that traverses were still challenging. He also continues to try to summarize the broader outline of the law. For example, he provides a brief but clear outline of the effects of the statute of 36 Edw. III, c.14 on traversing which compares favourably with Frowyk's convoluted discussion.[201] His discussion of proving age and suing livery generally follows Frowyk's and continues to call on the authority of Frowyk, as well as Kebell, Bracton, and Fortescue.[202] Overall, however, in this section Port refers to authorities less frequently, whether because the material was less controversial, or because he was gaining in confidence. His references to authorities decline as the reading progresses, though they continue to appear.[203]

Thus Port's reading is a fairly faithful adaptation of Frowyk's; he makes an occasional attempt to clarify the points made by Frowyk, and he is willing to raise questions about the validity of Frowyk's arguments, but generally only when supported by another authority. The reading is thus neither new nor confident, and it does little to move the law forward, but it makes two important points. Its complete omission of Constable's name suggests that Frowyk's reading had a greater impact than Constable's, though the value of this point may be mitigated by the fact that Port came from Frowyk's Inn. It also confirms that *Prerogativa Regis* remained an important topic at the end of Henry VII's reign, one that an ambitious junior reader might try to tackle, though with some care.

201 *Ibid.*, f.150; Frowyk, f.8.

202 Frowyk at f.151 and f.151v and Kebell, Bracton, and Fortescue at f.152v.

203 Frowyk remains a central figure, with Vavasour close behind and Townshend a clear third. There are also incidental references to Kebell, Brown, Brygges, and Hankford.

4

SPELMAN, YORKE, AND THE CAMPAIGN AGAINST USES

The first reading of Henry VIII's reign came in 1521, when John Spelman, another serjeant-elect giving his third reading, chose to revive the topic. In the circumstances of Henry VIII's rule, a new treatment of the law was necessary, one which would take into consideration both the earlier readings and the changes of his reign. The timing of this re-reading requires some consideration. It was not simply a response to the new monarch, for Henry VIII had already been on the throne for twelve years. The vagaries of the calls of serjeants may go some way to explaining why *Prerogativa Regis* had not been treated earlier in the reign, but, as Port's reading demonstrates, it was possible, though not particularly useful, for a more junior reader to take on the topic. However, a consideration of the king's policies early in his reign suggests reasons for both the gap and the renewed interest in the topic in 1521.

When Henry followed his father to the throne of England there was a sense of a new beginning, but, as far as the administration of the prerogative was concerned, the changes were more apparent than real. Henry VII's financial policy had been cordially disliked, and his son clearly set out to soothe public opinion on this matter. On his accession, Henry confirmed the pardon granted by his father shortly before his death and proclaimed a more ample pardon, but in true Tudor style he excepted debt.[1] His imprisonment of the hated Empson and Dudley was one of the most visible "repudiations" of his father's methods. Spelman was one of many who took note, commenting that "the king by the advice of his Council committed

[1] *Letters and Papers, Foreign and Domestic, of the Reign of Henry VIII*, vol. 1, 1509–1514, arr. and cat. J. S. Brewer (London: Longman, Green, Longman & Roberts, 1862), No. 2. The proclamations are dated 23 April 1509 and they are followed on 30 April by a list of persons excepted from the pardon, including Empson, Dudley, the informer John Batist Grimaldi, and others. *Ibid.*, No. 12.

Edmund Dudley and Sir Richard Empson . . . to the Tower of London, with various other promoters who did not look after the common wealth but sought only to fulfil the covetous purpose of the said King Henry VII."[2] This imprisonment, together with their subsequent execution, went a long way towards convincing onlookers that the financial exactions of the previous reign were at an end. The chronicler Hall, for example, notes that "in this yere kyng Henry the .vii. his executours made restitucion of great sommes of money, to many persons taken against good conscience to the sayde kynges vse, by the forenamed Empson and Dudley."[3] In reality, however, as Miller points out, "so far as is known, no money was refunded for the payments already made, although Edmund Dudley, in the Tower, had recalled that Henry VII had wanted restitution to be made to anyone wronged by him, and the king in his will had instructed his executors to make reparation where necessary."[4] The king's executors did hear cases brought by those who felt that they had been badly treated, but, as the duke of Buckingham discovered, they were not easily convinced.[5]

Henry did relieve some of those burdened by recognizances made during the previous reign, but he carried out no wholesale repudiation of his father's methods. In fact, in the early months of his reign, he cancelled only a handful of recognizances, many of which had simply been fulfilled, and there is no reason to believe that those who received genuine relief did not remain burdened by other bonds.[6] For example, the duke of Buckingham had a bond for £400 cancelled, but in 1515 he pleaded before the late king's executors that he had been wrongfully charged with debts of £7,179 and that he

[2] John Spelman, *The Reports of Sir John Spelman*, ed. J. H. Baker, 2 vols., Selden Society vols. 93 and 94 (London: Selden Society, 1976 and 1977), vol. 1, 175.

[3] Edward Hall, *Hall's Chronicle*, ed. Henry Ellis (London, 1809), 514.

[4] Helen Miller, *Henry VIII and the English Nobility* (Oxford: Basil Blackwell, 1986), 208.

[5] John Caryll, *Reports of Cases by John Caryll*, ed. J. H. Baker, 2 vols., Selden Society vols. 115 and 116 (London: Selden Society, 1998 and 1999), vol. 2, 670. See chapter 3, p. 147 above.

[6] See, for example, *Letters and Papers of Henry VIII*, vol. 1, Nos. 22, 266, 258, 275, 296, 313, and 380. Most of the recognizances were made by groups rather than individuals and the sums at stake range from £20 to 2,000 marks. This latter sum was owed by Lord Dacre and was just part of his list of wrongful exactions. The number of remissions granted to northerners is striking. Since it is unlikely that Henry was particularly generous to them, this supports the argument that his father had in fact taken particular care to bind the northerners to him through financial obligations. See chapter 3, pp. 151–54 above.

had lost a further £3,554 in legal expenses.[7] Though £400 was a substantial sum and the remission of such a debt might give a nobleman cause to be grateful to the king, the remaining burden kept him securely within the king's power.

There were some real changes in the administration of the prerogative when Henry VIII became king. The new king was as untrained in the business of kingship as his father had been at his accession, though for different reasons. This meant that the system required some immediate change. As Dietz points out, Henry VII

> had worked fundamental changes in the organization of the financial system, as a result of which the king in person was his own chief treasury official. He personally knew all his receipts and expenditures; he personally gave acquittances or discharges to the special treasurers, and to him, as the final officer of audit the great treasuries and revenue courts themselves submitted their accounts. The independence of the Exchequer was broken down in all its essential parts, and it, together with the new revenue bodies, were brought under the unified control of the monarch himself.[8]

This worked well under Henry VII, but his son had no intention of investing the time in administration that such a system required, and so the first parliament of his reign passed legislation to place it on a statutory basis. The exchequer had already launched an attempt to regain the ground it had lost under Henry VII and was harassing receivers who continued to pay their money to John Heron, treasurer of the chamber, and to account for it before the General Surveyors. The new act relieved the receivers and ordained that "all Acquitaunces and Billes of Receyte heretofore made by the seid John Heyron, in the time of the seid late noble Kyng [Henry VII], and in the tyme of our Souveraign Lorde that nowe ys and hereafter to be made by the seid John Heyron, . . . be a sufficient discharge to every suche Persone ayenst the Kyng . . . Aswell in the Kynges Eschequiour as in eny other of the Kinges Courtes."[9]

The same parliament continued the policy of making concessions to public opinion by passing an act which condemned the activities of Empson and Dudley and allowed those who had suffered from untrue inquisitions to traverse them, even if they had already

[7] *Letters and Papers of Henry VIII*, vol. 1, Nos. 765 and 835; Carole Rawcliffe, *The Staffords, Earls of Stafford and Dukes of Buckingham 1394–1521* (Cambridge: Cambridge University Press, 1978), 36.

[8] F. C. Dietz, *English Government Finance 1485–1558* (2nd edn, London: Frank Cass, 1964), 60.

[9] 1 Hen. VIII, c.3, *Statutes of the Realm*, 11 vols. (London, 1810–22), vol. 3, 2.

sued livery.[10] Though such a concession might prevent land-holders from suffering in the future by changing the record, the effectiveness of the act as a remedy for past ills was reduced by a proviso which stated that tenants who traversed an inquisition successfully would not receive the money they had lost in the meantime.[11] It is possible that this proviso rendered the act effectively useless to those who had suffered, or that the time and expense of traversing an inquisition on land that had already been liveried was more trouble than it was worth, but the fact remains that there was no rush to take advantage of the statute. Though trouble and expense may have been a factor in this, it also supports the argument that Empson and Dudley did not work outside the law, and it indicates that any moral outrage their methods might have caused could not be expected to stand up in court. It is clear that it was generally believed that there had been something rotten in the conduct of inquisitions, and another statute of the same parliament set out the rules to be followed by escheators and commissioners, because

> diverse of the Kynges Sugiectes lately have ben sore hurte troubled and some disherited by Escheatours and Commyssyoners causyng untrue offices to be founden, and sometyme retornyng into the Courtes of [recordes] offices and inquisicions that warre never founde, And sometyme changyng the mater of the Offices that were truely founden to the greate hurte troble and disheryson of the Kynges true Sugiectes, that lyke before tyme have nott ben sean in this realme.[12]

If we can say nothing stronger, however, the quiet reception of the statute granting traverses at least indicates that Empson and Dudley's activities were less burdensome than the process for reversing them.

Beyond the act which confirmed Heron's role in the financial administration of the prerogative, no further statutory changes were made in that year. Henry's policy of appeasement was so successful, in fact, that in 1510 there were rumours that Sir John Hussey was to be removed from his office of master of the wards, as part of a general dismantling of Henry VII's system.[13] Nevertheless, the chamber system continued to function. Sir Robert Southwell and Bartholomew Westby acted as surveyors of royal lands from

[10] 1 Hen. VIII, c.12, *Stat. Realm*, vol. 3, 7.

[11] *Ibid.* [12] 1 Hen. VIII, c.8, *Stat. Realm*, vol. 3, 4.

[13] H. E. Bell, *An Introduction to the History and Records of the Court of Wards and Liveries* (Cambridge: Cambridge University Press, 1953), 8.

at least the middle of 1510 onwards, and in 1511 the king issued a commission to them to survey and approve the royal lands in Wales, Cornwall, Chester, Flint, York, March, and Richmond as well as other lands in royal hands through attainder or forfeit.[14] This does not seem to have been enough to restrain the exchequer, and in the parliament of 1511–12 Southwell and Westby were given "a further and strenger auctorite" when parliament "ordeigned, established and enacted . . . that the said Sir Robert Southwell knight and Bartholomew Westby bee fromhensfurth general Surveiours and Approwers of all and singuler the Kings [lands]."[15] The statute opens by rehearsing the system established by Henry VII and pointing out its advantages, namely, that it was quicker and cheaper than the old procedure through the exchequer. There is no attempt to distance the new regime from the chamber machinery; in fact, the act states that the new king desires "the same and semblable order of accompte to contynue to be had and used . . . and to be answered of his revenues in his Chambre in maner and fourme abovesaide."[16]

Though statutory regulation gave the chamber system authority, it also greatly reduced its flexibility. Under Henry VII, the chamber system took its authority directly from the king and it needed no other. By removing the chamber from the personal direction of the king, Henry VIII made it both more independent and less powerful. It managed to resist the claims of the exchequer, but by 1515 the royal income from land had fallen to about £25,000 per annum, compared to £40,000 per annum at the death of Henry VII.[17] Without the personal interest of the king and the stimulus of his own immediate political and financial plans, the chamber was just another financial office. The chamber system, and prerogative finance, would not receive much of Henry's attention until money once again became a major issue.[18]

[14] *Letters and Papers of Henry VIII*, vol. 1, 217.

[15] 3 Hen. VIII, c.23, *Stat. Realm*, vol. 3, 45. Bartholomew Westby was one of the barons of the exchequer. The earlier commission under privy seal of June 1510 is referred to in this act.

[16] *Ibid.*

[17] B. P. Wolffe, *The Crown Lands 1461–1536: An Aspect of Yorkist and Early Tudor Government* (New York: Barnes & Noble, 1970), 85.

[18] However, the system continued to work to protect the king's rights. For example, the Attorney-General investigated all collusive recoveries to ensure that the king's fiscal rights were not infringed and "filled several rolls each term in the Common Pleas with recognizances taken from deforciants to ensure against any prejudice to the king's wardships." Baker, *Spelman's Reports*, vol. 2, 208.

Henry's grandiose foreign policy ensured that it was only a matter of time before he needed to make the most of his financial resources. There was a new interest in the reorganization of the administrative structure, particularly in the administration of the prerogative, in the years after 1518. Bell points to new appointments to wardship offices between 1518 and 1520 as evidence of the revitalization of that area, and argues that it was made necessary because of the decay of Henry VII's system.[19] He refers to a memorandum, undated but probably of this period, which complains that the practice of selling the lands of wards as well as their bodies had greatly reduced the king's profits from his prerogative. It recommends that the king should rebuild an official structure to manage the lands of wards and guard his interests. The memorandum's most telling point, however, comes at the end, when the author comments that:

> onles yt may plese your grace to be at some comynycation in yt yourself And to haue certen articles drawen and subscrybed for the spedynes of the same yt is supposed it wulbe long or this mater woll forward or come to eny good purpose.[20]

The problem was not so much in the structure of the administration, which had not changed greatly from Henry VII's days, as in the attitude of the king himself.

It is clear that around this time the king's attitude changed. At some time around 1519 Henry seems to have decided to take governing seriously, and he had a programme of reform drawn up which would have allowed him to rule in person. The reforms dealt with a variety of matters, and they included orders for John Heron and William Compton to make monthly reports of receipts and payments in the chamber, and for the surveyor of the king's lands to make a yearly declaration.[21] These plans were intended to restore the kind of government established by Henry VII; as Scarisbrick comments, "it appeared that . . . Henry had turned his back on the past and was preparing to become an industrious, working

[19] Bell, *Court of Wards and Liveries*, 9–10.

[20] SP 1/159, f.47. Printed in full in Bell, *Court of Wards and Liveries*, Appendix 1, 187–89.

[21] *Letters and Papers of Henry VIII*, vol. 3, 197. The memorandum also provides for such matters as the administration of the duchy of Lancaster, the settling of Ireland, and regular reports from the justices of the central courts.

monarch bent on high purposes. Never had he looked so like his father."[22]

Whether the impulse for reform came from Henry himself or, more likely, from Wolsey, there is no doubt that it was both genuine and short-lived. Though Wolsey did his best, there was no return to the personal government of Henry VII. Nevertheless, the reform proposals were born out of genuine need, and, while Henry did not transform himself, there was a recognition of the need for more efficient government. As Richardson points out, by 1521 the chamber treasury was basically empty, and, while this was not a cause for alarm as yet, it meant that the government needed to re-evaluate its financial resources.[23] This concern was clearly connected with the military capacity of the country, for in 1522 Wolsey carried out a military survey, noted by Hall, who remarks that at "this tyme commission was geuen throughout the realme, for general musters to be had, to knowe what power might be made within thesame, & also men sworne of what substaunce and landes thei wer of. And the Cardinal aduertised of thesame; not without grudging of the people, and marueilyng why thei should be sworne for their awne goodes."[24] This survey was unusual, because for the first time in a hundred years it gave the exchequer a detailed listing of individual wealth, and it obviously annoyed a land-holding population which questioned the government's rights and motives.[25] There was clearly a new concern with the financial state of the kingdom and a desire to establish a certain knowledge of both the wealth of the people and their military obligations. Thus Spelman's reading, delivered in Lent of 1521, was a timely contribution to the growing interest in the reformation of the prerogative administration. Though the government of his time was concerned with financial retrenchment rather than political manipulation, once again a serjeant-elect chose to read on *Prerogativa Regis* at a time when the text was of great political interest.

Spelman is the first Gray's Inn reader known to have addressed the prerogative after the recent Inner Temple dominance of the

[22] J. J. Scarisbrick, *Henry VIII* (Berkeley: University of California Press, 1968), 125.

[23] W. C. Richardson, *Tudor Chamber Administration 1485–1547* (Baton Rouge: Louisiana State University Press, 1952), 233.

[24] Hall, *Chronicle*, 630.

[25] R. W. Hoyle, "Crown, Parliament and Taxation in Sixteenth-Century England," *English Historical Review* 109 (1994): 1178.

topic. Nevertheless, Spelman built on the readings delivered by his predecessors in the traditional manner. He was well placed to develop Frowyk's arguments, for in 1516 he acted as executor of Frowyk's widow, and in that capacity he acquired some of Frowyk's manuscripts.[26] Though much of his reading does in fact follow Frowyk's interpretation, it is clear that he also had access to Constable's ideas, and he prefers Constable to Frowyk on occasion.

The surviving manuscript of Spelman's reading is much shorter than that of either Constable or Frowyk, suggesting that it might be seen as a commentary on, or perhaps a supplement to, the earlier expositions, though Spelman does not make direct reference to his predecessors as Port had done. It is possible that Spelman's reading differed in its structure from the earlier readings, but this is unlikely, for it faced the same need to be comprehensible to a mixed audience. It is more likely that the auditor who recorded the notes made the choice to preserve them in this form, retaining only the information of interest to one already familiar with the issues. Thus the manuscript does not cover the more basic topics, such as forms of landholding, but deals only with the issues surrounding the prerogative. In keeping with this, rather than examining Spelman in the same detail as the earlier readers, we will consider him only as he comments on and continues their work.

Spelman's treatment of *Prerogativa Regis* also allows us a closer glimpse into the process of constructing a reading. By the time he delivered the reading, his third, in 1521, Spelman had been at Gray's Inn for about twenty years.[27] During that time he had been engaged in collecting reports of cases argued in the courts as well as discussions which took place around the Inns. His reports were arranged in alphabetical order, and a large part of the section titled *Prerogative* is made up of notes from a reading.[28] The notes begin with chapter one of the text, but are quickly interrupted by a memorandum on the death of Henry VII, the accession of Henry VIII, the imprisonment of Empson and Dudley, and the swearing-in of the justices. More notes from a reading follow the memorandum, and they again begin with chapter one of the text. It is possible that

[26] Baker, *Spelman's Reports*, vol. 1, xiii. It is not exactly clear which manuscripts Spelman owned. Baker cites a year book (BL MS Add. 37659) which belonged to both Frowyk and Spelman. Spelman maintained his connection with the Frowyk family, marrying Frowyk's niece, Elizabeth, in the late 1520s.

[27] Baker, *Spelman's Reports*, vol. 1, ix. [28] *Ibid*., vol. 1, 174–83.

they are a continuation of the earlier notes, but there is no clear evidence either way, and the reading is undated and anonymous. Baker argues that this is not Spelman's own reading, but speculates that it is a paraphrase of Frowyk's reading, or of a reading which drew heavily on Frowyk.[29] If the paraphrase is contemporary with the memorandum, it suggests that Spelman's interest in the topic dated from early in his legal career. A rough contemporaneity might also suggest that the paraphrase is Port's reading, or an early copy of it, since it seems unlikely that Spelman was visiting readings in other Inns at this early stage in his career. However, there is no discernible relationship between the surviving manuscript of Port's reading and the paraphrase, and we know from Port that manuscript versions of Frowyk's reading were in circulation at the time. The paraphrase does not cover an entire reading, but it gives us an idea of the material available to Spelman when he went to construct his reading and allows us to see some of the places where he consciously chose to deviate from the interpretations of his predecessors. The reasons for the choices he made vary from topic to topic, suggesting that, like the earlier readers, Spelman was not driven simply by the desire to make a particular political point, but by the need to expound the law.

Spelman opens with the same central issue as the earlier readers, namely, what kind of tenure brings the royal prerogative. It is clear from the beginning of the lecture that Spelman is not following any one reader. He states that anyone who holds land which has escheated to the crown for felony, treason, or failure of heirs, or which has come to the crown through purchase or descent, does not hold in chief.[30] This statement is marked with a *quere* in the text, as it might well be, for it disagrees with both Frowyk and Constable. Spelman goes on to consider whether, when a mesnalty held of the king in chief escheats to the king, the tenant should hold of the king in chief as the mesne lord had done. He rehearses a variety of possibilities, as Constable had done, but he reaches no firm conclusion, for the issue turns on a difficult principle. His discussion ends with a succinct statement of the problem: "it is not reason to cause the tenant to be in worse condition against the king than he was against the mesne where there was no fault in him. And others say that it is better for the tenant to suffer loss than the

[29] *Ibid.*, vol. 1, 174, n.1.
[30] Spelman, Gray's Inn MS 25, f.303.

king and it is not reason that the king shall lose the advantage of his lordship where there is no fault in him, and therefore the law favours the king."[31] Spelman's explicit concern for the welfare of the tenant most closely echoes Boteler's position in *Stonor's Case*,[32] though he does not go so far as to place the tenant's rights above those of the king. Here Spelman takes the arguments made by the previous readers and reduces them to a point of principle, but he comes no closer to solving the problem.

When it comes to wardship Spelman's interpretation does borrow from both of the earlier readers. He believes that *Prerogativa Regis* "is only a confirmation of the common law" but that before the text "if one held of the king as of an escheat which is in his hands and not part of his crown, there the priority held as between common persons."[33] Thus he reaches much the same conclusion as Constable, that part of *Prerogativa Regis* is a declaration of the common law, and part is new, though he approaches it from a slightly different angle. Spelman appears to be evading the question of the status of *Prerogativa Regis*. He begins by stating that it is a declaration of the common law, but then he adds that it changes the law. He does the same thing in chapter one, where he says that "the beginning of this letter is a declaration of the common law and that this was the common law appears by Magna Carta cc.22 and 29 and common reason gives this to the king . . . And by the exception *de feodis archiepiscopi* etc. all this branch is a statute, for before this time the king had the wardship of lands held of such persons."[34] Thus he is unwilling to follow Constable completely and state that *Prerogativa Regis* is a statute rather than a treatise, but he admits that parts of the text establish new law. If we were to follow this to its logical conclusion, that a treatise by the sages of the law could change the law, the implications for the law-making powers of the legal profession, and by extension for the readers, are enormous. Spelman does not make such grandiose claims, but both his argument and the fact that it occasions no comment suggest that the inhabitants of the Inns were accustomed to think of themselves as law-shapers. By emphasizing that the text is a treatise, Spelman is placing himself among those who would wish to restrict the growth of the prerogative, but his recognition that part of the text makes new law is a concession

[31] Spelman, f.304. [32] See chapter 2, p. 82 above.
[33] Spelman, f.304. [34] Spelman, f.303.

to the reality of the situation. It demonstrates that both Constable's and Frowyk's readings had affected his perception of the text. It may also indicate that by 1521 the non-statutory nature of the text needed less emphasis and that Frowyk's reading had done its work in inclining the profession towards a strict interpretation.

Although there is no substantive relationship between their readings, Spelman does pick up on Port's concerns with regard to the wording of grants. For example, he argues that, when the king grants custody, this implies "the profits of the land etc., yet if the king grants the wardship of the body without speaking of marriage, the grantee cannot marry him."[35] Similarly, he is at pains to explain the implications of the different forms of grant. He points out that "if the king grants a [male] ward *durante minore etate sue* this is until 21 years and after this the grantee shall not have the ward, even if [he] does not sue livery for 10 years; but it is otherwise if he is granted *quam diu in manibus nostris fore contigerit.*" This is fairly straightforward, but Spelman then asks the obvious question: "whether after he is of the age of 21 years the king can grant the wardship afterwards *quam diu in manibus nostris fore contigerit*?"[36] There is clearly a desire to establish the exact implications of the various kinds of grant, and to determine how far the king can push the logical implications of his rights. The distinction Spelman makes between grants *durante minore etate* and *quam diu in manibus nostris fore contigerit* is quite logical, and the implication that a ward granted under the latter form of words would remain in the grantee's hands until he sued livery is not unreasonable. After all, it was up to the ward to sue livery, and such a provision would simply be an added incentive to do so without delay. To suggest, however, that the king might be able to grant wardships of those over the age of majority who had not sued livery, was to open a completely different issue. If applied, it would mean that wardships discovered years after the fact could be claimed and granted, and, theoretically at least, heirs well advanced in age could find themselves in ward to the king and granted to others. There is no doubt that this would provide a powerful incentive to sue livery, but it would also arouse enormous resentment. It is unlikely that it was ever seriously considered for general use, but Spelman's discussion of the issue raises some questions. It may simply reflect a shifting emphasis in the law; it

[35] Spelman, f.303. [36] Spelman, f.304v.

is notable that both Port and Spelman pay more attention to wording and the detail of administrative procedure than either Frowyk or Constable, and this may reflect a greater concern for the practical administrative details of a well-developed office. It is also possible that this office was engaged in pushing the implications of the administrative structure as far as it could go.

Spelman addresses other issues which also suggest a search for new wardships. He argues that the king will have the wardship of the body of the heir of one who held land of him in chief or in escheat, even if his ancestor held land of the bishop of Durham or others mentioned in chapter one of the text, since chapter one refers only to lands. From this point he goes on to question whether the king would have the wardship of the body of the heir when the king had bought, or inherited from a collateral ancestor, the manor from which the ancestor held.[37] It was agreed that he did not have his prerogative in the lands of such manors, but did that prevent him from claiming wardship of the body? Spelman does not explicitly claim such rights for the king, nor does he suggest that he thinks that they would be appropriate. The simple fact that such tortuous claims were being raised, however, is an indication that they were at least being considered, possibly as a result of the revitalization of the wardship office. It is likely that Spelman's reading was a testing ground for some new interpretations, though whether those interpretations were already being used in practice or were still in the realm of theory is not at all clear.

When it comes to primer seisin, Spelman follows Frowyk in broad terms. He does not accept Constable's idea that the king should have primer seisin of lands held of him in escheat, and he has clearly given the question some thought. The paraphrase of the earlier reading notes that "the king shall have primer seisin of all the lands whereof his tenant died seised, if any parcel is held of the king *in capite*, whether held in socage or in chivalry. But it must be held *in capite*."[38] Similarly, in his reading Spelman states that the king has primer seisin of all the lands his tenant held of him by knight service or socage and of the lands he held of other lords by any kind of service, as long as he held any parcel of the king in chief.[39] Thus Spelman's reading, taken with his notes from

[37] Spelman, f.304.

[38] Baker, *Spelman's Reports*, vol. 1, 181.

[39] Spelman, f.306.

the earlier reading, make it clear that on this question he followed Frowyk. Like Frowyk, he argues that *Prerogativa Regis* extends the statute of Marlborough by applying primer seisin to lands held in socage in chief and lands held of other lords. While Frowyk, concerned to prove that *Prerogativa Regis* is not a statute, argued that this had always been the case and Marlborough had simply been too narrowly interpreted, Spelman is quite happy to present the provisions of *Prerogativa Regis* as an innovation.[40]

There were some issues raised by this question of primer seisin over lands held in socage in chief which continued to be of interest from 1495 until after Spelman's reading. The paraphrase notes that "if one holds of the king in socage *in capite*, and of another by knight service, and dies, his heir aged fourteen years: in this case the king shall have primer seisin of the lands held of himself, and the other person shall have the wardship of the other land."[41] Port also made this point, differing with Frowyk.[42] There was, however, a problem with this, as Spelman noted, for the statute said that the king should have primer seisin of everything of which his tenant died seised, the argument which Frowyk supported. Spelman did not consider the issue in his reading, or at least no discussion has survived, but it was again raised at a later date and Brudenell, Coningsby, and Fitzherbert agreed with the paraphrase and argued "that the statute must be taken [to mean] that the king shall have primer seisin of all the lands etc. where the land held of him is held by knight service and not otherwise."[43] Thus, though the king's rights to primer seisin were extended to include lands held in socage, they were limited by the normal patterns of socage holdings. Though this may seem obvious, it is still worth noting that primer seisin was trimmed to fit with socage, rather than the reverse.

Spelman's interest in this issue and his general fidelity to Frowyk's views suggest that he would incline towards limiting the king's rights, and this is indeed the case. Probably the most convincing proof that Spelman did not accept Constable's view of primer seisin is the fact that he provides no discussion of lands held of the king as of escheat. His concern, like Frowyk's, is with the

[40] Spelman, f.306.

[41] Baker, *Spelman's Reports*, vol. 1, 183. [42] Hargrave 87, f.146.

[43] Baker, *Spelman's Reports*, vol. 1, 183. The date of the discussion is not noted, but Baker suggests that it took place in the exchequer chamber or Serjeants' Inn between 1523 and 1531.

relationship between the king's rights to primer seisin and his rights to wardship, though, unlike Frowyk, he mixes the king's rights to wardship and primer seisin. In discussing primer seisin, he often limits the king's rights more than Frowyk had done. For example, he argues that, if the king's tenant-in-chief also holds lands in borough English and has two sons and dies, the king will not have primer seisin of all, but only of that to which his tenant is heir.[44] Frowyk gave the king the right to primer seisin of all,[45] but in limiting primer seisin thus, Spelman is reducing it to the same range as the king's right to wardship under the same circumstances. He makes the same argument where lands held of the father in chief and of the mother (not in chief) descend to the heir. In this case, he argues, the king will not have primer seisin of the land inherited from the mother.[46]

Spelman's reading does not merely reproduce Frowyk, or even intensify Frowyk's restrictions on the king. There are places in Spelman's lecture where he rejects the arguments made by the earlier readers, even when they were in agreement. Both Constable and Frowyk had argued that, if the king's tenant enfeoffed another of land held in chief in fee, or was disseised of it, the king would not have primer seisin of that land when the tenant died, and Port agreed. Spelman agrees with them in the former case, because the deceased tenant is not a tenant of the land by right.[47] He disagrees, however, in the case of disseisin, because the king's tenant was a tenant by right in that case, even though he was out of possession.[48] Thus Spelman is reversing Frowyk's stand and arguing that right alone, without possession, is enough to give the king primer seisin, at least in the land held of him.[49] However, where the tenant gives away his right, even through a feoffment made without licence, the king has no claim to primer seisin. This differs from the paraphrase, which states that "if the tenant is disseised, and dies, the king shall not have primer seisin thereof, but he shall have wardship. And if the heir enters, then the king shall have primer seisin."[50] Thus the paraphrase represents the position taken by Constable, Frowyk, and Port, and there is no query or argument appended to it. By the time

44 Spelman, f.306. 45 See chapter 3, p. 117 above.

46 Spelman, f.306. 47 Spelman, f.306. 48 Spelman, f.306.

49 If the king's tenant was disseised of land held of another, the king would not have primer seisin of it, but only of the land held of him.

50 Baker, *Spelman's Reports*, vol. 1, 182.

of his reading, Spelman's view had changed, or developed, to the point where he believed that the king should have primer seisin in this case. He uses the same principle, i.e. that the king should have primer seisin of whatever his tenant held on the day of his death, whether in possession or in right, to argue that when the king's tenant "makes a lease for years or for life etc. and dies seised of the reversion and of lands held of others, the king shall have the primer seisin of the reversion and also of all the other lands."[51]

Spelman also argues against Constable's theories on the issue of leases. He says that "it is said that if the king's tenant-in-chief makes a lease for term of life to my tenant, with the reversion over in fee, in this case if my tenant dies the king shall have the primer seisin of the land whereof he was tenant for term of life, because he was his tenant thereof. And therefore he shall also have the lands held of me."[52] This argument was Constable's,[53] and Spelman believes that it is not valid because "the remainderman shall have livery of this and my tenant [shall have] livery of the land held of me, and because the king's tenant shall not have livery of everything at the one time, it seems that he shall only have primer seisin of that whereof his own tenant may sue livery."[54] Thus Spelman is rejecting Constable's argument that such tenants would first sue *ouster le main* of the king, and then, presumably, livery from their own lord. He returns to Frowyk's principle that the king can only have primer seisin when he can give livery, though he applies it even more strictly than Frowyk. He does not mention Constable's argument that the tenant should sue livery whenever the land changes hands, whether the change in possession was temporary or permanent, but in his reports he takes care to note that "after the death of a joint tenant the king shall not have primer seisin. And if the wife inherits and dies, and the husband has it by the curtesy, the king shall not have primer seisin."[55] Though, as we have seen, the notes from Spelman's reports do not necessarily represent his own position, it is unlikely that any support given by him to Constable's argument would have gone unnoticed in his reading, especially since it would have gone against his general inclination to interpret the text strictly. Constable's interpretation was clearly novel in 1495 and would not have been standard by 1521.

[51] Spelman, f.306. [52] Spelman, f.306. [53] See chapter 3, pp. 118–19 above.
[54] Spelman, f.306. [55] Baker, *Spelman's Reports*, vol. 1, 182.

In dealing with this question of leases, Spelman was considerably clearer than his predecessors, probably as a result of having time to consider their arguments. In the end, Spelman and Frowyk agree on the final result, though their principles differ, and Spelman's position was the more logical of the two. Frowyk would not have accepted Spelman's statement that the king can have primer seisin even when his tenant dies only with either possession of, or right to, land, but Frowyk's own reading shows him to have been somewhat inconsistent. It is hard to blame him for theoretical weaknesses, for Frowyk's reading shows little attempt at a consideration of the principles involved in the law under discussion. He is concerned mainly to show how the law worked in practice and to begin an examination of the theory. Spelman, on the other hand, had many years in which to consider the principles behind the law which Frowyk and Constable had expounded and to develop a clearer theory on which to rest his argument.

Spelman's reading, following on Port's, indicates that the legal profession was not convinced by Constable's interpretation of *Prerogativa Regis*, or that it was worried by the rigorous application of the prerogative under Henry VII, and that it was more inclined to follow a strict interpretation of the text. In practice, this meant the rejection of any attempt to allow the king to seize lands which were not inherited directly by his tenant-in-chief, which were not changing hands permanently, and of which the king could not give livery.[56] Like Frowyk and Constable, however, Spelman was directed more by his interpretation of the law than by his attitude to royal rights. Although he regularly seeks to restrict the king's claims, in relation to both primer seisin and wardship, he is quite happy to extend his rights where the logic of the law dictates that he should. Thus, having determined that the king can claim primer seisin when his tenant dies having land in possession or in right, he applies that principle equally. Spelman's reading seems to be oriented more towards a consideration of the principles underlying the king's rights than either of his predecessors, suggesting that the profession was developing a more sophisticated interpretation of the prerogative.

[56] Spelman does note a situation where the king could have primer seisin without a descent: if the tenant died without an heir, so that the lands escheated to the king, the king would still have primer seisin. Baker, *Spelman's Reports*, vol. 1, 182.

Besides furthering the discussion of issues raised by his predecessors, Spelman also highlights issues to which the earlier readers had devoted little attention. His examination of the wording of wardship grants is one such example, and it indicates the increased concern with exactitude in the administration of the prerogative.[57] Another area which figures prominently in Spelman's treatment is uses and their effect on the prerogative. Spelman's discussion of uses makes it clear that the statute of 1490 had significantly changed the way in which land was handled and devised, in a way which had not been obvious to the readers in 1495, and which Port seems to have wished to avoid. The earlier readers did not deal with uses in any detail and they did not consider the impact of wills on land held in use. Spelman's treatment, on the other hand, reflects the dispute presented in *Stonor's Case*, and the resolution noted by Caryll.[58]

Unlike the other readers, Spelman discusses uses in his lecture on chapter one of the text, treating them simply as another way of holding land. He points out that though "the letter [of the text] is that he [the deceased tenant] must be seised in fee . . . the statute is not taken this way, for if there is a tenant in tail with the remainder in fee to another, it is all one."[59] Thus, even though the king's tenant did not hold the land in fee, as long as he held it at the time of his death the king would have his prerogative in it. The same logic is extended to land in use, so that, if lands held of another were in use to the king's tenant, the king could claim his prerogative in them. He also argues that, if lands held of the king and lands held of another were in use, the king would have his prerogative in them all.[60] By treating uses as simply another form of landholding, Spelman is opening them up to the kind of extension the earlier readers had made, and allowing uses to attract the prerogative in both directions.[61] Thus, when the king's tenant was the feoffor, the king would have his prerogative, and, when the king's tenant was the feoffee, the king also benefited. This is a logical conclusion, based both on the decision of 1506 and on his own principle that the king should have his prerogative whether the tenant died in possession

[57] This is also reflected in the king's bench material concerning prerogative cases. As the years go on, the records become increasingly precise and detailed, taking care not to omit anything which might make the case *minus sufficiens in lege*. Though such a change is largely impressionistic and difficult to detail, it is quite clear.

[58] *Caryll's Reports*, vol. 2, 530. See chapter 2, pp. 105–11 above.

[59] Spelman, f.303. [60] Spelman, f.303. [61] See chapter 2, pp. 94–96 above.

of the land, or simply with a right to it. This interpretation also seems to have been generally accepted by the profession, for in 1522 Newdigate noted that, if the feoffor or the *cestui que use* died with his heir under age, the lord would have the wardship in either case "and thus he shall have two wardships for one tenancy."[62]

However, Spelman does retain his desire to restrict the king's rights to the letter of the law. Though the decision in 1506 had allowed the king wardship "as well of the lands of which his [the tenant's] ancestor died seised in use as in possession, as well of land held in socage as by knight service," Spelman seems to have responded against the king's claim to land in socage.[63] His reading does not emphasize the point, but his reports note that:

> though the land held of the king is in use, or in reversion, and the land held of the other is in possession, the king shall have the prerogative. But it is always necessary that the land held of the king should be held of him by knight service and *in capite*, and not in socage. And if one acre is held of the king as of his Duchy of Lancaster, by knight service, and another acre of the king by socage, yet he shall not have prerogative.[64]

Though the manuscript of his reading does not develop the distinction between the king's rights to land in chief and in socage, it does echo the report in its argument that "if the land is held of the duchy and also other land is held of the crown in socage, the king shall not have them."[65] It thus seems likely that Spelman did in fact oppose the general view that the statute of 1490 gave the king prerogative rights over all lands in use, and this fits with the argument above that the king should generally not have prerogative rights in socage land.

Spelman's discussion thus far is based on the assumption that the tenant had not made a will. If the tenant had made a will, the situation was changed somewhat. If lands held of others were in use and the king's tenant disposed of them by will for a term of years, the king would have no prerogative in them for that term. If, however, the tenant merely disposed of part of the profits from such lands, the king would have whatever was left. If the tenant held land of the king and of another in use and disposed of the profits of the land held of the king without any mention of the other land,

62 YB Mich. 14 Hen. VIII, f.5, pl.5.

63 *Caryll's Reports*, vol. 2, 530. 64 Baker, *Spelman's Reports*, vol. 1, 176.

65 Spelman, f.303.

the king would have his prerogative in that land.[66] Again, Spelman is assuming that the land in use, because it is held of the king, will transmit a right to the prerogative in the lands held of the other lords, though presumably only where the lands were held of the king in chief.

Besides the king's general rights to lands in use, Spelman also considers the more specific questions of wardship and primer seisin. The statute of 1490 allowed the king to retain the wardship of the body of his tenant, and this led to some complications in process. For example, how were the feoffees to regain possession of the land held of the king? It seems that the most common method was by suing special livery, a method which would avoid many awkward questions, for the feoffees would simply pay a fee in order to get a blanket livery. Spelman argues, however, that "the law is that they shall have *ouster le main*."[67] He does not elaborate on the reasons why *ouster le main* is more appropriate than livery, but clearly he believes that, since the feoffees hold the land in use rather than in fee, the king has no right to seize the land or to grant livery of it to them. Once again, he is reacting against the kind of argument made by Constable that the king should grant livery of land held of him every time it changes hands and is favouring the more restrictive idea that the king should grant livery of land only when it passes by descent.

Wardship also allows Spelman another opportunity to present uses as simply another form of landholding. He questions what will happen if a tenant with feoffees to his use dies leaving an heir under age, who goes on to take the profits from the land during his nonage. If, when the heir comes to his full age, an inquisition finds that he was under age at the time of the death of his father, and now he is of full age, will he be able to sue livery or not? Spelman argues that, under normal conditions, if an heir intruded without suing livery, the king would re-seize the lands, as would also happen if an heir intruded after the death of a tenant in dower. Though he does not state it explicitly, the implication is clearly that the heir of the *cestui que use* should also be subject to this penalty.[68]

Though, in discussing wardship, Spelman tries to reduce uses to simply another form of landholding, it is clear that this was not

[66] Spelman, f.303. [67] Spelman, f.306v.
[68] Spelman, f.306v. The manuscript, which is always difficult, is particularly obscure at this point, but this is quite clearly the general gist of his argument.

universally true. Uses still retained some of the functions which had made them popular in the first place, and which had not been changed by the statute of 1490. Quite simply, as the paraphrase puts it, "if the lands were in feoffment to use, then the king shall not have primer seisin, for this is not remedied by any statute [in the way that] wardship is remedied."[69] This, along with Spelman's treatment of wardships, indicates that the king still had much to do if he was to eliminate the effects of uses on his feudal revenue. His position was much stronger than Frowyk had allowed, and by 1521 there was no doubt that the statute of 1490 applied to his tenants. However, it helped him only when his tenant held land in knight service, had died without making a will, and left an heir under age. On the other hand, while Spelman makes it clear that Frowyk was over-ruled in his exclusion of the king from the statute, he makes it equally clear that Constable's over-enthusiasm for the king's rights was also rejected. Uses had long been a standard element of landholding patterns, and, by the time that Spelman lectured, the effects of the statute of 1490 had been thoroughly integrated into those patterns. He treats uses as a regular part of the system, and one which brought many of the same benefits and burdens as other methods of holding lands, but which retained its own peculiarities. Uses were still a convenient method of avoiding certain feudal burdens, despite royal attempts to curb them.

Spelman's treatment of uses as part of the common law was made possible largely through statutes of 1484 and 1490. Richard III's statute allowed the *cestui que use* to make a feoffment of land binding at common law. This was intended to protect the purchaser, but it had the effect of allowing titles to land to pass through uses and thus it presented the *cestui que use* as in some way the owner of the land. The statute of 1490, in allowing the devise of land held in use, had a different, but still profound, effect. Though it made no statement on the status of the use, by allowing devises it tacitly accepted the situation and provided common law protection. Thus, as the years passed, lawyers brought uses into the common law family.

That the fresh interest in the prerogative reflected in Spelman's reading continued unabated is clear from the administrative changes of the following years. A statute of 1523 bolstered the office of the king's general surveyors and laid out in detail both their

[69] Baker, *Spelman's Reports*, vol. 1, 181.

scope and their authority, re-affirming their independence from the exchequer.[70] In 1526, the crown went beyond this when it began a new campaign to recoup its losses, with the appointment of William Paulet as joint master of the king's wards. Although he shared the office, he combined it with that of receiver-general, prompting Bean to regard this as the development of a new phase in the administration of the prerogative and the beginning of the Court of Wards.[71] In the same year, "alienations by tenants in chief were only permitted on condition that prospective fiscal loss to the crown was indemnified. Penal recognizances were devised in the case of each and every such permitted alienation, which were enrolled in chancery."[72] These methods are familiar, and they show the crown relying on the combination of its traditional feudal right to license alienations and the more recent development of the use of recognizances to enforce those rights. The campaign quickly moved beyond these fairly passive activities, and in June 1526 a meeting of the king's council commanded the king's attorney and solicitor "that they shall have all such in accion as alieneth any lands which are houlden of the king as of his Crowne ymmediately and also as well those which selleth lands wherof the kinge is in the Reversion as them which maketh Alienacion whereby the king looseth livery or primer seisin."[73]

Though the implementation of these traditional methods of enforcement shows a renewed interest in the exploitation of the prerogative, they had little effect on the problems generated by uses, and by the end of the decade Henry VIII had decided that a frontal assault on uses themselves was necessary. There were many arguments against uses. The fact that they interfered with feudal incidents was a major irritant for the king, but that irritation was less for other lords, who compensated for the loss of their feudal incidents by depriving the king. Other facets of uses were of more concern to

[70] 14 & 15 Hen. VIII, c.15, *Stat. Realm*, vol. 3, 219–30. In 1535–36, the statute 27 Hen. VIII, c.62, *Stat. Realm*, vol. 3, 631–32, reinforced this and made it perpetual.

[71] J. M. W. Bean, *The Decline of English Feudalism 1215–1540* (New York: Manchester University Press, 1968), 237.

[72] J. A. Guy, *Christopher St. German on Chancery and Statute*, Selden Society supplementary series vol. 6 (London: Selden Society, 1985), 78.

[73] Phillips MS lot 581, sold at Sotheby's 26 June 1967. Quoted in Guy, *St. German on Chancery and Statute*, 79; cf. also E. W. Ives, "The Genesis of the Statute of Uses," *English Historical Review* 82 (1967): 675.

the general landholding public. The ability to direct land to others than the legitimate heir, which was one of the benefits of uses, was also one of its problems, and the obscured titles it caused increased the possibility for fraud.

Rather than seeking simply to enforce royal rights, two documents of this time sought to reform the way in which uses were administered by dealing with all of these problems. The documents are undated, but clearly belong to the period between 1529 and 1532. One is in the form of a draft bill, though its provenance is disputed, and the other is an agreement between the king and the nobility.[74] The former sets out to deal with the confusions in title caused by both entails and uses, and would do this by abolishing entails entirely and invalidating uses unless they were recorded in the common pleas.[75] The clear purpose of the bill is to ensure publicity in the transfer of lands. Not only does it require that uses be recorded, it also seeks to have all purchases of land read aloud in church on the Sunday following the sale and it prevents noblemen from selling any of their land without a licence from the king. Though this bill, if passed, would have done much to clear away the confusion surrounding titles to land and would have allowed the king to see clearly what was owed to him, it in no way helped him to get his due.[76]

The second document, the king's agreement with the nobility, was closely connected with the first, and went a long way towards achieving the king's wishes. The agreement would allow the nobility to continue to enjoy many of the benefits of uses, while giving the king guaranteed access to a certain proportion of his feudal rights. It opens with two statements, one clearly based on *Prerogativa Regis* and the other on the statute of 1490, which present the situation as it

[74] Holdsworth and Bean believe that the draft bill is of government origin, while Ives sees it as the work of an enthusiastic amateur. W. Holdsworth, *A History of English Law* (3rd edn, London: Methuen, 1966), vol. 4, 450; Bean, *Decline of English Feudalism*, 259–61; Ives, "Genesis of the Statute of Uses," 677–80.

[75] Holdsworth, *History of English Law*, vol. 4, 572–73. The bill mitigates the abolition of entails by allowing nobles to continue to use them. It was thus intended to preserve primogeniture purely within the nobility in order to maintain the power of the landed classes. See T. F. T. Plucknett, "Some Proposed Legislation of Henry VIII," *Trans. Royal Hist. Soc.*, 4th ser. 19 (1936): 122–25; A. R. Buck, "The Politics of Land Law in Tudor England, 1529–1540," *Journal of Legal History* 11 (1990): 204–07.

[76] This seems to be the main reason why Ives dismisses the possibility of an official origin for this bill.

then stood.[77] The agreement went on to state that feudal incidents would remain the same on land which was not in use or settled by will, but, where land was so settled, the king would receive his dues on one-third of the land. Similarly, if a ward sued livery within three months of attaining his majority and guaranteed to pay the crown one-third of a year's profit on the lands in the crown's hands, he would be free from assessment on the rest. An heir of full age suing livery would be exempted on paying half a year's profit.[78] The agreement was meant as the foundation of a new piece of legislation, but until the legislation was passed, the signatories were to be bound by the terms of the agreement. The purpose of the arrangement was clear: the king was willing to concede the right to devise two-thirds of an estate in return for a guarantee of his rights on the remaining one-third. It had the added benefit, from the king's point of view, of dealing with the livery of land under uses, something not covered by the statute of 1490, as both Frowyk and Spelman pointed out. It gives some indication of the current level of evasion of feudal incidents that the king was willing to settle for a guaranteed one-third of his ostensible rights. The document also contained a provision against any attempt to manipulate the agreement, which states that:

> if any manner of person . . . make or cause to be made any guift in taile to his heyre apparant or to any other to his use of any of his landes or tenementes or an other thing doe or cause to be done whereby the Kinge his heyres or successors should or might be evicted or excluded from any benefitt or profitt of ward primier seison or liverie contrarie to the effect and plaine meaninge of any of the Articles above written, Or if any other imaginacion or invencion hereafter shall be found contrived or devised contrarie to the same, yet, that or any such thing notwithstandinge, the Kinges heighnes . . . shall have the full benefitt and effect of his wardes of the bodyes and landes and primer seisons and liveries, accordinge to the plaine and true intent of the said Articles and every of them.[79]

The agreement not only binds the nobles not to seek loopholes, it also obliges the king to settle for his one-third as stated. This provision, like the rest of the agreement, foreshadows the king's policies over the next several years. Henry's desire was clearly to remove this

[77] BL MS Cotton Titus B. IV, ff.114–18. Printed in full in Holdsworth, *History of English Law*, vol. 4, 574–77.

[78] Ives, "Genesis of the Statute of Uses," 680–81.

[79] Holdsworth, *History of English Law*, vol. 4, 575–76.

gentlemen's agreement from the hands of the lawyers and the realm of the common law and the interpretation and manipulation that that would imply. He wanted his wishes to become law and to mean what he wanted them to mean. Trying to remove one piece of projected legislation from the body of the common law was completely unrealistic, as it went against every principle of legal interpretation. As we will see, however, Henry continued to insist on intervening personally in the interpretation of his law.

The agreement, signed by thirty peers, i.e. a majority of the lay lords, states that it was to be introduced into parliament at the next session, but, because the agreement is not dated, it is difficult to be sure whether this happened.[80] Contemporaries, including Eustace Chapuys, the imperial ambassador, and Edward Hall, the chronicler, make it quite clear that, when the bill did arrive, it did not have an easy passage in the Commons. In March 1532, Henry spoke sternly to a Commons delegation, warning them that "if you wyll not take some reasonable ende now when it is offered, I wyll serche out the extremitie of the lawe, and then wyll I not offre you so moche agayne."[81] Once again, Henry's words were prophetic, but for the moment nothing much happened.[82] This resistance is not surprising. The Commons was traditionally hostile towards taxation bills, and this was in effect an insidious and long-term tax, since, if it passed, the bill would make for the easier and more efficient collection of the king's feudal dues. Though in appearance the king was giving up part of his rights, in reality he would not have been so anxious to have the bill pass if he did not expect it to increase his total yield. As Ives points out, "a substantial number of the House clearly felt that the king was bluffing – the law was on their side, it was fixed and certain, and without the consent of the Commons it could not be changed."[83]

[80] Ives dates the bill to 1529–30, which would have seen the bill destined for the 1531 session. It was not, however, introduced until 1532, and Ives explains this by arguing that the government was unwilling to commit itself to an unpopular bill in 1531. Ives, "Genesis of the Statute of Uses," 681–82. Bean makes the more plausible argument that the various members of the nobility signed the agreement over a period of time up to January 1532. Bean, *Decline of English Feudalism*, 265–66.

[81] Hall, *Chronicle*, 785.

[82] Parliament was prorogued for Easter and met again in April. Henry again submitted the bill, and this time it received two readings.

[83] Ives, "Genesis of the Statute of Uses," 684.

The Commons had good authority for resisting the royal demand, since the law on the prerogative had been confirmed quite recently. This whole debate may have helped to direct the attention of the legal profession to the issue once again, for the serjeant-elect Roger Yorke chose it as his topic in 1531, confirming its provenance as a serjeant's topic, and continuing the Gray's Inn interest in the subject. Yorke's reading has survived only in fragments, but those fragments and Yorke's casebook can give us some indication of his knowledge of the prerogative and the probable direction of his reading.

It is readily apparent that Yorke relied heavily on Spelman in compiling his reports: the numerous mentions of Spelman's name in the section on "Gardes and Liveries," in particular, suggest that Yorke had access to Spelman's reading, as we might expect. The casebook has notes on many of the issues raised in the readings, most of which serve to clarify or confirm the direction in which the law was moving. For example, Yorke moves one step further in solving the problem of the service due when a mesnalty held in chief escheats to the crown. Spelman's dilemma was to determine whether the tenant should render the same service as his lord had previously done, thus placing a heavier burden on the tenant when he had committed no fault, or whether the tenant should render the crown the same service he had rendered the lord, thus depriving the king. Spelman's reading left the question unanswered, but Yorke is quite clear on the issue. He says that, when a mesnalty held of the king, but not held in chief, escheats for lack of heirs, the tenant will hold of the king as he held of the lord. If the mesnalty is held in chief, the tenant will hold as the lord held. However, he goes on to argue that, if, in the former case, the land escheated for treason "so that the king had this by reason of his prerogative and by reason of his crown and not by reason of any tenure, then all the tenants who previously held of such lords now hold of the king in chief."[84]

Yorke attributes the note to Frowyk and Spelman, but in fact it is an amalgamation of the principles and practices enunciated by three of the previous readers, for his conclusion on escheat for treason clearly relies much more heavily on Constable than either Frowyk or Spelman. Yorke's collection covers other similar

[84] Yorke's Casebook, BL MS Hargrave 388, f.243.

issues, such as the effect on tenure when a lordship purchased by the king escheats, and this time he attributes his conclusions to Spelman.[85] Yorke obviously considered Spelman the best authority on the prerogative, but he also couples his name regularly with that of Richard Hesketh, also of Gray's Inn, who does not seem to have read on the prerogative.[86] He mentions Frowyk only once, and Constable not at all, even though he had been influenced by him. Yorke clearly relied primarily on Gray's Inn exercises for his knowledge, but his inclusion of Frowyk as an authority suggests that he was aware of other arguments. The absence of Constable from his references suggests that the legal profession had rejected his overall interpretation of the prerogative, though some elements of his reading had been incorporated into the general knowledge of the law.

Yorke also displays the same kind of detailed interest in wording that Spelman had done. He notes the points concerning the difference between grants of wardship *ad plenam etatem* and *quam diu in manibus nostris fore contigerit* made by Spelman in his reading, but he adds other notes. Where Frowyk had dismissed the requirement that land should be held *ab antiquo de corona* noting that he had never seen issue taken on that question, but only whether land was held in chief or not,[87] Yorke goes out of his way to note that tenure *ab antiquo* is "where continually he [the tenant] held of the king by knight service."[88] Throughout the material, however, Yorke does not interpolate anything striking, nor does he query many of the notes. Though his expression of the law is a little more refined than Frowyk's, his direct line to the earlier reader and the traditional view of the prerogative is clear.

Though, as the comparison between Spelman's reports and his reading displayed, a casebook cannot be taken to represent a reader's views exactly, in Yorke's case it does indicate that much of his knowledge of the prerogative came from Spelman and largely followed his teaching. The fact that his reading did not survive is a further indication that there was nothing new or significant to be learned from

[85] *Ibid.*, f.246v.

[86] Hesketh gave his second reading, probably on Merton, in the Lent vacation 1515, the year after Spelman gave his first. J. H. Baker, *Readers and Readings in the Inns of Court and Chancery*, Selden Society supplementary series vol. 13 (London: Selden Society, 2001), 30–31. Spelman refers to Hesketh twice in his collection, under traverse and petition of grace.

[87] Frowyk, f.1. See chapter 2, pp. 84–87 above.

[88] Yorke's Casebook, f.246.

it. While we cannot recover most of the content of Yorke's lectures in 1531, if we assume that he understood and represented the law on the prerogative as it was generally accepted, his casebook can be of further use in elucidating some of the implications of uses for the prerogative as he understood them.

Quite apart from the king's concern with feudal dues, the single most obvious danger with uses was that the feoffee held the legal title to the land, and any claims on his estate could be taken from the feoffor's land. Thus, as Yorke noted, if the feoffee granted a rent charge to a stranger, or died leaving a widow, the rent or the dower could be taken from the land he held to the use of the feoffor. In this case, the grantee of the rent would be seised to the use for which the land had been enfeoffed and so the feoffor would not lose too much, but there were other situations in which he would not be so lucky. If the feoffee died leaving no heir and his land escheated to the lord, the lord would get the feoffor's land, but he would hold it to his own use. Similarly, if the feoffee was attainted or outlawed, the feoffor's land was vulnerable.[89] The usual method of avoiding these problems was to enfeoff land to a group of feoffees, so that if one suffered the others could safeguard the use.

Of course, one of the reasons for feoffments to uses was the benefit to be gained if any of these dangers threatened the feoffor. Yorke notes that "a use cannot be forfeit, for the lord is not able to have this, nor the king, except in a special case as where the use goes into mortmain."[90] Similarly, if the feoffor died without an heir, then the feoffee would hold the land to his own use.[91] This had the benefit of preventing the land from falling into the lord's hands and allowing the tenant to redirect it to a beneficiary of his choice.

Besides trying to avoid the dangers of confiscation or escheat, this was the main benefit of the use: it allowed the feoffor to dispose of his land by will after his death. However, there were some limitations to the way in which he could do this. If the feoffor put land in use and made a will ordering his feoffees to enfeoff his son and heir, and then died leaving his heir under age, the son would be in ward, even though his father had made a will in accordance with the statute of 1490. The reason, according to Yorke, was that "this will is as though void, for if he had not made such a will the son would

[89] Yorke's Casebook, f.234.
[90] Yorke's Casebook, f.234v.
[91] Yorke's Casebook, f.234.

still have the land."[92] If, however, the will directed the feoffees to convey the land to the son in estate tail, the body would be in ward, but not the land. There were also problems with willing uses in tail, however, as a later case demonstrates. Yorke reports a case where the tenant has a use in fee and makes a will that one J.S. should have the land to him in tail. The tenant then dies, leaving an heir under age. According to Yorke, the tenant's heir will be in ward to the lord for the fee simple, while the heir of J.S. will be out of reach, because "these cases go according to the order of the common law so that there must be a will of the fee simple or otherwise the old tenant remains tenant to the lord."[93] This was an updated version of the problems the early readers faced in deciding the wardship of land in remainder or reversion, and a reminder that very basic issues remained of concern.

While all of these cases show that a landholder seeking to dispose of his land through uses had to be very careful that his wishes did not backfire through careless conveyancing, they also demonstrate that uses were clearly becoming part of the mainstream of common law, as Yorke argued in the example above. Though Yorke was a regular practitioner in chancery,[94] and thus might be expected to display more interest than most in uses, there is nothing in his casebook which indicates an unusual attitude to uses or which indicates that they threatened the common law. Indeed, there is no reason to expect the majority of lawyers to object to uses on professional grounds. While the judges of the common law courts lost the business which was drawn to chancery, other legal practitioners were as happy to work in chancery as elsewhere. Moreover, the conveyancing requirements for uses must have greatly increased the business available to some sections of the legal population.

In fact, the only reasons to object to uses were those already named: the loss of feudal dues, which affected the king most of all and troubled few others; the confusion of titles which could harm the unwary buyer; and legal purism, which did not want to accept uses as part of the common law. Though the proposed bill of 1532 would have dealt with the first two to some extent, it was clearly not having an easy passage through the Commons, and so the crown seems to have turned to the final argument against uses,

[92] Yorke's Casebook, f.234v. [93] Yorke's Casebook, ff.248–248v.
[94] Guy, *St. German on Chancery and Statute*, 66.

legal purism, to get its way. This approach had first appeared in the autumn of 1526 when Thomas Audley, of the Inner Temple, read on the statute of 1490.[95] Audley first seems to have attracted royal attention in the parliament of 1523, and he quickly began to gather offices. In 1525, he was appointed to Princess Mary's council, and in 1526 he was appointed attorney of the duchy of Lancaster, a position closely associated with the enforcement of the prerogative.[96] Given this background, we might expect Audley to object to the employment of uses, and indeed this is the case, though he approached the issue with some subtlety. He pointed out that uses defrauded lords of their feudal rights, but he emphasized most the problem of uncertainty, which for him was caused by the fact that uses were not governed by the common law. He argued that:

> notwithstanding that these uses were at first imagined for good purpose . . . nevertheless for the greater part they were pursued and connived at of ill purpose, to destroy the good laws of the realm, which now by reason of these trusts and confidences is turned into a law called "conscience," which is always uncertain and depends for the greater part on the whim ["arbytrement"] of the judge in conscience; by reason whereof no man is certain of knowing his title to any land. For now land passes by words and bare proofs in the Chancery, whereas by the common law it could pass only by solemn livery on the land or something tantamount, or by matter of record or writing. Also the trial of title to land in this realm was never by proofs, but by verdict: but now it is contrary.[97]

Audley's argument, as Yorke makes clear, was not really in the mainstream of legal opinion. It most likely represents an idea under consideration in government circles in the late 1520s, which seems to have gathered appeal as the agreement with the nobility foundered in the Commons. It also attracted some attention in the debates of the period and both sides of the argument were expressed in pamphlets written between 1530 and 1532. In the *Replication of a Serjeant*, the serjeant argues that uses:

95 By this time it was no longer unusual for a reader to choose to read on any statute which interested him.

96 Stanford E. Lehmberg, "Sir Thomas Audley: A Soul as Black as Marble?," in *Tudor Men and Institutions: Studies in English Law and Government*, ed. Arthur J. Slavin (Baton Rouge: Louisiana State University Press, 1972), 7.

97 BL MS Hargrave 87, f.438, translated in Baker, *Spelman's Reports*, vol. 2, 198.

beganne of an untrewe and a crafty ynvencion to put the king and his subgyettes from that [which] they aughte to have of righte by the good, trewe common lawe of the realme: as the kinges highnes from his escheetes, his wardes, and his prymer seasons, and from other thinges that nowe cumme not to my mynde; and his subgiettes from theyre escheetes and wardes . . . the whiche they aughte to have by the lawes of this realme.[98]

St. German's *Little Treatise Concerning Writs of Sub Poena* responds to this, though not with much conviction. Though the treatise in general is a strong defence of the chancery jurisdiction through *sub poena*, St. German's argument in support of uses falls rather flat. He distinguishes between depriving someone of a right which is already his and preventing that right from coming to him. The former is wrong, the latter perfectly justified. Thus, if a man is dying and arranges the marriage of his under-age heir to reap the financial benefits, "he doth no wronge to ye lord."[99] The same principle applies "in al ye cases that be spokyn of in ye seid treatyce, where such titles be put awey by meanes of uses. And lyke wyse yf a man that hath no heir, general nor specyal, sellyth his lande, or gyvyth it awey, to ye intent that it shuld not eschete, he doth no wronge to the lorde."[100] St. German did not convince either side in the debate with this response, but the exchange indicates that Audley's argument against uses was gaining attention. A few years later, another tract, entitled *Damna Usuum*, made the same point, and suggested that "if the usez, which is in Regard but ye shadowe of the thyng and not ye thyng Indeyd, were clene put out of the lawe men y[at] had right should hereaftur come to there remedyes."[101]

Henry's threat to the Commons in 1532 that he would "serche out the extremitie of the lawe" suggests that the government was planning a move along these lines. In 1533, with the agreement with

[98] *The Replication of a Serjeant at the Laws of England*, in Guy, *Christopher St. German on Chancery and Statute*, 103. Guy speculates that the text was written by St. German, but notes that its attack on uses is one of the arguments against his authorship, since he does not reply effectively to this in his *Little Treatise*. Guy, *St. German on Chancery and Statute*, 57. Baker appears to suggest that it was actually by Audley, pointing to the similarity of the views expressed in the tract and Audley's earlier reading. Baker, *Spelman's Reports*, vol. 2, 199.

[99] Christopher St. German, *A Little Treatise Concerning Writs of Subpoena*, in Guy, *Christopher St. German on Chancery and Statute*, 114.

[100] *Ibid.* [101] Holdsworth, *History of English Law*, vol. 4, 578.

the nobility apparently dead in the Commons, the government got the opportunity to make good on the king's threat. In that year, Lord Dacre, one of the crown's major tenants-in-chief, died. Lord Dacre had not signed the agreement, and so his heirs were not bound by it, but he died leaving much of his estate in use and willed to others than his heir. The inquisition post mortem, held in January 1534, found that he had devised land in tail in order to defraud the king, but the feoffees protested that the will was not collusive, and this simple question became the central issue. Lord Dacre's will was valid according to the orthodoxy of the day, but the government set out to prove that land could not be willed through uses. The case was argued in chancery in 1535 and the judges of both benches were present by the command of the chancellor, that same Thomas Audley whose reading previously argued against uses.[102] Serjeant Yorke, the reader, represented the feoffees, and once again presented the general understanding of the law, that:

> a use was at common law, for a use is nothing but a trust which the feoffors put in the feoffee upon the feoffment; and if we were to say that there was no use at common law, it would follow that there was no trust at common law, which cannot be: for trust or confidence is a thing which is very necessary between man and man, and at least no law prohibits or restrains a man from putting his confidence in another.[103]

As proof that uses did exist at the common law, Yorke listed statutes made from the time of Richard II onwards dealing with uses in various ways. Because of this, he concluded, "it has been held for many years that a use was at common law, by the common opinion of the whole realm; and so it seems to me that it is no longer to be disputed for it cannot be said that all statutes made before now concerning uses are all void."[104] Yorke also tried to separate the use from other methods of holding land by pointing out that "the use does not pass as land passes; for land cannot pass without livery, but uses [pass] on a bare word."[105]

Yorke's statement was countered by Pollard, who attempted to cut the ground from under Yorke's feet by arguing that:

[102] Baker, *Spelman's Reports*, vol. 1, 228–30.
[103] YB Pas. 27 Hen. VIII, f.8, pl.22, translated in Baker, *Spelman's Reports*, vol. 2, 201.
[104] YB Pas. 27 Hen. VIII, f.8, pl.22, translated in part in Baker, *Spelman's Reports*, vol. 2, 201.
[105] YB Pas. 27 Hen. VIII, f.8, pl.22.

it seems that there is no use: for if there was any use, it must, of necessity, have its foundation either in the common law or by statute; and it seems that there was no use at common law, for it is impertinent that I should enfeoff you of the land, and so part from it, and that I should still have it, contrary to my feoffment and gift. There is no mention made of any use in old year books, and if there had been any use at common law it would have been specifically mentioned in the old books of our law . . . [also] no statute was made by which the use was made and thus there is no use.[106]

Serjeant Pollard further covered his position by adding that, even if the use did exist at common law, land in use could not be willed, for the common law did not allow wills of land.[107]

Pollard was followed by Montague, who spoke on the nature of wills, and argued that uses did exist at the common law, for both uses and the common law are founded on reason. Leaving legal history aside, however, he concluded that the most important point was that:

for a long time the law has been held thus and continuance of this makes a law. And if no reason proves this, in the civil law it is said that common error makes law. And it would be a great mischief to change the law now, for many inheritances in the realm at this time depend on uses, so that there would be great confusion if this was done [Dacre's will overturned].[108]

Thus Montague followed Yorke and the common view in arguing that uses did exist at common law, but he recognized that the law could develop in unexpected ways, owing nothing to statute or to the ancient common law, but much to the necessities of the time and the ingenuity of the common lawyers. He recognized the larger problems which would follow a victory for the crown and pleaded for a pragmatic acceptance of the legal developments of the previous fifty years.

Yorke, Pollard, and Montague present the three central views of *Lord Dacre's Case*: the tradition that uses had acquired validity at common law; the royal argument that they had no legitimate foundation and were fraudulent; and the pragmatic assertion that so much depended on them that any academic concern over their origins was out of place. The year book report gives no conclusion to the discussion, but, according to Spelman, the case was argued for a long time by the apprentices and serjeants and was then adjourned

106 *Ibid.*, f.9. 107 *Ibid.* 108 *Ibid.*, f.10.

to the exchequer chamber, where the chancellor, Cromwell, all the justices, and the chief baron gave their views.[109] Spelman identifies two questions in the debate. The first repeated the focus of the year book discussion, i.e. whether uses upon feoffments existed at common law, and "many of the justices were of opinion that this word 'use' was in old times called 'trust' or 'confidence'."[110] This seemed to dispose of this fairly satisfactorily, but the second issue was more troublesome. This was the simple question, "can *cestui que use* make a will of his lands?"[111] On this point, the group divided, with five, including Audley and Cromwell, arguing that such a will was void "for no land is devisable by will except by custom, since it is against the nature of land to pass in such a way."[112] Four justices, however, were of the contrary opinion.[113] According to Spelman, who was in the latter group, Justice Port also agreed with them,

> but he spoke so low that the said Chancellor and Secretary understood him to be of the other opinion, and therefore they thought that the greater number of justices were of [the same] opinion as themselves. Therefore all the justices were commanded to appear before the king, who commanded them to assemble to agree in opinion, and those who were of opinion that the will was void would have the king's good thanks.
>
> Then the justices reassembled before the said Chancellor and Secretary, and debated this question. And FITZJAMES, FITZHERBERT and SPELMAN, observing the opinion of the Chancellor, Secretary, and other justices, who were men of great reason (and the number of them was greater), conformed with their opinion. But Shelley was not there because he was sick.[114]

It is impossible to know whether Shelley's illness was strategic, and we can only sympathize with him if it was, for the pressure placed upon the judges was immense. It is easy to conclude that the judges buckled under the royal will and abandoned their professional impartiality. However, it is difficult to argue that the situation was so clear cut. Though there is no doubt that the judges gave the king the result he wanted, there was clearly a strong argument for the king's

[109] The only exception was Englefield, who was in Wales.

[110] Baker, *Spelman's Reports*, vol. 1, 229. [111] *Ibid.*

[112] *Ibid.* The others who held this view were Lyster, chief baron, Baldwin, chief justice of the Common Pleas, and Luke, justice of the King's Bench.

[113] Spelman, justice of the King's Bench, Shelley and Fitzherbert, justice of the Common Pleas, and Fitzjames, chief justice of the King's Bench.

[114] Baker, *Spelman's Reports*, vol. 1, 230.

position. While Spelman's account makes clear the royal bullying, it also demonstrates the justices' discomfort with the whole issue. Under normal circumstances, the case would probably have been left unresolved and the parties encouraged to come to terms, but the circumstances were not normal. Not only was the king taking a personal interest in the conduct of the case, he wanted a unanimous decision from the judges, something of a rarity in any case. Nothing could more clearly demonstrate the importance of the case and the fact that the king intended it to have repercussions beyond this one estate, large though it was.

Indeed, the repercussions from *Lord Dacre's Case* were immense. The judgment itself was ironic, for, while it had begun with the question of whether uses could exist at common law, it was decided on the basis that they could and did, that they therefore followed the nature of common law and thus could not be devised. The effect of the decision was certainly as Hall, a reader at Gray's Inn himself, reports: "that lande coulde not be wylled by the ordre of the common law."[115] The decision in *Lord Dacre's Case* must have caused a general panic, for it was retrospective, and, as Montague had predicted, meant that any landholder in England who traced his title through a feoffment to uses would be vulnerable. Something had to be done quickly to save the situation and the king was more than willing to comply, on his terms. *Lord Dacre's Case* led directly to the Statute of Uses, which gave the king far more than he had originally sought in his agreement with the nobility. Rather than abolishing the use, the statute turned it from an equitable into a legal estate. The statute pursued the idea that uses followed the common law to the extreme and turned uses into a common law estate, joining the possession to the use. The *cestui que use* got no relief in his feudal incidents and land was no longer devisable by will. Though in his discussion of the negotiation over the proposed bill of 1532 Hall describes Henry as "an indifferent Prince, not willyng to take all, nor to lose all," it is clear that the king preferred the former alternative to the latter.[116] It was a harsh settlement, but parliament passed it with hardly a murmur, for the alternative was too terrible to contemplate.

[115] Hall, *Chronicle*, 785.

[116] *Ibid*. Hall also suggests that there were others at the time who recognized how far the king could carry the law against them.

The preamble to the Statute of Uses makes no mention of *Lord Dacre's Case*, nor of the pressure under which the statute was framed. Instead, it reads as a textbook exposition of the evils of the use, one which must have rejoiced the heart of the author of the *Damna Usuum*.[117] The need for the statute, and its connection to *Lord Dacre's Case*, are expressed most clearly in section nine of the statute, which states that:

> for asmoche as great ambyguytes and doutes may aryse of the validyte and invalidite of wylles here to fore made of any Landes Tenementes and Hereditamentes to the great trouble of the Kynges subjectes . . . [all wills of persons dying before 1 May 1536] shalbe taken and accepted good and effectuall in the Lawe after such fashyon maner and fourme as they were comonlye takyn and usid at any tyme within forty yeres next afore the makyng of thys act; any thyng conteynid in thys acte or in the preamble therof or any opynyon of the common Lawe to the contrary therof notwithstonding.[118]

Parliament was eager enough to pass the statute at the time, in order to nullify the recent "opynyon of the common Lawe," but opposition to it grew quickly. The statute effectively restored compulsory primogeniture and thus, as Hall remarks, it "sore greued the Lordes and Gentlemen that had many chyldren to setfurth."[119] The re-imposition of primogeniture also made it difficult to satisfy creditors in a will and this had the effect of reducing the financial flexibility of many families and jeopardizing their future economic stability.

Though the principle on which the statute was based was simple, it seems that conveyancers soon began to find possible ways around it. Indeed, opposition to the change was not confined to attempts to evade the statute, but quickly moved into a more dangerous arena, that of rebellion. The Statute of Uses has the distinction of being one of the few English statutes to contribute to an armed rising, and the reaction can be blamed largely on its harshness.[120] Given the compulsion under which the statute was passed, Henry was adding insult to injury when he deplored rebellion against "those lawes and Statutes, which by all the Nobles, knightes and gentilmen of

117 27 Hen. VIII, c.10, *Stat. Realm*, vol. 3, 539–40.

118 *Ibid.*, 541. 119 Hall, *Chronicle*, 785.

120 See M. L. Bush, *The Pilgrimage of Grace: A Study of the Rebel Armies of 1536* (Manchester: Manchester University Press, 1996), 110–11.

this realme whom the same chiefly toucheth hath ben granted and assented to."[121] Smith comments on the number of men, most obviously Aske, with a common law education among the leaders of the Pilgrimage of Grace, and suggests that they may have been concerned about Henry VIII's new interpretation of the relationship between kingship and law.[122]

It is clear that Henry VIII preferred to manipulate the law more directly than his father had done. Some members of the legal profession were vehemently opposed to this encroachment on their territory by the king or by any of his representatives. The *Replication of a Serjeant at Law*, though focused on the iniquities of the *sub poena*, indicates how narrowly the proper sphere of influence of the king and chancellor could be construed. The serjeant marvels at the chancellor's ability to make a writ of *sub poena*, which can halt process in the common law courts, "the whiche the kinge hym self cannot doo righte wiselye, for he is sworne the contrary, and yt is said hoc possumus quod de iure possumus."[123] He goes on to point out the obligations of the judges "to mynystre his lawes of this realme indeferentely to the kinges subgiettes" and of the serjeants to ensure that the king's subjects are "justifiede by the lawes of the realme."[124] Much to his disgust,

> this notwithstandinge, if the kinges subgiettes, upon a surmysede bill put yn to the chauncerye, shalbe prohibite[d] by a sub pena to sue according to the lawes of the realme, and be compellede to make aunswere before my lorde Chauncellor, then shall the lawe of the reame be sette as voyde and takyn as a thing of non effecte, and the kinges subgiettes shalbe ordrede by the discrecion of the Chauncellor, and by no lawe, contrary to all goode reason and good pollycy.[125]

The serjeant's distinction between the practices of chancery and the common law of the realm, though it might appeal to his colleagues,

121 PRO E 36/118, ff.99–99v, quoted in Ives, "Genesis of the Statute of Uses," 693; Hall, *Chronicle*, 821. As the king pointed out, the matter of uses "in no maner of thynges . . . toucheth you the basse commons of our Realme" (Hall, *Chronicle*, 821), supporting the argument that some of the gentry were involved in the rebellion as a consequence of the statute.

122 R. B. Smith, *Land and Politics in the England of Henry VIII: The West Riding of Yorkshire 1530–46* (Oxford: Clarendon, 1970), 208–09. It is worth noting that two of the fragments of Yorke's reading survive in a manuscript (BL MS Add. 38133) that belonged to Aske. The hand of the reading does not appear to be Aske's, but he was admitted to Gray's Inn in 1527 and could well have been present at the reading. Baker, *Readers and Readings*, 317.

123 *Replication of a Serjeant*, 100. 124 *Ibid.* 125 *Ibid.*, 100–01.

was not really justified, and St. German had little trouble in dispatching this argument with the rejoinder that "the kinges othe yn that poyncte is this, that he shall graunte to holde the lawes and custumes of his realme; and then if the lawes and custumes of his realme shall be understaunde aswell to be the lawes and custumes usede yn the chauncery as at the common lawe, as I suppose they be... then it is not againste the kinges othe."[126] St. German is returning to the basic premise that the king is the foundation of all law and whatever law is practised under his authority is part of the law of the realm, no matter where it is practised. In reality, the law has developed as the common law, administered by the judges and the serjeants, but, under St. German's scheme, this is merely a matter of convenience. If the king wished to change the method of administration, he could, theoretically, do so and if he wanted to take over administration of the law himself, this could also constitute fulfilling his oath.

Though this had been a fundamental constituent of legal authority for centuries, it had also been largely a fiction. According to Britton, Edward I invoked this power when he appointed judges, and added "that our jurisdiction be superior to all jurisdictions in our realm; so that in all kinds of felonies trespasses and contracts, and in all manner of other actions personal or real, we have power to give, or cause to be given, such judgment as the case requires without any other process, whenever we have certain knowledge of the truth, as judge."[127] Though intervening kings had retained that authority, they exercised it rarely. Henry VIII, however, was keenly aware of this role, referring in 1532 to the "offyce of a Kyng which is a Iudge" and his duty to "geue... sentence."[128] Not only was Henry enamoured with his role as a judge of the existing law, however, he was also convinced that he had the ability to change the law. His fascination with the imperial idea is well known[129] and it extended to the imperial right to make law. In the *Collectanea satis copiosa*, a collection of sources gathered in the course of Henry's campaign against the church, Bracton's famous passage on the relationship between the king and the law was changed to increase royal

126 St. German, *Little Treatise*, 122.
127 *Britton*, ed. F. M. Nichols, 2 vols. (Oxford: Clarendon Press, 1865), vol. 1, 2–3.
128 Hall, *Chronicle*, 784.
129 See, for example, J. A. Guy, *Tudor England* (Oxford: Oxford University Press, 1988), 81.

power: from the statement that "the king should be under God and under the law, because the law makes the king," it has been altered to read that the king should be "under God. Not under the law, for the king makes the law."[130] Furthermore, it seems that Henry even thought that the king could operate completely outside the bounds of the law. In his corrections to the Bishops' Book of 1537, which stated in its exposition of the fifth commandment that princes could kill and coerce their subjects "but by and according to the just order of their laws," he altered the passage to mean that only "inferior ministers," i.e. servants of the crown rather than princes, were restricted in this way.[131] The change did not survive Cranmer's scrutiny, but, though the archbishop moderated Henry's claims, his own interpretation of the commandment gave the prince a broad competence. Though he accepted that the prince must act according to justice, he relied heavily on the idea that the prince was the source of law, arguing that:

> when princes give pardons, placards, protections, and licences, contrary to the common order of their laws, yet that also is done by the law, so that it be never done against justice and equity between party and party. And moreover it is not amply spoken that the inferior rulers should do nothing, but by the order of their laws; for the laws be not theirs, but the princes, instead of whom they do minister the same justice, that he would do himself by the common order of his laws, if it should happen him to take the judgment thereof in his own hands.[132]

Although Cranmer does not come out in favour of the king's views, his statement would certainly not have gained favour with the serjeant of the *Replication*, nor even, we can assume, with St. German.

This sweeping and somewhat simplistic view of the king's right, by returning to a practical emphasis on the king's role as creator of law, ignored the whole area of administration of the law which had grown into a complex block of learning, outside the understanding of the monarch. Quite apart from the bureaucratic nightmare it presented for the professional lawyers, the idea of a king taking the law into his own hands would have received little support

[130] *Collectanea satis copiosa*, BL Cotton Cleopatra E VI, f.28v. The Latin has been changed from "Rex debet esse sub Deo et sub lege, quia lex facit regem" to "Ipse [rex] non debet sub homine sed sub Deo. Non sub lege, quia Rex legem facit."

[131] Thomas Cranmer, *Miscellaneous Writings and Letters of Thomas Cranmer*, ed. John Edmund Cox (Cambridge: Cambridge University Press, 1846), 105.

[132] *Ibid.*, 105.

among the educated sections of the populace. Indeed, Sir Thomas Elyot, just a few years earlier, approvingly related the story of the emperor Alexander, who, informed that the emperor did not have to obey his own laws, replied that he would never devise any laws for his people which he would not himself obey.[133] Elyot's moral is directed at lesser governors, but by taking the emperor as his model he exhorts all rulers to "know the bounds of your authority, know also your office and duty."[134] Elyot gives an interpretation of imperial rule radically different from the one Henry desired, and one probably more in tune with that of the political community. Cranmer also allowed less than the king would have wished, but more than the lawyers can have been comfortable with. More importantly, Cranmer's interpretation was impeccably orthodox, and his moderation of the king's somewhat blunt statement provided a possible avenue down which Henry could pursue his view of the relationship between the king and the law.

Ambitious as Henry's view was, it was neither practical, nor likely to gain general acceptance. Henry had no real interest in the general administration of the law, and even stalwart royal supporters like St. German believed that "princes were not learned enough to discover their power by themselves: they needed assistance lest they presume too much."[135] The legal profession was indispensable and would remain in charge of the law, but Henry seems to have been determined to redress the balance of power within the legal system in order to gain the initiative in controlling its operation. There are various examples of Henry's determination to bend the lawyers to his will and their ability to resist. In 1530, when a gathering of lawyers at Hampton Court decided that parliament could not enact that the king's divorce should be granted by the archbishop of Canterbury, the king was furious and prorogued the next session of parliament, apparently to give him time to change the lawyers' minds.[136] The king also took steps to remove the lawyers from political influence, excluding them from the conciliar role they had held under his father, until, by 1540, the lord chancellor was the only legal officer in the privy council.[137]

133 Sir Thomas Elyot, *The Book named The Governor*, ed. S. E. Lehmberg (New York: E. P. Dutton, 1962), 166.

134 *Ibid.* 135 Guy, *St. German on Chancery and Statute*, 40. 136 *Ibid.*, 24–25.

137 M. M. Condon, "An Anachronism with Intent?: Henry VII's Council Ordinance of 1491/2," in *Kings and Nobles in the Later Middle Ages*, ed. R. A. Griffiths and James Sherbourne (New York: St. Martin's, 1986), 233–34.

Not content with limiting the political role of the lawyers, Henry took the battle into their own camp. In 1540, he instituted an enquiry into the state of the Inns of Court. While this report provides much of our knowledge of the Inns at that date, the king's reason for commissioning it is nowhere stated. It has often been seen as an expression of Henry's interest in education, even a preliminary to the establishment of a new Inn under royal patronage which would discard the barbarities of traditional legal education in favour of a more "renaissance" approach. Rather than reflecting the king's interest in education, however, it is more likely that the king was concerned with curbing the influence of the existing Inns. If he was thinking of establishing a new institution, it was most probably as a model Inn teaching the law under royal supervision and patronage, in the royal interest, rather than as an altruistic gesture to the new learning.[138] Though we cannot prove Henry's intentions with regard to the enquiry, we have ample proof of his concern over the activities and influence of the Inns, particularly in matters concerning the prerogative. In 1540, Sir Humphrey Browne, king's serjeant, Sir Nicholas Hare, speaker of the Commons, and William Coningesby, the attorney of the duchy of Lancaster, were committed to the tower for giving advice to one Sir John Shelton of Norfolk on ways to avoid the provisions of the Statute of Uses.[139] The king's wrath was clearly roused by the fact that his serjeant and the attorney of the duchy of Lancaster were involved in trying to defraud him of the rights confirmed with such effort in the recent statute. Once again, the king made clear his determination that the law should mean what he wanted it to mean, regardless of the subtleties of legal learning, and he took the opportunity to warn the entire legal community against opposing his will. In an extraordinary speech the chancellor

> opened this day the king's majesty's will and pleasure unto the readers of the inns of court and chancery and other learned men . . . admonishing and warning them in his majesty's behalf not only truly and justly to interpret and expound his laws and statutes in the readings and moots but also to

[138] See D. S. Bland, "Rhetoric and the Law Student in Sixteenth-Century England," *Studies in Philology* 54 (1957): 500. The same interpretation can be placed on his establishment of the Regius professorships in the same year.

[139] See Charles Wriothesley, *A Chronicle of England During the Reigns of the Tudors, from AD 1485 to 1559*, ed. William Douglas Hamilton, vol. 2, Camden Society new ser. vol. 20 (London: J. B. Nichols, 1877), 116; Hall, *Chronicle*, 837; Baker, *Spelman's Reports*, vol. 2, 351.

instruct, advise and counsel all the king's loving subjects repairing to them for counsel in the law according to the very, just and true meaning of the laws and good statutes of the realm, without subtle practice, imagination, or deceit, and specially in such laws and statutes as be made for the maintenance aswell for the king's right and prerogatives as for the interest of the nobles and other his loving subjects of the realm for wardships, primer seisins, reliefs, and such like services . . . so that thereby our said sovereign lord, nor any his nobles or other subjects, should be defrauded of their rights and interests that is due to them by reason of their tenures, by any subtle practices, or invention of crafty wits, contrary to the true and just intents of the statutes provided in that behalf, as they would avoid the king's majesty's high indignation and displeasure, and the danger of the laws.[140]

The surviving reports present Browne and his companions as humble penitents to the king, willing and eager to hand over their possessions and their persons in reparation for their impertinence. Browne got no relief, for it seems to have been generally agreed that he had advised the deceased Shelton and that he was wrong to do so, and so he was ordered to pay £1,000 in compensation. This was Browne's second offence against the king's coffers, however, and that may have contributed to the severity of his treatment.[141]

Serjeant Browne's case set an ominous precedent, and, though it was an unusually blatant example, it does not seem to have been the only time the king interfered in the activities of the Inns. A few years later, in the common pleas, while the lawyers were discussing whether a copyholder could be ousted by his lord, Judge Browne noted that "in the time of the present king this matter was appointed to be argued; but on account of the mischief that would ensue thereby, if it had been adjudged as your opinion is [that he has no remedy], a command was sent by the King's Council that it should not be argued."[142] Though Browne does not mention the Inns, he can only be referring to a learning exercise, and the casual mention of royal interference in the business of the Inns suggests

[140] Baker, *Spelman's Reports*, vol. 2, 351. Though Hall's account is not nearly as detailed as Spelman's, he echoes the central points of the chancellor's complaint, that the lawyers acted "to the greate hynderaunce of the Kynges prerogatiue, and the true meanyng of thesaied [*sic*] statute, and also to the euill example of all other, that shoulde defraude the lordes of their seigniories." Hall, *Chronicle*, 837.

[141] In 1532, Browne was accused of advising felons to sell their goods to avoid forfeiting them. He was briefly imprisoned and lost his office of king's serjeant. He regained it in 1535. See Baker, *Spelman's Reports*, vol. 1, 184; Amanda Bevan, "The Role of the Judiciary in Tudor Government, 1509–1547" (PhD diss., Cambridge, 1986), 29–30.

[142] Baker, *Spelman's Reports*, vol. 2, 186.

that Henry was successful at some level in imposing his authority on the lawyers. The simple fact that Serjeant Browne had become a justice of the common pleas in 1542, however, indicates that the weight of the king's displeasure was not enough to ruin a legal career. Though Browne was stripped of his position as king's serjeant in 1532 and 1540, he quickly recovered, and it seems likely that the lawyers discreetly rallied around him.

The ambiguity at the heart of the lawyers' role is made clear in these years: acting under the king's authority, but required to keep the king obedient to the law, their position could easily become untenable if the king refused to submit to their professional judgment and instead insisted on encroaching upon their territory. Without any independent source of authority, the lawyers had no choice but to bend to the king in any open and sustained conflict. However, though they held their authority from the king, they seem to have retained an influence apart from his control. Henry's very concern to muzzle the Inns and punish individual lawyers argues for their ability to act independently of royal authority. The Inns, as an institution, had a long memory and the ability to act as the repository of legal learning far beyond the exigencies of the day. In this context, it is significant that Hall specifies that, when the chancellor assembled the lawyers to hear the king's message in 1540, he called "foure readers . . . of euery house of the foure principall Innes of Courte one."[143] If the king was to usurp the lawyers' position or to cow them effectively, he had to do so by dealing with the Inns as an institution. Individual lawyers could be imprisoned or fined, but the whole body could not be silenced, at least not indefinitely.[144]

[143] Hall, *Chronicle*, 837.

[144] The serjeants' rings provide an interesting sidelight on this question. It was the usual practice for the serjeants to distribute a large quantity of rings on the occasion of their elevation to the coif. The rings were engraved with an appropriate motto, but were common to each serjeant. Relatively few of the serjeants' rings have survived, and they are rare before the seventeenth century. The earliest surviving rings, from the late fifteenth and early sixteenth century, have the motto "Vivat rex et lex." The motto for the 1531 call was "Rex est anima legis," reinforcing the orthodoxy of the king's centrality to the law. The motto for either the 1521 or the 1540 call, and it would be fascinating to know which, was "Legis executio regis preservatio," again perfectly orthodox, but perhaps emphasizing the lawyers' role in the enforcement of the law. For a full exposition of the history of the serjeants' rings, see J. H. Baker, *The Order of Serjeants at Law: A Chronicle of Creations, with Related Texts and a Historical Introduction*, Selden Society supplementary series vol. 5 (London: Selden Society, 1984), 94–99.

The final scene in the battle over uses effectively demonstrates the limits of the king's power. In 1540, parliament passed the Statute of Wills, which ameliorated the harshness of the Statute of Uses. Its provisions are strikingly similar to those contained in the agreement with the nobility of 1529–31, for it allowed those who held land in knight service to devise two-thirds of their land, with the king retaining one-third in wardship or primer seisin. Land held in socage could be devised in its entirety.[145] Though the terms were much the same as those proposed earlier, the events of the intervening years meant that this statute left mesne lords in a much better position than they were before the Statute of Uses. With the conversion of uses to a legal estate, mesne lords regained access to wardships over lands which their tenant had enfeoffed to uses. The king was the loser under the Statute of Wills, and he lost a great deal.

There is some mystery surrounding the enactment of this statute in 1540. It was passed in the same parliament as the bill setting up the Court of Wards, but, though both bills dealt with aspects of the prerogative, they were not introduced together. Bean has connected the Statute of Wills with Cromwell's fall, arguing that the bill clearly had nothing to do with the minister and was hurriedly introduced at the time of his arrest.[146] He points out that the bill did nothing to prevent the kind of conveyances made by Sir John Shelton, but merely reverted to the terms of the earlier agreement, thus necessitating a further statute in 1542 "for thexplanation of the Statute of Wills."[147] By removing the statute from Cromwell's influence, Bean gives a convincing explanation for its failings, and he provides a plausible agent in the duke of Norfolk. What Bean does not explain, and what still remains obscure, is why the king suddenly gave up all the benefits he had acquired at such cost in 1536.

The obvious answer is that the reaction against the statute was so great that it forced him to back down, and without doubt that was a factor. The Pilgrimage of Grace was the most overwhelming expression of that reaction, but it was satisfactorily put down in 1536, suggesting that it was not an immediate impetus to change in 1540. The attempts of the lawyers to find ways around the statute

145 32 Hen. VIII, c.1, *Stat. Realm*, vol. 3, 744–46.
146 Bean, *Decline of English Feudalism*, 298–99.
147 34 & 35 Hen. VIII, c.5, *Stat. Realm*, vol. 3, 901–04.

may also have been a factor. Aske, a leader of the Pilgrimage of Grace, was already suggesting possible conveyancing methods for avoiding the rigour of the statute in the aftermath of the Pilgrimage, and his suggestions, though inaccurate, are strikingly similar to those suggested to Sir John Shelton by Browne, Hare, and Coningsby in 1540.[148] The royal response on that occasion was swift and severe, but the realization that even royal officials charged with enforcing royal rights were counselling clients on ways to avoid the prerogative may have helped to convince the king that his original programme was the more effective one. Besides this, the constant legislative activity necessary to keep up with new methods of evasion may not have worried Cromwell, but most administrators must have baulked at such a task. If Bean is correct in seeing Norfolk's influence in the bill, it may also represent a move on the part of noble counsellors to restore the situation they had agreed to in 1529, for they had much to gain.

The change of heart seems to have been sudden, as evidenced by the timing and the content of the bill. The 1529–31 agreement had involved an understanding that neither side would try to evade the provisions of the bill, and this statute seems to have envisaged the same situation, since it did not make any provision for the kinds of evasion practised by Shelton and others. It is difficult to believe that the king could have been so naïve as to believe that, after the bitterness engendered by the Statute of Uses, tenants would not have tried all means possible to evade their obligations. The Statute of Wills may have been a sweetener to make the establishment of the Court of Wards more palatable, or a concession to the nobility in the wake of Cromwell's fall, but it served to place the relationship between the king and his tenants on a firm, maintainable, and reasonably satisfactory footing for the first time in many years. The Statute of Uses had been the result of a clever manipulation of the law, but it was a political mistake. The Statute of Wills restored the balance between the king's rights and his subjects' willingness to pay, though it did so with some inefficiency.

The whole controversy over uses kept the royal prerogative in the limelight throughout the 1530s. It is impossible to pretend that the new legislation did not affect the prerogative, since it fundamentally altered one of the most popular methods of landholding in the

[148] See Bean, *Decline of English Feudalism*, 295 and 296–97.

country. Similarly, the Statute of Wills changed the situation by officially limiting the extent of the king's rights to reasonable levels. The overall effect of these statutes on the king's prerogative rights was not as significant as it might seem at first glance, however. The Statute of Wills limited the amount the king could claim, but it did not affect the type of claims he could make, while the Statute of Uses restored the prerogative to many lords who had long since lost it. Though the practical application of the prerogative was changed by the statutes, the law contained in *Prerogativa Regis* was not.

The process of passing the statute demonstrates the natural limits of the lawyers' authority. Though the common law was moving to absorb uses, there was an argument against them, which was catapulted to the fore when it became expedient. The application of political weight to the minority side shifted the balance of opinion within the profession and allowed for the radical change in the law. In this way the controversy over uses also serves to bring the legal profession into the limelight, for it saw the king attempt to manipulate both the law and the legal profession in the most blatant manner. Though the lawyers appeared to bend before the king, both in *Lord Dacre's Case* and *Serjeant Browne's Case*, a closer examination of their behaviour is revealing. In the first case, the king had a good argument in law to support his position, while in the second case he was relying on the weaker, but hallowed orthodoxy of the king's role as judge. In both cases, the position adopted by the king was undermined. *Lord Dacre's Case* was the more significant of the two, at least as far as the realm at large was concerned, and in going against the tide of the common law the king was forcing approval of a politically dangerous position. Though the lawyers had little choice but to give in, the political nation took up the opposition to the king's actions. *Serjeant Browne's Case* is of more limited interest, but it demonstrates both the king's fervent desire to control the lawyers and their ability to protect their own. Neither case presents the lawyers in a particularly favourable light, and it is clear that they had no inclination towards political martyrdom. However, it is equally clear that they were bound by their interpretation of the king's law, and that they had the political sense to bend to the king's wishes and live to fight another day.

5

THE EDWARDIAN READERS AND BEYOND

Though the Statutes of Uses and Wills answered many of the legal controversies surrounding *Prerogativa Regis*, the text was aired again in the Inns in 1549 and 1551. These readings themselves are limited in what they can tell us, but once again the context is of some interest. The 1540s saw the distribution of ex-monastery lands, most of which were given to be held in chief of the crown, thus potentially creating a new group of feudal landholders. In the abstract, this is an unlikely activity in the mid-sixteenth century, and it raises certain questions about the nature and extent of the feudal bond at the time. The last chapter showed that though the feudal system might well be bastardized by this time, it remained a powerful element in political and economic matters. Though its importance in these areas is clear, the more intangible effects of the feudal bond on the nobility demand some further consideration. As the chief landholders of the kingdom, the nobility bore the greatest burden of the prerogative, though, in theory at least, they were also the greatest beneficiaries of royal generosity.[1] The reciprocal nature of the feudal bond implied both that the lords paid feudal dues and gave service to the king in return for his grants of land to them, and that the lords would alleviate this burden by the imposition of similar requirements on their inferiors. Leaving aside the question of the "moral and historical justification"[2] of feudalism, we must consider whether the feudal bond between the crown and the nobility still existed in a recognizable form in the sixteenth century, and to what extent it was still marked by this reciprocity, as well as

[1] See K. S. H. Wyndham, "Crown Land and Royal Patronage in Mid-Sixteenth Century England," *Journal of British Studies* 19 (1980): 18–34.

[2] A. R. Buck, "The Politics of Land Law in Tudor England 1529–1540," *Journal of Legal History* 11 (1990): 201.

the effects on the feudal bond of a changing market in land as the century wore on.

The nobility of the 1520s and 1530s was still largely cast in the medieval mould, something well within the Tudor tradition. Henry VII has traditionally been viewed as an administrator-king, but Gunn has pointed out that, despite his rather colourless reputation, the monarch took an active part in the chivalric exhibition of his court, for "Henry VII, like Henry VIII, like Maximillian or Francis I, aspired to be the perfect knight as well as the perfect patron of learning, the perfect lawgiver, and so on."[3] Henry VIII surpassed his father in formal chivalric activity, and there is evidence that his nobility paid serious attention to both the practical and formal knightly rituals. Thus, in 1517–18, the duke of Buckingham took an aid from his tenants to knight his son (as indeed Henry VII had tried to do in 1504), and both Buckingham and Northumberland kept private heralds.[4] As Gunn points out, these noblemen were neither unusual nor anachronistic in their habits, for many of Henry VII's close associates retained private officers of arms.[5]

The idea that Henry VIII in particular set out to create a courtier nobility is attractive, but, as Miller has pointed out, there is no real justification for it.[6] The ceremonial around the court was essential for royal magnificence, and Henry VIII demanded noble attendance on formal occasions, but there is no evidence that he attempted to dislodge the nobility from their local power by enforcing attendance at court, or even that he consciously used the court to strengthen ties with the nobility. Maintaining the personal care of noble wards would be one obvious way of inculcating loyalty, but, as Miller points out, Henry did not do even that much.[7] The ceremonial at court was necessary for royal prestige, but it advanced noble prestige at the same time. There were some members of the nobility, like the Howards and the Dudleys, who sought and made their fortune through advancement at court, but on the other extreme there were some, like the Lords Ogle, who never attended either court or parliament, but served their king by maintaining

[3] S. J. Gunn, "Chivalry and the Politics of the Early Tudor Court," in *Chivalry in the Renaissance*, ed. Sydney Anglo (Suffolk: Boydell, 1990), 123.

[4] *Ibid.*, 125. [5] *Ibid.*

[6] Helen Miller, *Henry VIII and the English Nobility* (Oxford: Basil Blackwell, 1986), 100.

[7] *Ibid.*

order in the locality.[8] Both the Howards and the Dudleys demonstrate that the dangers of court life were as great as the rewards and perhaps the peaceful obscurity of the Ogle family had its benefits, but in reality the majority of the nobility fell between the two extremes. The court was the centre of the political nation, and any noble family seeking advancement was well advised to maintain a presence there. This had long been so, and, though Henry's court may have been more lavish than some of his predecessors, it was not staffed by a "courtier nobility" to any greater extent than those of his predecessors had been.

Henry's personality, his promotion of an imperial image, and the momentous changes of his reign combine with Holbein's portraits to produce an almost irresistible "renaissance monarch," but, while there is reality as well as power in that perception, Henry retained a strong medieval streak. Loach points out that, at his accession, Henry displayed himself both in the crown of Edward the Confessor and on the chair in Westminster Hall that was the king's bench.[9] Both were powerful images of kingship, but they were also ancient images which suggested a sacral and judicial king. Henry continued to play with the medieval role as well as the renaissance one throughout his life, and even at the end, Loach argues, by using the same funeral ceremonies as the nobility, the king stressed his "role as leader of a feudal band."[10]

Knighthood itself, that most medieval of institutions, was still the perquisite of the well-born warrior; Leonard has calculated that of the 336 knights alive in 1523, 151 owed their knighthoods to war, 65 to ceremonial occasions and only 26 were known to be "civil knights," i.e. those honoured for administrative services.[11] Civil knights were made in ones and twos, while large batches of knights were made only on occasions of war and ceremony. Knights could be made in order to confer prestige on the monarch; Leonard suggests

8 S. J. Gunn, "Off with Their Heads: The Tudor Nobility 1485–1603," in *The House of Lords: A Thousand Years of British Tradition*, ed. Robert Smith and John S. Moore (London: Smith's Peerage, 1994), 53.

9 Jennifer Loach, "The Function of Ceremonial in the Reign of Henry VIII," *Past and Present* 142 (1994): 51, 52.

10 *Ibid.*, 60.

11 H. H. Leonard, "Knights and Knighthood in Tudor England" (PhD diss., London, 1970), 106. Leonard could find no records for the remaining eighty-seven, but he argues that, even if all of them were civil knights, which is unlikely, civil knights would still have made up only one-third of the knightage of 1523.

that both Henries may have felt impelled to create large numbers for this reason, and that Henry VIII, in particular, may have needed to create knights to satisfy his image of himself as a successful warrior king.[12] Knighthoods could also serve as an incentive to service for those who received one, even in times of peace. Thus, in 1532, the earl of Northumberland asked the king for permission to knight some men in the Marches, thus "encoraging the hartes of gentilmen to serve me better under your gracious Highness."[13]

Northumberland's request expresses perfectly not only the martial value of knighthoods, but the relationship between such a nobleman, the king and the "gentilmen" of his area. The nobility were still the effective governors of their localities, though they governed them under the watchful eye of the king. This was traditionally the most effective method of government, particularly for the extremities of the kingdom, and it remained so under the Tudors. Bernard notes that "in some senses early Tudor England was a federation of noble fiefdoms," and this is the case, though the individual members of the federation had no rights of secession and only a fraction of the power of the king.[14] Both Henry VII and Henry VIII used their noblemen to rule the country, for there was no realistic alternative. Gunn, though characterizing Henry VII as an anti-noble king, points out that nevertheless he appointed noblemen he trusted to rule in regions where they were available, men like Thomas Stanley, earl of Derby, in the north-west; John de Vere, earl of Oxford, in East Anglia; Giles, lord Daubeney, in Somerset; and Jasper Tudor, duke of Bedford, in Wales.[15] There were, of course, dangers inherent in such a policy, and both kings were careful to prevent the rise of over-mighty subjects. The fiscal policies of the early Tudors ensured that no nobleman had either the financial flexibility or the discretion to build up the extensive estates necessary to threaten the throne; this, combined with provisions against retaining, restricted the growth of private armies.

Though these policies worked fairly well in the southern and south-eastern portions of the kingdom, they could be counterproductive on the frontiers. Frontier lords needed a large, well-armed, and well-trained following if they were to protect the

[12] *Ibid.*, 109. [13] Quoted in *ibid.*, 241.
[14] G. W. Bernard, *The Power of the Early Tudor Nobility: A Study of the Fourth and Fifth Earls of Shrewsbury* (Totowa NJ: Barnes & Noble, 1985), 180.
[15] Gunn, "Off with Their Heads," 63.

borders efficiently. Lords like Dacre and Northumberland were essential to the preservation of the north, but they were furthest from effective governmental control. This reality posed a chronic problem for both Henry VII and Henry VIII: how could they acquire and maintain effective control over these lords, reducing them as political threats while preserving them as powers in their localities? As we have already suggested, Henry VII used inquisitions in the north to remind both Northumberland and Clifford and their tenants that he himself was the ultimate source of their power and authority. Hanging a financial and tenurial sword of Damocles over the head of a northern lord was an effective way to remind him and his tenants of their allegiance without compromising their martial ability. As Northumberland expressed it in 1532, the military power of the north would then serve the king through their local lords.

The reality was far more complicated, for northern lords themselves were under conflicting pressures in their efforts to carry out their duties. Lord Dacre, for example, tolerated a good deal of cross-border lawlessness among his followers in order to maintain their military support in times of crisis. Some of his dealings with the Scottish nobility were technically treasonous, but they were part of the reality of guarding border security. Dacre was a powerful feudal lord in the traditional mould, and there was nothing anachronistic about this, for he was carrying out his duties to the crown in the only effective way possible. Though this was the case, Henry VIII, far from the northern border, was concerned about the growth of Dacre's power. As Ellis argues, Henry "at times refused to acknowledge the simple fact that the effective exercise of these border offices was heavily dependent on a strong local following based on extensive landed possessions in the region."[16] As his reign progressed, Henry became increasingly unwilling to tolerate the power of a lord like Lord Dacre, and so he tried to remove him from political influence and replace him with a lesser lord under direct royal control. In thus moving outside the traditional feudal hierarchy, Henry left himself open to failure. Following the disgrace of Dacre in 1534, the government lurched from one failure to another in its increasingly expensive attempts to manage the north. A feudal

[16] Steven G. Ellis, "A Border Baron and the Tudor State: The Rise and Fall of Lord Dacre of the North," *Historical Journal* 35 (1992): 276; Steven G. Ellis, *Tudor Frontiers and Noble Power: The Making of the British State* (Oxford: Clarendon Press, 1995), 261.

magnate like Dacre could not simply be replaced, for his following was something more than a collection of employees.

No one was more aware of this reality than the first earl of Cumberland, given the brunt of the burden of replacing Dacre. As Hoyle argues, Cumberland had an unenviable task to perform in trying to control the northern borders; he was an ineffective replacement for Dacre, not because of personal, or even political, conflicts, but simply because he was the "friend and creation of the king."[17] The mere delegation of royal authority, even when accompanied by a large measure of royal favour, was not enough to rule a turbulent area without a solid base of local political and economic power. As Dacre's career displays, it was infinitely preferable to have both, but local power was more crucial to the maintenance of order on the borders than royal support.

The Pilgrimage of Grace, on the other hand, demonstrates that mere local authority was not enough to overcome the power of the crown. Disturbing as the rebellion was, there was no real possibility that it would unseat the dynasty, and to that extent the policies of Henry VII and Henry VIII bore fruit: there was no single overmighty subject and not even any coalition of nobles in the north with the power to overcome royal authority. As Smith points out, however, the Pilgrimage was more than just a failed feudal rebellion. Though the structure of the rebel armies was predominantly feudal and their demands were conservative, the presence of four men trained at the Inns of Court among the leaders of the rebellion indicates that this movement had a new element.[18] Smith argues that the Pilgrimage of Grace "represents an important step in the transition from tradition towards modernity in political life. To say that by 1536 ideology had begun to count as a factor in politics is to draw attention to a neglected but very important aspect of the decline of feudal lordship."[19] Smith's point is that, by seeking to have all his subjects swear allegiance to him, Henry was breaking the feudal ties between his lords and their tenants which had threatened the monarchy in the past. This seemed like a positive achievement, but in weakening the feudal bond between lords and tenants the

[17] R. W. Hoyle, "The First Earl of Cumberland: A Reputation Re-assessed," *Northern History* 22 (1986): 94.

[18] R. B. Smith, *Land and Politics in the England of Henry VIII: The West Riding of Yorkshire 1530–46* (Oxford: Clarendon Press, 1970), 208–09.

[19] *Ibid.*, 261.

crown was effectively weakening the feudal bond between the crown and its chief lords. The feudal bond, in a practical sense, was alive and well throughout England during the reign of the early Tudors. It is part of the ambiguity of Henry VIII's policies that, while he sought to exploit and even extend the financial reach of feudalism, he was attempting to undermine its effective exercise.

The single greatest opportunity to extend fiscal feudalism and to change the structure of the nobility came with the dissolution of the monasteries. The king's great matter and the religious changes that flowed from it are not part of our concern here, but the ancillary economic and political consequences are of vital importance. Indeed, though the dissolution of the monasteries is usually examined as part of the Reformation, Hoyle argues that it was predominantly and primarily an economic issue. He points out that there was a movement to suppress the monasteries in the 1529 parliament, long before the religious changes had begun. This idea was linked to a memorandum of Thomas, Lord Darcy, which called for the examination of all knights' fees, baronies, and earldoms to see how many of them were held by the church.[20] In the militaristic mood of the 1520s, there was clearly a concern that the military strength of the kingdom was being enervated by the extent of church landholding.

The idea went nowhere in 1529, but when a dissolution was proposed again in 1534 it was couched as an attempt to re-endow the monarchy with clerical lands. Once again, nothing came of the plan; Hoyle argues that it was presented to parliament and rejected in favour of the act for first fruits and tenths.[21] This act led to the first group of visitations of the monasteries, for the combined purposes of valuing the properties for taxation and evaluating their moral state. The decline of morals was then used as an excuse for the dissolution of the smaller monasteries, but this left the crown in a difficult position when it came to covet the larger institutions. The failure of the 1534 proposal made it apparent that there would not be widespread support for a dissolution on purely financial grounds, but the 1536 act specifically praised the state of religious observance in the larger monasteries, precluding the possibility of using moral

[20] R. W. Hoyle, "The Origins of the Dissolution of the Monasteries," *Historical Journal* 38 (1995): 287.

[21] *Ibid.*, 291–93.

decline as an excuse for dissolution.[22] It was at this point that the crown moved to the policy of "voluntary" submissions.[23] According to this interpretation, as Hoyle points out, the history of the dissolution bears a striking resemblance to the history of the Statute of Uses, both of which had important financial implications.[24] In both cases, the crown, faced with parliamentary opposition to its demands, resorted to extra-parliamentary methods to achieve its aims.

1536 saw not only the Statute of Uses and the act for the dissolution of the smaller monasteries, but also the establishment of the Court of Augmentations.[25] The court was necessary, not simply because of the anticipated profits from the confiscations, as the act stated, but because of crown policy from the reign of Henry VII onwards. Crown lands had been increasing steadily, even before the Reformation, through the accumulation of attainted property and estates acquired through purchase and exchange. The monastery lands and the lands attainted following the Pilgrimage of Grace, though they vastly augmented crown holdings, were an extreme example of the general fiscal policy.[26] Although all three acts had different origins, together they had the potential to revolutionize the finances of the Tudor monarchy through the exploitation of the prerogative. The act establishing the Court of Augmentations stated that all grants of any estate of inheritance were to be held by knight service in chief, and that the king was to reserve a yearly rent of one-tenth of the annual value of the property.[27] Thus, when the king granted out monastery lands, they would be held in knight service, guaranteeing to the king his full feudal prerogative without possibility of evasion, thanks to the Statute of Uses, and he would, moreover, have a guaranteed yearly rent.

It is assumed that the early destination of the confiscated lands was the re-endowment of the crown, and it was only as a result of the

[22] 27 Hen. VIII, c.28, *Statutes of the Realm*, 11 vols. (London, 1810–1822), vol. 3, 575–78.

[23] Hoyle, "Origins of the Dissolution," 300. As the dissolutions became a reality, the reluctance to use religious lands to endow the crown faded. See 37 Hen. VIII, c.4, *Stat. Realm*, vol. 3, 988.

[24] Hoyle, "Origins of the Dissolution," 301.

[25] 27 Hen. VIII, c.27, *Stat. Realm*, vol. 3, 569–74.

[26] W. C. Richardson, *History of the Court of Augmentations, 1536–1554* (Baton Rouge: Louisiana State University Press, 1961), 3.

[27] 27 Hen. VIII, c.27, *Stat. Realm*, vol. 3, 572.

financial pressure accompanying the wars with Scotland and France that large quantities of land were sold off.[28] The early proposals for confiscation focused on the possibilities of using the monasteries for re-endowment, and indeed, during the three years following the dissolution, only about one-eighth of the confiscated lands, totalling about £11,633 per annum, was granted out, mostly to servants of the crown.[29] Not all of the grants were free gifts, but even those which were purchased were granted on favourable terms. Even though these grants represented only a small proportion of the lands in royal hands, they could have a significant impact on the balance of power. Although most of the lands granted went to the high nobility, most noble families received nothing. As Miller points out, members of the high nobility already advanced by Henry VIII, mostly important office-holders or men known to the king through service at court, got grants, but only a couple of barons were so fortunate.[30] The grant of lands could dramatically alter the balance of power in the localities, but Henry seems to have paid little attention to this, demonstrating once again an indifference to the realities of local politics. The main beneficiaries of royal munificence, then, were those with influence at court.

Even leaving aside the implications of the royal grants in the localities, the simple logistics of royal grants caused problems. As long as every grant and long-term lease had to be made by the king himself, the pressure on him was immense. As well as being time-consuming, it was often difficult for him to refuse requests without causing political damage, either to himself or to the petitioner. The solution was to sell lands rather than giving them away, and the move was more significant than it might appear at first glance. As Miller argues, this meant anyone could now acquire land from the king; money was as effective as influence or service.[31] Gifts to favourites

[28] G. O. Woodward, *The Dissolution of the Monasteries* (New York: Walker & Co., 1966), 124; F. C. Dietz, *English Government Finance 1485–1558* (2nd edn, London: Frank Cass, 1964), 148–49 and 213; Joyce Youings, "The Terms of the Disposal of the Devon Monastic Lands, 1536–58," *English Historical Review* 69 (1954): 22.

[29] Dietz, *English Government Finance*, 148. Wyndham calculates that between 1536 and 1540 the top magnates got more than 80 percent of the property conveyed by the Crown in Somerset and more than half of the favourable grants. K. S. H. Wyndham, "In Pursuit of Crown Land: The Initial Recipients of Property in the Mid-Tudor Period," *Somerset Archaeology and Natural History* 123 (1979): 66.

[30] Miller, *English Nobility*, 246.

[31] *Ibid.*, 247.

did not cease entirely, but they became far less common.[32] This change had long-term ideological, as well as political, consequences. The large-scale sale of lands on the part of the crown removed any implication of a reciprocal relationship between king and nobility; grants of land were no longer related to any kind of service to the king, but simply to the payment of cold hard cash. Thus, Smith argues, "in the disposal of monastic property we see land not as a sacred trust but as the object of multifarious transactions whose ultimate object was to gain more wealth."[33] Though the concept of land as a sacred trust may seem a little idealistic, the divorce of grants of land from service had two important and related consequences for royal authority. First, land remained the primary source of power and influence in the localities, but the path to land was no longer necessarily through royal favour. This was bound to affect the role of the monarch as the source of power. Secondly, by removing the element of reward from grants of land, it was more difficult to expect grantees (effectively purchasers) to hold their land by the onerous burdens of knight service.

In spite of this, the crown departed from its policy of granting land to be held in knight service, stated in the act establishing the Court of Augmentations, with great reluctance.[34] Sales of monastic land began in earnest in 1539, and Dietz argues that by Michelmas of that year £80,622 had been received, but the official campaign began in December, when a commission was issued to Cromwell and Sir Richard Rich, chancellor of the Court of Augmentations, to sell crown lands of the annual value of £6,000 at twenty years' purchase, that is, for a capital sum of twenty times their recorded annual value.[35] The land was to be held by knight service and a

32 Wyndham, "In Pursuit of Crown Land," 66. Wyndham argues that, once the sale of crown lands began in earnest, the top nobility got far fewer grants than other grantees and less than one-fifth of the favourable grants.

33 Smith, *Land and Politics*, 259.

34 Both the larger monasteries in 1539 (31 Hen. VIII, c.13, *Stat. Realm*, vol. 3, 734) and the colleges and chantries in 1545 (37 Hen. VIII, c.4, *Stat. Realm*, vol. 3, 991) were expressly given into the administration of the Court of Augmentations, thus automatically coming under the statute of 27 Hen. VIII, c.27, which ordained that all land granted out from Augmentations would be held in knight service.

35 Dietz, *English Government Finance*, 148–49; Youings, "Terms of the Disposal," 23. This was the standard rate of purchase at this time. The work by Habakkuk, Kew, and Gray has demonstrated clearly that, with the exception of a few short periods in which the bureaucratic machinery took some time to catch up with the movements of the land market, the bulk of the monastery lands was sold

yearly rent of one-tenth the annual value of the lands was to be reserved. This gave the crown the prospect of having its cake and eating it: not only did it get the capital sum at the time of sale and the prospect of feudal incidents as they fell due, but it also had a guaranteed yearly income. Both elements of the bargain caused purchasers some concern, and as a result the terms of sale of monastic lands were moderated through legislation during the 1540s.

The reservation of military tenure on monastic lands was not a particularly heavy burden if the lands were granted to, or bought by, families who already held land by military tenure, but it represented a serious commitment for a family moving to build up a landed estate. The decision to reserve military tenure on these lands suggests that the crown was interested in extending the reach of the prerogative, or at least in establishing a clear title through newly granted lands. Although there has been no systematic study of the dispersal of monastic lands for the entire country, local studies suggest that a sizable proportion of the monastery lands went to small purchasers. Although the large transactions which established a new power in the localities, such as Russell's grants in Devon, have attracted most attention, Youings, for example, has discovered that most of the purchases in Devon were small, generally worth less than £20 per annum.[36]

This conclusion is supported by Kew, who has studied the land market in Devon for both monastic and private lands. He argues that the disposal of monastic lands was not as big an event on the land market as might be expected, because the land market was fairly active in Devon before the dissolution, though the actual extent of this activity is debatable.[37] Much of the market was for small parcels of land, and sales of this kind of property were not significantly affected by the dissolution, because the legal and administrative costs involved in purchasing directly from the crown were prohibitive for transactions of this size.[38] On the other hand, although the market in large estates was much more limited, it seems that purchasers

at current market prices. H. J. Habakkuk, "The Market for Monastic Property, 1539–1603," *Economic History Review* 2nd ser. 10 (1958): 362–80; J. Kew, "The Disposal of Crown Lands and the Devon Land Market, 1536–1558," *Agricultural History Review* 18 (1970): 93–105; Madeleine Gray, "Crown Property and the Land Market in South-East Wales in the Sixteenth Century," *Agricultural History Review* 35 (1987): 133–50.

[36] Youings, "Terms of the Disposal," 31.

[37] Kew, "Disposal of Crown Lands," 95. [38] *Ibid.*, 96.

interested in large-scale purchases did not have too much difficulty in finding lands for sale, as long as they were in a position to know when important landlords wanted to sell. The biggest gap in the land market seems to have been for medium-sized properties, worth between £5 and £15 per annum, properties which would sell for between £100 and £300. These properties would most likely be large farms or small manors, and they rarely appeared on the market, though they would be most likely to appeal to a successful merchant or lawyer seeking to establish a landed base. Kew discovered that only about 7 percent of the land purchases made in Devon before 1536 fit this description, while the proportion rose to 18 percent between 1536 and 1558, for much of the confiscated monastic property fell into this range.[39]

Important though the monastic lands were, then, the sale of monastic property probably did not dominate the land market in the 1530s and 1540s. Kew has calculated that between 1536 and 1558 there were approximately 3,000 to 4,800 transactions in the private land market in Devon, compared with 234 royal grants of land in the same period. The royal grants were generally of larger properties, as evidenced by the fact that the private transactions were worth about £8,000, while the royal grants were worth £6,000 to £6,500.[40] Thus about 25–30 percent of land by value in Devon changed hands in the period between 1536 and 1558. This impressive figure is less startling, however, when we remember that up to 20 percent of Devon landowning families failed in the male line in each generation, causing a comparable volume of property to change hands for purely demographic reasons.[41]

Though these findings for Devon cannot, of course, be generally applied to the entire kingdom, they do suggest that the impact of the disposal of monastic property was less significant than has sometimes been assumed. Kew suggests that the main appeal of monastic lands lay in the range of property available for purchase, in terms of both size and location, since the majority of purchasers were consolidating or extending their estates, rather than establishing new ones. Thus the sale of monastic lands probably stimulated activity on the private land market, as landholders sold small, scattered properties to raise the necessary capital to buy larger, more

[39] *Ibid.*, 96–97. [40] *Ibid.*, 102–03.
[41] *Ibid.*, 103 and 105. It is also likely that some properties were sold more than once.

compact holdings.[42] Other purchasers were from local landowning families who, having made their money in the law or some kind of royal service, took this opportunity to establish themselves in their home area, or to extend small patrimonies. Still other purchasers seem to have been tenants of monastery lands, who took the opportunity to purchase the lands they had previously been leasing. As Habakkuk points out, the simple fact that compact manors with a high proportion of demesne lands attached, the type of property described by Kew as most difficult to acquire before the dissolution and most suitable for the establishment of a new family, were sold at the standard rate of purchase, rather than above, indicates that they were not in particular demand.[43] Most of the scholars who have looked at this question have concluded that the dispersal of the monastic lands did not in fact generally lead to the establishment of a new group of landholders. Though some of the purchasers were merchants or lawyers seeking to move into the landed classes, even many of this group seem to have been junior members of landed families, and in most cases were quickly absorbed into their local gentry community.[44] There is no doubt that the sale of monastic lands stimulated the land market, but it does not seem to have greatly changed the patterns of landholding, though it may have altered the balance of power between existing landholders.[45] The overall picture of the effect of the sale of monastic property is less dramatic than we might have expected. It is clear that some landed families did establish themselves in this period, and some scholars choose to emphasize this point,[46] but in general it seems that the

[42] *Ibid.*, 101.

[43] Habakkuk, "Market for Monastic Property," 380. It is also clear that the lands were not sold off at bargain prices, as was once thought.

[44] Madeleine Gray, "Change and Continuity: The Gentry and the Property of the Church in South-East Wales and the Marches," in *Class, Community and Culture in Tudor Wales*, ed. J. Gwynfor Jones (Cardiff: University of Wales Press, 1989), 33; J. A. Youings, *The Dissolution of the Monasteries* (New York: Barnes & Noble, 1971), 129–30; G. R. Elton, *Reform and Reformation: England 1509–1558* (Cambridge MA: Harvard University Press, 1977), 247–48.

[45] Habakkuk, "Market for Monastic Property," 380.

[46] Bettey, for example, points out that, "of the 211 leading families of Dorset at the beginning of the seventeenth century, 103, or nearly half the total number, had appeared for the first time in the ranks of the gentry between the meeting of the Reformation Parliament in 1529 and the end of the reign of Elizabeth in 1603." J. H. Bettey, *The Suppression of the Monasteries in the West Country* (Gloucester: Alan Sutton, 1989), 146. Given the decline of landed families through natural causes, this does not seem to be as dramatic a statement as its author seeks to imply.

monastic lands were absorbed into the land market in a remarkably orderly fashion, and its purchasers were absorbed into the ranks of the gentry, from which most of them hailed in the first place, with equal ease.

Though the sale of monastic property may not have led to a social revolution, it probably did enlarge the number of tenants holding land in military tenure for the first time. Military tenure was a heavy burden for prospective purchasers, particularly those intending to buy only small parcels of land. For those who already held land in chief of the king, it was largely immaterial, since their lands already carried the burden of prerogative wardship, but for those branching out into the property market for the first time, or seeking to add to land held in socage or burgage, the prospect of becoming a tenant of the king can have held little attraction. Presumably in response to this, in 1544 an act was framed which gave commissioners selling lands worth less than 40s per annum the discretion to sell the land in knight service in chief or in socage or burgage, though the one-tenth annual payment was retained.[47] This act alone does not seem to have been enough to reassure prospective purchasers, and in 1545 another act was passed which confirmed that any land worth less than 40s annually, sold under any tenure other than knight service, was held in socage or burgage and would descend from father to son without livery or *ouster le main*.[48]

This concession seems to have helped in the process of selling lands, and it quickly became an established policy. The commission for sales of 1546 did not give the commissioners the choice of selling smaller plots of land in knight service or socage; instead it ordered that all lands worth less than 40s per annum should automatically be sold with a socage tenure.[49] Again, however, the buying public required confirmation, and they received it in a statute of 1 Edw. VI, which clarified the terms of holding land. It laid out that all tenants holding land of the king as of a dukedom, barony, or honour did not hold of the king in chief, thus effectively confirming that they were not subject to the burdens of prerogative wardship by re-stating the principle established in Magna Carta. The statute was careful, however, to point out that this only applied to lands obtained by

[47] 35 Hen. VIII, c.14, *Stat. Realm*, vol. 3, 973.

[48] 37 Hen. VIII, c.20, *Stat. Realm*, vol. 3, 1012–3.

[49] Joel Hurstfield, "The Greenwich Tenures of the Reign of Edward VI," *Law Quarterly Review* 65 (1949): 76.

the crown through attainder, outlawry, and ecclesiastical surrender, and then re-granted.[50] It did not affect older tenures, either lands held in knight service in chief as of the king's person, or anyone whose ancestors had previously sued livery or *ouster le main*.

The beginning of Edward's reign saw a further concession to prospective purchasers, for the commissions of 1548 once again allowed commissioners to grant lands in knight service or socage, but this time the limit was raised to land worth £4 per annum. This, combined with the statute of 1547, quickly had an effect on the tenure under which land was granted to buyers. The granting of lands to be held "as of the manor of east Greenwich" seems to have become the standard for parcels of land worth under £4, and the purchasers were usually careful to have the monetary value of the purchase clearly stated also.[51] It was worth their while to be careful: though the Statute of Wills of 1540 had ameliorated the effects of the Statute of Uses, the establishment of the Court of Wards made evasion of the royal prerogative increasingly difficult for those who fell under its jurisdiction.

Land was still sold in military tenure whenever possible, and, of course, all land granted as a reward for services carried the burdens attendant on knight service, for the king had no need to make the package attractive to the grantee. For ordinary purchasers, however, the crown was forced to continue granting land in socage, and by the end of Mary's reign the limit had gone up to £10, while by the end of Elizabeth's it was £20.[52] Though there is no doubt that the sale of monastic lands extended the reach of the royal prerogative, the change was not as dramatic as Hurstfield suggested.[53] If some of the purchasers of this land were subject to the claims of the prerogative through land they already owned, and others bought lands below the limit of £2 or £4 in socage, then the king's gains would be limited.

Besides tenure, the other problem facing buyers of monastic lands was the yearly rent, but the crown abandoned this with even greater

50 1 Edw. VI, c. 4, *Stat. Realm*, vol. 4, 9.

51 Hurstfield, "Greenwich Tenures," 77. Hurstfield suggests that much of the land sold to London entrepreneurs, for example, was intended for re-sale and thus was sold in parcels of less than £4 with a clear socage or burgage tenure. *Ibid.*, 78–79.

52 *Ibid.*, 80.

53 Joel Hurstfield, "The Revival of Feudalism in Early Tudor England," *History*, new ser. 37 (1952): 137.

reluctance than it sold land in socage. Youings suggests that the reserved rent was intended to replace the clerical tenth lost with the dissolution of the monasteries, but it had added benefits beyond this. The ongoing rent allowed the crown to maintain a regular tenurial contact with these tenants, thus reinforcing the pseudo-feudal bond, while it also helped to avoid the evasion of feudal dues on lands held in knight service.[54] However, the rent was burdensome for purchasers and from the mid to late 1540s it began to be omitted from commissions for sale entirely. In December 1544, tenants were allowed to buy up the rent reserved on lands purchased since June of that year, and in May 1546 the offer was extended to all lands bought since 1536.[55] For a short while in the mid-1540s, therefore, the crown was reserving rents on the land it sold at the same time that it was allowing tenants to buy up the reserved rent on land sold at an earlier date. This represents one of the more obvious attempts on the part of the government to make the monasteries provide both immediate cash and long-term income, though it seems to have given up the latter in preference for the former. The decision to drop the reserved rent made sound financial sense, because it not only increased the amount to be made from the immediate sale, but it reduced the administrative cost associated with gathering large numbers of small rents. As Youings discovered, however, tenants did not rush to take advantage of the offer, and some of these rents continued to be paid into the next century.[56] Burdensome though the rents were, it is likely that tenants simply did not have the cash reserves to pay off the rent as well as the purchase price.

The sale of monastic lands, though it provided an immediate cash windfall and the prospect of long-term financial stability, was not an unmixed blessing for the crown. There was no social revolution in the ranks of landowners, but the sale created a new class of military tenants who had no direct connection to the medieval tradition of feudal landholding, and could not even regard the burdens attached to their lands as a consequence of royal generosity. For those who continued to owe reserved rents, this reminder of their burden must have been a constant irritation, while the possibility of wardship was an ever-present fear. This frustration is strikingly expressed by Henry Spelman, who graphically describes

[54] Youings, "Terms of Disposal," 27. [55] *Ibid.*, 27. [56] *Ibid.*, 28.

> that immortal and incurable wound, which every day bleedeth more than other, given to us and our posterity by the infinite number of tenures by knight's service *in capite*, either newly created upon granting out of these monasteries and lands, or daily raised by double *Ignoramus* in every town almost of the kingdom. For as the abbeys had lands commonly scattered abroad in every of them, in some greater or lesser quantity, according to the ability of their benefactors, so the leprosy of this tenure comes thereby as generally to be scattered through the kingdom. And whereas before that time very few did hold on that manner besides the nobility and principal gentlemen that were owners of great lordships and possessions . . . now, by reason that those abbey lands are minced into such infinite numbers of little quillets, and thereby privily sown (like the tares in the parable) almost in every man's inheritance, very few . . . can assure themselves to be free from this calamity.[57]

Although the unwelcome obligations attached to knight service cannot be ignored, for our purposes Spelman's outburst is equally important as evidence that, for at least a substantial proportion of the landholders of the later sixteenth century, this was an unfamiliar tenancy. The statute passed by Edward VI in 1547 is one indication that the tenurial law needed to be restated, and the plethora of self-help law books coming from the printing press in the same period suggests that many of the new owners wanted to learn something for themselves about the obligations and rights attached to their new property.

It is not surprising to discover, then, that *Prerogativa Regis* appeared in the readings in this period. George Willoughby of the Inner Temple read on it in Lent of 1549, breaking the recent Gray's Inn monopoly of the topic. Only the first three lectures of the reading survive, covering chapters one and two of the text, on tenures and wardship. The manuscript of the reading covers the usual material, but it appears to be the work of a more senior member of the Inn, for it does not cover as wide a range of topics as the earlier expositions, and the majority of the points noted are marked with a *quere*, as though the writer was interested mainly in the more difficult and controversial issues, rather than the basics of the law.

Willoughby places himself squarely behind Frowyk at the opening of his lecture, declaring that the text is "only a treatise and

[57] Henry Spelman, *The History and Fate of Sacrilege . . .*, ed. C. F. S. Warren (4th edn, London, 1895), 130–31. He goes on to complain about the establishment and activities of the Court of Wards.

declaration of the king's prerogative at the common law."[58] His fidelity to Frowyk is undermined, however, in his introduction to the material on wardship. Frowyk, when faced with the problem of reconciling *Prerogativa Regis* and Magna Carta, without allowing that the former granted the king new rights (which would have made it a statute), argued that the king had always had the rights stated in *Prerogativa Regis*, but that they had previously been interpreted too narrowly.[59] Willoughby, on the other hand, recounts the developments in Magna Carta and Westminster II and adds the changes caused by *Prerogativa Regis* to this account, arguing that "by this article of the prerogative it is declared that the king shall have the marriage of the heir being under age who holds of him in chief, or by any escheat or because the lord of the heir is in the king's ward, having no respect to the priority of feoffment."[60] This pattern is typical of the reading as a whole: it is largely a recapitulation of Frowyk, but with some significant differences. In this case, the discrepancy is not very logical, and it gives the impression that Willoughby has not really thought through the implications of the two statements. It is difficult to tell whether his departures from his model are simply misinterpretations, or whether he is attempting to present the most recent ideas on the topic, without having integrated them fully into the material he has taken from Frowyk.[61]

Willoughby opens his reading with the usual material on tenures, discussing escuage, grand serjeanty, cornage, and so on.[62] His reliance on Frowyk is confirmed by his attention to the idea of tenure *ab antiquo*, which he defines as knight service which had continued from time immemorial, and his distinction that, if the king purchases land and gives it to hold of him, it is in chief, but not *ab antiquo*.[63] Though Willoughby does not comment on the relevance of this distinction, even to point out that it was no longer relevant, it is marked with a *quere* in the text, indicating either that the auditor did not see the point of the distinction, or did not agree with it.

58 Willoughby, BL MS Harley 1691, f.197.
59 See chapter 2, p. 88 above. 60 Willoughby, f.200v.
61 Although there were some inconsistencies in the earlier readings, and the manuscript of Willoughby does not preserve a complete text, the standard of learning in the readings given by the serjeants-elect does seem to be superior.
62 The manuscript does not deal with the more basic elements of tenure, again suggesting that the note-taker was fairly senior.
63 Willoughby, f.197v.

Willoughby's debt to Frowyk is equally clear in his interpretation of the king's rights when land escheats to him for felony or treason. He argues that, when a mesnalty held in chief of the king escheats for felony, the tenant holds of the king in chief, but, when it escheats for treason, the tenant will not hold in chief.[64] This is because the mesnalty which escheats to the king for felony was held of the king, and so the king will keep the tenure he had, while lands held of other lords may escheat to the king for treason. This argument goes against both Constable, who gave the king everything in chief, and Spelman, who gave nothing in chief, and, as with many of the other points, the writer has marked the disagreement.

Although Willoughby generally follows the pattern established by Frowyk, he does raise one issue absent from the earlier readings. He notes that, when "one who holds of the king in chief holds also certain lands of another in socage and dies, his heir under age, the king shall have his prerogative of the lands held in socage until the full age of the heir and yet the words of the prerogative are only *de quocunque tenuerit per* [*huiusmodi*] *servicium*."[65] Thus, according to the strict words of the statute, the king should have custody only of the land in knight service. This issue had not been raised by any of the earlier readers, who all agreed that the king would have custody of all the lands passed from the tenant to his heir, no matter how they were held, as long as he held something of the king in chief.[66] It is tempting to see here a new issue raised by those purchasers of monastic land who had previously only held land in socage and who resented their vulnerability to the imposition of the prerogative, particularly if the land held in chief represented only a small part of their total holdings. There is no way to prove this point, and Willoughby does not specifically refer to the monastic lands at any place in the surviving reading. This argument does stand out as one of the few places where Willoughby diverged significantly from the pattern of his model, and, not surprisingly, it is marked with a *quere*.

Though he relies on Frowyk, it is clear that Willoughby was not unthinkingly following his model, for, besides adding to and moderating some of Frowyk's views, he actively disagrees with him

64 Willoughby, f.198. 65 Willoughby, f.199.

66 Spelman had argued that the king's rights over land held in socage should follow the rules for socage lands, and re-emphasized the need for the tenant to have land in knight service in chief in order for the king to claim his prerogative, but he never went so far as to suggest that he would not get land held in socage.

in his discussion of collusion. Frowyk and Constable agreed that, where a tenant aliens land held of the king by collusion, and this is found in the inquisition, then the king would have everything, and Willoughby also accepts this.[67] Frowyk, however, goes on to argue that, if the tenant aliens land held of other lords, the king has no remedy, since he cannot aver covin under the statute of Marlborough, the usual practice, because the statute is only available to the lords. Willoughby, on the other hand, argues that the king can aver covin under the statute of Marlborough, and will have his prerogative in the land.[68] Again, the auditor does not seem to have been convinced, and it is an odd argument. The most likely explanation for Willoughby's divergence here is the impact of the statute of 4 Hen. VII.[69] Frowyk discounted this as an element in the interpretation of the prerogative for the same reason that he discounted the statute of Marlborough, because it did not name the king. Over the course of time, however, it was established that the 1490 statute did in fact apply to the king, and it is possible that Willoughby applied the same principle retroactively to Marlborough, as they had been linked by Frowyk. If this is the case, it is a small, but curious example of re-interpretation of the old law to conform with the new.

Willoughby, then, has little new to tell us about the development of the prerogative in the 1540s. The section of his reading that survives is a fairly faithful reprisal of Frowyk's lectures. Given the level of similarity between the two readings, it seems that Willoughby worked from some version of Frowyk's material, probably a manuscript in circulation at the Inner Temple. Willoughby's only original contribution, his questioning of the king's right to claim lands his tenants held in socage, does not seem to have had any immediate impact, though we will see it appear again. The survival of Willoughby's truncated lectures in a single manuscript further suggests that they were not considered particularly valuable at the time, though given the vagaries of manuscript survival this is not a particularly compelling point.

The last reader in this period to handle *Prerogativa Regis* was William Staunford of Gray's Inn, who probably read on it in Lent

[67] See chapter 2, p. 95 above; Willoughby, f.199v.

[68] Willoughby, f.199v. Constable does not deal explicitly with this issue. He says that if the tenant aliens land held of the king and other lords the king will recover it all, but he does not specify what would happen if the tenant aliens only land held of other lords by collusion.

[69] See chapter 2, pp. 105–11 above.

of 1551.[70] There is no surviving manuscript of Staunford's reading, but we do have his treatise on the topic, the *Exposicion*.[71] The relationship between the treatise and his probable reading is not clear, however. The treatise was dedicated in 1548, and seems to have circulated within the legal profession soon after that, though it was not published until 1567.[72] Thus the treatise predates his presumptive reading, and apparently remained more valuable than it. It is also rather different from the usual readings, most obviously because it is in English, but also for its extensive use of authorities.

Staunford makes it clear in the title that he is relying heavily on the material in Fitzherbert's *Graunde Abridgement*, and he presents the treatise almost as a digest of the abridgment, though he does use other sources. One of the surviving fragments of Yorke's reading also refers to Fitzherbert, and this points to the impact of his abridgment on the legal profession in general, and legal education in particular.[73] The inclusion of Fitzherbert's name in the title of Staunford's treatise may indicate a new concept of authority, but it is worth remembering that Port also leaned heavily on authorities. Neither man read as a serjeant-elect, and, while Staunford is certainly the product of a new age, and is probably also using Fitzherbert's name as a marketing ploy, there may also have been a certain comfort in his name. Besides using the most recent authorities, Staunford also uses Bracton and Britton more consistently than most of the readers on this topic. This impression of antiquarian learning is reinforced by his (very) occasional references to classical authors like Seneca.[74]

[70] J. H. Baker, *Readers and Readings in the Inns of Court and Chancery*, Selden Society Supplementary Series vol. 13 (London: Selden Society, 2001), 38–39.

[71] William Staunford, *An Exposicion of the Kinges Prerogatiue, collected out of the great Abridgement of Iustice Fitzherbert, and other olde Writers of the Lawes of Englande* . . . (London, 1567).

[72] The popularity of the treatise is attested by its publication in 1567, 1568, 1573, and 1577. S. E. Thorne, ed., *A Discourse upon the Exposicion and Understandinge of Statutes* (San Marino: Huntingdon Library, 1942), 92.

[73] J. H. Baker, ed., *The Reports of Sir John Spelman*, 2 vols., Selden Society vol. 93 and 94 (London: Selden Society, 1976 and 1977), vol. 2, 162. In using the abridgment, Staunford was closing a circle, for both Fitzherbert and Brooke regarded readings as suitable sources for their collections. L. W. Abbott, *Law Reporting in England 1485–1585* (London: Athlone Press, 1973), 59.

[74] Staunford, *Exposicion*, f.5. Baker comments that Staunford "wrote books so crammed with references and quotations that he seemed incapable of venturing an opinion unless it could be derived from someone else. In that sense Staundford [*sic*] was the first modern legal textbook writer." J. H. Baker, "English Law and the Renaissance," *Cambridge Law Journal* 44 (1985): 59.

Though he follows the usual practice of the readings in explaining each chapter of the statute in turn with the use of examples, Staunford's examinations are much shorter than the usual treatment in the readings, his examples are fewer, and he separates his discussion of process from his consideration of the law. All of these peculiarities suggest that Staunford intended his treatise for a different audience than the reading, presumably for the new holders of land in knight service. Staunford's reader would have required some knowledge of the law, but his book does limit itself to the situations and problems most likely to arise regularly, rather than dealing with more technically challenging settlements.

All of these factors cast some doubt on the utility of comparing Staunford's treatise with the earlier readings, but, though it is rather more difficult to relate him to those treatments, Staunford remains part of their tradition. First, even though his book is limited in the topics it covers, he remains true to the Inns by pointing out and examining the places where the law was, and remained, unclear. The *quere*s in his treatise demonstrate both the habit of disputation in the Inns, and how unsettled the law on the prerogative remained, even at this late date. Secondly, the treatise seems to have found some favour with the legal profession. In his address to Nicholas Bacon, which prefaces the work, Richard Tottell notes that the "woorke . . . is thought well of by the Sages of the law, and well worthy to be printed."[75] Though Tottell might simply be promoting his new product, there is a good deal of truth to his claim, and Staunford does seem to have become the standard reference on the topic: Egerton owned the treatise in both manuscript and print and one of the few clearly intelligible words in one fragment of Yorke's reading is the word "Staunford."[76] Though this may partly have been because it was the only printed work on the topic, Staunford's eminence, and the place of his treatise in the dissemination of knowledge of the prerogative, would alone justify consideration of his work.[77] It is also worth remembering that a good proportion of the audience at the Inns did not intend to become

[75] Tottell, in Staunford, *Exposicion* (no pagination).

[76] Thorne, ed., *Discourse upon the Exposicion and Understanding*, 92; BL MS Hargrave 253, f.77v.

[77] Staunford was attorney-general of the Court of Surveyors from 1542 to 1546, created serjeant in 1552, and became a justice of the common pleas in 1554. Baker, *Readers and Readings*, 38.

professional lawyers, and Staunford recognizes this, pointing out that, if treatises such as this make the acquisition of legal knowledge easier, students "might both as they went and after they come to their iorneis end gather some other knowledge, not onely therewith to garnish theire owne science, but also the better to serue in such honorable rome as they be called to serue the kinge and soueraigne lord in."[78]

Despite the differing format of Staunford's work, its handling of the first chapter of the statute covers the same kinds of issues as the readings, establishing what kinds of tenures on what kinds of holdings bring the prerogative. Thus he points out that the prerogative applies to tenants by estate of inheritance or for term of life, to tenants in possession or reversion, and to services as well as lands.[79] In all of these cases, and throughout this section, Staunford emphasizes that the usual interpretation goes beyond the words of the statute; for example, he points out that, though the words of the statute are "*in dominico suo*," "this woorde demeane is not here taken to bee the verie possession or takyng of the profits, for if the kinges tenaunt dye seased but of a reuercion or of a remainder in landes holden of a common person and duringe the minoritye of his sonne the particuler tenaunte dyethe, the kynge (this notwithstanding) shall haue this lande in warde as he hath the rest."[80] Staunford does not pursue the difference between a remainder and a reversion here, but he follows this point with a discussion of whether the tenant must die seised, as the statute says, in order for the king to claim his prerogative. He points out that, if a tenant dies seised but a stranger then intrudes on the land, the heir will still be in ward. From here, he makes the logical progression to the question of whether, if the king's tenant is disseised and dies, the king should have the prerogative, and concludes, with some trepidation, that he should.[81] In this way, Staunford follows Spelman in concluding that the heir's right to the land, even without possession, will bring the prerogative, though the words of the statute limited it to cases where the tenant died seised in his demesne.

Staunford seems to place himself with those who believe that *Prerogativa Regis* should be interpreted narrowly, for he argues that parliament "maketh no part of the kinges prerogatife, but long time

[78] Staunford, *Exposicion*, preface to Nicholas Bacon.
[79] *Ibid*, ff.6v–7v. [80] *Ibid*., f.8. [81] *Ibid*., ff.8–8v.

before it had his being by thorder of the commen law."[82] He does not make the point explicitly, but his constant reminders that the statute is not being interpreted literally in practice suggest that he disapproves of the practice of extending the prerogative. Staunford emphasizes this issue in a particularly striking manner when he remarks that the statute gives the king custody of the lands the tenant held of other lords.

> *Per huiusmodi seruicium*, that is to saye, by lyke seruice. Bye these woordes the landes that are holden of other muste bee holden allso by knyghtes seruice or els the statute extendes not to them, and yet the lawe is taken to the contrarye, for yf the lands holden of other bee holden but in socage or free burgage the kynge shal haue prerogatiue in them as it appearethe in 24 E3 for this statute is but a confirmacion of the common lawe, and therefore shallbee taken by equities and namelye when the lawe was so taken in 9 H3 whiche was longe time before the makyng of this statut. Howebeit Bracton & Britton dothe extende this prerogatiue no further then to landes holden of other by knightes seruice, therefore enquire for the cause and reason thereof.[83]

Staunford is raising the same doubt as Willoughby did here, though none of the earlier readers had questioned the king's right to this land. The fact that Staunford had to go back to the thirteenth century to raise controversy over this matter indicates the difficulty of finding a contrary authority, while he himself recognizes that this issue was settled even before the statute came into existence, and so there is no real suggestion that it can, even if it should, be changed. Nevertheless, the coincidence of the two Edwardian readers raising this same obscure issue is too much to ignore, and it reinforces the earlier suggestion that it was raised at the behest, or at least under the stimulus, of purchasers of monastic lands.

Though Staunford seems to believe that the words of the text should be limited to a strict interpretation, his understanding of the prerogative as an element of the common law causes him to

[82] Staunford points to writers like Glanvill, Bracton, and Britton, who discussed the prerogative before the statute existed, to demonstrate that it came from the common law, and argues that *Prerogativa Regis* was simply a declaration made by parliament to clarify the situation.

[83] Staunford, *Exposicion*, ff.8v–9. Staunford's argument that the text should be interpreted broadly because it was an affirmation of the common law was not unusual: Mordant made the same point in *Stonor's Case*. M. Hemmant, ed., *Select Cases in the Exchequer Chamber before all the Justices of England*, vol. 2, Selden Society vol. 64 (London: Bernard Quaritch, 1948), 165.

expand it on occasion. In considering wardship, he asks whether, since "there bee diuers statutes concernynge wardeshyppe made aswell beefore as since the time of kynge Edwarde the seconde... this prerogatiue wyl extende to those statutes or not, and it seemethe it dothe."[84] To support his point Staunford gives the example of the statute of 4 Hen. VII, which "prouidethe that the heire *cesty que vse* shall bee in warde."[85] He argues that, if the king's tenant-in-chief made a feoffment of lands which he held of another lord to the use of himself and his heirs, and then died before the making of the Statute of Uses, the king would have his prerogative in those lands, and he cites *Stonor's Case* in support of his argument.[86] As the arguments in *Stonor's Case* demonstrate, it took the lawyers some time to reach the conclusion that the king should have the benefit of that statute, with some disagreement on the issue continuing until the early sixteenth century. Staunford makes no mention of the debate, simply taking the final interpretation as supporting a broader reading of the king's rights to wardship.[87]

Staunford also opens up the king's right to claim wardship over the lord by priority. He argues that according to Bracton and Britton "no lorde can be more auncienter than the kynge, for all was in hym and came from hym at the begynninge. And therefore his highnesse muste haue prerogatiue in the bodye of whosoeuer the infaunte holdeth besides."[88] For this reason, Staunford gives the king the right to wardship of the body in preference to the lord by priority, not only when the tenant held of the crown, or of a new escheat[89] or when a tenant was in wardship by reason of wardship, but even when the king purchased a segniory, or a manor held of one of his new escheats.[90] In general terms, Constable and Frowyk agreed that the king had this prerogative where land was held of the crown or by escheat, and Constable extended it to a wardship by reason of

[84] Staunford, *Exposicion*, f.9. [85] *Ibid.*, f.9.

[86] *Ibid.*, ff.9–9v. He makes an identical point later, in his discussion of primer seisin, where he points out that before the Statute of Uses the heir of the *cestui que use* had to sue an *ouster le main sine exitibus*, which he describes as "in nature of a livery for the heire of *cestuy que use* which had bene in ward." *Exposicion*, ff.15–15v. Staunford's mention of the Statute of Uses in these two places highlights the otherwise complete omission of the topic from his treatise.

[87] See chapter 2, pp. 105–11 above. [88] Staunford, *Exposicion*, f.10.

[89] As opposed to the "old escheats," which had belonged to the crown since shortly after the conquest. See chapter 2, p. 84 above.

[90] Staunford, *Exposicion*, ff.10–10v. He does concede that this gives the king wardship only over the body, and not the lands held of the other lords.

wardship.[91] On the specific question of wardship, Constable argued that the king should also be preferred to the lord by priority whenever he held land as king, such as a forfeiture for treason, or the land of an idiot, though Frowyk did not take this view.[92] In attaching the prerogative to land purchased by the king, Staunford seems to be pushing the prerogative in the same way as Constable, but with less justification. One possible reason for Staunford's new approach to this issue is the framing of the act establishing the Court of Augmentations, which gave jurisdiction over land purchased by the king to the court.[93] The inclusion in the act of lands purchased by the king, as well as lands coming to the king through dissolution, may have encouraged Staunford to assume that they would carry the same obligations, especially since he inclined towards blending statutory provisions. It was possibly this kind of confusion which led to the statute of 1547 to clarify tenures.

On the question of primer seisin, Staunford has little new to say. He does confirm indisputably the failure of Constable's attempt to apply the claim to primer seisin to lands held of the king only by escheat, for he opens his discussion of this section with the statement that, if the tenant does not hold of the king in chief, "the kynge can haue noe primer seisin."[94] In fact, Staunford does not even raise the issue of lands held as of escheat. He does remark that this rule was questioned because a tenant holding lands in burgage in the city of London of the king had had his lands seized and sued livery, but he points out that this precedent was rejected by Markham, chief justice of the king's bench, in 1467, with the agreement of all the judges. He concludes from this that the tenant "must holde of the kynge in capite, but whether he holde of the kyng by knights seruice or by Socage in capite it makethe noe matter so that he holde in capite, for the kinge in bothe cases shall haue primer seisin althoughe not wyth so large a prerogatiue in thone case as in the other."[95]

Staunford's treatment of primer seisin also demonstrates that, while Constable's attempt to extend primer seisin to lands held in escheat had failed, Frowyk's attempt to avoid a coincidence of the claims of primer seisin and wardship had also failed. He points out

[91] Constable, 27–28. [92] See chapter 2, pp. 100–01 above.
[93] 27 Hen. VIII, c.27, *Stat. Realm*, vol. 3, 571.
[94] Staunford, *Exposicion*, f.13. [95] *Ibid.*, f.13v.

that, where the tenant held land of the king by knight service in chief, "the kynge shall haue the same prerogatiue when the heire is of full age at the deathe of his auncester as he should haue hadde yf hee hadde beene wythin age,"[96] i.e. prerogative in all the lands of the tenant, those held of other lords as well as the king, both in knight service and in socage. If the tenant held land in socage in chief of the king, on the other hand, the king had no claim to the lands held of other lords if they were held by knight service, while he had no right to primer seisin on the lands held even of himself in socage in chief if the heir was under the age of fourteen. In both cases, the guardian of the body of the heir, in the first case the lord of whom the land was held in knight service, and in the second case the *prochein amy*, would come and sue *ouster le main cum exitibus*.[97] It was only where the heir of land held in socage in chief was over the age of fourteen at the death of his ancestor that the king could have primer seisin and the heir must sue livery. Staunford speculates that in this case the king will also have primer seisin of the lands held of other lords, even if they are held in socage, but he is unsure if this is so. His doubt on this issue comes from his attempt to reconcile the statute of Marlborough with *Prerogativa Regis*, and this demonstrates again the desire of the lawyers to integrate the various statutes into a coherent interpretation of the law. It was this process which led to the identification of the king's rights to wardship and primer seisin, for Staunford consistently mingles the instructions of the statute, arguing that "these wordes [on primer seisin] may bee conferred and coupled with the firste chapiter of this statute of prerogatiue whiche hath the verye self same wordes. And therefore looke in what cases noted vppon the firste chapiter the king hath his prerogatiue by reason of wardship, In al the same cases shall his highnes haue prerogatiue by reason of primer seisin."[98]

Having discussed primer seisin, Staunford moves on to suing livery, and again he gives a short, pithy, and relevant discussion of the topic, providing the information most likely to be of general use. For example, he points out that, even if an heir was in ward, the king would still have primer seisin and relief, and the heir would

[96] *Ibid.*, f.13v.

[97] *Ibid.*, ff.13v–14. Cf. Spelman, chapter 4, p. 117 above, on wardship of heirs in socage. Willoughby also makes the point that an heir to land held in socage in chief will not be in ward, but will have to sue livery.

[98] Staunford, *Exposicion*, f.14. The only exception he makes is for collusion.

still have to sue livery, though in this case he would only pay half a year's profit for primer seisin, while if he was not in ward he would pay a full year's profit.[99] Staunford also lists other heirs whose lands might be seized by the king, such as wards by reason of wardship and tenants of bishops' temporalities in the king's hands because of vacancy, and he describes their responsibilities.[100] Most of this material is fairly straightforward, but Staunford does raise a couple of disputed points. He asks, for example, if the king's tenant-in-chief dies, leaving an heir of full age, and one that holds of the heir dies before he has sued livery, does the king have primer seisin of the lands of the second heir, i.e. primer seisin by reason of primer seisin? Staunford concludes that he should, as a logical extension of his identification of the king's rights to wardship and primer seisin, but he recognizes that the point is doubtful.[101] He also questions whether, if a tenant dies seised of a reversion with a rent reserved, the heir should sue livery immediately, or should wait until the reversion falls to him. He argues that the normal procedure with a reversion is to allow the heir to choose: if he decides to sue livery immediately, he only pays half a year's profit, while, if he elects to wait for the death of the tenant in possession, he must pay a full year's profit. When there is a rent reserved, however, he believes that the heir suing livery during the life of the tenant should pay a year's profit of the rent as well as the half year's profit on the land, though again, he is not entirely sure if this is the case.[102] Besides demonstrating the administration's concern to take its share of every part of the heir's income, this argument also highlights its preference for money in the hand rather than in the bush.

With the establishment of the Court of Wards and Liveries, the process involved in holding inquisitions and suing livery was tightened up, and Staunford makes some reference to this. He points out that by a statute of 1542 (the Act concerning Wards and Liveries) it was ordered that no one holding land worth more than £5 per annum could sue livery before an inquisition was held by the escheator or

99 *Ibid.*, f.14v. 100 *Ibid.*, ff.14v–15.

101 In 1516, it had been argued that the king would not have primer seisin by reason of ward, which makes it unlikely that primer seisin by reason of primer seisin would be accepted. John Caryll, *Reports of Cases by John Caryll*, ed. J. H. Baker, 2 vols., Selden Society vols. 115 and 116 (London: Selden Society, 1998 and 1999), vol. 2, 669.

102 Staunford, *Exposicion*, f.13.

other commissioner, under the authority of the Court of Wards.[103] This opened up the holders of these lands to the activities of the officials of the court, and, following the redistribution of monastic lands, the commissioners must have been eager to establish who had become a tenant of the king. They may in fact have been too eager, and their position certainly gave them the potential to greatly disrupt their neighbours' lives. Such activities may well account for one of the demands of Kett's rebellion that "nomen shalbe put by your Esthetory and Ffeodarie to ffynde eny office unles he holdeth of your grace in cheffe or capite above x[li] by yere."[104] It is striking that the issue centred around the king's interest in lands worth £5–10 annually, the very parcels which seem to have been of most interest to those entering the monastic land market.

The process of suing special livery for lands worth more than 20 marks per annum seems to have become standard by this period, for Staunford addresses the question of whether the heir who holds lands in various counties and sues special livery must have an inquisition, and answers in the affirmative, "for the kinge can neuer be fulli enformed of his title vnlesse ther be an office found in euery shere, & also by finding of seueral offices one record may be better for the kinge then another, whereof his grace may take auantage, for the best shal be taken for the kinge."[105] The new court was clearly developing new protocols for the holding of inquisitions, and, though it encouraged the suing of special livery for larger estates, thus reducing the risk of a technical error in the proceedings holding up the livery, it clearly had no intention of allowing this concession to undermine the king's right to examine his tenant's lands in detail.

Staunford's approach to the prerogative confirms the attitude among the other readers, and indeed highlights it. We have seen

103 *Ibid.*, f.50v. 33 Hen. VIII, c.22, *Stat. Realm*, vol. 3, 861. 1542 saw a good deal of rationalization of the administration of prerogative income. Besides this statute, an act was also passed establishing the Court of Surveyors to supersede the office of surveyors. 33 Hen. VIII, c.39, *Stat. Realm*, vol. 3, 879–90.

104 F. W. Russell, *Kett's Rebellion in Norfolk* (London, 1859), 52. The enmity between Kett and the local escheator, John Flowerdew, may have made this a more prominent issue than it otherwise would have been, but it is still striking that it was important enough to be included in the list of the rebels' grievances. See S. T. Bindoff, *Kett's Rebellion, 1549* (London: Historical Association, 1949), 15–16.

105 Staunford, *Exposicion*, f.51.

that Constable, in presenting *Prerogativa Regis* as a statute, went on to extend the prerogative in the king's favour in many ways, most notably in his treatment of primer seisin, while Frowyk, by insisting that the text was simply a declaration of the common law, limited it to a strict interpretation. Both readers, however, restricted or extended the law where their understanding of the material dictated it, even when such an interpretation ran contrary to their usual approach. Although their attitude to the law was consistent, neither reader sought to grant or withhold privileges that their reading of the law would not support, thus indicating that, though they may have had sympathies in one direction or the other, their first loyalty was to the integrity of the law. Both Spelman and Willoughby followed Frowyk, though Spelman was a little more lax in his definition of the text, accepting that at least part of it made new law, but again they diverged from their predecessors on occasion, not on ideological grounds, but on their interpretation of the law. Staunford, though he accepts that the king's prerogative rights come from the common law, looks on *Prerogativa Regis* as a parliamentary confirmation of those rights, and thus he is positioning himself between the two groups. In presenting the text as a confirmation of the common law, Staunford is indicating his belief that it must be interpreted closely, except where it affirmed the common law, when it could be extended. By constantly drawing attention to the ways in which the text is not interpreted literally, Staunford seems to indicate a dissatisfaction with the extension of the prerogative, but, at the same time, he seeks to extend the prerogative in some areas left untouched by the previous readers. Staunford again indicates the way in which the lawyers tried to balance their own feelings and inclinations with their understanding of the law, sometimes with incongruous results. He also demonstrates that the law continued to remain unclear in places, and the lawyers continued to debate it, even after the readings on the topic ended, and even in works directed at a more general audience.

Staunford's *Exposicion* is not only shorter and simpler than the readings, it is quite obviously in a different category for another reason. The readings sought, not only to expound the law, but to develop the legal sense of the students, their "forensic agility."[106] The numerous cases given as examples by the readers served not

[106] E. W. Ives, "A Lawyer's Library in 1500," *Law Quarterly Review* 85 (1969): 108.

only to highlight issues that the apprentices might expect to see in practice, but to develop their ability to interpret the law in various situations. Staunford's book, though it points out areas of disagreement, is less concerned with this development of legal sense, than with giving a clear and practical overview of the prerogative as it was then understood. His treatise is indicative of one kind of change taking place in the teaching of the prerogative in the second half of the sixteenth century. The reading given by James Morice in the Middle Temple in 1578 suggests another.

Morice's text has some features in common with Staunford's treatise: it is in English, and it survives in the writer's own words. Though the introduction states very clearly that it was given as a reading in the Middle Temple and apologizes that it has not been polished since delivery, the fact that the text is addressed to William Cecil (supposedly at his request) throws some doubt on the accuracy of this statement. The modesty topos carries over to the opening of the reading itself, where Morice apologizes to the assembled audience for his choice of text, and proceeds to justify himself with a display of humanist learning. Though it was never published, Morice's reading is a treatise as surely as Staunford's, and one which demonstrates the shift in the prerogative from the feudal to the constitutional.

Though he set out to discuss the royal prerogative, Morice did not read on *Prerogativa Regis*, but on Westminster I c.50. In his reading he explains quite clearly why he made this choice: in his view *Prerogativa Regis* is not a statute, and it does not effectively cover the royal prerogative, since it contains "only a very few of them, and those not the chiefest."[107] To prove the first assertion, he repeats familiar arguments: it is not named or dated;[108] "the authoritie of Bookes and learned men" shows that it is not a statute;[109] and

[107] BL MS Egerton 3376, f.7.

[108] He adds that it should not be excused on this account by its age, since "the makers of Statutes of former tyme have ever had especiall regard certainly to sett downe necessary circumstances requisite and convenient for matters of record." *Ibid.*

[109] For this he gives the usual year book references to YB Trin. 43 Edw. III, f.22, pl.12, and Littleton and Choke in YB Mich. 15 Edw. IV, ff.12–13, pl.17. He refers to Fitzjames' reading, as reported by Brooke, and to Frowyk's, and points out that in the *New Commentaries* it is called a treatise. Finally, he warns the reader not to be confused by its appearance in the "Common booke of Statutes," since other non-statutory texts, like the *Expositiones vocabulorum* and the *Dies Communes in Dote* also appear there. *Ibid.*, f.7v.

"Mr. Stamford in his treatice therevpon hath said that all or the most part of the Prerogatives therein declared were before at the Common Law."[110] He recognizes that the earlier readings imply that the text is a statute, and deflects argument by suggesting that those readers used the text because of "the excellent matter therein conteyned and Common opinion which often prevaileth."[111] However, *Prerogativa Regis* does not serve his purposes, which he lays out very clearly in his introduction.

Morice opens the text with a discussion of royal power which differs strikingly from the earlier readings. Describing the king as the head of the body politic, he asks "what can a right or Prerogative Royall more aptly signifie and expresse vnto vs then that a lawfull Prince by Iustice and not by pleasure doth rule and governe the people comitted to his charge."[112] From here, he moves into a discussion of the relative merits of democracy, oligarchy, and monarchy, complete with references to Athens and Rome. He concludes with a rousing vindication of monarchy bounded by law, but

> least peradventure it may be thought that while wee bind and linck the king to law, wee derogate over much thereby vnto his Royall Matie and seeme to sett forthe a Venetian Duke or Spartane King, we are to learne by this our Statute with what ample soveraigne and honorable rightes preheminences, dignities and prerogatives the wise and politike lawes of this Realme haue adorned and enriched the Royall Throne and imperiall diademe of this soe flourishing a kingdom . . .[113]

Thus Morice's reading has little interest in the nitty-gritty of the king's feudal prerogatives, but is focused much more on the broader conception of the royal prerogative, of which wards and liveries were only a small, and perhaps not very interesting, part. Morice doubtless recognized the practical value of wardships and liveries, and in 1589 he became attorney of the Court of Wards.[114] Nonetheless, his clear and quite conscious rejection of *Prerogativa Regis* as a useful topic for discussion would seem to mark the end of the active and controversial phase of its history.

The last text on the topic in this period only confirms this assessment, for it is not an exposition of the prerogative, but a treatise on wards and liveries. Sir James Ley became attorney of the Court of Wards in 1608, and his *A Learned Treatise concerning Wards and Liveries* was written during his tenure of that office, though it was

110 *Ibid.*, f.7v. 111 *Ibid.* 112 *Ibid.*, f.3v.
113 *Ibid.*, f.5v. 114 Baker, *Readers and Readings*, 165.

not published until 1642. Ley's connection with the court makes him particularly well equipped to write this treatise, and the dedication directs it specifically to the students of the law who hope to practice there. Like the dedication of Staunford's *Exposicion*, it remarks on the amount of labour needed to digest the law on any topic from the various year books and abridgments, and offers the work as a way around such a tedious task. Ley's treatise puts us in a new era in legal education, for by the end of the sixteenth century the readings had often declined, partly because of treatises like his and Staunford's, into expositions of obscure and arid knowledge, rather than useful guides to the realities of practice.

Ley's text is clearly related to Staunford in structure as well as intent, for it also separates its discussion of the law from the discussion of process, but it is further removed from the readings than Staunford's. Ley does not structure his treatise around *Prerogativa Regis*, and he avoids the earlier practice of beginning his discussion of each new segment with the words of the statute. Although he covers similar material, his work is more clearly presented as a textbook; for example, it breaks the question of tenures into separate sections under headings such as "Tenure *in Capite* by Knights service" and "Common Knights service of the King." Like Staunford, Ley is also much more limited in the range of material he covers; his work is intended as an introduction to the principles of the law, but does not use examples to illuminate those principles.

Although Ley is clearly not within the tradition of the readings, it is worth taking a quick look at his treatise, for it is the last statement of the law in this period, and demonstrates the conclusions the legal profession had reached on the prerogative. Ley has little to say on the more basic questions of tenure, for they had remained the same through all the readings. He restates some of the basic points made by Frowyk and particularly relevant to the active land market of the later sixteenth century, for example that, when the king grants lands out, it was customary for him "to restore the ancient Tenure of the Subiect, and if a grant had beene made otherwise, hee of whom the lands were holden before, had his remedy by petition to the King."[115] Similarly, he negates Staunford's extension of the king's rights over land he had purchased with the simple statement that if "the King purchase a Mannor, of which I.S. holds, hee shall

[115] Sir James Ley, *A Learned Treatise concerning Wards and Liveries* (London, 1642), 4.

hold as hee held before, and shall not sue Livery, nor pay Primer seisin, nor hold *in Capite*."[116]

Ley also indicates some changes made in the reign of Edward VI which Staunford did not cover. These changes support the idea that the process governing the administration of the prerogative was tightened up under the Court of Wards. Thus he discusses the statute of 1549 which ordained that, when an inquisition could not discover the tenure by which land was held, or from whom it was held, it would not automatically be taken as a tenure for the king, as had previously been done. Instead, a *melius inquirendum* would issue, to inquire further, but, if the information was still not available, the king would then claim his traditional rights.[117] The act also redressed a nagging injustice, remarked upon by the earlier readers, by allowing an heir of full age found to be under age to traverse the mistaken inquisition. The statute did not really deprive the king of anything, but it was intended to restrain the administrators of the prerogative from anticipating too much. Its preamble suggests that royal officials were, as usual, presuming on their office, for it states that the statute was framed expressly because copyholders and leaseholders were being ejected from their lands by inquisitions which found that the land was held of the king, and then had no remedy. The passing of the statute indicates a desire to conciliate these tenants by curbing the enthusiasm of the royal officials, but it must also be considered in conjunction with the rebellions of 1549.

Though Ley does cover the same kinds of issues as the readers, his simple formulations of the law seem to be miles away from the complex discussions of Frowyk and Constable. His statement that

> To Knights service *in Capite*, are incident not only Ward, Marriage, Primer seisin, Reliefe, Livery, and Licence to alien, but also Prerogative to Wardships, and Primer seisin of all other Lands holden of common persons in Knights service, or in Soccage, and of all other services, whereof the Tenant *in Capite* dyed sole seised in Fee, and Fee taile in his owne Right, or in the Right of his wife in Possession, Reversion, Remainder, or in Right which descended to the Kings Ward, and not to any other customary heire, as the younger sons in Gavellkindes etc.[118]

[116] *Ibid.*

[117] *Ibid.*, 6. Ley dates the statute to 1 Edw. VI, but it is actually 2 & 3 Edw. VI, c.8, *Stat. Realm*, vol. 4, 47–48.

[118] Ley, *Learned Treatise*, 10.

covers all the issues usually discussed by the readers and answers the simple question of what the king can claim, but with no indication of why or when. He does discuss some elements of the prerogative in a little more detail, but only as much as is necessary to make his point clear. Despite the indication in the dedication that this work is intended for students of the law, it is not a teaching tool in the same way as the readings.

The readings delivered after Henry VIII's reign, then, do not represent any significant development in the law. The changes that had the largest impact on the prerogative took place outside the Inns and outside the scope of *Prerogativa Regis*. With the Statute of Uses, the law on the prerogative was returned to an earlier state, while the Statute of Wills represented a practical compromise between the needs of the king and the landholders of England. These changes meant that the law was largely settled and the need to re-interpret the old statute had faded. The only significant changes left within the scope of *Prerogativa Regis* were procedural, and they were handled by the Court of Wards and Liveries. Much of the vibrancy of the early readings disappeared in these later renditions, for the drama of the earlier period had disappeared. The law moved from readings designed to test and train the minds of the legal profession into textbooks for landowners uninitiated in the mysteries of the prerogative.

As both Staunford's and Ley's treatises demonstrate, this new market was looking for business-like texts which would guide them through the intricacies of the processes of the various courts which dealt with crown land. This growing administrative structure, though necessary to deal with the burgeoning land market following the dissolution, made it increasingly difficult for the king's tenants to feel any personal connection with their lord, even if they had been inclined to do so. The prerogative became a royal business, rather than a royal tool. Though Henry VII's administration of the prerogative was highly developed and efficient, it retained the flexibility produced by the king's personal involvement. It could be shaped and manipulated to produce the results most politically helpful as well as financially rewarding. His lords felt the weight of royal rather than bureaucratic attention. This change in procedure accentuated and accelerated the falling value of the feudal bond.

The Pilgrimage of Grace and the treatment of Dacre demonstrated a change at the top of the feudal chain, but the disruptions of

1549 were more indicative of the diminishing bond at the lower end of the scale. The rebellions of Edward's reign centred on religious and economic issues, but good lordship was also a concern, especially among those affected by enclosure. As the west-country rebellions demonstrate, there was a feeling that good lordship had declined, and that the lord who would provide for his tenants with fair rents, secure employment, and legal protection had been replaced by the agricultural entrepreneur.[119] The ideal of traditional good lordship was often more of a myth than a reality, and the older nobility was just as likely, in the economic circumstances of the mid-century, to impose high entry fines and enclose lands, but the emergence of a new group of gentry following the dispersal of the monastic lands seems to have highlighted the change. As Bush points out, many of the risings were sparked by hostility to an individual figure "who was not of the long-established gentry but on the make as a landowner," such as John Flowerdew in Norfolk.[120] From this origin, they could come to focus on the shortcomings of the aristocracy as a whole, the group who had failed to protect them from the economic turmoil of the period.

Kett's rebellion, in its effort to turn the clock back and return to an earlier form of feudalism, is indicative of the failure of the ideal in the new circumstances of the period. In light of the changes associated with Henry VII's reign, it is significant that the rebels seek a commission "to redresse and reforme all suche good lawes, statutes, proclamacions, and all other your procedyngs, whiche hath byn hydden by your Justices of your peace, Shreves, Escheatores, and other your officers, from your pore comons, synes the first yere of the reigne of your noble grandfather King henry the seventh."[121] The rebels had other demands relating to the feudal structure, indicating both how widely the reach of the royal prerogative could be felt, and the weight of the burden of local lordship. In the first category, they asked that fishermen should be allowed to keep the profit from all of their catch, including whales or sturgeon (reserved to the king under *Prerogativa Regis*), and though this was a provision particularly relevant to the Norfolk fishermen, others had wider

119 Barrett L. Beer, *Rebellion and Riot: Popular Disorder in England During the Reign of Edward VI* (Kent OH: Kent State University Press, 1982), 70–71.

120 M. L. Bush, *The Government Policy of Protector Somerset* (Montreal: McGill-Queens University Press, 1975), 85.

121 Russell, *Kett's Rebellion*, 55–56.

application. The request that the feodary, the local officer of the Court of Wards, should not simultaneously serve as counsellor to any individual, with the corollary that the feodary should be appointed by the local community, indicates the power this official had in the shire, and his potential for inconveniencing his neighbours or protecting his employer. The same concerns are demonstrated by the request, already mentioned, that no one holding land worth less than £5 should be subject to inquisitions. Royal rights were not the rebels' only concern, however. Local tyranny is suggested by their desire to prevent anyone holding a manor on his own behalf from acting as bailiff to another, and in their concern that no one should be allowed to sell the wardship of any infant, but rather that the infant should choose his own marriage. They except the royal right to wardship from this latter demand.[122] This concession to royal rights may have been intended to curry favour, but given the impractical nature of many of the rebels' demands, this is unlikely. It is more likely that the distinction represents a recognition of the king's rights over his lords, along with the rejection of the local lords' rights over the rebels given their failure of lordship. The reciprocity of the feudal bond was once again a source of weakness: as one party failed in their duty, the other party rejected their obligations.

There seems to have been some recognition of this failure among the gentry, and Sir Thomas Smith made the connection with monastery lands, when he had the knight in his *Discourse of the Commonweal* "confess that some of us, that had lands either given us by the King's Highness that belonged heretofore to abbeys and priories and were never surveyed to the uttermost before, or otherwise descended to us, have enhanced, many of them, above the old rents."[123] The connection between the changing attitude to land and the purchase of monastery lands was not only apparent to tenants or observers like Smith, but was also accepted amongst the older gentry. The anonymous author of *The Institucion of a Gentleman*, for example, accepted that one of humble background could achieve gentle status through virtue and learning, but warned his readers against thinking that this could include those who "obteigned

[122] *Ibid.*, 51–55.

[123] Sir Thomas Smith, *A Discourse of the Commonweal of this Realm of England*, ed. Mary Dewar (Charlottesville: University Press of Virginia, 1969), 40.

the name of gentleman, the degree of Esquiers, and the title of Knightes" by sharp dealing in monastic lands.[124]

Though the gentry may have recognized that this new attitude to land was not appreciated by either their traditional dependants or their more conservative peers, there was little incentive for them to conform to the older ideal, as the times were clearly changing. The value of good lordship as a road to political or administrative advancement was fading with the centralization of the Tudor state. As the role of the nobles became less important with the decline in their role as arbitrators, local peace keepers and representatives of their locality, their value to those on the way up also fell. Military participation in the retinue of a lord became less appealing when the likely result was a summons to Star Chamber.[125] Even the military importance of the nobility in the defence of the country, the original foundation of the feudal system, suffered a crucial blow in this period. English armies were traditionally formed by the nobility raising their tenants, and this remained the case until 1544. In that year, Henry VIII fatally wounded the system by summoning 4,000 militiamen to France to reinforce the army there. This was largely a measure of convenience, for most of the nobility were still in action in France and could hardly be sent back to England to raise men, but, as Miller points out, it marked the end of the quasi-feudal army.[126] The older system did not disappear immediately, for between 1544 and 1558 it was still the more common method of raising an army, but by the middle of the century it was apparent that it was not working properly. By 1560, armies were normally recruited on a county basis by muster-masters appointed by commission, rather than by royal letters to noblemen.[127] This whole shift was mainly due to the changing composition of the landed classes. The crown had once been able to raise an army by sending out letters to a small number of lay and ecclesiastical magnates who held large estates and maintained a considerable retinue. By the 1540s, with the decline of some of the great aristocratic families, the success of the royal campaign against retaining, and the dissolution

[124] *The Institucion of a Gentleman* f. B vi a. Quoted in Leonard, "Knights and Knighthood," 23.

[125] Gunn, "Off with Their Heads," 64.

[126] Miller, *English Nobility*, 159–60.

[127] Jeremy Goring, "Social Change and Military Decline in Mid-Tudor England," *History* 60 (1975): 188; Miller, *English Nobility*, 159.

of the monastic estates, it was no longer clear who had the resources or the obligation to provide men for the army.[128]

On the other hand, it appears that, as the change in landholding obscured the obligations of the gentry to provide men, tenants were becoming increasingly unwilling to accept their duty to serve in the army. Goring points to a number of examples of tenants refusing their landlords' demands to serve in the army, on the ground that their tenure did not oblige them to do so. Tenants of the manor of Ackleton in Shropshire, for example, argued that, since they did not hold their lands "by knight's service nor by any such service . . . for which they ought to go with them [the lords of the manor] in the wars," their duty was only to the king and his commissioners.[129] The prevalence of the problem is indicated by the fact that parliament attempted to deal with it by a clause in the Act against Unlawful Assemblies of 1549, which ordered that copyholders or fermors who refused a military summons from the sheriff, justice of the peace, or their lord should be punished with the loss of their lands for the term of their lives.[130] Henry VIII's policy of requiring his subjects to swear allegiance directly to him and thus break the traditional chain of feudal loyalty was coming home to roost. The weakening of the loyalty between tenant and lord, the entry of a new group into the landholding class, and more business-like methods of farming all combined to reduce the influence of feudal ideals and the practical value of feudal obligations.

As the military value of the feudal system declined, to be replaced by a more bureaucratic army, so too the feudal idea of knighthood underwent the transformation into a civil honour. By 1550, the number of civil knights had risen from the 26 of 1523 to 141, and

[128] Goring, "Social Change and Military Decline," 188–89. Goring points out that the crown, when preparing its army in 1543, sent out letters to all those in the southern part of the kingdom thought to have the resources to provide soldiers, but it turned out that many of the addressees were dead or deficient in resources, while many of those who could have supported the obligation did not receive a letter.

[129] Goring, "Social Change and Military Decline," 189.

[130] 3 & 4 Edw. VI, c.5, *Stat. Realm*, vol. 4, 107. The statute was directed against attempts to attack privy counsellors or enclosures and was thus obviously a response to the turmoil of the rebellions. The fact that those objecting to enclosures seem often to have been of the same group as those refusing to serve in the army suggests that the act was aimed at two problems and may have been ineffective in both.

the number continued to grow.[131] Under Elizabeth, as the possibilities for knightings in time of war and on ceremonial occasions fell, the numbers of civil knights grew in both absolute and proportional terms.[132] Knighthood came increasingly to be seen as a social distinction rather than a military honour, and by 1589 Elizabeth had formulated a conscious policy of knighting men of good birth and sufficient wealth who had served her well, in order to establish a small and honourable group below the nobility.[133] To maintain the value of the honour, it was necessary to restrict the number of knighthoods, and this, Leonard argues, was the reason for the queen's anger when Essex knighted large numbers at war: such knightings caused resentment among those who had stayed behind in civil service in the hopes of earning advancement.[134] Though the policy served the needs of the government well, it further highlights the decline in the feudal ideal through the sixteenth century.

The 1530s and 1540s, then, saw a sharp decline in both the theoretical and practical value of feudalism. The active land market led to a shift in the ownership of property, with greater numbers of "new" gentry becoming lords and more members of the lower orders buying their lands. As the lords became less lordly, and tenants became more substantial landholders, the boundaries between the various levels of the feudal hierarchy were becoming increasingly blurred. The shift towards more business-like agricultural practices further accentuated the new nature of lordship in the mid-sixteenth century, while the declining military role of the nobility reduced the practical value of the feudal system. Though these changes would probably have occurred in any case, the coincidence of the sale of monastic lands, the growth of enclosures, and the decline of lordship served to highlight the shift.

At the same time that feudalism was declining in practice, it was being established on completely new foundations by the administration. The elements of *Prerogativa Regis* which had occupied the earlier readers, such as the king's rights over lands held of escheat and the relationship between the king's rights to wardship and primer seisin, had been largely settled by the 1530s, while the other big question, that of uses, was covered by the statute of 1536. By the time that Willoughby and Staunford came to look at *Prerogativa*

131 Leonard, "Knights and Knighthood," 106.
132 *Ibid.*, 113. 133 *Ibid.*, 116. 134 *Ibid.*, 117–18.

Regis, the administration of the prerogative had been revolutionized by the Statutes of Uses and Wills, the establishment of the Courts of Wards and Augmentations, and the sale of monastery lands. Though all of these innovations depended on the basic concepts of *Prerogativa Regis*, they went far beyond the words of the text. Rather than trying to incorporate all of this new material into their readings, Willoughby and Staunford seem to have settled for a restatement of the work of their predecessors. The lawyers dealt with the changes through a more direct treatment of the new material; by the middle of the sixteenth century the taboo on introducing new material into the cycle of readings had disappeared, probably due to the pressure and importance of Henrician legislation. Readings on the Statutes of Uses and Wills were a more appropriate and innovative method of dealing with the changes of recent years than another treatment of the time-worn *Prerogativa Regis*. The treatises of Staunford and Ley demonstrate that *Prerogativa Regis* had largely passed from the world of legal dispute to that of lay landowners and law students.

CONCLUSION

The purpose behind the earliest readings on *Prerogativa Regis* is unclear. Without a definite name and a clear date to attach to them, it is hard to do more than speculate about why a reader in the mid-fifteenth century, or thereabouts, would choose to lecture on the topic. All we can say for certain is that the early readings were shorter and simpler than the later texts, and that they focused primarily on the problems of the delivery of land from ancestor to heir and the issues that this raised for the king's rights. They establish some of the central topics for discussion, but there is no urgency in them. There is little concern with issues of fraud, and not much focus on the niceties of procedure in these early texts.

The readings given by Frowyk and Constable in 1495 raised the stakes. It is striking that the first time we have readings which can be securely named and dated, they are given in the same year by two serjeants-elect. This alone indicates that the text was topical, and it is clear that these readings on *Prerogativa Regis* were delivered in response to a more intensive application of the prerogative by the servants of the king. The purpose behind that application is not as clear. The result of the investigations was to increase the royal income, and it was this aspect of their activity which has attracted most attention, then and now, but it is not entirely clear that this was their primary objective. The acquisition of money alone would not seem to explain the assiduous attention the king paid to his tenants-in-chief. Rather, his inquisitions and commissions were intended to establish exactly who those tenants were, and how they held their land, as part of a necessary evaluation of the king's resources.

The readings of 1495 cast a certain amount of light on contemporary legal attitudes to the king's rights. Constable and Frowyk are representative of two approaches to the prerogative. Both accepted that the king's prerogative gave him the right to seize the lands of his tenants-in-chief on their death and to hold them until the heir was of age, performed homage, and sued livery. They also agreed that these rights were a result of the king's position as feudal lord and resulted from the tenure by which the land was held. Thus, they both approached the subject of the prerogative in the same light, but they differed on their interpretation of the details. Constable was far more inclined to extend the king's rights over both wardship and primer seisin. He was willing to help the king to cast his net ever more widely, through a broad interpretation of both *Prerogativa Regis* and more recent statutes such as 4 Hen. VII, c.17. Frowyk, on the other hand, was much more inclined to limit the king's rights. He did not deny the king's prerogative – no lawyer of the period would – but he resisted the attempt to make more of it than the text of the law would allow. Frowyk was much more concerned than Constable to balance the rights of king and tenant, and he did not hesitate to object to recent changes in practice which were not justified by the law, but simply by the fees they garnered in the chancery.

If we characterize Constable as a royalist, we might expect to see him receiving the advancement which Thorne speculated would follow a pro-royal reading in 1495. In fact, Constable rather faded away in the years before his death in November 1501, with little evidence that he was rewarded with offices or grants. Frowyk, on the other hand, flourished, becoming chief justice of the Common Pleas before dying in the summer of 1506 "in florida juventute sua."[1] Furthermore, Bacon singles Frowyk out as a particular servant of Henry VII. Commenting on the king's willingness to employ men of ability, Bacon includes Frowyk in a list with Morton, Fox, Bray, and Warham.[2] How are we to explain this favour for the conservative Frowyk? One likely explanation of the phenomenon might lie in the fact that Frowyk's reading found greater favour with the legal profession than Constable's. Although he did not carry the profession with him on every issue, the later readings follow Frowyk's lead rather than Constable's. Frowyk's reading, though it did not seek as much for the king, may have achieved more for him. It gave

[1] John Caryll, *Reports of Cases by John Caryll*, ed. J. H. Baker, 2 vols., Selden Society vols. 115 and 116 (London: Selden Society, 1998 and 1999), 2: 529.

[2] Francis Bacon, *The History of the Reign of King Henry the Seventh*, ed. Jerry Weinberger (Ithaca: Cornell University Press, 1996), 208.

a clearer view of what the king could realistically hope to get, given the limitations of the administrative and political situation of the day. Thus the readings caution us against falling into the trap of believing that the more "royalist" reading of the law would necessarily reflect royal wishes or attract greater royal favour.

Why did the more conservative view of the law find favour with Henry? Bacon's comment that "as he governed his subjects by his laws, so he governed his laws by his lawyers,"[3] may provide part of the answer. Henry was determined to get everything that was due to him, but he was not seeking to oppress his subjects. It is generally recognized that Henry was concerned to re-establish the power and prestige of the monarchy, and his interest in his feudal prerogatives has been seen as the pursuit of wealth to that end. However, it is likely that the king was just as interested in the means as in the final result. The process of seizing land and granting livery of it was a profound expression of lordship, and the exercise of prerogative lordship was an equally profound expression of kingship. Welcome though the income was, the prerogative that allowed Henry to flex his royal muscles in every shire in the country must have been more welcome. It provided him with an economical way of reminding his tenants of the pervasiveness of royal power effectively applied, a point that needed to be made at the end of the fifteenth century.

The revival of a more active form of feudal kingship was not only a means for inculcating a healthy fear of royal power, it also had a positive value. With hindsight, we are fully aware that the demands of sixteenth-century warfare and the stimulation of sixteenth-century humanism would combine to leave medieval feudal ideals in the dust, but the inexorability of progress was not so apparent at the end of the fifteenth century. K. B. McFarlane has pointed out that any usurper had to struggle to "restore and reimpose the crown's shaken authority."[4] The forms of feudal intercourse may have appeared as a valuable aid to such a recovery. Though the shifting allegiances of the fifteenth century may argue against placing much faith in oaths of homage or fealty, the simple fact that they were still

[3] *Ibid.*, 133.

[4] K. B. McFarlane, "The Wars of the Roses," in *England in the Fifteenth Century: Collected Essays*, ed. K. B. McFarlane (London: Hambledon, 1981), 255.

being made suggests that they continued to have some meaning.[5] This particular currency must have been devalued by the turmoil of the period, but the essential connection between the taking of the oath and the holding of land ensured that the ceremony of homage and fealty would not become a completely empty formula. Historians of bastard feudalism have come to accept that phenomenon as "an adaptation of the forms of feudalism rather than as the manifestation of a radical change in social organisation."[6] If we accept "fiscal" feudalism as an analogy to bastard feudalism, it is clear that the same can be said of it. The forms of fiscal feudalism, both in its financial claims and in the ties on which those claims were based, served as an active reminder of the bonds between king and tenant.

The simple fact that Henry VII exploited his feudal rights more efficiently than his immediate predecessors has suggested that he was exploiting an illegitimate or unacceptable power, but that was not necessarily the case. Even those lawyers who sought to keep the king's rights within bounds accepted that he had those rights, and, despite the loud complaints against the activities of the commissions, the broader population felt much the same way. While the extent of the king's rights was being debated, the exercise of those rights kept his role as feudal sovereign very much at the forefront of the political stage.

The readings delivered in the reign of Henry VIII took place in a different context. By 1521, when Spelman lectured, the novelty of the prerogative administration had faded. Constable's and Frowyk's readings had provided a solid basis on which to develop the law, and John Port had delivered one fairly unobjectionable reading as part of that process. The machinery of the prerogative administration was more firmly established, though rather less efficient than Henry VII's system. The political drive behind the prerogative was also less urgent. In the 1520s Henry VIII was firmly established on the throne and not yet worried about the future of the dynasty.

[5] P. S. Lewis, in looking at feudal forms in France, argues that "the difference between the old, the 'feudal' form of contract, and the new, the 'non-feudal' form, seems to find its crux simply in the question of whether or not homage was done." "Decayed and Non-Feudalism in Later Medieval France," *Bulletin of the Institute of Historical Research* 37 (1964): 160.

[6] G. L. Harriss, "Introduction," in McFarlane, *England in the Fifteenth Century: Collected Essays*, ix.

He was concerned more with the financial possibilities of the prerogative than with the political value of the feudal bond.

Spelman's reading reflects these points. His text, as it survives, is shorter than either Frowyk's or Constable's, but it is more sophisticated. He has taken their introduction to the law and moved it to a greater level of coherence; rather than simply presenting a demonstration of the law as it is, he tries more often to bring out the principles motivating it. Furthermore, Spelman's reading picks up on one innovation from Port's lectures: a greater concern with the specific wording of prerogative procedure. This suggests that the administration was testing the limits of the law, while the kind of technicalities he discusses supports the idea that economics rather than politics were driving the policy. Finally, Spelman spends more time on lands held in use than either of his predecessors, indicating a growth in interest in the relationship between uses and prerogative finance.

Though he differs from both Constable and Frowyk in places, Spelman's treatment is clearly based on theirs, and indicates the continuing line of development of the law within the structure of the Inns. He reflects Frowyk's desire to contain the king's rights, but he is clearly aware of the tradition represented by Constable. His reading follows neither completely, but presents Spelman's own idea of the law at that time. His focus on uses indicates an element of the law which stands against any royal interest in increased prerogative income, and suggests that a change in the law was imminent. Spelman's reading and reports, together with Yorke's reports, demonstrate the quiet and continuous development of the law on uses, a process which was soon to be rudely interrupted. The political negotiations and debates in the years before the Statute of Uses, on the other hand, show lawyers of various political persuasions presenting their arguments for and against the historical validity of uses and demonstrate the interaction of intellectual opinion, legal activity, and political pressure in the effort to change a politically and economically sensitive topic. Taken together, these sources indicate the way in which the smooth development of the law could be interrupted by the intervention of political necessity.

Audley's reading and the arguments in court in *Lord Dacre's Case* make it clear that this was not a simple question of king against lawyers, however. The complexity of the relationship between the variety of the arguments presented by the lawyers and the end sought by the king indicates that the lawyers held a multivalent position in the political and administrative structure. Although they succumbed to the king's wishes in the end, the body of justices was almost equally divided between two equally plausible interpretations of the law. Spelman's report makes it clear that the king promised his favour to those who returned the result he sought, but there is no suggestion that those who presented the opposite view would suffer. Browne, Hare, and Conyngesby were later arrested and imprisoned on a related question, but their fault was not in holding an opinion contrary to the law, but in advising a tenant of the king on how to evade the law. Moreover, their punishment was exemplary rather than severe, since all were quickly released, their fines may have been remitted, and there is no evidence that their careers suffered in the long term.[7] Browne was removed on two occasions from his position as king's serjeant, but this did not prevent him from reaching the bench.[8] There is no event in the reigns of Henry VII or Henry VIII comparable to Edward IV's removal of Markham from the bench in retribution for an unfavourable verdict.[9]

The lawyers thus seem to have had the benefit of a certain level of immunity from punishment, if not entirely from pressure. In this way, they largely exemplified Dudley's idea of a body which would preserve the law against the prince, when necessary.[10] They also seem to have maintained a healthy balance between the needs of the king and the community. In all of the major disputes through the period the justices seem to have been fairly evenly divided between those who wished to concede more to the king and those who wished to limit his claims. Individual readings also tended to be finely balanced, with Frowyk, Port, Spelman, and Staunford all tending to restrict the king's rights while allowing latitude in some areas. This creative conservatism served to maintain an equilibrium

[7] Amanda S. Bevan, "The Role of the Judiciary in Tudor Government, 1509–1547" (PhD diss., Cambridge, 1986), 30–31. Hare was released within two days, while Conyngesby was promoted from attorney-general of the duchy of Lancaster, being created serjeant in June 1540 and a justice of king's bench shortly afterwards.

[8] *Ibid.*, 31.

[9] For a contemporary reference to this event, see Sir Thomas More, *The History of King Richard III*, in *The Complete Works of St. Thomas More*, ed. Richard S. Sylvester (New Haven: Yale University Press, 1963), vol. 2, 70.

[10] See introduction, p. 14 above.

within the system, allowing a moderate development of the law, while preventing the advantage from moving either to the king or his tenants. The lawyers' role was not heroic, but it was nonetheless important. As Baker comments, "the new law of the renaissance period was made, not by flouting the old learning, but by sneaking round it."[11]

This apparent calm within the common law in a period of general turbulence raises an important issue. Law is a fundamental expression of the nature of the society in which it functions; if the society undergoes fundamental change, surely the law must display some upheaval? Legal historians have long been proud of the uniqueness of the common law tradition, but its uniqueness comes embarrassingly close to insularity if the members of this intellectual elite remained untouched by a Europe-wide revolution in thought. However, as Thorne points out, law "cannot fall victim . . . to sudden changes in mere intellectual fashion, for it finds its justification independently in its success in dealing with the problems life presents to it."[12] Thus law is not simply an academic subject, but a reflection of society which, "however abstract it might become, . . . was essentially an expression of contemporary life."[13] As society was convulsed by changes in religion and politics, law continued to express and direct the fundamental secular structure of English life; the common law, after all, governed land. The lawyers could not ignore the events of their day, and the readers clearly responded to the changing circumstances around them, but neither could they bend the necessities of the law to the wishes of the moment. They were bound by the logic of a fairly inflexible system which "has rarely admitted openly to the possibility of change."[14] The slow and cautious extension of the words of *Prerogativa Regis* by the readers gives an indication both of the unwillingness of the profession to admit the possibility of change, and of the method by which change was achieved. Political and economic issues obviously played a role in the explication of the text, but all of the readers were

[11] J. H. Baker, ed., *The Reports of Sir John Spelman*, 2 vols., Selden Society vols. 93 and 94 (London: Selden Society, 1976 and 1977), vol. 2, 163.

[12] S. E. Thorne, "English Law and the Renaissance," in *Essays in English Legal History* (London: Hambledon Press, 1985), 194.

[13] F. M. Powicke, "Reflections on the Medieval State," *Trans. Royal Historical Society*, 4th ser. 19 (1936): 8.

[14] J. H. Baker, "English Law and the Renaissance," *Cambridge Law Journal* 44 (1985): 50.

restricted in their arguments by their understanding of the law; the final abandonment of the topic highlights the limits beyond which the lawyers could not go. Thus the insularity of the law in the face of broader cultural change can be seen as an expression of the integrity of its principles.

If the law did express the fundamental structure of English society, then the readings indicate that that structure was still feudal in the first half of the sixteenth century. Moreover, there is no indication that even the English humanists had any real desire to change that. Thus, when Richard Morison, for example, argued for a reformation in the laws of England, his interest was in form rather than content. Like most of the humanists who sought such a reformation, his primary concern was with the barbarity of law French and the confusion of the year books. He advocated a concordance of the existing law, rendered into Latin, and, for those who argued that it was impossible, he drew "a rude plat in the Latin tongue of the tenures of land and of services that your subjects, being tenants, by the common laws of this your realm owe unto their lords."[15] For Morison, the basic structure of tenure and service was assumed. Indeed, his ideal was a hierarchical structure, in which "everyone is content with his degree, glad to do that that he may lawfully do, gladder to do that which he seeth shall be for the quietness of the realm, albeit his private profit biddeth him do the contrary."[16] The higher levels of the hierarchy were to be occupied by those distinguished by virtue rather than simply birth, but there was no question that the hierarchy would continue to exist, or that it would continue to function in the same way. The scramble for land, wealth, and title among the Tudor "new men" indicates that there was no rejection of the feudal ideal, or of the idea that service to the king would be rewarded through the grant of lands, though the type of men taking the path to the top might have changed. For those further down the social scale, even this level of change was unacceptable. Morison writes, more in sorrow than in anger, that the rebels of 1536 were "angry that virtue should be rewarded when she cometh to men that had no lords to their fathers. They will that none rule but noblemen

15 Sir Richard Morison, "Discourse Touching the Reformation of the Laws of England," quoted in Thorne, "English Law and the Renaissance," 191.

16 Sir Richard Morison, *A Remedy for Sedition*, in *Humanist Scholarship and Public Order*, ed. David Sandler Berkowitz (Washington: Folger Shakespeare Library, 1984), 112.

born."[17] Thus, despite the changes of the 1530s, it seems that the law expounded by the readers was not out of step with common assumptions about the structure of society.

By the time that Willoughby and Staunford lectured in Edward's reign, the context had once again changed dramatically. Finance was now a less immediate issue, for the changes of the Reformation had brought the king a substantial income. Though the exploitation of this income depended largely on the manipulation of his prerogative rights, the establishment of the Courts of Wards and Augmentations took the pressure off *Prerogativa Regis*. Furthermore, the Statutes of Uses and Wills had solved the problem of land held in use. Many of the issues considered by the earlier readers were transformed by these pieces of legislation, but the prerogative was still in the limelight. The distribution of monastic land to be held in knight service had the potential to create a new class of feudal tenants, bringing a larger number of the king's subjects into a direct feudal relationship with him.

As the second Tudor saw his dynasty hover on the edge of extinction, it is not surprising to find a growing emphasis on personal loyalty to the monarch. Henry VIII's insistence that all his subjects take an oath of allegiance to him is well known, but it is associated with the Reformation changes, rather than with a broader concern for the structure of society. This oath further seems to move us into a more modern era, for the allegiance is not based on a feudal relationship or sworn to the king as lord, but is based on loyalty to the king as king. It seems, however, that older ideas of swearing allegiance were still circulating in Henry's reign. In his reading on uses in 1526, Thomas Audley describes homage as "an actual and corporal service to be made . . . in the person of he who ought to perform it to the person of him who ought to receive it and not by deputy or attorney."[18] He follows this with a description of the process where the man comes and "kneels etc. and his lord sits and he puts his hands between the hands of his lord. And as Bracton says the placing of the tenant's hands etc. implies obedience and the closure of the lord's hands etc. implies defence and the tenant says I will be your man etc."[19]

Such a description is more consonant with our concepts of the height of feudalism than with its close. We can explain it away as

[17] *Ibid.*, 115. [18] BL MS Hargrave 87, f.430v. [19] *Ibid.*, f.431.

an antiquarian flourish, or the words of an inveterate and romantic conservative, but Thomas Audley, the epitome of the Tudor man, does not fit either description. Nor does the setting support such suggestions, for the readings were oriented towards the practical. Audley was by this time in government service, and this suggests the most interesting possibility, that this picture of the forging of the feudal bond came from the government of the day. This is not to say that this was the practice in the 1520s or before; Constable's and Frowyk's descriptions of the heir running from administrative office to office to fulfill the various demands for suing livery of his lands sounds more realistic.[20] Both Frowyk and Constable refer to the performance of homage, and Constable even describes how the heir will "kneel before the king and put his hands together between the king's hands and the chamberlain will take his oath. And then he will kiss the king's cheek and pay his fees to the chamberlain."[21] Constable's mixture of the administrative and the feudal is echoed in Frowyk's description, but both readers agree that "to avoid the costs the heirs are accustomed to purchase a privy seal directed to the chancellor to respite homage."[22] Thus the performance of homage was an option as far as the earlier readers were concerned, but the suggestion is that even if the heir chose to exercise it, it was less personal and thus less attractive than the picture painted by Audley.

This picture of feudalism rising sits uneasily with the idea of Tudor monarchy, and indeed it seems that Henry VIII tried to exploit the forms of feudal intercourse without accepting their logic. His new class of feudal tenants did not have the links to royal service or royal tenancy which would promote a feudal connection. Nor was the personal basis of the feudal relationship easily transferred to a broader group of tenants. The king could not possibly be good lord to all the numbers of landholders of the crown, and without the element of personal loyalty to mitigate the burdens of lordship, the imposition of feudal tenure on a new group seems to have acted as an irritant. Starkey expresses both sides of the argument in his *Dialogue*

[20] Thomas Frowyk, CUL MS Hh.2.1, f.6v; Robert Constable, *Prerogativa Regis: Tertia Lectura Roberti Constable de Lincolnis Inne Anno 11 H. 7*, ed. S. E. Thorne (New Haven: Yale University Press, 1949), 63–64.

[21] Constable, 63.

[22] Frowyk, f.6v. Constable, 64, does not describe the process, but he assumes that the heir can dispense with homage in this way.

between Pole and Lupset. Lupset points out that when William the Conqueror came into England he gave out lands to be held in return for service "under such condycyon that when so ever they decessyd levyng theyr heyrys wythin age that then thes landys duryng the nonage schold retorne to the superior agayne by whose benefyte hyt cam to the famyly & stoke . . . the wych me semyth much resonabul consyduryng they benefytys come al from hym by the wych the hole famyly schold be mainteynyd."[23] This was the traditional rationale behind feudal dues and one which was generally accepted.

Nevertheless, by the mid-sixteenth century few tenants could claim a tenure dating back to the Conquest, or to time immemorial. Newer tenants of the crown were more likely to identify with Pole's testy response, that "they wych gave theyr landys to theyr servantys myght put so such condycyon both of ward & maryage & so hyt may appere somewhat resonabul al theyr successorys to be bounden aftur that maner, to them wych consydur the tyme of the tyranne, but we must loke a lytyl hyar & consydur the tyme of nature."[24] This dispute suggests a transitional view: those who had held of the crown for any considerable period could reasonably be expected to render the dues which were a natural part of that system, but, for those who had acquired land in recent years, a more enlightened approach was required. The readings of Willoughby and Staunford both suggest a new interest in the restriction of primer seisin and wardship solely to land held in knight service in chief of the king, which must have appealed to this group of landholders who were accustomed to holding land in socage and newly exposed to the prerogative.

The tensions between the new aims of monarchy and the old methods of achieving those aims suggest that a further consideration of the impact of the redistribution of monastery lands on the political and tenurial framework of landholding might repay investigation. The sixteenth century saw enormous changes on the land, with the redistribution of Church lands,[25] enclosures, agrarian development, and geographical and social mobility of population.

23 Thomas Starkey, *A Dialogue Between Pole and Lupset*, ed. T. F. Mayer, Camden Society 4th ser. vol. 37 (London: Royal Historical Society, 1989), 77.

24 *Ibid.*, 78.

25 Estimated by Cooper at 20–25 percent of the land of England. J. P. Cooper, "The Social Distribution of Land and Men in England, 1436–1700," *Economic History Review*, 2nd ser. 20 (1967): 421.

Economic historians have paid a great deal of attention to the lower levels of the rural population and their attitudes to the land. They have also examined the effects of feudal conditions such as fines and rents on the exploitation of land by the peasantry, and the importance of such considerations relative to demographic change.[26] There has been less consideration of the effects and extent of royal lordship. The cumulative effect of centuries of escheat, division of land held in chief between co-heirs, and the distribution of monastic lands placed a large proportion of the land of England under the direct lordship of the crown, and brought a large number of landholders, from the higher nobility to holders of land worth £5–10 per annum, into direct contact with royal administration. Attitudes to both land and lordship changed dramatically during the course of the sixteenth century, and it seems unlikely that the attitudes and practices of the crown had no impact on these shifts. If the remarks of Henry Spelman are to be believed, they suggest that an upwardly mobile population was purchasing land held of the crown and resenting the burden of feudal dues. This has both political and economic implications which deserve further study.

It is not hard to see why there were no readings on *Prerogativa Regis* after the 1550s, for the relative blandness of the later readings indicates that the centre of interest had moved elsewhere. The law had been placed on a new footing by the legislation of the 1530s and 1540s, and *Prerogativa Regis* was looking increasingly irrelevant. Elton argues that "the land law was revolutionized; despite the continued existence of the 'feudal incidents', the Statutes of Uses and Wills terminated the truly feudal era in its history."[27] By now it should be apparent that any attempt to identify a "truly" feudal era is pointless, but there can be no denying that the landscape of the feudal law had been radically remodelled. The old idea

[26] Many of these issues were raised during the Brenner debate and the historians involved in that extended discussion present some of the central issues of agrarian economic development in England and across Europe in the medieval and early modern period. See T. H. Aston and C. H. E. Philpin, ed., *The Brenner Debate: Agrarian Class Structure and Economic Development in Pre-Industrial Europe* (Cambridge: Cambridge University Press, 1987). The debate has continued to inspire research which has taken note of the tenurial issue: see R. W. Hoyle, "Tenure and the Land Market in Early Modern England or a Late Contribution to the Brenner Debate," *Economic History Review*, 2nd ser. 43 (1990): 1–20.

[27] G. R. Elton, *Reform and Renewal: Thomas Cromwell and the Common Weal* (Cambridge: Cambridge University Press, 1973), 160.

of the prerogative was rather outdated, and the new conception, with which we are more familiar, was only beginning to emerge. It is striking that the readers betray no knowledge of the kinds of issues we associate with the later royal prerogative. There is no discussion of the distinction between the king's absolute and ordinary prerogative, little consideration of why he has these rights and no attempt to provide any theoretical justification for them, beyond the simple fact of tenurial obligation and kingship. In fact, there is no theory of the prerogative evident in the readings, but rather a list of the specific prerogatives to which the king has a right. The discussion of Frowyk's and Constable's readings in chapters two and three best conveys the sense that the king's dues were a rather miscellaneous collection of rights gathered together in the text of *Prerogativa Regis*, rather than a coherent body of privileges derived from an overarching right.[28] Thus, from 1495 through to 1551, the readers were looking backwards to the king's feudal rights, rather than forward to his absolute rights. It is not until we reach Morice's reading in 1578 that we can start to see some of those issues taking shape in this forum, and this simply makes his choice to turn from *Prerogativa Regis* to Westminster I more striking. Although Constable's more royalist outlook might at times tempt us to look for a proto-absolutism in the readings, it is clearly not there, and it was not possible for a reader interested in the political theory of the prerogative to read it into this text.

Though the eruption of parliamentary legislation in the sixteenth century has deservedly attracted much attention, it seems that the regular cycle of activity at the Inns of Court has a claim to some of that notice. Striking as the legislation of Henry VIII was, it affected only a small proportion of the litigation taking place in England at the time, and it had to be interpreted in the context of the body of existing law. Moreover, once it had been passed by parliament, it was handed over to the lawyers to be refined and applied. Their development of the prerogative displays an example of their capacity to fine-tune the law on their own initiative and to resist the temptation to do more than fine-tune. If Constable's

[28] Glenn Burgess comments that Staunford's *Exposicion* is an example of the tendency of the common lawyers to list the king's rights rather than theorizing on them, but he shows no awareness of the origin of the *Exposicion* in the Inns. Glenn Burgess, *Absolute Monarchy and the Stuart Constitution* (New Haven: Yale University Press, 1996), 152.

attempt to exchange old law for new had succeeded, the implications for law-making and for the role of parliament would have been vast. His attempt failed, not because of any particular heroism on the part of the lawyers, but simply because such a change required the whole body of the profession to accept that his was a reasonable interpretation of the law. His words were not authoritative in any way, and they were, in the final analysis, subjected to the test of reason and found wanting.

Thus the lawyers seem to have followed their mandate to speak with the authority of the king, but to speak against the king when the law required it. Though they were the king's servants, they proved that the law was not the king's law, but that of king, parliament, and people, or, perhaps more properly, that of custom and reason. Henry VIII's proposed changes to the coronation oath indicate the direction in which he wanted to take both the formation and preservation of the laws. He was willing to swear that:

> he shall graunte to holde lawes and *approvyd* customes of the realme and *lawfull and not preiudiciall to hys crowne or imperiall Jurisdiction* to his power kepe them and affirme them which the nobles and people haue made and chosen *with hys consent*, And the evill Lawes and customes hollie to put out, and stedfaste and stable peax to the people of his realme kepe and cause to be kept to his powre *in that which honour and equite do require.*[29]

Such a model of kingship would have placed England securely in the category of absolute monarchy and might have made Henry's power in the temporal realm equal to his power in the spiritual realm. However, the simple fact that the monarch had to share both the making of law and the preserving of law meant that England had a structural safeguard against absolutism.

[29] Leopold G. W. Legg, ed., *English Coronation Records* (Westminster: A. Constable, 1901), 241. Italics indicate Henry's additions.

NOTES ON THE APPENDIXES

With the exception of Constable's text, the readings on *Prerogativa Regis* survive only in manuscript. Considerations of length have prevented me from including all of them, but it seemed important to include examples to illustrate the genre as well as the material. They are given here in translation, for ease of access. I have chosen to provide Frowyk's and Spelman's texts for a number of reasons. Frowyk's reading was clearly the most important text of the period, judged both by its impact on the later readings and the number of copies of it which have survived (all of the other readings survive only in a single copy). Spelman's reading is a valuable indication of the further development of the law in the next century.

This version of Frowyk's reading is in CUL MS Hh.2.1, ff.1–10, though it has been compared with other manuscripts, and readings have been supplied in a few instances from HLS MS 1037 and HLS MS 14 where they help to clarify the meaning. These additions are noted. This is generally a good version of his text, in a clear hand. Spelman's reading is preserved in only one manuscript, Gray's Inn MS 25. This is the most technically challenging of the manuscripts, in a heavily abbreviated and rather cramped cursive hand of the mid-sixteenth century, and some portions of it are quite illegible. These passages are indicated with [...]. In general I have followed the words of the text closely, but in both translations I have supplied some words for clarity, and these are indicated by [ ]. The punctuation and capitalization has been standardized, and both texts have been divided into paragraphs. I have corrected the statute and case references given by the readers, but since these are not intended as full editions I have generally not corrected the text, except in a small number of instances where the error was obvious. These are indicated with <>.

Appendix 1

THOMAS FROWYK'S READING ON *PREROGATIVA REGIS*, cc.1–3, INNER TEMPLE, LENT 1495

[**f.1**] *Dominus rex habebit custodiam* [The lord king shall have the wardship] etc. Before now there have been several opinions about whether this is a statute or not, or a declaration of the prerogative of the king by the authority of parliament; Prysott said on this in 35 Hen. VI[1] that it is a statute and there is the same opinion in 43 Edw. III[2] in the case of the prior of Lanthony, but afterwards in 15 Edw. IV[3] the contrary is held, that is that it is not a statute but rather a declaration of the king's prerogatives. I think that this is not any statute nor declaration as above, but a treatise made by some men wise in the law, just like *Bracton*, *Visus Franciplegii*, *Modus Calumniandi Essoniorum*, *Hengham*, and other similar works. And if it were a statute, it would be entirely observed in every point; and many articles of this are not held to be law and many were law before the making of it. In this it is like the statute of 25 Edw. III[4] of treason, for that is only an exposition of the common law; also it is not like Magna Carta for that was made a statute by Marlborough, c.4.[5] Further, if it was a statute that would appear in the wording of it, such as "in the parliament held at" etc. or similar words. These are prerogatives which are given at the common law, as I understand. And this may be [consistent with reason]; for the judges have prerogatives before many others; and each judge derives his authority from the king and he is the supreme judge and head of the law whereby he may reasonably have such prerogatives. The basis of the prerogatives is tenure in chief, and the effect of this article is that if one holds of the king by knight service, that the king shall have the wardship of all the lands of which his tenant died seised.

1 YB Hil. 35 Hen. VI, ff.40–42, pl.2.

2 YB Mich. 43 Edw. III, f.22, pl.12.

3 YB Mich. 15 Edw. IV, ff.11–14, pl.17.

4 Stat.5, c.2, *Stat. Realm*, vol. 1, 319–20.

5 *Recte* c.5, *Stat. Realm*, vol. 1, 20.

For this reason we must see which lands shall be said to be held of the king in chief and which not.

A man holds of the king by knight service which has continued from time immemorial; this is expressly tenure in chief by the words of this article, that is *ab antiquo de corona*, yet I have not seen any issue taken on this, that is, whether it is held *ab antiquo de corona* or not, but whether it was held in chief or not.

If the king purchases a lordship, the tenant does not hold of him in chief. If a barony or honour escheats to the king for felony, every tenant who holds of the said barony or honour holds of the king by the same services as he held of the barony before. And this is by the statute of Magna Carta c.30[6] and also the name of the barony [remains] in the king and in such cases he shall not have his prerogative.

It is otherwise if the mesnalty which is held of the king in chief escheats, for there he shall have the mesnalty in the same way as he had the lordship, and thus diversity. Still, if the mesnalty escheats to the king for treason, the tenant does not hold in chief, for the king would have had this by such an attainder if the mesnalty had been held of someone else. Thus there is a diversity between attainder for felony and treason and this appears in 5 Edw. III[7] where an acre held of a manor in the hands of the king which escheated for felony was held to be a parcel of the manor and that for treason was not.

The king purchases land and gives it to hold of him; he shall hold in chief and yet this is not *ab antiquo de corona*. It is otherwise if the prince purchases land and gives it to hold of him, and then he is king, it is not held in chief. But if he gave these in tail or for term of life and then when he is king he releases to the tenant [all his right], then the tenant shall hold in chief.

A lordship descends to the king from any collateral ancestor, the tenant shall not hold in chief. If the king gives any parcel of the duchy of Lancaster under the seal of the duchy as he should, the tenant shall not hold in chief. It is otherwise where the king grants a parcel [**f.1v**] of an honour or barony by his great seal.

The king purchases a lordship and releases it to the tenant, he shall hold in chief. The law is the same if there are various mesnes between the king and the tenant paravail and the king releases to the

[6] *Recte* c.31, *Stat. Realm*, vol. 1, 117. [7] Reference not found.

tenant all his right, the mesnalties are extinguished and the tenant holds in chief.

The king's villein purchases a lordship which is found by inquisition, the tenant does not hold in chief.

In all these cases of tenure in chief if they hold by knight service the king shall have his prerogative.

A man confesses in a court of record to hold of the king in chief, the lord of whom he holds in fact shall not be bound by this acknowledgment.

The law is the same if a man estops himself by suing livery or otherwise, yet if he holds in socage of a stranger and confesses to holding in chief, the king shall not have his prerogative for the stranger shall not suffer any loss.

The king gives land to hold of one J.S. by knight service, he shall hold of J.S. and also of the king in chief and also the king shall have the prerogative of both: *quaere* because it was argued.

And just as he can give land reserving a rent to a stranger, he is able to reserve a lordship to a stranger. But if the king has lands by forfeiture under the statute *De Religiosis*[8] there he must give over the lands to hold of the chief lord and may not grant them to hold of any other stranger, *causa statuti*.

A man [is] attainted [of treason] by authority of parliament with a proviso in the same act that every lord shall have his services as before the attainder, and then the king grants the same land to another, the tenant holds of the king and also of the other lords.

The letter is *per servicium militare* [by military service] and this has been shown [already] by other words, and so etc. But in the case of the king, if he grants land and expresses no service the grantee shall hold by knight service.

If the grant is *absque aliquo reddendo*, or rendering 12^d a year and fealty, if it does not say or express in the grant "for all services" he shall hold by knight service and this appears in 44 Edw. III.[9]

The article is *omnium terrarum* [of all lands]: yet he shall have rents, advowsons in gross, commons in gross, villeins, profits à prendre, for which things an assize lies, and an office of inheritance, and if he is not able to occupy it himself he shall make a deputy, as with the office of the sheriff of [Worcester], yet these things do not lie in the tenure of any other. But he shall not have the wardship

[8] 7 Edw. I, *Stat. Realm*, vol. 1, 51. [9] YB Mich. 43 Edw. III, f.45, pl.59.

of an annuity for this is not real, but something which follows the person.

The words of the *diem clausit extremum* are *tam in dominico quam in servicio* which proves that the king shall have more than lands.

The article speaks further *de quocunque tenuerunt per huiusmodi servicium* [of whatever they held by service of this kind]: yet if the tenant holds land in socage or in burgage the king shall have them, as appears in 24 Edw. III,[10] until the full age of the heir. The king does not have prerogative of a ward who belongs to him by reason of ward. The article is *per servicium militare*, yet if the tenant holds by grand serjeanty the king shall have his prerogative, because grand serjeanty gives the king the wardship. However, grand serjeanty is not knight service, for he shall not pay an aid to marry his daughter and also he shall not pay the same relief as a tenant by knight service, for he shall pay the value of his land by the year: as appears Trinity 2 Hen. IV.[11]

In dominico suo ut de feodo [In his demesne as of fee] etc. yet if the tenant dies seised of lands in tail he shall have his prerogative. And so it is if the king's tenant gives land in tail with the remainder in fee and the remainder escheats to the king, the tenant in tail holds of the king in chief, and the king shall have the wardship of the land.

[**f.2**] In some cases where the king's tenant does not die seised the king shall have the prerogative and in this case where he dies seised he shall have nothing, as where the king's tenant is disseised of land held of others, there he shall have his prerogative. The law is the same where lands held of others are leased for term of life and the tenant dies and then the tenant for term of life dies. Thus if the king's tenant has a remainder of lands held of another and dies and after this the tenant for term of life dies the king shall have his prerogative of this land, for which see the case of Skrene 15 Edw. IV.[12]

The reason why the lord shall have the wardship of the issue of his tenant is for the defence of the realm and the king shall have the wardship because the entire defence of the realm is in him and he shall have all the land because he cannot have a joint tenant with him.

[10] YB Pas. 24 Edw. III, f.47v, pl.33. [11] *Recte* Mich. 11 Hen. IV, f.34, pl.64.
[12] YB Mich. 15 Edw. IV, ff.10–11, pl.16, and ff.11–14, pl.17.

Lands descend from a collateral ancestor to the king's ward held of another; the king shall not have his prerogative and this was held in Skrene's case by all the justices.

The king's tenant leased certain lands held of others for term of life rendering certain rent and dies, the king has the reversion and the rent, and [when] the tenant for term of life dies the king shall have the land and this was in 7 Hen. VI.[13] The king's tenant leased for term of life, the remainder in fee, the remainderman dies seised of other lands held of another, the lord shall have the lands held of him; and if the tenant for term of life dies, the king shall only have the lands held of himself alone.

The king's tenant has land in tail held of another and discontinues and dies; his son, being in the king's ward after his death, recovers by formedon: the king shall not have the wardship of the recovered lands, for the heir after the death of his father had only a right to this land. Query, because it was argued. The law is the same if the king's tenant is disseised of land held of others and the heir of the disseisor is in by descent and the heir of the disseisee recovers. And so it is if the heir recovers by any ancestral action; someone who has an acre held of the king and a mesnalty of another purchases the tenancy for term of life and dies, the king shall have the mesnalty which is revived.

The king's tenant is [seised] of a mesnalty in general tail and purchases the tenancy to him and to his heirs female and has issue a son and a daughter and dies; the king shall have the mesnalty which is revived by the death. A man holds a mesnalty of the king in tail and purchases the tenancy in fee and has issue a son and daughter by one womb and a son by another womb and dies; the elder son, in the king's ward or out of it, dies without issue: the king shall have the mesnalty which descends to the younger son and he shall not have the lands which descend to the daughter.

The king's tenant aliens the lands held of others by collusion, the king cannot aver covin by the statute of Marlborough, because the statute was made for the advantage of the lords, and here the lords do not have a remedy for this, because if the tenant had died [seised] they would not have the ward, and thus the feoffee shall hold the land against all of the lords. The law is the same where the king's tenant makes a feoffment to his use of lands held of another; neither

13 YB Mich. 7 Hen. VI, ff.2–5, pl.7 (*Gascon's Case*).

the king nor his lords shall have advantage of the new statute made in 4 Hen. VII,[14] but if he aliens by collusion the acre held of the king in chief, the king shall have advantage of it and shall have both acres.

A man enfeoffs the king's tenant and another, and the king's tenant dies, the king shall not have that of which he was joint tenant, but the other [shall have it] by survivorship. It shall be otherwise if the feoffment had been to the king's tenant and to the other and to the heirs of the king's tenant, for if the one who had the estate for life survives and dies, the king shall have the lands by the prerogative.

The king's tenant has lands in borough English and has issue two sons and dies, the king shall not have the land in borough English, and even if the elder son dies afterwards without issue, still the king shall not have the wardship of the lands in borough English. [**f.2v**] Lands are given to the king's tenant and to his heirs male and he has issue a daughter; the king shall not have these lands.

The king's tenant has lands in gavelkind and has issue two sons; the king by his prerogative shall only have the half which belongs to the elder son. A man who holds land in tail of the king in chief and holds other lands in fee of a stranger has issue a son and daughter by one womb and a son by another womb and dies; the elder son dies without issue in the ward of the king or outside the king's ward, the king shall only have the land in tail.

Various lands descend to a feme covert which are held of the king and other lands of other lords, the husband has issue within age and enters in the lands held of the king, but not into the lands of the other lords; when the woman dies the lord enters into the lands held of him, and when the tenant by curtesy dies, his heir under age, the king shall not have the land held of others. But if the [other] lands were held in socage, query.

The king's tenant disseises his son and dies, the son under age, the king shall only have the land held of him; the law is the same if the son has a title for action, for he is remitted in both cases.

The king's tenant is disseised and dies, his heir under age, and before the inquisition the disseisor dies, his heir also under age, and this is found by various inquisitions; the king shall have his prerogative of both. The law is the same where the king's tenant aliens by covin and dies, his heir under age, and his feoffee dies, his

[14] c.17, *Stat. Realm*, vol. 2, 540–41.

heir under age; the king shall have the prerogative of both as in the other case above.

The article is *exceptis feodis Archiepiscopi Cantuarensis Episcopi Dunolmensis inter Tyne et Tise* [except the fees of the archbishop of Canterbury, the bishop of Durham between Tyne and Tees] etc. and this is understood where the king's tenant purchases land held of their ancient fees. For if the bishop [*sic*] of Canterbury purchases a lordship and the king's tenant dies seised of any land held of such a lord, the king shall have his prerogative. Also the bishop of Durham has a county palatine within which, if the king's tenant has any lands, [the king] shall not have his prerogative of them. Also, if the king's tenant dies seised of any lands held of the prince within the county of Chester, the king shall not have his prerogative, because within the same county the prince shall have prerogative, as the king has.

And note that he said afterwards that if my tenant makes a gift in tail with the remainder in fee and the remainderman dies without an heir, my lordship is extinct. It is otherwise if the king gives lands in tail, remainder in fee and the remainderman dies without an heir, so that the remainder escheats to the king, for the tenant in tail held of the king in chief, which note well.

Rex habet maritagium heredum [The king shall have the marriage of an heir]: The effect of this prerogative is that the king shall have the marriage of the heir of his tenant under age who holds by knight service or grand serjeanty in whatever manner he held, according to the words and effect of the letter, even though the tenant does not hold of him in chief, and the statute of Magna Carta c.28[15] was not made to exclude the king from the wardship of the body; for before this statute the common law was that the king should always have the wardship of the body, but rather this statute was made solely for the lands.

And if the king had disseised a baron, and someone who holds of the same barony and of another dies, the king, being in by disseisin, shall have the wardship of the body.

And the king would have had it so before the statute of Westminster II c.16,[16] which statute was made before this treatise, and by the same statute it is made certain that the lord by priority shall have the wardship of the body, *nullo habito respectu* as the said

[15] *Recte* c.27, *Stat. Realm*, vol. 1, 117.   [16] *Stat. Realm*, vol. 1, 82.

statute expresses. Yet the king is not bound by the statute, inasmuch as he is not named in the said statute.

The article is that the king shall have the wardship of the body and what shall be called priority or posteriority has been shown before, and so etc. and how priority can be changed and how not. If someone has held two acres severally of two men and held one by a more ancient feoffment of the one than he had the other acre of the other, he is the lord by priority.

[**f.3**] In some cases one shall have the wardship of the body before the king, as when there is a father and a son and lands descend to the son held of the king, the son under age; the father shall have the wardship of his own son, for he does not claim by any tenure, and the king shall only have the lands which have descended; thus to this intent he [the father] is in a better condition than another person, yet to another intent he is the father and in a worse condition, for he is not able to grant the wardship of his son to another. And in the same manner the father shall have the wardship of his daughter and heir, see 9 Edw. IV.[17]

Father and son, and lands held of the king descend to the son while the father is living, the father is attainted of felony; the king shall have the wardship of the body while the father is living. And if the land is held of a common person then he shall have it as above. The father has issue a daughter and land held of the king descends to her, the king shall have the land and not the body; but if afterwards the father takes a second wife and has issue a son, now the king shall have the wardship of the body of the daughter. Lands held of the king descend to my villein, the king shall not have the body, but if he is manumitted afterwards, the king shall have him. It is otherwise if lands descend to an infant who is made an apprentice, for there the common law shall be preferred: 8 Edw. IV, 22.[18]

Also it has been agreed that a lord shall oust the termor and have the wardship of the tenancy, and yet in some cases a common person shall have the wardship of the body. As when the lord has a ward, and lands held of the king descend to the same ward; the king shall not have the body because it was lawfully vested.

But if lands held of the king and lands held of a stranger descend at the same time the king shall have his prerogative of the body, as appears in the case of the earl of Warwick. Lands descend to

[17] YB Hil. 9 Edw. IV, f.53, pl.16. [18] YB Mich. 8 Edw. IV, f.23v, pl.38.

an infant while the father is living and then lands held of the king descend to the same infant, then the father dies; the king shall have the wardship of the body.

A man seised of a remainder of land held of the king and of lands held of another dies seised, the lord seizes the ward, the particular tenant dies afterwards; the king shall only have the land and not the body. It would be otherwise if the king had granted the remainder to be held of him, for there by the death he shall have everything: *quod nota bene*.

An infant in the ward of a common person recovers lands held of the king by an ancestral action; the king shall not have the wardship. The law is the same if an infant enters into lands held of the king by reason of any condition made by any of his ancestors, for it was lawfully vested before. But if this infant, being in ward as appears in all these cases above, enters on his father's disseisor, the king shall have everything.

A woman has issue and takes a husband and then lands held of the king and held of others descend to the same woman; the husband enters only in the lands held of the king and the woman dies and the other lord seizes the ward, and then the husband, tenant by the curtesy, dies; the king shall only have the lands held of himself.

A man has issue two sons under age, the elder enters into religion in the life of his father and the father dies seised of land held of a lord who seizes the wardship of the younger son, and then lands held of the king descend to the same ward, and the elder son is deraigned; the king shall have the wardship of him and shall oust the other lord from the land (query, because it was argued) and if the elder dies afterwards the king shall have the wardship of the younger and also of the land which the lord had. The law is the same if the tenant has issue a daughter and his wife is secretly pregnant with a son and he dies seised of lands held of a common person who seizes the wardship of the daughter and then lands held of the king descend to the same daughter and then the son is born; the king shall have the wardship of the son of the tenant.

[**f.3v**] The tenant dies having issue a daughter, and his wife secretly pregnant with another daughter, and lands held of the king descend to the same daughter being in the lord's ward; the second daughter is born; the king shall have the wardship of the second daughter. The law is the same if a woman has issue a daughter and takes a husband and has another daughter and his wife dies, after which lands descend to the same daughters, held of a stranger, the lord seizes the wardship of the elder, and then land held of the king descends to the same daughter and then the husband dies; the king shall have the second daughter.

A man who holds two acres of land, the one by priority and the other by posteriority, dies seised, the lord by priority seizes the ward, and then other lands held of the king descend to the same ward, and then the land which the lord by priority has is evicted by a recovery or otherwise; the king shall have the wardship of the body, even though the title of the lord by priority[19] was before the king's title, and in this case, if the issue brings a writ of error and reverses the judgment against him, the lord by priority shall be restored to the wardship out of the possession of the king. But if the lord by priority had married the child or if the child had satisfied him for the marriage before the land was thus divested the king shall not have the wardship, yet if the lord had granted the wardship of the body to a stranger before the land was thus divested the king would have the wardship.

A man is seised of two acres, the one by priority, the other by posteriority, the lord by posteriority is outlawed in a personal action; the king shall not have the wardship of the body, because the ancestor did not hold of him. The king grants to my tenant in knight service by his letters patent an acre of land to hold of him for twenty years in socage and after that in knight service and then the tenant dies within the twenty years, the heir under age. The lord seizes the ward, then the twenty years expire; the king shall not have the body. The law is the same where any such lordship which was made before the statute escheats to the king.

The article is that the king shall have wardship by reason of wardship. Yet if some one holds of the second ward and dies, his heir under age, the king shall have the wardship of the third ward, and so on infinitely.

If the king grants a lordship of lands held in chief for term of life the grantee shall not have the prerogative as to any other lands; it is otherwise for the body, and this appears in 5 Edw. III 4[20] and I understand the reason is that the grant of the lordship does not change the priority or posteriority and it is thus in the case of a

[19] *Recte* posteriority, HLS MS 1037, p.7.

[20] YB Hil. 5 Edw. III, ff.4–5, pl.17.

common person. But if the king grants his lordship for term of life and the tenant makes a feoffment and takes back again to himself an estate in fee of the land held of the king, and dies, the king's grantee shall not have the wardship of the body.

If the king grants a ward, the committee shall have the prerogative of any other ward just as the king himself shall have, for he continues the king's possession as appears in 12 Hen. IV, 25,[21] in the case of the earl of Arundel and in that case if the tenant changes the tenancy, as by feoffment and taking back an estate, it is not material. Thus there is a divers[ity]. But if such a committee has wardship by reason of wardship and a tenant who holds of the second ward by posteriority and of another by priority dies, his heir under age, the grantee shall not have the body of the third ward, because he had the second ward in his own right.

There is a lord by priority and a lord by posteriority: the lord by posteriority is attainted of treason and before any inquisition is found the tenant dies, his heir under age; the lord by priority shall have the wardship. The law is the same if the king's villein has a lordship by posteriority; before any inquisition is held the tenant dies, the heir under age; the lord by priority seizes the body and then the king seizes the lordship of the villein, the king shall not have the wardship of the body.

The king has wardship by reason of wardship and the first ward sues his livery out of the hands of the king: the second ward dies under age; the king shall not have the wardship of his heir, but he who sued livery shall have it. And such a case was in 13 Edward IV.[22] **[f.4]** The king has a wardship by reason of a lordship of the principality, and then the prince was created and restored to the principality, and then the said ward died under age, the prince shall have his heir in ward and not the king.

There is a lord, mesne and tenant and each holds by knight service. The mesne has issue a son and a daughter and purchases a tenancy to him and the heirs female of his body and dies seised of an acre held of the king: the king shall have the wardship of both; that of the son because the mesnalty is revived in him by the death of his father and the wardship of the daughter by reason of the

[21] YB Hil. 12 Hen. IV, ff.18–19, pl.20; YB Trin. 12 Hen. IV, f.25, pl.12.
[22] YB Pas. 13 Edw. IV, f.10v, pl.6.

wardship of the son. The law is the same where the mesnalty is to the heirs male[23] and the tenancy is given to the mesne and his heirs female[24] and he has a son and a daughter and dies.

The law is the same if such a mesnalty is in tail to someone who purchases the tenancy in fee and has issue a son and a daughter by one womb and a son by another womb and dies seised and the elder son enters and dies without issue; now the mesnalty is revived in the younger son and the lands descend to the daughter, and thus the king shall have the wardship of the son by reason of the mesnalty and of the daughter by reason of the wardship of the son.

There is the king, a mesne lord and a tenant, and the mesnalty is in tail to the heirs female; the mesne purchases the tenancy and before the statute of *Quia emptores terrarum*[25] he enfeoffs another to hold of him by knight service and has issue a son and a daughter and dies; the king shall have the wardship of the daughter and of the son by reason of wardship.

Item habebit primam seisinam [Also he shall have primer seisin] etc. The effect of this article which was [made] in the late time of King Edward I is that the king shall have primer seisin of all lands and tenements which his tenant held of him and of which he died seised as long as he held of him in chief, which affirms the common law, and this appears by the statute of Marlborough c.16[26] which says *quod dominus Rex habeat liberam seisinam ut prius habere consuevit*, which proves that this was an ancient prerogative of the king; *liberam seisinam* and *primer seisin* are the same and the said statute says that the heir shall sue livery out of the hands of the king as had been the usage before. Yet this statute mistakes one thing, which is that this is understood where the king's tenant holds by knight service and the law is that the king shall have primer seisin where his tenant holds of him in socage if he holds of him in chief but he shall not have the wardship [of the heir's body] unless he holds of him by knight service.

Also it appears by the statute of Magna Carta, c.27,[27] that if the tenant holds of the king in socage and of another by knight service, the king shall not have the wardship; but the words of the same statute are *nisi ipsa feodi firma debeat nobis servicium militare* etc. by

[23] Female HLS MS 1037, p.8.

[24] Male HLS MS 1037, p.9.

[25] *Stat. Realm*, vol. 1, 106.

[26] *Stat. Realm*, vol. 1, 24.

[27] *Stat. Realm*, vol. 1, 117.

which words is implied that the common law was that he should have had the prerogative where the tenant had held by knight service; and so the said words prove that the common law is affirmed by the two preceding articles. How the king's title shall be found and the party's title, and how he shall have the land out of the king's hand, I shall show on the next day.

The king's tenant leases land for term of life rendering certain rent and dies, the king shall not have primer seisin of the reversion, nor of the rent until after the death of the tenant for term of life: 7 Hen. VI in the case of Gascon.[28] Otherwise if he has other lands held of others and leases the lands held of the king for term of life and dies, for there the king shall have primer seisin of the other lands. But he shall not oust the termor as the ward shall do. The king's tenant gives land in tail rendering certain rent and dies, the king shall have primer seisin; and even if the heir has sued livery, if the tenant in tail dies without issue afterwards, the king shall have primer seisin of the land. And in the same case, if no rent had been reserved, still the king shall have primer seisin of the lordship.

I showed on the last day that if the king's tenant has lands in borough English and has issue two sons and dies, the king shall only have the wardship of the lands of the elder, yet in the same case he shall have primer seisin of everything. Thus it is if lands are given to the king's tenant and the heirs male of his body and the tenant dies without male issue, the king shall have primer seisin of everything and there he shall not have the wardship of everything and the donor shall sue *ouster le main* of the land in tail.

[**f.4v**] Next the article is *post mortem* etc. yet if the king's tenant leases to a stranger for term of life with the remainder in fee, and the remainderman dies, the king shall not have primer seisin.

In some cases the king shall have the wardship and not primer seisin, as when the king's tenant aliens by covin and dies with his heir of full age, the king shall not have primer seisin; it is otherwise if he was under age, for there he shall retain the land until livery is sued. The law is the same if the king's tenant enfeoffs a stranger to his use and dies with his heir of full age, he shall not have primer seisin; it is otherwise if he was under age, for there he would have the wardship by the statute of the present king, Henry VII.[29]

[28] YB Mich. 7 Hen. VI, ff.2–5, pl.7.

[29] 4 Hen. VII, c.17, *Stat. Realm*, vol. 2, 540–41.

The king gives lands in tail and the tenant [in tail] aliens in fee and dies; the king shall have primer seisin of this land, for he cannot discontinue the king's reversion.

The article is *cuiuscumque ætatis* [of whatever age] yet if the tenant dies seised of land held of others and dies without an heir, the king shall have primer seisin of everything.

If a man recovers land held of the king by an ancestral action, the king shall not have primer seisin. It is otherwise if he recovers by assize of *mort d'ancestor*. The king's tenant leases for term of life with the remainder in fee, and the remainderman dies, the king shall not have primer seisin; yet if the heir recovers by a writ of waste, the king shall have primer seisin.

The king's tenant dies seised of land held of others and in the same land held of others a stranger abates, the king shall have primer seisin of all; yet in 10 Ric. II[30] the contrary is held.

The king's tenant is disseised and dies, there shall be no primer seisin and yet he shall have the wardship, for he shall not have primer seisin for a right only, without possession.

The article is *cuiuscumque ætatis*, yet if he is under age he shall have the wardship and after full age this possession shall serve him for a seisin until livery.

The king's tenant as of his duchy dies seised, his heir of full age, the king shall not have primer seisin, but the heir shall enter without suing livery; yet the contrary is held 2 Hen. VI.[31]

The use in the chancery is that the king shall have primer seisin of the lands which are held of his ward, which is against reason as it seems, though there was such a precedent in 28 Hen. VI[32] that such a one sued livery.

The article is *omnibus terris et tenementis* [all lands and tenements] etc., yet the king shall have primer seisin of advowsons, commons in gross, rent charges and rent seck and all such things.

The article is *capiendo exitus* [*omnes*] *donec facta fuerit inquisitio prout moris est* [taking all the issues until an inquisition is held according to custom] etc., by which it appears that the king is able to seize without an inquisition, which is neither law nor good reason, now or at that time yet by the statute of 8 Hen. VI[33] it appears that

[30] *Recte* YB Trin. 12 Ric. II, Anthony Fitzherbert, *La Graunde Abridgement* (London, 1516), Livery 28.

[31] YB Hil. 2 Hen. VI, ff.5–7, pl.5.

[32] YB Trin. 28 Hen. VI, f.11, pl.23.

[33] c.16, *Stat. Realm*, vol. 2, 252.

he was able before the same statutes to seize without an inquisition, which was never right, for two reasons; one, a man can have nothing from the king by a matter of fact and for the same reason the king can have nothing by a matter of fact: and also if the king were able to seize without an inquisition, the party would be without remedy because the king's title must appear as a matter of record to which the party can respond and now by the said statute of 18 Hen. VI[34] it is ordained that the king cannot grant any ward without an inquisition, by which it is implied that he cannot have the ward without an inquisition. Yet at the common law the king could have seized the wardship of the body, for it is only a chattel, like wreck and such things.

If the escheator seizes before etc. he shall be punished by assize, yet he has sufficient warrant by the words of the *diem clausit extremum* to seize at the outset, but this is only the form of the writ from ancient times just like the words of the *grand cape*. Also it appears by the statute of Lincoln that if one sues livery out of the king's hands and then a new title is found for the king, still the king shall not re-seize without a *scire facias* and this title must be found by an inquisition.

The article is *primer seisin*. If the tenant who holds of the king in chief dies, the king shall not seize the land without an inquisition. It is otherwise if he holds as of the duchy or of another lordship, for there he shall seize without an inquisition. A man holds an acre in chief and another of the duchy and dies seised, the heir under age, the king seizes the acre held of the duchy and grants this to another [and then] it is found by an [**f.5**] inquisition that he died seised of the other acre held in chief; now the king shall re-seize and recover the lands held of the duchy, for now the king shall have them until the heir has sued livery, for he was deceived in his grant. In the cases [above] where the king seizes without an inquisition, the heir does not need to sue livery but rather enters.

A man seised of a ward is outlawed in a personal action, the king shall seize without an inquisition. The law is the same of a termor who is outlawed in this way. A man holds a lordship of the king and is outlawed for felony and then a wardship falls to him, the king shall seize the ward without an inquisition, but not the lordship. The law is the same if a wardship falls to the king's villein; the king shall

[34] c.6, *Stat. Realm*, vol. 2, 306–07.

seize the ward without an inquisition but not the lordship which the villein has, nor lands purchased by him.

The king's tenant dies without an heir, the king shall enter without an inquisition, because the law casts the freehold on him and no one else is able to take it, and to this purpose he shall have the same advantage as a common person.

The king presents to a church without title and his clerk is instituted and inducted, the one who has the right shall have a petition.

The king grants lands in tail or for term of life, the tenant dies without issue of his body; the king shall enter without an inquisition. The law is the same if lands descend to the king by a collateral ancestor. The king grants a lordship for term of life, to which the tenancy escheats, and then the term expires; he shall seize without an inquisition.

A man is attainted of treason by authority of parliament, and in the same act it is ordained that the king shall grant his lands to another in tail, and then the king grants them accordingly and then the tenant dies without issue; the king shall enter without an inquisition and have the land. Yet if the king's tenant aliens in mortmain the king shall not seize without an inquisition.

And in cases where a man is able to give [lands] to the king without a matter of record, as in leases for term of life, the remainder to the king, [this remainder is good] without a deed enrolled. Also a grant made to the king of a wardship of the body is good without a matter of record.

Lands escheat to the king's villein which he has by reason of the duchy of Lancaster; the king shall enter without an inquisition. It is otherwise if [the villein] purchases lands.

The king presents to a church without title and his clerk is instituted and inducted; the king shall have the advowson by the matter in fact, and the one who has the right shall have a petition.

In no case shall the king have primer seisin of tenants who hold of him in chief without an inquisition, for he has this as king.

The king is entitled by an inquisition which does not give him clear title, still he shall seize: as where it is found that he holds of the king, and it is not expressly found that he holds in chief, the king shall seize. The law is the same if it is found that he holds of the king, *sed per quae servicia ignorant*. The law is the same if it is found that the tenant died seised, *sed de quo et quibus ignorant*. Thus where no tenure is found the king shall seize, as the law is taken, yet I understand that this is only a bare and single title for the king.

It is found by an inquisition that someone died, his heir of full age, and that he held of one J.S., and it appears as a matter of record in chancery that the land is held of the king; the king shall have primer seisin. The law is the same if it is found by an inquisition in one county that some one is heir to the king's tenant, and by another inquisition in another county that the tenant died seised of certain lands [without an heir];[35] the king shall have primer seisin.

It is found by inquisition that the king's tenant is attainted of felony or treason; if there is no such attainder the inquisition is void.

A man in a court of record confesses that his father held of the king in chief and died; this is sufficient title for the king to seize and the king shall have all the issues after the death of the ancestor. [**f.5v**] In *praecipe quod reddat* the tenant says that he holds for term of life with the remainder to the king, and dies; the king shall enter without an inquisition.

In some cases the king is not able to seize with only an inquisition, as when an abbot of the king's foundation alienates land and this is found by an inquisition, yet he may not seize without a *scire facias*. And in every case where a common person is put to his action, the king may not seize by an inquisition alone, but shall have a *scire facias*. As where it is found by inquisition that the tenant who held of the king for term of life had made waste, or that the king's tenant had ceased [to perform services]; the king shall not seize without *scire facias*. Yet in special cases this does not hold. As when the king's tenant aliens by covin and dies and this is found by inquisition; he shall seize without *scire facias*, and the reason is because the king is not bound by the statute, inasmuch as he is not named.

The article is *capiendo exitus* [*omnes*] *donec facta fuerit inquisitio* [taking the issues until an inquisition is held] etc. yet the king shall have all the issues of the land from the time his title accrues until the inquisition is found, for in each case where the king is entitled to any land, he shall be answered for the issues, except where the tenant sues an *ouster le main cum exitibus* or in special cases. As when the king's tenant aliens without licence and this is found by an inquisition a long time afterwards; the king shall seize and shall not have the

35 HLS MS 1037, p.13.

issues in the meantime, for the king only has the land as a pledge for the fine for alienation.

Where the king shall have the issues he shall have them according to the inquisition found before the escheator, the transcript of which shall be sent into the exchequer, and thereupon process shall issue against the tenant or the heir and he shall have an answer to this by saying that it does not amount to so much, and also he should only be charged for his own occupation; thus each tenant of the land in the meantime shall answer for the issues for his time and shall have the same answer.

The king's tenant dies seised, his heir of full age, who enters and dies seised, and this is found by inquisition; if he died [seised] of an estate in fee simple, then his next heir shall answer for the issues accrued after the king's title, as well in his father's time as in his own time, but if he died seised of an estate tail, he shall only be charged for his own time and his father's executors for his time.

The king's tenant dies seised, the heir shall not be charged for the issues from cutting the wood. It is otherwise if the king is entitled to the land by escheat and the stranger cuts the wood, for there he has the title to have the same wood. The king's tenant dies, his land being of the value of £10, and the heir amends or improves the land to the value of £20, the king shall have his issues according to this value. But if the heir runs the land down the king shall be answered according to the value which the land had at the time of the tenant's death etc.

The king shall be answered for the casual profits that he himself could have taken if he himself were in possession. As where the king's tenant has a *villein regardant* and dies with his heir of full age, which villein purchases land, and the heir enters, and all this matter is found by inquisition; the king shall have the land purchased by the villein; but if the heir had alienated before the inquisition the king would be answered according to the value of the land. The law is the same of a wardship which fell to him.

It is used in the chancery that the king shall have primer seisin after the death of the tenant for term of life, with the remainder over, which is not warranted by the law, but only by their fees in the chancery. And the statute of Marlborough says *quod dominus habeat simplicem seisinam ut pro domino cognoscatur*, which words are void, and the other case can be called simple seisin. Also it has been used that if two joint tenants hold of the king and the one dies, the other shall sue livery, which is not reasonable. But if a husband and wife are joint tenants and the husband dies, the wife shall sue livery and this is in 11 Edw. III[36] and query this.

In the article the last day I showed how the king shall have the primer seisin which he had at the common law, as appears by the words of the said article, which are *prout moris est* and also by [**f.6**] the statute of Marlborough, c.17,[37] which says *quod dominus rex inde habebit liberam sesinam ut prius habere consuevit*, which words imply that primer seisin was at the common law and also the words of the same statute are *ne heredes vel alius se intrudat in hereditatem priusquam [illam] de manibus ipsius domini Regis recipiat* [nor shall the heir, or any other, intrude in the inheritance, before he has received it out of the king's hands] etc. by which words it appears that the heir shall sue livery at the common law. Now I will show how and by what writs the heir shall sue livery, and also how the king can be entitled; for every inquisition which can entitle the king shall not be sufficient to entitle the heir.

The king can be entitled by an inquisition found before the escheator *virtute officii* or *virtute brevis* or by a general or special commission to others or by no writ.

The article is *donec facta fuerit inquisicio prout moris est* [until an inquisition is held as is usual]; yet [the heir] can have livery without any office or inquisition, as by special livery and this can be under age as in the case of the duchess of Buckingham in the second year where the king granted her the wardship *quam diu in manibus suis fore contigerit*, and afterwards the king gave the ward a special livery, and thereby the duchess was without remedy. It would have been otherwise if the king had granted to her the ward *durante minori aetate et quam diu in manibus suis fore contigerit* and then the king made a special livery to the ward.

And in another way the heir can have his livery without an inquisition, as where the king's tenant dies, his heir of full age enters, and before any office found the king pardons him all intrusions. But if an inquisition is found before the pardon, then the pardon shall only serve for the profits taken before. Still by right one shall never have livery except when an inquisition is found for him by writ and not *virtute officii*.

36 Hil. 15 Edw. III, pp.273–74, pl.6 (Rolls series).
37 *Recte* c.16, *Stat. Realm*, vol. 1, 24.

The king's tenant dies, the heir shall have *diem clausit extremum* whether he is under age or of full age, and this writ shall be a livery for the heir and therefore he shall see at his peril that his title is well found, for otherwise he shall never have livery.

The king's tenant dies seised of two acres and by the *diem clausit extremum* it is found that he died seised only of one *et quod non habuit plures terras nec tenementa*. The heir at full age sues livery and then by another inquisition it is found that he died seised of two acres; the king shall re-seize and there is no remedy for the heir for the two acres.

If the heir has a *diem clausit extremum* and then the escheator is discharged from his office, the new escheator can enquire by virtue of the same writ, and if he will not do so, the heir can sue a writ called *amotus* within the year to the new escheator, and if the escheator is associated he can also have within the year a special commission and also a *supersedeas* to the escheator. And if the inquisition found by the *diem clausit extremum* is insufficient in part or in whole the heir shall have a *melius inquirendum*.

If in the *diem clausit extremum* these words "*et non habet plures terras nec tenementa*" are not returned the heir can have a writ called *que plura* [to inquire] about the lands omitted in the first inquisition, and he shall have livery on both writs, and after the year and day or twenty years after the heir shall have the writ called *mandamus*. And if the heir being in the king's ward dies, his next heir shall have the writ called *devenerunt*; and by this writ they can find more lands than were in the first inquisition, as when the king's ward has lands by purchase.

If the heir's title is found by a general commission he cannot sue livery on this, which I know by experience, but it is otherwise by a special commission.

There is also a commission of concealed lands, as when the king's tenant dies seised of two manors and the one is found by inquisition and the other concealed, and the heir sues livery; then the said commission shall issue, and after this matter is found the king shall have *scire facias* against the tenant and seize it back, and there is no remedy for him [the heir]. Also there is a writ called the writ of concealed lands, and this shall only be granted [**f.6v**] on a matter of record in chancery proving the concealments.

A man shall only have one writ of *diem clausit extremum* or *mandamus* or *devenerunt* if it is properly returned. The heir can have his land by general livery. There is also an *ouster le main cum exitibus*, *ouster le main sine exitibus* and *amoveas manum*.

If the heir of the king's tenant is found of full age he shall not have *aetate probanda*; it is otherwise if he is found under age, in which case the writ of *aetate probanda* shall not be granted to him until the time when it appears by the inquisition that the heir is of full age. It is found in the inquisition that the heir is 16 years and more; he shall not have the advantage of this word "more" and if he is found under age by an inquisition and of a younger age by another inquisition, he shall not have the said writ until he appears of full age by every inquisition, but if at full age he purchases the said writ and before his age is proved it is found by another inquisition that he is under age, a *supersedeas* shall issue to the escheator to stop the process concerning his age. Still when his age is proved before the inquisition he shall have livery, because this is a perfect trial between the king and him.

This writ of *aetate probanda* may be directed to the escheator or to the sheriff and shall only be directed to one county alone, and the heir shall come and show the place of his birth and the writ shall be directed to that county; and this inquisition shall be by twelve men and also by witnesses. And if a son brings the said writ each of the witnesses must be of the age of 42 years at least, since the witnesses must have a reasonable memory of his birth as appears 2 Ric. II;[38] and if a woman brings the action they must be of the age of 37, for the female heir shall have this writ at the age of 16 years.

A woman can be proved in this trial and if the jury finds her of full age and the witnesses find her under age she shall not have her livery but shall be taken under age, and then when she comes to full age according to that which the witnesses found, she shall have her livery without another writ of *aetate probanda*. And the witnesses in their verdict must show specially the circumstances of her age, as the year, day and hour and place, and other signs of the year following, like thunder or earthquake or such things; but the verdict of twelve shall be generally that the heir is under age or of full age without more.

The sheriff returns two witnesses and the one says that the heir is aged 23 years and the other that he is 22 years, the heir shall not have livery because the two witnesses must agree. It is otherwise

[38] *Recte* 21 Ric. II, Fitzherbert, Livery 5.

if the jury finds him to be 22 years and the witnesses 23 years, for there he shall have livery. There are three witnesses and the jury, and two of the witnesses prove him of full age and the third finds him under age, he shall have his livery. There are four witnesses and the twelve, and two witnesses find the heir of full age and the other two witnesses that he is under age, the heir shall not have his livery for the testimony of two is sufficient for the king. Thus before such a livery the heir must have this writ.

The article is *homagium eius ceperit* [taking his homage]: The order for doing homage when age is proved [is] to have a writ from the clerk of the rolls to the keeper of the privy seal testifying the age, and from him a privy seal to the king's chamberlain to receive his homage, and when he has done this he shall have a writ from the chamberlain to the chancellor testifying that he has received his homage, and thereupon the chancellor shall award to the heir his writ of livery directed to the escheator etc. But to avoid the costs, heirs are accustomed to purchase a privy seal directed to the chancellor to respite homage and send a transcript of this into the exchequer, after which process shall be awarded out of the exchequer annually for him to make his homage.

[**f.7**] Note that such an heir shall never have livery except where his title is found sufficient by their writ.

The king's tenant aliens land held of the king by covin and dies seised of another parcel and this is found by inquisition, the heir at full age shall sue livery of that of which the ancestor died seised and the feoffee shall sue *ouster le main sine exitibus* and if the heir does not wish to prove his age the feoffee shall have no remedy. The law is the same where the king's tenant makes a feoffment to his use of a parcel, for the king or lord shall have the ward by the statute made 4 Hen. VII,[39] yet if the king's tenant makes a feoffment by covin of everything the feoffee shall have *aetate probanda* unless a special *ouster le main* is granted to him.

A man has lands in borough English [held] of a common person and dies seised of other lands held of the king and has issue two sons and dies and this is found by an inquisition; the elder shall have livery and the younger son shall have *ouster le main sine exitibus*, for no one shall have a livery of the lands but the king's tenant. The king's tenant has other lands held of another lord to him and his

[39] c.17, *Stat. Realm*, vol. 2, 540–41.

heirs female of his body and has issue a son and a daughter and dies; the son shall sue livery of the land held of the king and the daughter shall have *ouster le main*.

And in all these cases where a stranger is heritable to the land held of others of which the king's tenant died seised and the heir to this is not heritable, he [the stranger] shall have *ouster le main*; and this can be by an inquisition found without a writ, that is, *virtute officii*. And in the previous case if the daughter is under age the king shall not have the wardship and she shall have *ouster le main* under age.

The king's tenant has lands held of others in gavelkind and has issue two sons and dies, the younger brother shall have *ouster le main* of his part, even if the matter is found *virtute officii* as before and on the *ouster le main* the younger shall have partition: and how this shall be done I intend to show hereafter. Two sons, both hold of the king; the elder gives his part to the younger in tail who dies without issue of his body and this [is found] good, the elder sues livery for the share of his brother, to whom he is heir, and for the other share he shall have *ouster le main* because he does not claim this as heir but rather by reason of his reversion.

The mesne who holds of the king dies with his heir of full age, and after the inquisition is found the tenancy escheats to the king; the heir has no remedy to have livery of the land, for to him the inquisition shall not serve for the tenancy: (Query, because it was argued). It would have been otherwise if the heir had entered in [the lands by] escheat before the inquisition was found, for there he would have livery of the land and also the king would have and be answered for the profits of the seignory before the escheat and for the profits of the land after the escheat.

The king's tenant has other lands held of the king in chief in borough English, and has issue two sons and dies; the two shall have separate liveries by an inquisition found *virtute brevis*, but they must have two writs of *aetate probanda*, and if in this case they are both found of full age and afterwards by an inquisition held *virtute officii* [it is found] that the elder is under age the younger shall not have livery until it appears by the last inquisition that the elder is of full age. But if the younger had proved his age by *aetate probanda* before the said last inquisition was found, he shall have the advantage of that and the elder shall wait. It is found by an inquisition *virtute brevis* that the king's tenant died, the heir of full age, and on this the heir sued livery, and then it is found by another inquisition *virtute officii* that the heir is under age, the king shall re-seize. It is otherwise if the age was proved by *aetate probanda*.

The king's tenant has lands in fee simple and in fee tail held of the king, and has issue a son and a daughter by one womb and a son by another womb, and dies, and the inquisition is found *virtute brevis*; and then the elder son dies without issue, and then this matter is found by a *devenerunt*, the sister shall sue livery as heir to her brother for the fee simple, because the king's possession was sufficient possession to make her heir to her brother, and the brother of the half-blood shall sue livery of the lands in tail.

[**f.7v**] The king's tenant leases for life, remainder in fee, the remainderman dies with his heir of full age, the heir must have an inquisition found by writ; and then the tenant for term of life dies: the heir shall not have livery until another inquisition *virtute officii* is found proving his death.

The king's tenant has other lands for term of life also held of the king; the reversion descends to his heir by another ancestor and then the father dies. There the heir must have two writs of *diem clausit extremum*: yet in the judicial register it appears that he can have one writ for both lands. The king's tenant is tenant by the curtesy of other lands also held of the king and dies, his heir must have a writ as heir to him and another writ as heir to his mother, yet the course in chancery is the contrary. But if someone is heir to the husband and another is heir to the wife, there they must have separate writs otherwise they shall not have livery.

Note that if the heir of the king's tenant sues livery it is necessary that all inquisitions in all counties and all the parcels to which he is heritable and of which his ancestor died seised must be found by writ, and that he sues livery in all the counties, and if any are omitted the livery is worthless.

Lands held of the king given to a man and his wife in special tail and they have issue a daughter and the wife dies: the husband has issue another daughter by another wife and dies, and it is found by inquisition that he died seised of that land in fee, and the elder daughter was daughter and heir, whereupon she had livery, and then by another inquisition it was found that the father had another daughter, and thereupon a *scire facias* was awarded against the sister by the statute of Lincoln, which wishes the special tail to be shown: and it was not allowed, because the special matter was not found by the writ, and thereupon the king shall re-seize, and for this reason the writ of *diem clausit extremum* shall be delivered to the heir. But if it had been found by the inquisition that the king's tenant died seised of an estate in fee simple and only had issue a daughter and sued livery, and then by another inquisition the truth is found, the king shall not re-seize.

The king's tenant has lands in another county held of the king in borough English and has issue two sons and dies, and by an inquisition the younger is found heir in the county where the lands by the custom are, and by another inquisition the elder is found heir in another county, the king shall re-seize by *scire facias* because the custom was not found by the inquisition, for he [the younger] is not heir by blood; yet in the above case if there is only one son, and the custom is not found in the inquisition, the king shall not re-seize.

A livery must be made entirely, as above.

The king's tenant dies seised of two manors and by the inquisition it is found that he only died seised of one, if the heir sues his livery and then it is found by another inquisition that he died seised of the other manor, he [the king] shall re-seize all and there shall be no remedy for the heir, for he shall only have a *diem clausit extremum* in which it shall be entirely found and he shall not be able to have a commission because the *diem clausit extremum* is returned.

The king's tenant of an acre disseises another of another acre and dies seised, and when this is found the heir sues livery of everything, still by a special <dis>agreement he shall discharge him of the damages for the acre by disseisin.

If a parcel is omitted, the livery is worthless as in the case of 44 Edw. III, 25,[40] where the heir made omission of an advowson in gross, and for this the king re-seized. Yet in some cases the heir shall sue livery by parcels, as when lands held of the king descend to him from different ancestors. The law is the same if the king's tenant dies seised of two acres in two counties and the king makes special livery to him of one, he shall sue livery of the other.

Also, whereas livery must be entire, yet nevertheless it may be found that the heir sues livery of all the land generally where it ought to be *retenta dote* [retaining dower] and the title of dower

40 YB Pas. 44 Edw. III, f.12, pl.17.

appears by the inquisition, the king shall re-seize; and if the title of the dower does not appear by the same inquisition but rather by another [**f.8**] the king shall re-seize, and if the title of dower appears by no inquisition, the woman can come into chancery and on that surmise she shall have *scire facias* against the heir, but in these cases <the king> the heir has remedy by a new livery.

The heir at common law sues livery of the lands at the common law and also of lands in borough English, and then it is found by inquisition that he has a younger brother, still the livery of the lands at common law is good, and it is not like the previous case of dower, for the woman has title in every part.

The heir sues livery and an inquisition is found afterwards to defeat the livery, the king shall not re-seize without a *scire facias*; but if he sues livery on an insufficient inquisition, the king shall re-seize without a *scire facias*, as in the case before, where the king's tenant died seised of two manors in two counties and the heir only sued livery of one.

Before livery the heir is certified a bastard, the king shall re-seize without a *scire facias*, and in this case if it is found by another writ that another is heir, the king can maintain against him that the one who is certified a bastard is the heir and against the bastard that he is a bastard, and neither of them shall have livery.

If the younger is found heir by writ, the elder must be found heir by another writ in another county, and then they shall interplead. If the elder is found heir *virtute brevis*, the younger *virtute officii*, the elder must transfer his inquisition before his livery. If the elder is found heir *virtute officii* and the younger by writ, there is no remedy for the elder.

The king's tenant has issue two sons, the elder enters into religion in his father's lifetime, the father dies, the younger is found heir by writ, the elder is deraigned and found heir *virtute officii*: neither of them shall have livery. The law is the same if a man has issue a daughter and dies, his wife being secretly pregnant: if the daughter is found heir by writ, [then the son is born][41] there is no remedy for the son.

The king has a wardship by forfeiture or by grant, the heir does not need to sue livery. The king has wardship by reason of wardship, the second ward shall sue livery by the course of chancery. The

41 HLS MS 14, f.17v.

king grants his lordship for term of years, a wardship falls in within the years and before full age the years expire; the heir shall not sue livery. The law is the same if the termor grants the wardship to the king. A man seised of a ward is outlawed in a personal action, the heir at his full age shall not sue livery because in these cases the king does not have the wardship by reason of any lordship.

And there is another writ which is called *amoveas manum* and this lies where the king is entitled by an insufficient inquisition.

A man holds lands of the king [in socage][42] and dies, his heir under age, the next friend shall sue livery *una cum exitibus*; but if he [the heir] is of full age he shall have livery *sine exitibus*.

I have shown how the king shall have primer seisin and how he shall have his prerogative in respect of the wardship, of the land as well as of the body, and also how and in what manner the heir shall sue livery out of the hands of the king. And now I intend to show how, when the king is entitled to any land by any false inquisition, the party who has right shall have his remedy, and in what case the party shall have his traverse or petition or his *monstrans de droit*.

The statute of 34 Edw. III, c.14,[43] provides that the party shall have a traverse of a false inquisition to entitle the king, as appears by the same statute; and the statute of 36 Edw. III, c.13,[44] provides that after the escheator has found such a false inquisition he shall show this in the chancery within the month, and if he does not wish [to do so] the party shall have a writ to him to certify this, and the party afterwards shall have his traverse or *monstrans de droit* at once, without waiting for another order, and also that the chancellor by his discretion may lease the land to the party at farm, finding surety as appears by the statute; see the statute.

Yet at the common law a man could have had a traverse for a chattel. As when the king's tenant had a lease, and an inquisition was found that he had aliened [**f.8v**] without licence, where he did not alien; in this case he had a traverse, but not without another inquisition found for the tenant that he did not alien: see 12 Edw. IV.[45] The law is the same if it is found by a false inquisition that my tenant held of the king in chief and died, his heir under age; if I have another inquisition found for me I shall have a traverse for the ward but now by the said statute the party shall have a traverse

[42] HLS MS 1037, p.22; HLS MS 14, f.17v. [43] *Stat. Realm*, vol. 1, 368.
[44] *Stat. Realm*, vol. 1, 374–75. [45] YB Mich. 12 Edw. IV, f.8v, pl.24.

without any inquisition, and so there is a distinction between the order of them.

Sometimes the heir traverses the inquisition, as when a stranger is found heir *virtute officii*; if the true heir is found afterwards by writ he shall have a traverse of the first inquisition, and he cannot traverse the first inquisition without another inquisition found for him, because then he would have livery on the first inquisition which did not give him any title.

But if it is found by inquisition that J.S. held of the king in chief and died, whereas he held of me, I shall have it without traverse, for this does not disaffirm the king's title and I shall have this traverse without any other inquisition found for [me; and] this by the said statute. The law is the same where it is found that my tenant held of the king and that his younger son is his heir, the heir [the elder] shall have a traverse without another inquisition.

Where the king's title in any parcel is found true by the inquisition the party shall not have remedy without petition, as where it is found that the king's tenant died seised and that such a one is his heir, and by another inquisition it is found that he died without an heir, there is no remedy but petition. [It is] otherwise if by the last inquisition it is found that the ancestor aliened in mortmain, for there the heir shall traverse the alienation in mortmain, because in the first case the inquisition entitled both the heir and the king and in the latter case the inquisition entitled the king alone, for by such an alienation the king is entitled and not the heir on either part.

It is found that the king's tenant died seised and that the lands are held by knight service and by another inquisition afterwards it is found that the lands are held in socage, which is true; if the heir is under age he shall traverse the inquisition and have livery *cum exitibus*, and if he delays until he comes to his full age the nature of his livery is changed for there he shall have livery *sine exitibus*.

In these previous cases the heir shall have a traverse if an inquisition is found for him, but now by the statute the heir shall have a traverse without any inquisition. Still in no case where the party affirms the king's title found by office shall he have a traverse. The said statute of 36 Edw. III[46] and the statute of 9 Hen. VI, c.16,[47] provide [that he shall have his traverse without any inquisition

[46] *Stat. Realm*, vol. 1, 375. [47] *Recte* 8 Hen. VI, c.16. *Stat. Realm*, vol. 2, 252.

found][48] as above and also that the escheator shall return his inquisition within the month on pain of £20 and that the said inquisition shall remain in the chancery for a month after the return, and furthermore as appears. And the statute of 18 Hen VI, c.6,[49] provides that no letters patent may be given to any person before the inquisition of the king's title is taken and the statute provides further etc.

A petition was at common law, where the king was entitled by a false record; and the order of a petition is that the party shall make a bill to the king comprising his own title and also all the king's titles, and when the king has endorsed the bill that right should be done to him, a commission shall be awarded to enquire into the party's title as comprised within the bill, which shall be returned into chancery, and there the king's attorney may maintain the king's title and traverse the party's title which was found before, and may put the party to a great delay and, at the common law, before the statute of 14 Edw. III,[50] to infinite delay, for he was able to show the court that various evidences were in the treasury concerning the king's title, and pray writs of search in the treasury, and if such writs were not returned, or if they were returned that they had not fully searched, this was no contempt, because these writs were sued for the advantage of the king; but now, by the said statute it is ordained that he shall not have more than four writs of search, and if the issue taken by the king's attorney is found against him the judgment shall be that the party shall recover *salvo iure regis*, to this purpose that where he [has] another right and it is not the same right which was found before, on this petition he shall not have his judgment *una cum exitibus* for it is his writ of right against the king, and just as he shall not have damages in a writ [**f.9**] of right against a common person, he shall not have *exitus* against the king by suing his petition.

In a traverse the party shall show a title for himself in the chancery and rehearse all of the inquisitions found for the king, even if there are 20, as to say *compertum est quod* etc. And in some cases the king must maintain all of the inquisitions which were traversed and in some cases not. And also the king can choose to maintain his inquisition or traverse the party's title, and he can take issue

48 HLS MS 1037, p.24.

49 *Stat. Realm*, vol. 2, 306–07.

50 c.14, *Stat. Realm*, vol. 1, 286.

and relinquish the issue and demur in law, but if after the issue he demurs in law he cannot resort to the issue again, and after the same issue he cannot take a new issue unless it is the same term, and if the twelve men are sworn he shall not demur in law afterwards.

If a title is found for the tenant by an inquisition there is no need to show any other title, as when it is found that the king's tenant aliened in fee without licence, he shall traverse the alienation without making any other title for himself. The law is the same if it is found that he aliened in mortmain. It is otherwise where no title appears in the inquisition for the party, and therefore in an assize if the tenant derives any title or interest from the plaintiff, there is no need for the plaintiff to make [any other] title, as when the tenant says that the plaintiff leased to him for term of life. And in all these cases of traverse the party must say that he was seised until he was disseised by the escheator *colore officii predicti*.

In the cases of petition or traverse, if the king has granted the lands before the petition or traverse, then the party shall have *scire facias* against the grantee or patentee [to show] whether he knows of anything to say whereby his patent should not be revoked. It is otherwise if, pending such a petition or traverse, the king had made such a grant. If in such a case the grantee or patentee makes a default on the day the *scire facias* is returned, after which he had been warned, he forfeits his patent, for by his default it shall be revoked at once.

The king may maintain every inquisition found for him which are consistent with each other, as when it is found that the king's tenant died, his heir under age, and by another inquisition that he aliened in mortmain: as appears 9 Hen. IV, 61.[51] It is otherwise if the inquisitions are repugnant, as if it is found by an inquisition that the king's tenant died, his heir under age, and by another inquisition that he made a feoffment by collusion; in this case the king maintains one of the inquisitions at his peril, for these are repugnant: see 11 Hen. IV, 80,[52] on this matter.

The person who tenders a traverse must traverse all the inquisitions found before the tender of his traverse but not an inquisition found while his traverse is pending, for that way there might be infinite delay; and if judgment is given for the one who tenders the traverse then a *scire facias* shall issue for the king on the inquisition

[51] YB Mich. 9 Hen. VI, ff.6–7, pl.20. [52] YB Trin. 11 Hen. IV, ff.80–81, pl.22.

found while the traverse is pending. Yet an inquisition can be found while the traverse is pending which shall put the party to his petition and abate this traverse.

And if the king and the party are at issue on the traverse, the record shall be sent into the King's Bench and the issue shall be tried, and the king's attorney shall have a *venire facias* and judgment shall be given by the statute of 34 Edw. III.[53] It is otherwise where a traverse is tendered in the exchequer on an inquisition found *virtute officii*, for there the barons of the exchequer shall not send the record to the [King's] Bench but shall rather try the matter themselves. An inquisition found by writ is returned into chancery and another inquisition is found for the same land *virtute officii*; the one who tenders the traverse shall have *certiorari* to the barons of the exchequer to send the inquisition found *virtute officii* into the chancery, and there the party shall tender his traverse to both.

There is no great difference in the process between a *monstrans de droit* and a traverse, but in the *monstrans de droit* he affirms the king's title and avoids it. And also one shall have a *monstrans de droit* when he is out of possession by the same inquisition, [**f.9v**] as when the king's tenant is disseised and [the disseisor][54] aliens in mortmain and the disseisee re-enters and all this matter is found by inquisition, he shall have a *monstrans de droit*, but if he did not enter before the inquisition he shall be put to his petition.

A disseisor enfeoffs the king by a deed enrolled, the disseisee shall only have a petition. The law is the same if the king's tenant is disseised and the disseisee dies, his heir shall have petition. The prince purchases lands to which I have a right and then is king, I shall have petition.

A false inquisition finds that a stranger died seised of my lands held of the king and that he died without an heir: I shall have traverse. It is otherwise if it is found that the stranger was attainted of felony or of treason and that he was seised of my lands held of the king, for there he shall have petition, because he cannot traverse the attainder which is a matter of record. The disseisor enfeoffs the king's villein and this is found by inquisition, the disseisee shall have petition; but if the disseisee had entered before the inquisition was found, then he shall have *monstrans de droit*. The law is the same if a disseisor enfeoffs an alien, for there the king is entitled to the

[53] c.14, *Stat. Realm*, vol. 1, 368. [54] HLS MS 1037, p.26.

freehold by a defeasible title. An inquisition found on a matter of record which entitles the king: the party shall be put to his petition and shall not have *monstrans de droit*.

If one disseises me of land held of the king and dies seised, the heir under age or of full age, and the inquisition is found, there is no remedy until the heir has livery, for if he is under age there is no petition against the king because a writ of right does not lie against the guardian, but the freehold is in the heir; yet if <he> [I] had made a continual claim and entered before the inquisition, I shall have *monstrans de droit* against the guardian. The law is the same if an infant is disseised of land held of the king, and the disseisor dies seised, and the infant enters before the inquisition, he shall have *monstrans de droit*.

In some cases the party shall not traverse unless an inquisition is found for him *virtute officii* or by commission out of chancery, as when a husband and wife are joint tenants of land held of the king, the husband dies seised, and it is found by an inquisition that he died sole seised: the wife shall not traverse this without another inquisition of her title found for her, as appears 15 Edw. III.[55] The law is the same if it is found that the one joint tenant died sole seised.

The king's tenant enfeoffs another and it is found that the feoffor died seised, the feoffee on this traverse shall show the king's licence for the purchase, or else the king shall re-take the land for the fine.

Tenant in tail, the remainder to another in fee, of land held of the king, and it is found by inquisition that he died seised in fee and that his brother is his heir; if the <reversioner> [remainderman] wishes to traverse the inquisition he must have another inquisition found for him.

If it is found that someone died seised of lands held of the king, his heir under age, where he held the lands of another lord by knight service, the lord shall have his traverse. The law is the same if it is found by a false inquisition that a stranger died seised of land held of the king whereof another is seised.

But a person who has rent charge or rent seck or other profits out of the land, and then the land comes into the king's hands by a false inquisition, the party shall not have traverse but rather shall be put to his petition of grace; yet if the title of the one who has the rent or

[55] Reference to Edw. III not found; YB Pas. 12 Hen. VI, Fitzherbert, Traverse 45.

such profits is proved in the inquisition, he shall have a writ to the escheator to pay him the rent or to suffer him to have the profits, and if the king makes a patent of the land the party shall distrain the patentee.

There are two joint tenants, one of them is attainted of treason, and it is found that he [holds] alone, the other shall sue by petition; but if the joint tenancy is found by inquisition, severance shall be made by the escheator, and yet for an entire thing of which they were joint tenants there is no remedy, because it is not severable.

It is found that the tenant of a stranger holds of the king and died seised, his heir of full age, the lord shall not have a traverse for this because he did not lose anything or any interest in the land. [**f.10**] Yet where it is found that the tenant of a stranger who only had a reversion holds of the king and died seised, the heir under age, the true lord shall have a traverse for the reversion and the body.

Three or four inquisitions are found for the king and the party traverses all except one, and it is found for him and adjudged, the king shall re-seize without *scire facias*, for the king's title is not fully answered, as appears by the traverse, but if he had traversed all the inquisitions as he should and had an erroneous judgment, the king would not re-seize but rather have a writ of error. The law is the same of an erroneous judgment given against the king in a petition, as appears 13 *Libr. Ass.*,[56] and it is not like a livery which it appears is not duly sued, for the king shall re-seize without *scire facias*: see 39 *Liber Ass.*, 18.[57]

A man tenders a traverse and does not maintain or pursue his traverse, this shall be peremptory and he shall never have another traverse, for the one who tenders a traverse is like a defendant against the king. It is otherwise where a man is non-suited in a petition. Two tender a traverse and one of them does not pursue it, the other shall pursue it alone and have *ouster le main* of the half by metes and bounds. Two lords tender a traverse for the wardship of the lands and body, and one of them does not pursue it, the other shall pursue and have the moiety of the lands, but for the body he is without remedy. Two tender a traverse and one of them does not pursue it, the other shall pursue alone and have *ouster le main*; but if it is for an advowson, and one of them does not maintain his traverse, the other has no remedy.

[56] Reference not found. [57] 39 Edw. III; 39 *Libri Assisarum*, pl.18.

Such an inquisition [is] found during the traverse as puts the party to his petition, the traverse shall abate. A traverse is tendered and the heir sues special or general livery pending the traverse, this shall abate the traverse. The law is the same where the party tenders a traverse and is at issue with the king, and while this is pending another stranger tenders another traverse and judgment is given for the first, the second traverse is abated by the judgment.

Appendix 2

JOHN SPELMAN'S READING ON *PREROGATIVA REGIS*, cc.1–3, GRAY'S INN, LENT 1521

[**f.303**] Spelman's lecture in Lent vacation 12 Henry VIII

Dominus rex habebit custodiam [The lord king shall have the wardship] etc. The beginning of this letter is a declaration of the common law and that this was the common law appears by Magna Carta cc.22 and 29[1] and common reason gives this to the king. And prerogative [. . .] other except lease given to his tenant [. . .] And by the exception *de feodis archiepiscopi* [the archbishop's fees] etc. all this branch is a statute, for before this time the king had the wardship of lands held of such persons as well as of others, except of the bishop of Durham, and in the counties of Chester [. . .] and in such places where the king's writ does not run. And this statute was made for this exception, for all of the rest is following the common law.

And by this word *custodiam* [custody] is implied the profits of the land etc., yet if the king grants the wardship of the body without speaking of marriage, the grantee cannot marry him.

Omnium terrarum [of all lands] is understood to be lands, tenements, rents, advowsons, commons, corrodies, and all profits appendant, offices, and all things of inheritance except annuities, for [he] will not have those.

Qui de ipso tenent in capite per servicium militare [who holds of him in chief by knight service]: in chief and of the crown are both one. Then it is to be seen who holds in chief. It seems that those who hold of any honour or lordship that is a part of the crown, as of Windsor, Dover etc., but those who hold of any honour or lordship which has escheated for felony or treason do not hold in chief; however query. The law is the same of those who hold of an

[1] *Recte* cc.2–7?, *Stat. Realm*, vol. 1, 114–15.

honour or lordship which escheats to the king for default of heirs, as Wallingford and Bolingbroke, or by purchase or descent.

If the king gives land reserving certain rent to a stranger, both shall be held in chief. It is otherwise if the king seizes lands for forfeiture in mortmain and gives them to hold of him, this is not in chief. And if land is forfeited for treason and by act of parliament, and there is a proviso in this, that is, when the king gives them that he [the tenant] shall hold them of the lords, and the king gives them to hold of him, still it is not in chief.

And if my tenant acknowledges in a court of record that he holds of the king in chief, yet this does not bind me. And if my tenant sues livery without inquisition I will not be bound by this. It is otherwise if there is an inquisition, for there I must traverse it.

If the king releases to the tenant paravail, the tenant now holds in chief. If one holds four acres for four pence and the king confirms his estate in two acres to hold for seven pence, then he holds the two acres in chief by knight service. If one who holds of the king in chief gives the land in tail etc. and the tenant in tail performs the services to the king, he holds in chief.

Per servicium militare [by military service] is by homage, fealty and escuage. If it was *salvo forinseco servicio* or *servicio domino regi per scutagium*, by castlegard, by cornage, or if the king gives the land *absque aliquo reddendo*, it is knight service; but if he gives the land to hold of him by fealty without service it is not knight service at all.

De quibus ipsi tenentes fuerunt seisiti in dominico suo ut de feodo [of which his tenants were seised in their demesne as of fee]: the letter is that he must be seised in fee, but the statute is not taken this way, for if there is a tenant in tail with the remainder in fee to another, it is all one. And the law is the same if the lands held of another are in use to the king's tenant, but if the lands held of another are enfeoffed by collusion the king shall not have them. Also if land is held of the duchy and also other land is held of the crown in socage, the king shall not have them. And if the land held of the king and also of others is in use, the king shall have everything. And the law is the same if the land held of the king is in reversion and the other in possession and vice versa. But if the lands held of others are in lease for term of years, the king shall not have them. And if the lands held of others are in use and the tenant by his will disposes of them for certain years the king shall not have them during the years, but if he disposes of only a part of the profits for term of years, the king shall have the rest. And if he disposes by his will of the profits of the land held of the king for term of years, and says nothing of the other lands, the king shall have the prerogative. If two joint tenants hold of the king, and one of them dies, the land shall pass to the survivor and the king shall have nothing.

Exceptis feodis [excepting the fees] shall be understood of the ancient lordships, for if they purchase lordships at this day the king shall have them; the law is the same if the archbishop aliens a lordship through the chapter seal and purchases it back; but it is otherwise if he recovers a manor by *cessavit* or by forfeiture in mortmain or it escheats through a mesne lordship.

And if a *villein regardant* to a manor which is parcel of the crown purchases a manor, and the king enters into it, then it shall be his in chief. And if the tenancy escheats to a mesnalty held in chief, the mesne shall hold as he held before, but if the mesnalty escheats to the king the tenant shall hold as the mesne held, however query. And if the mesne here is forjudged, the tenant shall hold in chief etc.

[**f.304**] *Rex habet maritagium heredum* [The king shall have the marriage of an heir] etc. Some say that by the common law before this statute the king had the marriage of the body where the ancestor held of him as of his crown, and thus with respect to the marriage *ab antiquo de corona* this article is only a confirmation of the common law, but before this statute if one held of the king as of an escheat which is in his hands and not part of his crown, there the priority held as between common persons and this seems well warranted by the statute of Magna Carta c.30,[2] which begins *si quis tenerit de nobis de honore* etc. Item, it seems that as for the body, if [the lands] are held in chief or by escheat of the king, he shall have the ward, even if the same tenant had lands within the bishopric of Durham or Canterbury etc. because the first article there [refers] only to the lands and not to the body. But query, if the king purchases a manor or honour or other lordship or has such a thing by descent, whether he shall have the body there without regard to priority, for the statute only speaks of where he holds by escheat etc., or if an alien purchases such a lordship and the king seizes this, for

[2] *Recte* c.31, *Stat. Realm*, vol. 1, 117.

such things are not escheats. And also some escheats are part of the crown. And various men have various opinions on this, so query.

Others hold that if [there is] the king, mesne lord and tenant, and the mesne holds of the king in chief and the mesnalty escheats to the king for default of heirs or for felony or because it is aliened in mortmain, or the king recovers by *cessavit*, or where the abbot aliens lands of the king's foundation, and the king enters: in all of these cases and others it seems that where the mesnalty comes instead of service which is parcel of the crown, it is part of the crown and all lands held of that mesnalty are held of the king as of his crown. Some say that by the escheat of the mesnalty the tenancy paravail shall not be held of the king as of his crown unless the services of the mesnalty were once part of the crown and began through the king, as well as the services of the paramount lord, as in the case where the king gives land, part of his crown, to hold of him as of his manor, now the services begin through the king and are part of the crown, and afterwards the king grants the same manor to be held of him, now this new lordship begins through the king also and now there is the king, mesne lord and tenant and if the mesnalty escheats the tenant holds of the king in chief, because he held of the king in chief at the beginning. But if the king's tenant before the statute gave the land to hold of him or at this day [gives it] in tail to hold of him, and the mesnalty escheats, they say that this lordship which began through another than the king shall not be part of his crown, so query, for it is not reason to cause the tenant to be in worse condition against the king than he was against the mesne where there was no fault in him. And others say that it is better for the tenant to suffer loss than the king and it is not reason that the king shall lose the advantage of his lordship where there is no fault in him, and therefore the law favours the king.

But if someone seised of a manor is attainted of treason, the king shall have the escheat even if he does not hold of the king immediately, and such an escheat does not go in lieu of service and therefore some say that these are escheats of which the king shall not have his prerogative, but as the tenant shall have who forfeits, according to the statute of Magna Carta as it seems;[3] but by this statute the king shall have the body of such an escheat. Query, however, for by such an escheat it is annexed to the crown, so if a tenant in tail or for term

[3] c.27, *Stat. Realm*, vol. 1, 117.

of life is attainted of felony, the king shall have their lands during their lives. And if a tenant who holds of them and of another man dies, the king shall have the wardship of the body by this statute, but if the king grants his lordship for a term or in fee, the grantee shall not have the prerogative for the prerogative cannot be granted.

Item, if the king has the wardship of the body in such a case by his prerogative by this statute and grants the ward to another and thus *de herede in heredem quousque* etc. [**f.304v**] *unus heredum veniat ad plenam etatem*, the grantee shall not have more heirs than the first, because the king is only entitled to them by his prerogative, which he cannot grant; however query. But if he makes such a deed of grant of his own lordship it is otherwise and if the king's tenant takes a husband and they have issue a daughter and the wife dies, the husband is tenant by the curtesy, and therefore the king shall not have the ward, for he is tenant to the king; but if the tenant by the curtesy takes my tenant to wife and has issue another daughter and the wife dies, and afterwards the husband dies, the king shall have the wardship of one daughter and I shall have the other, for they are heirs to separate fees. If, however, the king's tenant takes a husband and they have issue a daughter, and the husband dies, and she takes my tenant as husband and they have issue another daughter, whether the wife dies before the husband or vice versa, still the king shall have the wardship of both of the daughters, for both are heirs to his tenant who was their mother and one of them is the heir of my tenant who was her father etc.

If a woman under age is in ward and granted *durante minore etate*, if she is married still the grantee shall have her until 16 years, and then she shall sue livery. If the king grants a [male] ward *durante minore etate sue* this is until 21 years and after this the grantee shall not have the ward, even if [he] does not sue livery for 10 years; but it is otherwise if he is granted *quam diu in manibus nostris fore contigerit*. Query, however, whether after he is of the age of 21 years the king can grant the ward afterwards *quam diu in manibus nostris fore contigerit*?

[**f.306**] *Item habebit primam seisinam* [Also he shall have primer seisin] etc. Before this statute the king had primer seisin, as appears by the statute of Marlborough c.16, which begins *de hereditatibus que de domino rege tenentur in capite sic observandum est* etc. but there he has such a clause. *Et hoc intelligatur de terris et feodis que racione* *servicii militaris vel seriantie seu jure patronatus in manu regis esse consueverunt*. And thus as it appears by this statute the king shall not have primer seisin even though his tenant holds of him in chief by socage. And also by this statute he shall not have primer seisin of any lands but of those which are held of him. But this article enlarges the king's prerogative in these two points beyond the statute of Marlborough: that is, one is that the king shall have primer seisin if the tenant holds of him in chief by socage as well as by knight service, for the statute is general *qui de eo tenent in capite* [who hold of him in chief] and does not say by knight service; the other enlargement is that the king shall have primer seisin of all the land of the tenant who holds of him or another by socage or by knight service, if he holds any part in chief of the king, for the statute is general *de omnibus terris & tenementis de quibus* (*ut supra*) [of all lands and tenements of which]. So now he shall have primer seisin of all the lands held of himself by knight service or in socage and of the land held of others by any kind of service, if he holds any part of the king in chief etc.

De quibus seisiti fuerint in feodo [of which they were seised in fee] etc. Nevertheless in this case he shall not have primer seisin where his tenant was seised in fee; as, if his tenant made a feoffment in fee of lands held of the king in chief, by licence or without licence, the king shall not have primer seisin of any of the lands, for he was not his tenant by right. But if he was disseised of lands held of the king in chief, the king shall have primer seisin of all, because he was his tenant by right. But if perhaps he was disseised of lands held of another, the king shall not have primer seisin of them, but only of the lands held of himself. Query all the cases of disseisin etc.

The statute is *seisiti fuerint in feodo* [they were seised in fee] which shall be understood if he was seised the day of his death or was a tenant in right on the day of his death. Also the king shall have primer seisin in cases where he was not seised in fee on the day of his death, as where the king's tenant makes a lease for years or for life etc. and dies seised of the reversion and of lands held of others; the king shall have the primer seisin of the reversion and also of all the other lands, and thereupon the heir shall sue livery while the tenant for term of life is living, if he wishes.

And also it is said that if the king's tenant-in-chief makes a lease for term of life to my tenant, with the reversion over in fee, in this case if my tenant dies the king shall have the primer seisin of the land whereof he was tenant for term of life, because he was his tenant thereof. And therefore he shall also have the lands held of me. Query, however, for it seems hard, and therefore it seems that the remainderman shall have livery of this and my tenant [shall have] livery of the land held of me, and because the king's tenant shall not have livery of everything at the one time, it seems that he shall only have primer seisin of that whereof his own tenant may sue livery.

If the king's tenant is seised of a manor held of the king in chief and of another manor in borough English and has issue two sons and dies, it seems that the king shall not have primer seisin of all, but of that whereof his tenant is heir and not of that whereof the younger son is heir, unless the younger son is heir to the manor which is held of the king, as well as the elder. The law is the same if lands descend to my nephew from his father, held of the king in chief, and lands held of others descend to him from his mother, and he dies without issue; the king shall have primer seisin only of the land held of him in chief, and the other lands which descend to the heir from his mother shall not be in ward because he is not the king's tenant [for them]. The law is the same if the nephew is made heir to one part [and] this part escheats, and the king shall not have primer seisin because he is not his tenant, but in this case if he dies without an heir of the one part and of the other, the king shall not have primer seisin of anything, but he shall have the land held of him by escheat and the other escheats [shall go] to their lord.

Again, it was said that if a man recovers by a writ of entry sur disseisin in the post [**f.306v**] or by entry *dum fuit infra etatem* or *non compos mentis* or in such an action where by the death of the ancestor on whose seisin the action is brought, the king's avowry is changed, there the king shall not have primer seisin for he was not able to have this at the time of the ancestor's death; but if he recovers by an action where by the death of the ancestor the king shall have primer seisin, he [the king] shall have it [the land] afterwards, for *nullum tempus* [*occurrit regi*] etc., as in mort d'ancestor, aiel and cosinage etc., but this is if he recovers land held of the king, whereas if he recovers land held of others, query. And yet if he who recovers is under age he shall be in ward, and also if he is of full age he shall pay relief and also homage; but query how, for he shall not have the primer seisin etc.

The heir must sue a writ and have an inquisition in every county where he has lands or else everything shall be re-seised. The law is the same of an advowson on which livery was not sued 44 [Edw. III] f.17,[4] and feoffees [. . .] this petition.

If a man has feoffees to his use and dies, his heir under age and in the king's ward by reason of the use, it is usual that the feoffees shall have special livery, but the law is that they shall have *ouster le main*. And if a man who has feoffees to his use dies, his heir under age, who takes the profits during his nonage and when he comes to full age it is found by an inquisition that he was under age at the death of his father and that now he is of full age, query whether now he shall sue livery or not, for *Broke* recorder [of London] thought he shall, namely the feoffees, because at one time he was under age, and yet he had a pardon for all intrusions etc.

And if a woman who is a tenant in dower of lands held of the king dies and the heir enters before livery of them they shall be re-seised etc. C_ says that he knows by experience that a ward by reason of ward shall sue livery of all the lands which he holds of the ward who is in the king's ward *quod quere*. Query whether [if it is] socage in chief [he] shall not sue livery, and also of each knight service held of the king by reason of escheat or in another manner etc. query. It seems that it is a distinction whether a ward by reason of ward comes to these lands at the age of 21 or not: query if the king shall have prerogative of them, that is, this ward.

[**f.307v**] *Sine exitibus* [without the profits] And if the one acre is held of the king and the other is gavelkind, the elder shall sue livery of the acre held of the king and of half of the other and the younger shall sue *ouster le main*, for he shall not have livery unless he is the king's true tenant. And if the king's tenant has other lands held of others which are entailed to him and to his heirs female and he dies seised, the son shall have livery and the daughter shall have *ouster le main* and in this case the king shall not have the wardship of the daughter.

And if the mesne who holds of the king dies with his heir of full age and an inquisition is found etc. whereby the king has the mesnalty for primer seisin and then the tenancy escheats, the heir shall not have livery of the land because the inquisition did not find this. And if the king's tenant has lands in fee simple and in fee tail

[4] YB Pas. 44 Edw. III, f.12, pl.17.

held of the king and has issue a son and a daughter by one womb and a son by another womb and dies seised, and an inquisition is found *virtute brevis*, and then the elder dies without issue, and this matter is found by *devenerunt*, the sister shall sue livery of the fee simple and the son of the tail.

And he who wishes to have good livery must have an inquisition *virtute brevis* in each county where his ancestor had land, and every part to which he is inheritable must be found in them, and then sue livery in all the counties or the king shall re-seize, for if he omits even an advowson in gross it is a cause for re-seizure, and therefore it must be entire.

And if a title to dower is found in the inquisition and he sues livery of all and enters without *retenta dote* etc. or *salva dote*, the king shall re-seize, but it is otherwise if no mention is made of the woman in the inquisition. And if the heir at common law sues livery of the land at common law and also in borough English and then it is found by inquisition that he had a younger brother, still the livery shall remain good for the land at common law.

If the heir sues livery on a good inquisition and then another inquisition is found, the king shall not re-seize without a *scire facias*, but it is otherwise if the inquisition is insufficient. And if a stranger traverses the inquisition the heir shall not have livery pending this traverse. And if the king grants a lordship for term of years and a wardship falls in and then the years expire, still he [the ward] shall not sue livery. The law is the same if the termor grants the wardship to the king. And the law is the same if someone who has a ward is outlawed in a personal action etc.

[**f.318**] Prerogativa Regis lecture 5

Now it must be seen if the king is entitled by a false inquisition, how the party shall have a remedy. And it seems that in some cases he shall be helped by a traverse, in other cases by *ouster le main*, by petition, or by *monstrans de droit*. And if the king is entitled by an inquisition to a lordship in fee simple, there a petition lies, and not a traverse.

And there was no traverse before the statute of 36 Edw. III, c.13,[5] which provides that the escheator, after such a false inquisition

[5] *Stat. Realm*, vol. 1, 374–75.

found, should send this into the chancery within the month and if he will not do so, then a writ shall issue to him to certify it and immediately afterwards the aggrieved party shall put in his traverse or *monstrans de droit*, and that the chancellor may lease it to farm at his discretion. And if there were 20 false inquisitions the party must traverse them all. And it begins *Compertum est* etc. And the king's attorney can maintain the inquisition or traverse the party's title or join issue or demur etc. And also he can waive each of them in this term but not in another term.

And if an inquisition is returned in the chancery *virtute brevis* and another false inquisition is returned in the exchequer *virtute officii*, he can have *certiorari* out of the chancery to the exchequer to certify the inquisition there and then he shall traverse both.

And if one is found heir who is not heir in fact, the one who is the true heir shall not traverse the inquisition without an inquisition found for him, but the lord shall traverse the inquisition for the tenure without any inquisition found for him. And also the heir of full age shall traverse the tenure without an inquisition. And the law is the same if the inquisition finds that the king's tenant died seised of my land. And if the king's tenant aliens to me by licence and it is found by inquisition that he died seised, I shall show the feoffment with licence and traverse it without another inquisition. And in these cases they shall have *amoveas manum*, but in this case it shall be *sine exitibus*.

And those who have a rent charge or rent seck or other profits shall not traverse a false inquisition, but are put to a petition.

And if it is found by a false inquisition that my tenant held of the king and died seised and that the heir is of full age, the lord does not need to traverse this, but it is otherwise if the heir is under age. And on an erroneous judgment in a traverse or petition, the king shall not re-seize. And if an inquisition finds me under age when I am of full age, I shall not traverse this, even if I am found of full age by another inquisition. And if the true heir is found of full age, and by another inquisition in another county it is found that another is heir and under age, the true heir has no remedy.

If the king grants the land by patent to another before the traverse and then the traverse is tendered, the *scire facias* shall issue to the patentee, and if he is warned and does not come, his patent is void. And the issue joined in the chancery on an inquisition shall be tried in the King's Bench. It is otherwise if the issue is joined in the Exchequer.

And a person who sues a petition must make a bill to the king comprising the king's title as well as his title and then the king shall endorse it *Soit droit fait*, and then shall issue [a writ] to enquire as to the title etc. And when this is returned, still the king's attorney can traverse the points which were found. And then four writs of search shall be granted and if the title is found for the plaintiff then he shall have judgment *salvo iure*. And if he recovers a manor by petition and then the same title is found for 20 acres which are part of the manor, whereby they are seised, the party shall show the matter and aver that they are part of the manor, and if they are at issue on [whether] they are part or not part, the attorney shall have a writ of search. And in a petition he shall have judgment *una cum exitibus*, for it is like a writ of right.

And if it is found that such a one was attainted of felony and was seised of my lands at the time I must have a petition, for I cannot traverse the record. If a disseisor enfeoffs the king by an enrolled deed, the disseisee shall have a petition. And if the king's ancestor disseised me and dies seised, and it descends to the king, I must have a petition; and the law is the same if the disseisor dies without an heir and the king enters by escheat. And the law is the same if the prince purchases land to which I have a right and then is made king. And the law is the same if the disseisor enfeoffs the king's villein and this is found by an inquisition, but [it is otherwise] if the disseisee had entered before the inquisition and disseisin is found in the inquisition for then *monstrans de droit* lies. And the law is the same if the disseisor enfeoffs an alien, for the king is entitled to the freehold by a defeasible title. And if one disseises me of land held [**f.318v**] of the king and dies seised, his heir under age, and the dying seised is found by inquisition, there is no remedy until livery is sued, for no petition lies, for writ of right does not lie against the guardian; but if the tenure is found to be by knight service or is in socage, the heir shall have a traverse, for he would be disadvantaged in various ways. And the law is the same if he was seised of an estate tail and it is found that it was in fee simple.

Monstrans de droit lies if lands of my ancestor, who devised them to me, were held of the king and afterwards <I> [he] die[s] without an heir, whereby an inquisition is found that he died without heir and held of the king, I shall show this matter and confess the inquisition and have the lands out of the king's hands. And if it is found that he died without an heir where there is an heir, the heir shall show this etc. And if I recover against the king's tenant and before execution he dies and an inquisition finds his dying seised, I shall show this matter and have it out of the king's hands etc. And if the king's tenant disseises me and dies seised, and the disseisin is found, I shall have *ouster le main*.

BIBLIOGRAPHY

Primary sources

Manuscript readings

Anonymous
Bodleian MS Rawlinson C. 294, ff.205v–206v
Cambridge University Library MS Ee.5.22, ff.338–363v

Edward Grantham (tentative identification)
Cambridge University Library MS Hh.3.6, ff.55v–70

Thomas Frowyk (1495Q)
Cambridge University Library MS Hh.2.1, ff.1–26
Cambridge University Library MS Hh.3.6, ff.71–73
Harvard Law School MS 14, ff.9–44
Harvard Law School MS 1037 No. 6
Harvard Law School MS 203

John Port (1507A)
BL MS Hargrave 87, ff.142–76

John Spelman (1521Q)
Gray's Inn MS 25, ff.302–318v (Chaloner MS)
Bodleian MS Rawlinson B.432, ff.52–53v (tentative identification)

Thomas Audley (1526A)
BL MS Hargrave 87, ff.427–57 (on 4 Henry VII, c.17)

Roger Yorke (1531Q)
BL MS Hargrave 253, f.77v
BL MS Add. 38133, f.11v, f.13
BL MS Hargrave 388, ff.211–72 (casebook)

George Willoughby (1549Q)
BL MS Harley 1691, ff.197–201

James Morice (1578A)
BL MS Egerton 3376, ff.2–66v (on W. II, c.50)

Administrative and legal records

Public Record Office
King's Bench Rolls: KB 27
Common Law Pleadings in Chancery: C 43
Lord Treasurer's Remembrancer's Memoranda Rolls: E 368
Exchequer Accounts, Various: E 101
Treasury of the Receipt: E 36
Escheators Accounts: E 136

British Library
MS Add. 7099
MS Add. 7100
MS Add. 21480
MS Add. 21481
MS Cotton Cleo E iv
MS Cotton Cleo E vi
MS Harley 980
MS Harley 2051
MS Lansdowne 127

Printed

Baker, J. H., *Readings and Moots at the Inns of Court in the Fifteenth Century*, vol. 2. Selden Society vol. 105. London: Selden Society, 1989
ed. *Sources of English Legal History: Private Law to 1750*. London: Butterworths, 1986
Bayne, C. G., ed. *Select Cases in the Council of Henry VII*. Selden Society vol. 75. London: Bernard Quaritch, 1958
Benloe, William. *Les Reports de Gulielme Benloe, Serjeant de Ley, Des divers Pleadings et Cases en le Court del Comon-Bank, en le several Roignes de les tres Hault & Excellent Princes, le Roy Henry VII., Henry VIII., Edw. VI., & les Roignes Mary & Elizabeth*. 1689. In *English Reports*, vol. 123. London: Stevens & Sons, 1912
Bland D. S., ed. *Early Records of Furnivall's Inn*. Newcastle upon Tyne: Dept. of Extra-Mural Studies, King's College, 1957
Bracton. *On the Laws and Customs of England*. Translated by Samuel E. Thorne. 4 vols. Cambridge MA: Belknap Press of Harvard University Press, 1968–77

Britton. Edited by F. M. Nichols. Oxford: Clarendon Press, 1865

Brooke, Robert. *Some New Cases of the Years and Time of King Hen. VIII., Edw. VI., and Qu. Mary, written out of the Great Abridgement composed by Sir Robert Brook, Knight, &c. 1651*. In *English Reports*, vol. 73. London: Stevens & Sons, 1907

Calendar of Feudal Aids 1284–1431. Edited by H. C. Maxwell-Lyte. 6 vols. London: HMSO, 1899–1920

Calendar of Inquisitions Post Mortem and Other Analogous Documents Preserved in the Public Record Office: Henry VII. 3 vols. London: HMSO, 1898–1955

Calendar of the Patent Rolls Preserved in the Public Record Office: Henry VII. 2 vols. London: HMSO, 1916; Nendeln, Liechtenstein: Kraus Reprint, 1970

Campbell, William, ed. *Materials for a History of the Reign of Henry VII*. 2 vols. *Rerum Britannicarum Medii Aevi Scriptores* vol. 60. London: HMSO, 1873–77; Nendeln, Liechtenstein: Kraus Reprint, 1965

Caryll, John. *Reports of Cases by John Caryll*. Edited by J. H. Baker. 2 vols. Selden Society vols. 115 and 116. London: Selden Society, 1998 and 1999

Chancery Common Law Proceedings (C43, C44). List & Index Society vol. 67. London: private distribution, 1971

Constable, Robert. *Prerogativa Regis: Tertia Lectura Roberti Constable de Lincolnis Inne Anno 11 H. 7*. Edited by S. E. Thorne. New Haven: Yale University Press, 1949

Cranmer, Thomas. *Miscellaneous Writings and Letters of Thomas Cranmer*. Edited by John Edmund Cox. Cambridge: Cambridge University Press, 1846

Dalison, William. *Les Reports des divers Special Cases Adjudge en le Court del Comon Bank en les Reignes de les tres hault & Excellent Princes Hen. VIII, Edw. VI et les Reignes Mar. & Eliz*. 1689. In *English Reports*, vol. 123. London: Stevens & Sons, 1912

Dudley, Edmund. *The Tree of Commonwealth*. Edited by D. M. Brodie. Cambridge: Cambridge University Press, 1948

Dugdale, William. *Origines Juridiciales: Or Historical Memorials* . . . 2 vols. 3rd edn, London, 1680

Dyer, Sir James. *Abridgement des reports seignior Dyer*. London, 1590

Reports of Cases in the Reigns of Hen. VIII., Edw. VI., Q. Mary, and Q. Eliz., taken and collected by Sir James Dyer, Knt. some time Chief Justice of the Common Pleas. 1794. In *English Reports*, vol. 73. London: Stevens & Sons, 1907

Reports from the Lost Notebooks of Sir James Dyer. Edited by J. H. Baker. 2 vols. Selden Society vols. 109 and 110. London: Selden Society, 1993 and 1994

Elyot, Sir Thomas. *The Book named The Governor*. Edited by S. E. Lehmberg. New York: E. P. Dutton, 1962

Fitzherbert, Sir Anthony. *La Graunde Abbregement de le Ley*. London, 1577

The New Natura Brevium of the Most Reverend Judge Mr Anthony Fitz-herbert. To which is added a commentary supposed to be written by the late Lord Chief Justice Hale. 2 vols. 9th edn, London, 1794

Fortescue, Sir John. *De Natura Legis Naturae.* In *The Works of Sir John Fortescue, Knight, Chief Justice of England and Lord Chancellor to King Henry the sixth, Now first collected and arranged by Thomas (Fortescue) Lord Clermont.* London, 1869

The Governance of England. Edited by Charles Plummer. Oxford, 1885

De Laudibus Legum Anglie. Edited by S. B. Chrimes. Cambridge: Cambridge University Press, 1942

Gairdner, James, ed. *Letters and Papers Illustrative of the Reigns of Richard III and Henry VII.* 2 vols. *Rerum Britannicarum Medii Aevi Scriptores* vol. 24. London: HMSO, 1861–63; Nendeln, Liechtenstein: Kraus Reprint, 1965

Gardiner, Stephen. *The Letters of Stephen Gardiner.* Edited by James Arthur Muller. Cambridge: Cambridge University Press, 1933

Hall, Edward. *Hall's Chronicle.* Edited by Henry Ellis. London, 1809

Hatton, Sir Christopher. *A Treatise concerning Statutes or Acts of Parliament and the exposition thereof.* London, 1677

Hector, L. C. and Barbara F. Harvey, ed. *The Westminster Chronicle 1381–1394.* Oxford: Clarendon Press, 1982

Hemmant, M., ed. *Select Cases in the Exchequer Chamber before All the Justices of England*, 1377–1509. 2 vols. Selden Society vols. 51 and 64. London: Bernard Quaritch, 1933 and 1948

Henry VIII. *Answere to the Rebelles in Yorkshire.* London, 1536; Amsterdam: Theatrum Orbis Terrarum, 1977

Institutions or Principall Grounds of the Laws and Statutes of England. London: William Myddylton, 1543

Keilway, Robert. *Relationes quorundam Casuum selectorum ex Libris Roberti Keilway Armiger.* London, 1602

Kingsford, C. L., ed. *Chronicles of London.* Oxford: Clarendon Press, 1905

Legg, Leopold G. W., ed. *English Coronation Records.* Westminster: A. Constable, 1901

Letters and Papers, Foreign and Domestic, of the Reign of Henry VIII, 1509–1547. Edited by J. S. Brewer *et al.* 21 vols. London: Longmans, HMSO, 1862–1932

Ley, Sir James. *A Learned Treatise Concerning Wards and Liveries.* London: 1642

Littleton, Sir Thomas. *Littleton's Tenures in English.* Edited by Eugene Wambaugh. Washington: John Byrne & Co., 1903

Magna Carta in F. wherunto is added more statutes than euer was imprynted in any one boke before this tyme with an Almanacke & a Calendar to know the mootes. Necessarye for all yong studiers of the law. London: Robert Redman, 1529

More, Sir Thomas. *The Apologye of Sir Thomas More, Knyght.* Edited by Arthur Irving Taft. EETS original ser. vol. 180. London: Oxford University Press, 1930

The History of King Richard III. Edited by Richard S. Sylvester. Yale Edition of the Complete Works of St. Thomas More vol. 2. New Haven: Yale University Press, 1963

Utopia. Translated by Paul Turner. Harmondsworth: Penguin, 1965

Morison, Sir Richard. *A Lamentation in which is shown what pain and destruction cometh of seditious rebellion*. In *Humanist Scholarship and Public Order: Two Tracts against the Pilgrimage of Grace*, ed. David Sandler Berkowitz. Washington: The Folger Shakespeare Library, 1984

A Remedy for Sedition wherein are contained many things concerning the true and loyal obeisance that commons owe unto their prince and sovereign lord the king. In *Humanist Scholarship and Public Order: Two Tracts against the Pilgrimage of Grace*, ed. David Sandler Berkowitz. Washington: The Folger Shakespeare Library, 1984

Pauli, Reinhold, ed. *Drei Volkswirthschaftliche Denkschriften aus der Zeit Heinrichs VIII von England*. Göttingen: Dieterich'sche Verlags-Buchhandlung, 1878

Perkins, John. *A Profitable Book of Maister Iohn Perkins, felowe of the Inner Temple, treating of the Lawes of Englande*. London, 1565

Port, Sir John. *The Notebook of Sir John Port*. Edited by J. H. Baker. Selden Society vol. 102. London: Selden Society, 1986

Putnam, B. *Early Treatises on the Practice of the Justice of the Peace in the Fifteenth and Sixteenth Centuries*. Oxford Studies in Social and Legal History vol. 7, ed. Sir Paul Vinogradoff. Oxford: Clarendon Press, 1924; New York: Octagon Reprint, 1974

Rotuli Parliamentorum: ut et Petitiones, et Placita in Parliamento. 8 vols. London, 1780–1832

Smith, Sir Thomas. *A Discourse of the Commonweal of This Realm of England*. Edited by Mary Dewar. Charlottesville: University Press of Virginia, 1969

Sneyd, Charlotte Augusta, ed. and trans. *A Relation, or rather a True Account, of the Island of England, with Sundry Particulars of the Customs of these People, and of the Royal Revenues under King Henry the Seventh, about the Year 1500*. Camden Society vol. 37. London: John Bowyer Nichols & Son, 1847

Spelman, Sir John. *The Reports of Sir John Spelman*. Edited by J. H. Baker. 2 vols. Selden Society vols. 93 and 94. London: Selden Society, 1976 and 1977

John Spelman's Reading on Quo Warranto. Edited by J. H. Baker. Selden Society vol. 113. London: Selden Society, 1997

Starkey, Thomas. *A Dialogue Between Pole and Lupset*. Edited by Thomas F. Mayer. Camden Society 4th ser. vol. 37. London: Royal Historical Society, 1989

Statutes of the Realm. 11 vols. London, 1810–22

Staunford, Sir William. *An Exposicion of the Kings Prerogatiue, collected out of the great Abridgement of Iustice Fitzherbert, and other olde Writers of the Lawes of Englande, by the right Worshipfull Sir William Staunford Knight, lately one of the Iustices of the Queenes Maiesties Court of Comon Pleas*. London, 1567

St. German, Christopher. *Doctor and Student*. Edited by T. F. T. Plucknett and J. L. Barton. Selden Society vol. 91. London: Selden Society, 1974

A Little Treatise concerning Writs of Subpoena. In *Christopher St. German on Chancery and Statute*. Edited by J. A. Guy. Selden Society supplementary series vol. 6. London: Selden Society, 1985

St. German, Christopher [?]. *The Replication of a Serjeant at the Laws of England*. In *Christopher St. German on Chancery and Statute*. Edited by J. A. Guy. Selden Society supplementary series vol. 6. London: Selden Society, 1985

Thomas, A. H. and I. D. Thornley, ed. *The Great Chronicle of London*. London: George W. Jones, 1938; Gloucester: Alan Sutton, 1983

Thorne, S. E., ed. *A Discourse upon the Exposicion and Understandinge of Statutes*. San Marino: Huntingdon Library, 1942

Readings and Moots at the Inns of Court in the Fifteenth Century, vol. 1. Selden Society vol. 71. London: Selden Society, 1954

Vergil, Polydore. *The Anglica Historia of Polydore Vergil, AD 1485–1537*. Edited and translated by Denys Hay. Camden Society vol. 74. London: Royal Historical Society, 1950

Waterhouse, Edward. *Fortescutus Illustratus*. London, 1663

Wriothesley, Charles. *A Chronicle of England during the Reigns of the Tudors, from AD 1485 to 1559*. Edited by William Douglas Hamilton. Camden Society new ser. vols. 11 and 20. London: J. B. Nichols and Sons, 1875 and 1877

Year Books. *Les Reports des Cases en les Ans des Roys Edward V. Richard III. Henrie VII. & Henrie VIII. Touts qui par cy devant ont este Publies*. London, 1679

Secondary sources

Abbott, L. W. *Law Reporting in England 1485–1585*. London: Athlone Press, 1973

"Public Office and Private Profit: The Legal Establishment in the Reign of Mary Tudor." In *The Mid-Tudor Polity c.1540–1560*, ed. Jennifer Loach and Robert Tittler, 137–58. London: Macmillan, 1980

Adams, Simon. "Baronial Contexts? Continuity and Change in the Noble Affinity, 1400–1600." In *The End of the Middle Ages? England in the Fifteenth and Sixteenth Centuries*, ed. J. L. Watts, 155–97. The Fifteenth Century Series No. 6. Gloucester: Sutton, 1998

Alford, Stephen. "Politics and Political History in the Tudor Century." *Historical Journal* 42 (1999): 535–48

Alsop, J. D. "The Revenue Commission of 1552." *Historical Journal* 22 (1979): 511–33

"The Structure of Early Tudor Finance, c.1509–1558." In *Revolution Reassessed: Revisions in the History of Tudor Government and Administration*, ed. Christopher Coleman and David Starkey, 135–62. Oxford: Clarendon Press, 1986

Anglo, Sydney. *Images of Tudor Kingship*. London: Seaby, 1992

Baack, Ben. "The Development of Exclusive Property Rights to Land in England: An Exploratory Essay." *Economy and History* 22 (1979): 63–74

Bacon, Francis. *The History of the Reign of King Henry the Seventh*. Edited by Jerry Weinberger. Ithaca: Cornell University Press, 1996

Baker, J. H. "Counsellors and Barristers." *Cambridge Law Journal* 27 (1969): 205–29

"The Attorneys and Officers of the Common Law in 1480." *Journal of Legal History* 1 (1980): 182–203

"The English Legal Profession, 1450–1550." In *Lawyers in Early Modern Europe and America*, ed. W. Prest, 16–41. London: Croom Helm, 1981

The Order of Serjeants at Law: A Chronicle of Creations, with Related Texts and a Historical Introduction. Selden Society supplementary series vol. 5. London: Selden Society, 1984

"English Law and the Renaissance." *Cambridge Law Journal* 44 (1985): 46–61

"Dr. Thomas Fastolf and the History of Law Reporting." *Cambridge Law Journal* 45 (1986): 84–96

"Learning Exercises in the Medieval Inns of Court and Chancery." In *The Legal Profession and the Common Law*, 7–23. London: Hambledon Press, 1986

"Readings in Gray's Inn, Their Decline and Disappearance." In *The Legal Profession and the Common Law*, 31–38. London: Hambledon Press, 1986

"The Inns of Court and Legal Doctrine." In *Lawyers and Laymen*, ed. T. M. Charles-Edwards *et al.*, 274–86. Cardiff: University of Wales Press, 1986

"The Inns of Court in 1388." In *The Legal Profession and the Common Law*, 3–6. London: Hambledon Press, 1986

The Third University of England: The Inns of Court and the Common-law Tradition. Selden Society Lecture for 1990. London: Selden Society, 1990

"Personal Liberty under the Common Law of England, 1200–1600." In *The Origins of Modern Freedom in the West*, ed. R. W. Davis, 178–202. Stanford: Stanford University Press, 1995

Why the History of English Law Has Not Been Finished. Downing Professorship, Inaugural Lecture. Cambridge: Cambridge University Press, 1998

Readers and Readings in the Inns of Court and Chancery. Selden Society supplementary series vol. 13. London: Selden Society, 2001

The Law's Two Bodies: Some Evidential Problems in English Legal History. Clarendon Law Lectures. Oxford: Oxford University Press, 2001

Baker-Smith, Dominic. "Inglorious Glory: 1513 and the Humanist Attack on Chivalry." In *Chivalry in the Renaissance*, ed. Sydney Anglo, 129–44. Suffolk: Boydell, 1990

Barraclough, Geoffrey. "Law and Legislation in Medieval England." *Law Quarterly Review* 56 (1940): 75–92

Bartlett, Robert. "Lordship and Law in Medieval England." *Journal of British Studies* 30 (1991): 449–54

Barton, J. L. "The Medieval Use." *Law Quarterly Review* 81 (1965): 562–77

Batho, Gordon. "Landlords in England: The Crown." In *The Agrarian History of England and Wales*, vol. 4, 1500–1640, ed. Joan Thirsk, 256–76. Cambridge: Cambridge University Press, 1967

Baumer, Franklin Le Van. "Christopher St. German: The Political Philosophy of a Tudor Lawyer." *American Historical Review* 42 (1937): 631–51

The Early Tudor Theory of Kingship. New York: Russell & Russell, 1966

Bean, J. M. W. *The Decline of English Feudalism 1215–1540*. New York: Manchester University Press, 1968

Beer, Barrett L. *Rebellion and Riot: Popular Disorder in England During the Reign of Edward VI*. Kent OH: Kent State University Press, 1982

Behrens, Greg. "An Early Tudor Debate on the Relation Between Law and Equity." *Journal of Legal History* 19 (1998): 143–61

Bell, H. E. *An Introduction to the History and Records of the Court of Wards and Liveries*. Cambridge: Cambridge University Press, 1953

Bellamy, J. G. *Bastard Feudalism and the Law*. Portland: Areopagitica Press, 1989

Bellot, Hugh H. L. "The Exclusion of Attorneys from the Inns of Court." *Law Quarterly Review* 26 (1910): 137–45

Berman, Harold J. *Law and Revolution: The Formation of the Western Legal Tradition*. Cambridge MA: Harvard University Press, 1983

Bernard, G. W. *The Power of the Early Tudor Nobility: A Study of the Fourth and Fifth Earls of Shrewsbury*. Totowa NJ: Barnes & Noble, 1985

Bettey, J. H. *The Suppression of the Monasteries in the West Country*. Gloucester: Alan Sutton, 1989

Bevan, Amanda S. "The Role of the Judiciary in Tudor Government 1509–1547." PhD diss., Cambridge, 1986

Bindoff, S. T. *Kett's Rebellion, 1549*. London: Historical Association, 1949

Birks, Michael. *Gentlemen of the Law*. London: Stevens and Sons, 1960

Bisson, Thomas N. "The 'Feudal Revolution'." *Past and Present* 142 (1994): 6–42

Bland, D. S. "Rhetoric and the Law Student in Sixteenth-Century England." *Studies in Philology* 54 (1957): 498–508

"Henry VIII's Royal Commission on the Inns of Court." *Journal of the Society of the Public Teachers of Law* 10 (1969): 178–94

"Learning Exercises and Readers at the Inns of Chancery in the Fifteenth and Sixteenth Centuries." *Law Quarterly Review* 95 (1979): 244–52

Blatcher, Marjorie. *The Court of King's Bench 1450–1550: A Study in Self-Help*. London: Athlone Press, 1978

Bolland, W. C. "Two Problems of Legal History." *Law Quarterly Review* 24 (1908): 392–402

A Manual of Year Book Studies. Cambridge: Cambridge University Press, 1925

Brand, Paul. "Courtroom and Schoolroom: The Education of Lawyers in England Prior to 1400." *Historical Research* 60 (1987): 147–65

The Origins of the English Legal Profession. Cambridge MA: Blackwell, 1992

"Hengham Magna: A Twelfth-Century English Common-law Treatise and its Composition." In *The Making of the Common Law.* London: Hambledon Press, 1992, 369–91

Brenner, Robert. "Agrarian Class Structure and Economic Development in Pre-Industrial Europe." In *The Brenner Debate: Agrarian Class Structure and Economic Development in Pre-Industrial Europe*, ed. T. H. Aston and C. H. E. Philpin, 10–63. Past and Present Publications. Cambridge: Cambridge University Press, 1987

Brodie, D. M. "Edmund Dudley: Minister of Henry VII." *Transactions of the Royal Historical Society*, 4th ser. 15 (1932): 133–61

Brown, E. A. R. "The Tyranny of a Construct: Feudalism and Historians of Medieval Europe." *American Historical Review* 79 (1974): 1063–88

Brown, R. Allen. *Origins of English Feudalism.* New York: Barnes & Noble, 1973

Buck, A. R. "The Politics of Land Law in Tudor England, 1529–40." *Journal of Legal History* 11 (1990): 200–17

Burgess, Glenn. *The Politics of the Ancient Constitution: An Introduction to English Political Thought, 1603–1642.* London: Macmillan, 1992

Absolute Monarchy and the Stuart Constitution. New Haven: Yale University Press, 1996

Burns, J. H. *Lordship, Kingship, and Empire: The Idea of Monarchy, 1400–1525.* The Carlyle Lectures for 1988. Oxford: Clarendon Press, 1992

Bush, M. L. *The Government Policy of Protector Somerset.* London: Edward Arnold, 1975

"'Up for the Commonweal': The Significance of the Tax Grievances in the English Rebellions of 1536." *English Historical Review* 106 (1991): 299–318

"Tenant Right under the Tudors: A Revision Revised." *Bulletin of the John Rylands University Library of Manchester* 77 (1995): 161–88

The Pilgrimage of Grace: A Study of the Rebel Armies of October 1536. Manchester: Manchester University Press, 1996

Cam, Helen. "The Decline and Fall of English Feudalism." In *Liberties and Communities in Medieval England: Collected Studies in Local Administration and Topography*, 205–22. Cambridge: Cambridge University Press, 1944

"The Legislators of Medieval England." *Proceedings of the British Academy* 31 (1945): 127–50

Magna Carta – Event or Document? Selden Society Lecture for 1965. London: Bernard Quaritch, 1965

Cameron, A. "A Nottinghamshire Quarrel in the Reign of Henry VII." *Bulletin of the Institute of Historical Research* 45 (1972): 27–37

Carpenter, Christine. "Law, Justice and Landowners in Late Medieval England." *Law and History Review* 1 (1983): 203–37

Locality and Polity: A Study of Warwickshire Landed Society, 1401–1499. Cambridge: Cambridge University Press, 1992

"Henry VII and the English Polity." In *The Reign of Henry VII: Proceedings of the 1993 Harlaxton Symposium*, ed. Benjamin Thompson, 11–30. Harlaxton Medieval Studies V. Stamford: Paul Watkins, 1995

"Political and Constitutional History: Before and After McFarlane." In *The McFarlane Legacy: Studies in Late Medieval Politics and Society*, ed. R. H. Britnell and A. J. Pollard, 175–206. The Fifteenth Century Series No. 1. Stroud: Alan Sutton, 1995

Chrimes, S. B. *English Constitutional Ideas in the Fifteenth Century*. New York: American Scholar Publications, 1966

Henry VII. London: Eyre Methuen, 1972

"The Reign of Henry VII." In *Fifteenth-Century England 1399–1509*, ed. S. B. Chrimes *et al.*, 67–85. New York: Barnes & Noble, 1972

Chroust, A. "The Legal Profession During the Middle Ages." *Notre Dame Lawyer* 32 (1956); 85–140; *Notre Dame Lawyer* 33 (1957): 268–99

Clanchy, M. T. "Law, Government and Society in Medieval England." *History*, new ser. 59 (1974): 73–78

Condon, M. M. "Ruling Elites in the Reign of Henry VII." In *Patronage Pedigree and Power in Later Medieval England*, ed. Charles Ross, 109–42. Gloucester: Alan Sutton, 1979

"An Anachronism with Intent?: Henry VII's Council Ordinance of 1491/2." In *Kings and Nobles in the Later Middle Ages*, ed. Ralph A. Griffiths and James Sherborne, 228–53. Gloucester: Alan Sutton, 1986

Cooper, J. P. "Henry VII's Last Years Reconsidered." *Historical Journal* 2 (1959): 103–29

"The Social Distribution of Land and Men in England, 1436–1700." *Economic History Review*, 2nd ser. 20 (1967): 419–40

"Patterns of Inheritance and Settlement by Great Landowners from the Fifteenth to the Eighteenth Centuries." In *Family and Inheritance: Rural Society in Western Europe, 1200–1800*, ed. Jack Goody, Joan Thirsk and E. P. Thompson, 192–327. Cambridge: Cambridge University Press, 1976

"The Counting of Manors." In *Land, Men and Beliefs: Studies in Early-Modern History*, ed. J. P. Cooper, 1–16. London: Hambledon Press, 1983

"In Search of Agrarian Capitalism." In *The Brenner Debate: Agrarian Class Structure and Economic Development in Pre-Industrial Europe*, ed. T. H. Aston and C. H. E. Philpin, 138–91. Past and Present Publications. Cambridge: Cambridge University Press, 1987

Cornwall, Julian. "The Early Tudor Gentry." *Economic History Review*, 2nd ser. 17 (1964–65): 456–71

Coss, P. R. "Bastard Feudalism Revised." *Past and Present* 125 (1989): 27–64

"The Formation of the English Gentry." *Past and Present* 147 (1995): 38–64

Coward, Barry. *The Stanleys, Lords Stanley and Earls of Derby, 1385–1672: The Origins, Wealth and Power of a Landowning Family*. Chetham Society. Manchester: Manchester University Press, 1983

Croot, Patricia and Parker, David. "Agrarian Class Structure and the Development of Capitalism: France and England Compared." In *The Brenner Debate: Agrarian Class Structure and Economic Development in Pre-Industrial Europe*, ed. T. H. Aston & C. H. E. Philpin, 79–90. Past and Present Publications. Cambridge: Cambridge University Press, 1987

Cunningham, S. "Henry VII and Rebellion in North-Eastern England, 1485–1492: Bonds of Allegiance and the Establishment of Tudor Authority." *Northern History* 32 (1996): 42–74

Dawson, John P. *The Oracles of the Law*. Ann Arbor: University of Michigan Law School, 1968

Dietz, F. C. *English Government Finance 1485–1558*, 2nd edn, London: Frank Cass, 1964

Doe, Norman. *Fundamental Authority in Late Medieval English Law*. Cambridge, Cambridge University Press, 1990

"Legal Reasoning and Sir Roger Townshend, JCP (d. 1493)." *Journal of Legal History* 11 (1990): 191–9

"The Positivist Thesis in Fifteenth-Century Legal Theory and Practice." *Journal of Legal History* 11 (1990): 27–39

Dowling, Maria. *Humanism in the Age of Henry VIII*. London: Croom Helm, 1986

Du Boulay, F. R. H. "Gavelkind and Knight's Fee in Medieval Kent." *English Historical Review* 77 (1962): 504–11

Dunham, William Huse. "Regal Power and the Rule of Law: A Tudor Paradox." *Journal of British Studies* 3 (1964): 24–56

Ellis, Steven G. "A Border Baron and the Tudor State: The Rise and Fall of Lord Dacre of the North." *Historical Journal* 35 (1992): 253–77

Tudor Frontiers and Noble Power: The Making of the British State. Oxford: Clarendon Press, 1995

Elton, G. R. "The Commons Supplication of 1532: Parliamentary Manoeuvres in the Reign of Henry VIII." *English Historical Review* 66 (1951): 507–34

The Tudor Revolution in Government: Administrative Changes in the Reign of Henry VIII. Cambridge: Cambridge University Press, 1953

England Under the Tudors. London: Methuen & Co.; New York: Barnes & Noble, 1959

"State Planning in Early-Tudor England." *Economic History Review*, 2nd ser. 13 (1961): 433–39

"Problems and Significance of Administrative History in the Tudor Period." *Journal of British Studies* 4 (1965): 18–28

"The Rule of Law in Sixteenth Century England." In *Tudor Men and Institutions: Studies in English Law and Government*, ed. Arthur J. Slavin, 265–94. Baton Rouge: Louisiana State University Press, 1972

Reform and Renewal: Thomas Cromwell and the Common Weal. Cambridge: Cambridge University Press, 1973

"Henry VII: A Restatement." In *Studies in Tudor and Stuart Politics and Government, Papers and Reviews 1946–1972*, vol. 1, *Tudor Politics/Tudor Government*, 66–97. London: Cambridge University Press, 1974

"Henry VII: Rapacity and Remorse." In *Studies in Tudor and Stuart Politics and Government, Papers and Reviews 1946–1972*, vol. 1, *Tudor Politics/Tudor Government*, 45–65. London: Cambridge University Press, 1974

"Mid-Tudor Finance." *Historical Journal* 20 (1977): 737–40

Reform and Reformation: England 1509–1558. Cambridge MA: Harvard University Press, 1977

English Law in the Sixteenth Century: Reform in an Age of Change. Selden Society Lecture for 1978. London: Selden Society, 1979

"Politics and the Pilgrimage of Grace." In *After the Reformation: Essays in Honour of J. H. Hexter*, ed. Barbara C. Malament, 25–56. Philadelphia: University of Pennsylvania Press, 1980

"King Henry VII." *Transactions of the Honourable Society of Cymmrodorion* (1985): 131–45

Ferguson, A. B. "The Tudor Commonweal and the Sense of Change." *Journal of British History* 3 (1963): 11–35

The Articulate Citizen and the English Renaissance. Durham NC: Duke University Press, 1965

Fideler, Paul A. and Thomas F. Mayer, ed. *Political Thought and the Tudor Commonwealth: Deep Structure, Discourse and Disguise*. London: Routledge, 1992

Fisher, R. M. "Thomas Cromwell, the Dissolution of the Monasteries and the Inns of Court, 1534–40." *Journal of the Society of the Public Teachers of Law* 14 (1976–77): 111–77

"Thomas Cromwell, Humanism and Educational Reform 1530–40." *Bulletin of the Institute of Historical Research* 50 (1977): 151–63

"The Reformation in Microcosm? Benchers at the Inns of Court, 1530–1580." *Parergon*, new ser. 6 (1988): 33–61

Ford, Lisa. "Conciliar Politics and Administration in the Reign of Henry VII." PhD diss., University of St. Andrews, 2001

George, M. Dorothy. "Notes on the Origin of the Declared Account." *English Historical Review* 31 (1916): 41–58

Goodman, Anthony. *The New Monarchy: England 1471–1534*. Oxford: Basil Blackwell, 1988

Goodrich, Peter. "Poor Illiterate Reason: History, Nationalism and Common Law." *Social and Legal Studies* 1 (1992): 7–28

Goring, Jeremy. "Social Change and Military Decline in mid-Tudor England." *History* 60 (1975): 185–97

Graves, E. B. "Circumspecte Agatis." *English Historical Review* 43 (1928): 1–20

Gray, Howard L. *The Influence of the Commons on Early Legislation: A Study of the Fourteenth and Fifteenth Centuries*. Cambridge MA: Harvard University Press, 1932

Gray, Madeleine. "Crown Property and the Land Market in South-East Wales in the Sixteenth Century." *Agricultural History Review* 35 (1987): 133–50

"Change and Continuity: The Gentry and Property of the Church in South-East Wales and the Marches." In *Class, Community and Culture in Tudor Wales*, ed. J. Gwynfor Jones, 1–38. Cardiff: University of Wales Press, 1989

Griffiths, Ralph A. "Henry Tudor: The Training of a King." In *King and Country: England and Wales in the Fifteenth Century*, 115–36. London: Hambledon Press, 1991

"The Crown and the Royal Family in Later Medieval England." In *King and Country: England and Wales in the Fifteenth Century*, 1–10. London: Hambledon Press, 1991

The Reign of King Henry VI. Stroud: Sutton, 1998

Gross, A. J. "K. B. McFarlane and the Determinists: The Fallibilities of the English Kings, c.1399–1520." In *The McFarlane Legacy: Studies in Late Medieval Politics and Society*, ed. R. H. Britnell and A. J. Pollard, 49–75. The Fifteenth Century Series No. 1. Stroud: Alan Sutton, 1995

Grummitt, David. "Henry VII, Chamber Finance and the New Monarchy." *Historical Research* 72 (1999): 229–43

Gunn, S. J. "Chivalry and the Politics of the Early Tudor Court." In *Chivalry in the Renaissance*, ed. Sydney Anglo, 107–28. Suffolk: Boydell, 1990

"Literature and Politics in Early Tudor England." *Journal of British Studies* 30 (1991): 216–21

"The Accession of Henry VIII." *Historical Research* 64 (1991): 278–88

Review of *Locality and Polity: A Study of Warwickshire Landed Society, 1401–1499* by Christine Carpenter. *Historical Journal* 35 (1992): 999–1003

"The Courtiers of Henry VII." *English Historical Review* 108 (1993): 23–49

"Off with Their Heads: The Tudor Nobility: 1485–1603." In *The House of Lords: A Thousand Years of British Tradition*, ed. Robert Smith and John S. Moore, 52–65. London: Smith's Peerage Ltd, 1994

Early Tudor Government, 1485–1558. New York: St. Martin's Press, 1995

"The Structures of Politics in Early Tudor England." *Transactions of the Royal Historical Society*, 6th ser. 5 (1995): 59–90

"Sir Thomas Lovell (c.1449–1524): A New Man in a New Monarchy?" In *The End of the Middle Ages? England in the Fifteenth and Sixteenth Centuries*, ed. J. L. Watts, 117–53. The Fifteenth Century Series, No. 6. Gloucester: Sutton, 1998

Guth, DeLloyd J. "Enforcing Late-Medieval Law: Patterns in Litigation During Henry VII's Reign." In *Legal Records and the Historian*, ed. J. H. Baker, 80–96. London: Royal Historical Society, 1978

Guy, J. A. "A Conciliar Court of Audit at Work in the Last Months of the Reign of Henry VII." *Bulletin of the Institute of Historical Research* 49 (1976): 289–95

The Cardinal's Court: The Impact of Thomas Wolsey in Star Chamber. Sussex: Harvester Press, 1977

The Public Career of Sir Thomas More. Brighton: Harvester Press, 1980

Christopher St. German on Chancery and Statute. Selden Society supplementary series vol. 6. London: Selden Society, 1985

"The Privy Council: Revolution or Evolution?" In *Revolution Reassessed: Revisions in the History of Tudor Government and Administration*, ed. Christopher Colemen and David Starkey, 59–85. Oxford: Clarendon Press, 1986

"Thomas Cromwell and the Intellectual Origins of the Henrician Revolution." In *Reassessing the Henrician Age: Humanism, Politics and Reform 1500–1550*, ed. Alaister Fox and John Guy, 151–78. Oxford: Basil Blackwell, 1986

"Thomas More and Christopher St. German: The Battle of the Books." In *Reassessing the Henrician Age: Humanism, Politics and Reform 1500–1550*, ed. Alaister Fox and John Guy, 95–120. Oxford: Basil Blackwell, 1986

Tudor England. Oxford: Oxford University Press, 1988

"The Henrician Age." In *The Varieties of British Political Thought, 1500–1800*, ed. J. G. A. Pocock, 13–46. Cambridge: Cambridge University Press, 1993

Habakkuk, H. J. "The Market for Monastic Property, 1539–1603." *Economic History Review*, 2nd ser. 10 (1958): 362–80

Harrison, C. J. "The Petition of Edmund Dudley." *English Historical Review* 87 (1972): 82–99

Harriss, G. L. "Medieval Government and Statecraft." *Past and Present* 25 (1963): 8–39

Review of *The Crown Lands, 1461–1536* by B. P. Wolffe. *English Historical Review* 88 (1973): 172

"Introduction." In *England in the Fifteenth Century: Collected Essays*, by K. B. McFarlane, ix–xxvii. London: Hambledon Press, 1981

"Political Society and the Growth of Government in Late Medieval England." *Past and Present* 138 (1993): 28–57

"The King and his Subjects." In *Fifteenth Century Attitudes*, ed. Rosemary Horrox, 13–28. Cambridge: Cambridge University Press, 1994

"The Dimensions of Politics." In *The McFarlane Legacy: Studies in Late Medieval Politics and Society*, ed. R. H. Britnell and A. J. Pollard, 1–20. The Fifteenth Century Series No. 1. Stroud: Alan Sutton, 1995

Harvey, Sally. "The Knight and Knight's Fee in England." *Past and Present* 49 (1970): 3–43

Hastings, Margaret. "Sir Thomas More: Maker of English Law?" In *Essential Articles for the Study of Thomas More*, ed. R. S. Sylvester and G. P. Marc'hadour, 104–18. Hamden CT: Archon Books, 1977

Hazeltine, H. D. "The Renaissance and the Laws of Europe." In *Cambridge Legal Essays*, ed. Percy Winfield and Arnold McNair, 139–71. Cambridge: W. Heffer & Sons, 1926

Heal, Felicity and Clive Holmes. *The Gentry in England and Wales 1500–1700*. Basingstoke: Macmillan, 1994

Helmholz, R. H. "Continental Law and Common Law: Historical Strangers or Companions?" *Duke Law Journal* (1990): 1207–28

Henderson, E. F. "The Date of the 'Prerogativa Regis'." *English Historical Review* 5 (1890): 753–54

Hicks, Michael. "Attainder, Resumption and Coercion 1461–1529." *Parliamentary History* 3 (1984): 15–31

Hilton, R. H. "A Crisis of Feudalism." In *The Brenner Debate: Agrarian Class Structure and Economic Development in Pre-Industrial Europe*, ed. T. H. Aston and C. H. E. Philpin, 119–37. Past and Present Publications. Cambridge: Cambridge University Press, 1987

Hoak, Dale. "The Secret History of the Tudor Court: The King's Coffers and the King's Purse, 1542–1553." *Journal of British Studies* 26 (1987): 208–31

"The Iconography of the Crown Imperial." In *Tudor Political Culture*, ed. Dale Hoak, 54–103. Cambridge: Cambridge University Press, 1995

Holdsworth, Sir William. *A History of English Law*. 10 vols., 3rd edn, London: Methuen, 1966

Holt, James. "The Introduction of Knight Service in England." *Anglo-Norman Studies* 6 (1983): 89–106

Magna Carta and Medieval Government. London: Hambledon Press, 1985

Horowitz, Mark R. "Richard Empson, Minister of Henry VII." *Bulletin of the Institute of Historical Research* 55 (1982): 35–49

Hoyle, R. W. "The First Earl of Cumberland: A Reputation Re-assessed." *Northern History* 22 (1986): 63–94

"Monastic Leasing before the Dissolution." *Yorkshire Archaeological Journal* 61 (1989): 111–37

"Tenure and the Land Market in Early Modern England or a Late Contribution to the Brenner Debate." *Economic History Review*, 2nd ser. 43 (1990): 1–20

"Crown, Parliament and Taxation in Sixteenth-Century England." *English Historical Review* 109 (1994): 1174–96

"The Origins of the Dissolution of the Monasteries." *Historical Journal* 38 (1995): 275–305

"The Land-Family Bond in England." *Past and Present* 146 (1995): 151–73

"Taxation and the Mid-Tudor Crisis." *Economic History Review*, 2nd ser. 51 (1998): 649–75

Hoyt, Robert S. "The Nature and Origins of the Ancient Demesne." *English Historical Review* 65 (1950): 145–74

Hunnisett, R. F. "The Reliability of Inquisitions as Historical Evidence." In *The Study of Medieval Records: Essays in Honour of Kathleen Major*, ed. D. A. Bullough and R. L. Storey, 206–35. Oxford: Clarendon Press, 1971

Hurstfield, Joel. "The Greenwich Tenures of the Reign of Edward VI." *Law Quarterly Review* 65 (1949): 72–81

"The Revival of Feudalism in Early Tudor England." *History*, new ser. 37 (1952): 131–45

"The Profits of Fiscal Feudalism, 1541–1602." *Economic History Review*, 2nd ser. 8 (1955): 53–61

The Illusion of Power in Tudor Politics. The Creighton Lecture in History, 1978. London: Athlone Press, 1979

Ives, E. W. "Promotion in the Legal Profession of Yorkist and Early Tudor England." *Law Quarterly Review* 75 (1959): 348–63

"The Reputation of the Common Lawyer in English Society, 1450–1550." *University of Birmingham Historical Journal* 7 (1960): 130–61

"The Genesis of the Statute of Uses." *English Historical Review* 82 (1967): 673–97

"A Lawyer's Library in 1500." *Law Quarterly Review* 85 (1969): 104–16

"The Purpose and Making of the Later Year Books." *Law Quarterly Review* 89 (1973): 64–86

The Common Lawyers of Pre-Reformation England. Cambridge: Cambridge University Press, 1983

Jack, Sybil. "Henry VIII's Attitude Towards Royal Finance: Penny Wise and Pound Foolish?" In *Francois Ier et Henri VIII, deux princes de la Renaissance 1515–1547*, ed. Charles Giry-Deloison, 145–64. Lille: Centre d'Histoire de la Region du Nord et de l'Europe de Nord-Ouest, 1996

James, M. E. *A Tudor Magnate and the Tudor State: Henry Fifth Earl of Northumberland*. Borthwick Papers No. 30. York: St. Anthony's Press, 1966

"Change and Continuity in the Tudor North: Thomas First Lord Wharton." In *Society, Politics and Culture*, ed. M. E. James, 91–147. Cambridge: Cambridge University Press, 1986

"English Politics and the Concept of Honour, 1485–1642." In *Society, Politics and Culture*, ed. M. E. James, 308–415. Cambridge: Cambridge University Press, 1986

"The First Earl of Cumberland (1493–1542) and the Decline of Northern Feudalism." In *Society, Politics and Culture*, ed. M. E. James, 148–75. Cambridge: Cambridge University Press, 1986

Jeffries, Peggy. "The Medieval Use as Family Law and Custom: The Berkshire Gentry in the Fourteenth and Fifteenth Centuries." *Southern History* 1 (1979): 45–69

Jones, Neil G. "Tyrrel's Case (1557) and the Use upon a Use." *Journal of Legal History* 14 (1993): 75–93

"Long Leases and the Feudal Revenue in the Court of Wards, 1540–1645." *Journal of Legal History* 19 (1998): 1–22

Jones, Norman L. "Profiting from Religious Reform: The Land Rush of 1559." *Historical Journal* 22 (1979): 279–94

Kantorowicz, E. H. *The King's Two Bodies: A Study in Mediaeval Political Theology*. Princeton: Princeton University Press, 1957

Kelley, D. R. "Clio and the Lawyers: Forms of Historical Consciousness in Medieval Jurisprudence." *Medievalia et Humanistica*, new ser. 5 (1974): 25–49

"History, English Law and the Renaissance." *Past and Present* 65 (1974): 24–51

"*Vera Philosophia*: The Philosophical Significance of Renaissance Jurisprudence." *Journal of the History of Philosophy* 14 (1976): 267–79

Kern, Fritz. *Kingship and Law in the Middle Ages*. Translated with an introduction by S. B. Chrimes. New York: Blackwell, 1956

Kew, J. "The Disposal of Crown Lands and the Devon Land Market, 1536–58." *Agricultural History Review* 18 (1970): 93–105

Kitching, C. J. "The Quest for Concealed Lands in the Reign of Elizabeth I." *Transactions of the Royal Historical Society*, 5th ser. 24 (1974): 63–78

"The Disposal of Monastic and Chantry Lands." In *Church and Society in England: Henry VIII to James I*, ed. Felicity Heal and Rosemary O'Day, 119–36. London: Macmillan, 1977

Knafla, Louis A. "The Matriculation Revolution and Education at the Inns of Court in Renaissance England." In *Tudor Men and Institutions: Studies in English Law and Government*, ed. Arthur J. Slavin, 232–64. Baton Rouge: Louisiana State University Press, 1972

Lander, J. R. "Attainder and Forfeiture, 1453–1509." In *Crown and Nobility 1450–1509*, ed. J. R. Lander, 127–58. London: Edward Arnold, 1976

"Bonds, Coercion and Fear: Henry VII and the Peerage." In *Crown and Nobility 1450–1509*, ed. J. R. Lander, 267–300. London: Edward Arnold, 1976

The Limitations of English Monarchy in the Later Middle Ages. The 1986 Joanne Goodman Lectures. Toronto: University of Toronto Press, 1989

English Justices of the Peace, 1461–1509. Gloucester: Sutton, 1989

Lehmberg, Stanford E. *The Reformation Parliament, 1529–1536*. Cambridge: Cambridge University Press, 1970

"Sir Thomas Audley: A Soul as Black as Marble?" In *Tudor Men and Institutions: Studies in English Law and Government*, ed. Arthur J. Slavin, 3–31. Baton Rouge: Louisiana State University Press, 1972

The Later Parliaments of Henry VIII, 1536–1547. Cambridge: Cambridge University Press, 1977

Leonard, H. H. "Knights and Knighthood in Tudor England." PhD diss., London University, 1970

Lewis, P. S. "Decayed and Non-Feudalism in Later Medieval France." *Bulletin of the Institute of Historical Research* 37 (1964): 157–84

Lewis, T. E. "The History of Judicial Precedent." *Law Quarterly Review* 46 (1930): 207–24 and 341–60; *Law Quarterly Review* 47 (1931): 411–27

Loach, J. "The Function of Ceremonial in the Reign of Henry VIII." *Past and Present* 142 (1994): 43–68

Logan, F. Donald. "The First Royal Visitation of the English Universities, 1535." *English Historical Review* 106 (1991): 861–88

Luckett, D. A. "Crown Patronage and Local Administration in Berkshire, Dorset, Hampshire, Oxfordshire, Somerset and Wiltshire, 1485–1509." PhD diss., Oxford University, 1992

"Crown Patronage and Political Morality in Early Tudor England: The Case of Giles, Lord Daubeney." *English Historical Review* 110 (1995): 578–95

"Henry VII and the South-Western Escheators." In *The Reign of Henry VII: Proceedings of the 1993 Harlaxton Symposium*, ed. Benjamin Thompson, 54–64. Harlaxton Medieval Studies V. Stamford: Paul Watkins, 1995

"Patronage, Violence and Revolt in the Reign of Henry VII." In *Crown, Government and People in the Fifteenth Century*, ed. Rowena E. Archer, 145–60. The Fifteenth Century Series No. 2. New York: St. Martin's Press, 1995

"The Thames Valley Conspiracies Against Henry VII." *Historical Research* 68 (1995): 164–72

"The Rise and Fall of a Noble Dynasty: Henry VII and the Lords Wiloughby de Broke." *Historical Research* 69 (1996): 254–65

MacCulloch, Diarmaid. "Kett's Rebellion in Context." *Past and Present* 84 (1979): 36–59

Maclean, Ian. *Interpretation and Meaning in the Renaissance: The Case of Law*. Cambridge: Cambridge University Press, 1992

Maitland, F. W. *English Law and the Renaissance*. Cambridge: Cambridge University Press, 1901

"The *Praerogativa Regis*." In *Collected Papers*, vol. 2. Cambridge: Cambridge University Press, 1911

Mayer, Thomas F. "On the Road to 1534: The Occupation of Tournai and Henry VIII's Theory of Sovereignty." In *Tudor Political Culture*, ed. Dale Hoak, 11–30. Cambridge: Cambridge University Press, 1995

McConica, J. K. *English Humanists and Reformation Politics*. Oxford: Clarendon Press, 1965

McFarlane, K. B. "The Wars of the Roses." *Proceedings of the British Academy* 50 (1964): 87–119

The Nobility of Later Medieval England: The Ford Lectures for 1953 and Related Studies. Oxford: Clarendon Press, 1973

England in the Fifteenth Century: Collected Essays. London: Hambledon Press, 1981

McKisack, May. *Medieval History in the Tudor Age*. Oxford: Clarendon Press, 1971

Megarry, Robert. *Inns Ancient and Modern: A Topographical and Historical Introduction to the Inns of Court, Inns of Chancery, and Serjeants' Inns*. Selden Society Lecture for 1971. London: Selden Society, 1972

Miller, Helen. *Henry VIII and the English Nobility*. Oxford: Basil Blackwell, 1986

Milsom, S. F. C. "Law and Fact in Legal Development." *University of Toronto Law Journal* 17 (1967): 1–19

Historical Foundations of the Common Law. London: Butterworths, 1969

The Legal Framework of English Feudalism. Cambridge: Cambridge University Press, 1976

Studies in the History of the Common Law. London: Hambledon Press, 1985

"The Origin of Prerogative Wardship." In *Law and Government in Medieval England and Normandy: Essays in Honour of Sir James Holt*, ed. George Garnett & John Hudson, 223–44. Cambridge: Cambridge University Press, 1994

Mirov, Matthew Campbell. "Readings on Wills in the Inns of Court, 1552–1631." PhD diss., Cambridge, 1993

Morgan, D. A. L. "The House of Policy: The Political Role of the Late Plantagenet Household, 1422–1485." In *The English Court: From the Wars of the Roses to the Civil War*, ed. David Starkey *et al.*, 25–70. London: Longman, 1987

Newton, A. P. "The King's Chamber under the Early Tudors." *English Historical Review* 32 (1917): 348–72

"Tudor Reforms in the Royal Household." In *Tudor Studies Presented by the Board of Studies in History in the University of London to Albert Frederick Pollard*, 231–56. London: Longmans Green & Co., 1924

Nichols, F. M. "Observations upon the Nature of the Tenure or Service of Cornage." *Archaeologia* 39 (1863): 349–56

"On Feudal and Obligatory Knighthood." *Archaeologia* 39 (1863): 189–244

Nicholson, Graham David. "The Nature and Function of Historical Argument in the Henrician Reformation." PhD diss., Cambridge, 1984

Noyes, Arthur H. *The Military Obligation in Medieval England*. Columbus OH: Ohio State University Press, 1930

Ogilvie, Charles, *The King's Government and the Common Law 1471–1641*. Oxford: Basil Blackwell, 1958

O'Sullivan, Richard. "Sir Thomas More and Lincoln's Inn." In *Essential Articles for the Study of Thomas More*, ed. R. S. Sylvester and G. P. Marc'hadour, 161–68. Hamden CT: Archon Books, 1977

Outhwaite, R. B. "Who Bought Crown Lands? The Pattern of Purchases, 1589–1603." *Bulletin of the Institute of Historical Research* 44 (1971): 18–33

Palmer, R. C. "The Feudal Framework of English Law." *Michigan Law Review* 79 (1980–81): 1130–64

Payling, Simon. *Political Society in Lancastrian England: The Greater Gentry of Nottingham*. Cambridge: Cambridge University Press, 1991

"The Waning of Noble Lordship in Late Fifteenth Century England." *Parliamentary History* 13 (1994): 322–32

"The Politics of Family: Late Medieval Marriage Contracts." In *The McFarlane Legacy: Studies in Late Medieval Politics and Society*, ed. R. H. Britnell and A. J. Pollard, 21–47. The Fifteenth Century Series No. 1. Stroud: Alan Sutton, 1995

Pickthorn, Kenneth. *Early Tudor Government: Henry VII*. Cambridge: Cambridge University Press, 1949

Plucknett, T. F. T. *Statutes and Their Interpretation in the First Half of the Fourteenth Century*. Cambridge: Cambridge University Press, 1922

"The Lancastrian Constitution." In *Tudor Studies Presented by the Board of Studies in History in the University of London to Albert Frederick Pollard*, 161–81. London: Longmans Green & Co., 1924

"The Place of the Legal Profession in the History of English Law." *Law Quarterly Review* 48 (1932): 328–40

"Some Proposed Legislation of Henry VIII." *Transactions of the Royal Historical Society*, 4th ser. 19 (1936): 119–44

Legislation of Edward I. Oxford: Clarendon Press, 1949

A Concise History of the Common Law. 5th edn, Boston: Little, Brown, 1956

Early English Legal Literature. Cambridge: Cambridge University Press, 1958

"Ellesmere on Statutes." In *Studies in English Legal History*. London: Hambledon Press, 1983

Pocock, J. G. A. *The Ancient Constitution and the Feudal Law: A Study of English Historical Thought in the Seventeenth Century*. New York: W. W. Norton, 1967

Pollard, A. F. *Factors in Modern History*. 3rd edn, London: Constable & Co., 1932

Pollard, A. J. *North-Eastern England During the Wars of the Roses: Lay Society, War and Politics*. Oxford: Clarendon Press, 1990

Pollock, Sir Frederick. "The Origins of the Inns of Court." *Law Quarterly Review* 48 (1932): 163–70

"The History of English Law as a Branch of Politics." In *Jurisprudence and Legal Essays*, ed. A. L. Goodhart, 185–211. London: Macmillan, 1961

Pollock, Sir Frederick and Frederic William Maitland. *The History of English Law Before the Time of Edward I*. 2 vols. 2nd edn, Cambridge: Cambridge University Press, 1968

Post, Gaines. *Studies in Medieval Legal Thought: Public Law and the State, 1100–1322*. Princeton: Princeton University Press, 1964

Postan, M. M. and John Hatcher. "Population and Class Relations in Feudal Society." In *The Brenner Debate: Agrarian Class Structure and Economic Development in Pre-Industrial Europe*, ed. T. H. Aston and C. H. E. Philpin, 64–78. Past and Present Publications. Cambridge: Cambridge University Press, 1987

Powell, Edward. "Arbitration and the Law in England in the Late Middle Ages." *Transactions of the Royal Historical Society*, 5th ser. 33 (1983): 49–67

"Settlement of Disputes by Arbitration in Fifteenth-Century England." *Law and History Review* 2 (1984): 21–43

Kingship, Law and Society: Criminal Justice in the Reign of Henry V. Oxford: Clarendon Press, 1989

"After 'After McFarlane': The Poverty of Patronage and the Case for Constitutional History." In *Trade, Devotion and Governance: Papers in Later Medieval History*, ed. Dorothy J. Clayton, Richard G. Davies, and Peter McNiven, 1–16. Stroud: Alan Sutton, 1994

"Law and Justice." In *Fifteenth Century Attitudes*, ed. Rosemary Horrox, 29–41. Cambridge: Cambridge University Press, 1994

Powicke, F. M. "Reflections on the Medieval State." *Transactions of the Royal Historical Society*, 4th ser. 19 (1936): 1–18

Pugh, T. B. "The Magnates, Knights and Gentry." In *Fifteenth-Century England 1399–1509*, ed. S. B. Chrimes *et al.*, 86–128. New York: Barnes & Noble, 1972

Radin, Max. "Early Statutory Interpretation in England." *Illinois Law Review* 38 (1943): 16–40

Rawcliffe, Carole. *The Staffords, Earls of Stafford and Dukes of Buckingham 1394–1521.* Cambridge: Cambridge University Press, 1978

"Baronial Councils in the Later Middle Ages." In *Patronage Pedigree and Power in Later Medieval England*, ed. Charles Ross, 87–108. Gloucester: Alan Sutton, 1979

Rawcliffe, Carole and Susan Flower. "English Noblemen and Their Advisors: Consultation and Collaboration in the Later Middle Ages." *Journal of British Studies* 25 (1986): 157–77

Reynolds, Susan. *Fiefs and Vassals.* Oxford: Oxford University Press, 1994

Richardson, H. G. and G. O. Sayles. "The Early Statutes." *Law Quarterly Review* 50 (1934): 201–23 and 540–71

The Governance of Medieval England from the Conquest to Magna Carta. Edinburgh: Edinburgh University Press, 1963

Richardson, W. C. "The Surveyor of the King's Prerogative." *English Historical Review* 56 (1941): 52–75

Tudor Chamber Administration 1485–1547. Baton Rouge: Louisiana State University Press, 1952

History of the Court of Augmentations, 1536–1554. Baton Rouge: Louisiana State University Press, 1961

Richmond, Colin. "1485 and All That, or What Was Going on at the Battle of Bosworth?" In *Richard III: Loyalty, Lordship and Law*, ed. P. W. Hammond, 172–206. London, Alan Sutton, 1986

Robertson, Mary L. "Profit and Purpose in the Development of Thomas Cromwell's Landed Estates." *Journal of British Studies* 29 (1990): 317–46

Robinson, O. F. "Bracton & Hengham: The Wages of Virtue." *Journal of Legal History* 15 (1994): 73–76

Ross, Richard J. "The Commoning of the Common Law: The Renaissance Debate over Printing English Law, 1520–1640." *University of Pennsylvania Law Review* 146 (1998): 323–461

Russell, F. W. *Kett's Rebellion in Norfolk*. London, 1859

Sainty, Sir John. *A List of English Law Officers, King's Counsel and Holders of Patents of Precedence*. Selden Society supplementary series vol. 7. London: Selden Society, 1978

Savine, Alexander. *English Monasteries on the Eve of the Dissolution*. Oxford Studies in Social and Legal History, ed. Sir Paul Vinogradoff, vol. 1. Oxford: Clarendon Press, 1909

Sayles, G. O. "A Fifteenth-Century Law Reading in English." In *Scripta Diversa*, 301–12. London: Hambledon Press, 1982

Scarisbrick, J. J. *Henry VIII*. Berkeley: University of California Press, 1968

The Reformation and the English People. Oxford: Basil Blackwell, 1984

"Henry VIII and the Dissolution of the Secular Colleges." In *Law and Government under the Tudors*, ed. Claire Cross, David Loades, and J. J. Scarisbrick, 51–66. Cambridge: Cambridge University Press, 1988

Schoeck, R. J. "Rhetoric and the Law in Sixteenth-Century England." *Studies in Philology* 50 (1953): 110–27

"Sir Thomas More, Humanist and Lawyer." In *Essential Articles for the Study of Thomas More*, ed. R. S. Sylvester and G. P. Marc'hadour, 569–79. Hamden CT: Archon Books, 1977

Simpson, A. W. B. "The Reports of John Spelman." *Law Quarterly Review* 72 (1956): 334–38

"Keilway's Reports, temp. Henry VII and Henry VIII." *Law Quarterly Review* 73 (1957): 89–105

"The Circulation of Year Books in the Fifteenth Century." *Law Quarterly Review* 73 (1957): 492–505

"The Early Constitution of the Inns of Court." *Cambridge Law Journal* 28 (1970): 241–56

"The Source and Function of the Later Year Books." *Law Quarterly Review* 87 (1971): 94–118

"The Early Constitution of Gray's Inn." *Cambridge Law Journal* 34 (1975): 131–50

A History of the Land Law. Oxford: Clarendon Press, 1986

"The Common Law and Legal Theory." In *Legal Theory and Legal History: Essays on the Common Law*, 359–82. London: Hambledon Press, 1987

"The Rise and Fall of the Legal Treatise: Legal Principles and the Forms of Legal Literature." In *Legal Theory and Legal History: Essays on the Common Law*, 273–320. London: Hambledon Press, 1987

Slavin, Arthur J. "Lord Chancellor Wriothesley and Reform of Augmentations: New Light on an Old Court." In *Tudor Men and Institutions: Studies in English Law and Government*, ed. Arthur J. Slavin, 49–69. Baton Rouge: Louisiana State University Press, 1972

Smith, Llinos Beverley. "The Statute of Wales, 1284." *Welsh History Review* 10 (1980): 127–54

Smith, R. B. *Land and Politics in the England of Henry VIII: The West Riding of Yorkshire 1530–46*. Oxford: Clarendon Press, 1970

Somerville, R. "Henry VII's 'Council Learned in the Law'." *English Historical Review* 54 (1939): 427–42

History of the Duchy of Lancaster. London: Chancellor and Council of the Duchy of Lancaster, 1953

Spelman, Henry. *The History and Fate of Sacrilege, Discover'd by examples of Scripture, of Heathens, and of Christians, from the beginning of the world, continually to this Day*. Edited by C. F. S. Warren. 4th edn, London, 1895

Starkey, David. "Court and Government." In *Revolution Reassessed: Revisions in the History of Tudor Government and Administration*, ed. Christopher Coleman and David Starkey, 29–58. Oxford: Clarendon Press, 1986

"Which Age of Reform?" In *Revolution Reassessed: Revisions in the History of Tudor Government and Administration*, ed. Christopher Coleman and David Starkey, 13–27. Oxford: Clarendon Press, 1986

"Intimacy and Innovation: The Rise of the Privy Chamber, 1485–1547." In *The English Court: From the Wars of the Roses to the Civil War*, ed. David Starkey *et al.*, 71–118. London: Longman, 1987

Stevenson, E. R. "The Escheator." In *The English Government at Work 1327–1336*, vol. 2, *Fiscal Administration*, ed. J. F. Willard, W. A. Morris *et al.*, 109–67. Cambridge MA: The Medieval Academy of America, 1947

Sugarman, David. "Simple Images and Complex Realities: English Lawyers and Their Relation to Business and Politics, 1750–1950." *Law and History Review* 11 (1993): 257–301

Suggett, Helen. "The Use of French in England in the Later Middle Ages." *Transactions of the Royal Historical Society*, 4th ser. 28 (1946): 61–83

Thompson, Benjamin. "Monasteries and Their Patrons at Foundation and Dissolution." *Transactions of the Royal Historical Society*, 6th ser. 4 (1994): 103–25

"The Laity, the Alien Priories, and the Re-distribution of Ecclesiastical Property." In *England in the Fifteenth Century: Proceedings of the 1992 Harlaxton Symposium*, ed. Nicholas Rogers, 19–41. Harlaxton Medieval Studies IV. Stamford: Paul Watkins, 1994

"Introduction: The Place of Henry VII in English History." In *The Reign of Henry VII: Proceedings of the 1993 Harlaxton Symposium*, ed. Benjamin Thompson, 1–10. Harlaxton Medieval Studies V. Stamford: Paul Watkins, 1995

Thompson, F. M. L. "The Social Distribution of Landed Property in England Since the Sixteenth Century." *Economic History Review*, 2nd ser. 19 (1966): 505–15

Thorne, S. E. "Statuti in the Post-Glossators." *Speculum* 11 (1936): 452–61

"The Equity of a Statute and Heydon's Case." *Illinois Law Review* 31 (1936): 202–16

"Tudor Social Transformation and Legal Change." *New York University Law Review* 26 (1951): 10–23

"English Feudalism and Estates in Land." *Cambridge Law Journal* (1959): 193–209

"English Law and the Renaissance." In *Essays in English Legal History*, ed. S. E. Thorne, 187–95. London: Hambledon Press, 1985

"Livery of Seisin." In *Essays in English Legal History*, ed. S. E. Thorne, 31–50. London: Hambledon Press, 1985

"Notes on Courts of Record in England." In *Essays in English Legal History*, ed. S. E. Thorne, 61–73. London: Hambledon Press, 1985

"The Early History of the Inns of Court with Special Reference to Gray's Inn." *Graya* 50 (1959): 79–96; reprinted in *Essays in English Legal History*, ed. S. E. Thorne, 137–54. London: Hambledon Press, 1985

Thornton, T. "The Integration of Cheshire into the Tudor Nation State in the Early Sixteenth Century." *Northern History* 29 (1993): 40–63

Tout, T. F. *Chapters in the Administrative History of Medieval England*. Manchester: University of Manchester Press, 1928

Tubbs, J. W. *The Common Law Mind: Medieval and Early Modern Conceptions*. Baltimore: Johns Hopkins University Press, 2000

Turner, G. J. "A Newly Discovered Ordinance." *Law Quarterly Review* 12 (1896): 299–301

Van Caenegem, R. C. *The Birth of the Common Law*. Cambridge: Cambridge University Press, 1973

Walker, Greg. *Persuasive Fictions: Faction, Faith and Political Culture in the Reign of Henry VIII*. Brookfield VT: Scolar Press, 1996

Walker, Sue Sheridan. "Proof of Age of Heirs in Medieval England." *Medieval Studies* 35 (1973): 306–23

"Free Consent and Marriage of Feudal Wards in Medieval England." *Journal of Medieval History* 8 (1982): 123–34

Wallace, J. W. *The Reporters Chronologically Arranged with Occasional Remarks*. 3rd edn, Philadelphia, 1855

Watkin, Thomas Glyn. "The Political Philosophy of the Lord King." In *Communities and Courts in Britain, 1150–1900*, ed. Christopher Brooks and Michael Lobban, 1–12. London: Hambledon, 1997

Watts, John L. "'A Newe Ffundacion of is Crowne': Monarchy in the Age of Henry VII." In *The Reign of Henry VII: Proceedings of the 1993 Harlaxton Symposium*, ed. Benjamin Thompson, 31–53. Harlaxton Medieval Studies V. Stamford: Paul Watkins, 1995

Henry VI and the Politics of Kingship. New York: Cambridge University Press, 1996

Waugh, Scott L. *The Lordship of England: Royal Wardships and Marriages in English Society and Politics 1217–1327*. Princeton: Princeton University Press, 1988

Wolffe, B. P. "The Management of English Royal Estates under the Yorkist Kings." *English Historical Review* 71 (1956): 1–27

"Henry VII's Land Revenues and Chamber Finance." *English Historical Review* 79 (1964): 225–54

The Crown Lands 1461 to 1536: An Aspect of Yorkist and Early Tudor Government. New York: Barnes & Noble, 1970

The Royal Demesne in English History: The Crown Estates in the Governance of the Realm from the Conquest to 1509. London: George Allen & Unwin, 1971

Woodbine, G. E. "The Language of the English Law." *Speculum* 18 (1943): 395–436

Woodward, G. O. "A Speculation in Monastic Lands." *English Historical Review* 79 (1964): 778–83

The Dissolution of the Monasteries. New York: Walker & Co., 1966

Wyndham, K. S. H. "In Pursuit of Crown Land: The Initial Recipients of Property in the Mid-Tudor Period." *Somerset Archaeology and Natural History* 123 (1979): 65–73

"Crown Land and Royal Patronage in Mid-Sixteenth Century England." *Journal of British Studies* 19 (1980): 18–34

Youings, J. A. "The Terms of Disposal of the Devon Monastic Lands." *English Historical Review* 69 (1954): 18–38

"Landlords in England: The Church." In *The Agrarian History of England and Wales*, vol. IV, *1500–1640*, ed. Joan Thirsk, 306–56. Cambridge: Cambridge University Press, 1967

The Dissolution of the Monasteries. New York: Barnes & Noble, 1971

Zaller, Robert. "Breaking the Vessels: The Desacralization of Monarchy in Early Modern England." *Sixteenth Century Journal* 29 (1998): 757–78

Zeeveld, W. Gordon. *Foundations of Tudor Policy*. Cambridge MA: Harvard University Press, 1948

INDEX

Note: Names appearing in the bibliography appear as separate headings, as do kings, bishops and archbishops, and persons of outstanding significance such as Fortescue. Lawyers and justices are gathered under that heading. Passing references to persons are not indexed. To enable users to link the texts of the readings as reproduced in Appendixes 1 and 2 with treatment in the main body of the book, a very detailed breakdown of the issues discussed is to be found under "Frowyk, J." and "Spelman, Sir J." Other readers have not been indexed to this same level of detail.

www.ingramcontent.com/pod-product-compliance
Lightning Source LLC
LaVergne TN
LVHW052241200926
848481LV00002B/238
* 9 7 8 0 5 2 1 1 8 7 6 9 5 *